Advance praise for *A Nation of Farmers*

Sharon Astyk is one of the most interesting writers on the environment today. I strongly urge you to read her book.

— George Monbiot,
author of *Heat*,
www.monbiot.com

A hundred million new farmers! It's a daunting and invigorating challenge, and it's a damned good thing that someone is thinking about how it might actually happen. This book is more exuberant than scary, thank heaven — it's just w^ ve need.

— Bill McKibben,
author of *Deep Economy*

This c   .merica's biggest challenges in a
re   ation of Farmers* should be required
re   ooler. We don't have to wait on politicians
or \   it." This book empowers every person with an
action   ..s revolutionary in its simplicity and effectiveness.

— Joel Salatin, farmer, Polyface Farm,
and author of *You Can Farm* and
Everything I Want to Do is Illegal,
www.polyface.com

The world is sleepwalking into a food scarcity fiasco. Those Americans who want to continue eating regularly will have to take more responsibility for growing it themselves. This book is a forceful, sensible, and comprehensive treasure trove of knowledge about where food comes from and what to do with it.

— James Howard Kunstler
author of *World Made By Hand*
and *The Long Emergency*

Whether you are a full-time farmer or a backyard hobbyist, a city dweller or a budding back to the lander, *A Nation of Farmers* belongs on your bookshelf. If you eat, you need to read it.

— Kathy Harrison,
author of *Just In Case: How to be
Self-sufficient When the Unexpected Happens*

A Nation of Farmers offers an elegantly clear path to understanding how we have strayed so far from living within the Earth's limits, and also to finding simple ways to move into a prosperous life that regenerates, rather than depletes, this beautiful planet's bounty. Sharon and Aaron are to be congratulated on teasing apart, and then masterfully reassembling, complex issues of food, land, and livelihood. This book gives us tangible steps we can take to quiet our fears and live gracefully and in abundance at the end of the Oil Age.

— Toby Hemenway,
author of *Gaia's Garden*,
www.patternliteracy.com

A NATION *of* FARMERS

Defeating the Food Crisis on American Soil

Sharon Astyk & Aaron Newton

NEW SOCIETY PUBLISHERS

Cataloging in Publication Data

A catalog record for this publication is available from the National Library of Canada.

Cover design by Diane McIntosh.
Cover images: Beet © iStock/Natasha Litova; Pitchfork: © iStock/Daniel Goodings

Printed in Canada. First printing March 2009.

Paperback ISBN: 978-0-86571-623-0

Inquiries regarding requests to reprint all or part of *A Nation of Farmers* should
be addressed to New Society Publishers at the address below.

To order directly from the publishers, please call toll-free (North America)
1-800-567-6772, or order online at: www.newsociety.com

Any other inquiries can be directed by mail to:
New Society Publishers
P.O. Box 189, Gabriola Island, BC V0R 1X0, Canada (250) 247-9737

New Society Publishers' mission is to publish books that contribute in fundamental ways to
building an ecologically sustainable and just society, and to do so with the least possible impact
on the environment, in a manner that models this vision. We are committed to doing this
not just through education, but through action. This book is one step toward ending global
deforestation and climate change. It is printed on Forest Stewardship Council-certified acid-
free paper that is **100% post-consumer recycled** (100% old growth forest-free), processed
chlorine free, and printed with vegetable-based, low-VOC inks, with covers produced using
FSC-certified stock. Additionally, New Society purchases carbon offsets based on an annual
audit, operating with a carbon-neutral footprint. For further information, or to browse
our full list of books and purchase securely, visit our website at: www.newsociety.com

NEW SOCIETY PUBLISHERS
www.newsociety.com

Recycled
Supporting responsible use
of forest resources
www.fsc.org Cert no. SW-COC-1271
© 1996 Forest Stewardship Council

100%

Books for Wiser Living
recommended by *Mother Earth News*

Today, more than ever before, our society is seeking ways to live more conscien-
tiously. To help bring you the very best inspiration and information about greener,
more sustainable lifestyles, *Mother Earth News* is recommending select New
Society Publishers' books to its readers. For more than 30 years, *Mother Earth* has
been North America's "Original Guide to Living Wisely," creating books and mag-
azines for people with a passion for self-reliance and a desire to live in harmony
with nature. Across the countryside and in our cities, New Society Publishers and
Mother Earth are leading the way to a wiser, more sustainable world.

Contents

For
Salem, Keaton,
Asher, Isaiah, Simon & Eli

Acknowledgments

We owe many people a debt of thanks, including everyone who commented on the work in progress at our blogs, Hen and Harvest and The Oil Drum. To Ingrid Witvoet for midwifery and endurance, and Audrey Dorsch for patient editing, to all who contributed recipes, and to our kind transcriptionists: Jerah Kirby, Sarah Hartman, Meredith Funston and Hannah Roberson. Thanks to those whose wisdom we drew on: MEA, Steve Balogh, Carolyn Baker, Peter Bane, Albert Bates, Colin Beavan, Jason Bradford, Kathy Breault, Jeffery Brown, Kurt Cobb, Ron Danise, Julian Darley, Roger Doiron, Deanna Duke, Miranda Edel, Edson Freeman, Adam Grubb, Kathy Harrison, Richard Heinberg, Rose Hayden-Smith, Toby Hemenway, Rob Hopkins, Ilargi, Keith Johnson, George Kent, Gene Logsdon, Matt Mayer, Bill McKibben, Kathy McMahon, Pat Meadows, George Monbiot, Faith Morgan, Pat Murphy, Helena Norberg-Hodge, Alice Oldfather, Cassie Parsons, Dale Allen Pfeiffer, Thomas Princen, Megan Quinn-Bachman, Tom Philpott, Phil Rutter, David Roberts, Stoneleigh, Stuart Staniford, Gail Tverberg, Natalie Veres, Bob Waldrop, Chris Welch, and Judy Wick.

Sharon wishes to thank a crew of supportive friends/family including her parents, in laws, sisters and nieces, Alexandra, Steve, Joe, Susan, Ted, Miriam, Bess, Chris, Jesse, Jon, Steph, Jenn, George, Claudia, Elaine, Jamie, Carol and others who tolerated her nattering. Most of all, she is grateful to Eric, reluctant and beloved farmer, and her four farmers-in-training, Eli, Simon, Isaiah and Asher.

Aaron is grateful to Tony, Jon, Rebekah, Margaret and Howard for their support and to Joyce who taught him more by example than she can know. He is grateful to Chuck Borders, Lateef Jackson, Rebecca Necessary, Todd Serdula and Sandra Smith. Thanks to Keaton and Salem for the greatest motivation possible. Most of all Aaron is thankful for his wife, Jennifer who was supportive of his wild ideas and picked up his slack. Thank you.

Preface

You know, when you farm,
Your hands are dirty at the end of the day,
But your hands are clean.

— CLAYTON BRASCOUPE —

There was no way that we could ever write a book about transforming the American food system without a lot of help. When we took on this enormous project, we knew we'd have to invoke more voices, people who knew more than we did, who were already acting. Getting one-third of the American population involved in food production and preparation makes the whole thing very much a collaboration — with all of you and with experts who we met through their books and in person.

Scattered through each chapter you'll find interviews with some of the most significant figures in food, energy and environmental movements. Their work guided ours, and we wanted to give them a chance to speak for themselves.

When we interviewed these leaders, we asked each of them for a recipe that they make themselves, one that they felt best helped us grasp the future of food. I mean, who doesn't want to know what Bill McKibben or Richard Heinberg thinks we'll be eating in the coming decades? The exchange of recipes is very much a way of connecting people. We hope that this very ordinary and wonderful sharing of something from their tables will be a gift.

Aaron and Sharon wanted to share some of our favorites as well — the delicious and adaptable foods that our families love. And Sharon ran a recipe contest on her blog — more than 70 wonderful recipes for low-energy, low-cost meals poured in. We chose our favorite eight — and wish we had room for more. You can check out all the recipes and the full text of all the interviews for this book at anationoffarmers.com — just look for the tabs that say "interviews" and "recipes."

This book being as huge a project as it is, we needed to invoke not just others' thinking about these questions, not just the back fence culture of people sharing food and recipes, but also to recall the last time that we all pulled together to address a massive international crisis. So throughout the book you'll notice World War II posters exhorting us that we can do it, that we can grow our own food. Today we can take our place with the greatest generation and their work ensuring food security.

In a sense, all of these parts of the book — the posters, the recipes, the interviews — are part of the same project: getting a grip on something that is huge (the remaking of our agriculture and our cuisine) and simultaneously very ordinary and simple (making sure that everyone has a good meal). And just as most of us rarely get a whole meal from field to table alone, this particular plate has been filled with the help and hands of many others. We're grateful to them.

The Big Lie

*It is impossible to restore the sustainable societies of indigenous
and aboriginal peoples. But the values they embodied — careful
stewardship of earth, modest use of its riches, safeguarding the
future of the generations to come, restraint and as high a degree
of self-provisioning as possible — can reanimate ancient and
still unrealized dreams of a secure sustenance for all.*

— JEREMY SEABROOK —

From the first, let us dispense with the Big Lie. You know the one we refer to: the eternally repeated claim that we cannot make real and deep and radical change in our way of living, even if it is the right thing to do. The Big Lie narrows both our perspective and our perception of our alternatives, while making our failures seem natural and inevitable. The Big Lie claims that we are cowards, that we are weak, that we are no longer the inheritors of our revolutionary past and that we lack moral integrity. It is a slander, and yet we believe it. And until we stop believing it, we cannot lift our hands, our voices or our hoes and get on with the work of change.

We hear the Big Lie over and over again, from every side. It is told by authority, defiantly, in defense of the maintenance of power by the privileged, as when Dick Cheney announced, "The American way of life is non-negotiable" in response to questions about whether Americans should conserve energy. It is told by those who have grown frustrated with their failure to make change and who believe that the scope of change must be limited by our cowardice, as when climate change activist George Monbiot writes, "By 'feasibility' I mean compatibility with industrial civilization.... Whether or not we enjoy the soft life…it is politically necessary to discover the means of sustaining it."[1] We have been told it is true for so long that we believe it, and it shapes our thinking and prevents us from seeing the choices and answers that stand just outside of our reach.

But how do we know that it isn't true? One way is simply to look around us, at our history and at other people in our world. We might look back as far as the early Christians, who held their goods in common and stood in resistance to established cultures. Or perhaps we would look at our own American Revolution, which established that national democracies can succeed over the divine right of kings. Or to Gandhi's non-violent revolution in India, the march across the subcontinent and his demonstration that non-violent resistance can overcome armies. There are tens of thousands of such examples of human beings reimagining their society, and from those reimaginings creating something real and tangible. None of those people chose the easy path. Each of them chose what they believed to be right, despite a great cost to themselves.

But, we are told, we are somehow different than they. The Big Lie carries with it the false notion that acts of courage and rebellion are exceptional and not the work of people very much unlike ourselves. Those who stand up for justice and liberty are different, we are told in a thousand ways, each enforcing the Big Lie.

How do we know that we are still courageous and powerful people, that we are still able to re-envision our society and make it over, just as revolutionaries of all sorts have done in the past? We know this for two reasons. The first is that we recognize the theory of exceptionalism as false doctrine. We believe that we are like other people, that other people are like us. We look inside ourselves and see ordinary human beings, flawed and imperfect, capable of great foolishness and terrible mistakes, and also capable of a great deal of good. And we can make change. The people we know are like us — they are ordinary people, and thus capable of the ordinary acts of heroism that make revolutions possible.

The Big Lie tries to convince us that we are less good, less moral, less brave, less able than those who came before us. But we know that is false. We know in our hearts and deep in our guts what we are capable of.

The other reason we know we can transform our society is that when we look around us, again and again we see the Big Lie made false. We find acts of resistance and courage in every place, every town and state and nation. We see people who will lay down their lives for what they believe is right and people who have the courage to go on living for the same cause. We see people who go each week to church, mosque or synagogue, or out into the world and woods, and try to live honorably, doing not what is easy but what is right. We see those who will go to jail for what is right and give

up comfort and convenience for what they believe. That we have not unified our work and come to a whole and complete understanding of what is
right is a problem, in part shaped by the prevalence of the Big Lie. But that
fact does not mean we cannot, or should not, find a common answer and
change our society, our economy and our culture if it no longer serves us.

So let us dispense right this moment, today, now, with the Big Lie. We
can be the moral descendents of those who have chosen to remake their
cultures. We can be the inheritors of those who fought back against slavery and oppression, those who overthrew unjust rulers, who marched and
stood firm and said "No" and backed it with their action. We are those people — there is nothing inherent in us that makes us less courageous or less
good, strong or moral than the world's ordinary, heroic people. All we need
to do is to begin, to take up courage and honor, morality and strength as
our banner, and to bury the Big Lie beneath a thousand working hoes and
shovels.

CHAPTER 1

Groundwork for Victory
GROW MORE IN '44

A Fast Train

Food Security in Crisis

*Well you've been on a fast train and it's going off the rails
And you can't come back can't come back together again
And you start breaking down
In the pouring rain...
Well you've been on a fast train*

— VAN MORRISON —

SHARON: In 2006, on the first day of Rosh Hashana, the Jewish New Year, at the International Conference on Peak Oil put on by Community Solutions, I gave my very first talk about peak oil, climate change and the challenges we face in the future. I was a complete unknown, following famous speakers with more qualifications in their pinky fingers than I had in my whole body. I was terrified, and the more so because right before my talk, the marvelous Peter Bane stood up and said virtually everything I had put in my laboriously prepared speech — only better, funnier and wiser. I had about five minutes to come up with a half-hour talk, five minutes that I'd originally planned to spend throwing up with fear. Mostly I was just praying that I wouldn't leak milk all over my shirt, as I was away from my nine-month-old son for the first time.

Because it was Rosh Hashana, I thought I could kill some time by telling a story most people might not have heard. So I stood up and said that the rabbis told us that on Rosh Hashana God decides what the future of each human being will be in the coming year. Now, that part is simple enough, and probably part of the folklore of just about every culture with a divinity. But what's interesting is that Jews are told that even though God inscribes our future on

Rosh Hashana, God doesn't finalize that decision until Yom Kippur, ten days later. That is, there's a short period of time in which our future is written down — when we can see what is coming — but during which there is still hope for change, and our prayers and actions can still alter the future.

And that, I said, is where the whole world stands right now, religious or no. Climate change and peak energy and depletion of every sort mean that we are very close to having irrevocably inscribed a terrible, disastrous future for ourselves. If we don't look carefully, it might seem like it is too late to change our fate, that there isn't any hope. But the fact is, we have a very short window to change things. That doesn't mean we can keep the world from warming entirely or that we can go on using energy like there's no tomorrow. It doesn't mean that the future won't be difficult. But it would be just as big a mistake to believe that there is no hope as it is to believe that we are not on the cusp of disaster.

Where is the hope? The hope, I argued, is that there were more people in that room listening to us talk about what needs to be done than were in the room when the idea of the American Revolution first came up. The hope is that for all the evil done in human history, there are always powerful counterforces trying to do good, trying to change society, trying to overthrow bad ideas and replace them with good ones. And sometimes, just sometimes, as in the American Revolution, as in Gandhi's peaceful revolution, the good ideas actually win.

What radical idea did I have to offer anyone to base a revolution on? The only thing remaining out of that late, unlamented speech I'd labored over was one idea, a really simple one, but so far, no one had said it. I mentioned that if we are going to live with fewer fossil fuels, we are going to need to revert to a society in which meeting our own basic needs is normal — and what is more basic than feeding ourselves? Oil has replaced people in industrial agriculture, and now people have to come back and replace the oil. But the coming agrarian revolution is a good and hopeful thing, not the scary retreat to backbreaking peasant slave labor it has often been portrayed as.

I got kind of crazy and called for 100 million new farmers and gardeners to start a new revolution, to create new economies and lower-energy, sustainable societies, to get us better food and a better life, and more democracy. I'm not really sure exactly what I said — I was running on adrenaline and the fear that no one would ever let me back on a stage again after this, so I'd better take this chance to get it all out of my system.

And believe it or not, it wasn't a disaster. I got a lot of applause, and later on Richard Heinberg, pretty much the leader of the Peak Oil Movement, wrote a paper called "50 Million Farmers" and was kind enough to credit me with influencing him. And I got to meet Aaron, who was there as a journalist and interviewed me. And from there sprang the beginnings of a real question — and this book, which tries to answer it: Could you start a new American Revolution based on an agrarian dream? Or maybe more accurately, could you re-start the first American Revolution and Thomas Jefferson's dream of a Nation of Farmers? Could you get a better food system and some security in the face of disaster and maybe, just maybe, the kind of democracy we'd once imagined?

The Train Goes Off the Rails

I am writing
because we have an emergency…
— NAOMI WOLF —

In early 2008, the world's food, economic and energy train came off the rails. What was startling was that it didn't happen either gradually or in a linear way. Instead, things simply fell apart at an astounding rate, faster than anyone could have predicted without being accused of lunacy. Most of us didn't quite see it this way. This was a short-term shift, a minor downturn, we were told. So we didn't recognize the beginnings of disaster when we first saw them.

It started with biofuels and growing meat-consumption rates in developing economies. As poor people in growing economies attempted to get a share of the pie while rich people in the Global North kept a death grip on what they had, disaster ensued. The growing demand for food, for cars and cows drove the price of staple grains up at astounding rates. Scientists, estimating that biofuels were responsible for up to 60 percent of the growth in food prices, called for a moratorium on biofuel production.[2] In 2007 overall food inflation was at 18 percent,[3] which created a new class of hungry. But that was just the tip of the iceberg. In 2008 the month-to-month inflation for some commodities was higher than 2007's annual inflation. And despite a deflationary economy into early 2009, food prices were expected to remain high or rise, because farmers were unable to secure planting loans to enable them to grow food.

Rice, the staple of almost half the world's population, rose 147 percent, and wheat increased 25 percent in just one day. Price increases were inequitable (as was everything else), so while rice prices rose 30 percent in rich nations like the US, Haitian rice prices doubled.[4] The United Nations (UN) and the Organization for Economic Co-operation and Development (OECD) separately issued reports suggesting that over the next decade these trends toward higher food prices in proportion to income would continue and that, in fact, average food prices would be up to 65 percent higher than in the early parts of this decade, plunging millions into poverty and hunger. Haiti, desperately poor, was an early canary in the hunger coal mine. By early 2008 tens of thousands of impoverished Haitians were priced entirely out of the market for rice and other staples and were reduced to eating "cookies" made of nutrient-rich dirt, vegetable shortening and salt to quiet their hunger pangs.[5] Women stood on the street, offering their children to any reasonably well-fed passerby, saying, "Please, take one and feed them." Thousands of Haitians marched on Port Au Prince, yelling, "We're hungry." And indeed, the Haitian government was complicit, allowing food relief to rot on the wharves. But Haiti was just the start. More and more of the world's poor, including the poor of the US and other rich-world nations, found themselves in a disaster.

Forty nations either stopped exporting grains or raised tariffs to make costs prohibitive. Food prices rose precipitously as importing nations began to struggle to meet rising hunger. After riots over long bread lines threatened to destabilize Egypt, the Egyptian government set the army to baking bread for the hungry and raised wages to compensate for rapidly rising food prices. Mexico slashed tariffs and offered a subsidy to millions of hungry people to avoid outright starvation.[6] The UN warned that 33 nations were in danger of destabilizing, and the list included major powers such as Pakistan, Mexico, North Korea, India, Egypt and South Africa. Many of these hold nuclear weapons or are otherwise politically and strategically essential.

Food riots erupted all over the world in the first few months of 2008 —

in Bangladesh, Mexico, Ivory Coast, Uzbekistan, Pakistan, Thailand, the Philippines, Peru, Indonesia, Bolivia, Ethiopia and more. The government of Haiti was the first to experience radical change as a result of the food crisis, but others struggled with stability.[7]

The crisis didn't stop among the already poor, however. *The Economist* reported that the crisis extended well into the middle class of many nations. Joanna Sheeran, director of the World Food Project explained, "For the middle classes,... it means cutting out medical care. For those on $2 a day, it means cutting out meat and taking the children out of school. For those on $1 a day, it means cutting out meat and vegetables and eating only cereals. And for those on 50 cents a day, it means total disaster."[8] By late summer 2008, more than 175 million people who had managed to raise their incomes above $2 a day found themselves inexorably drawn back to the world poverty level,[9] while millions of those who called themselves "middle class" began, slowly, to realize that they were no such thing. Many of the supposed middle class in rich-world nations were actually the working poor who had overextended their credit to keep up appearances. As credit tightened because of a growing financial crisis, appearances were fraying. Pawnshops started to do booming business with Americans and Canadians who could no longer meet basic needs for food and gas.[10]

In 2007, a major United States newspaper reported the growing problem of seasonal malnutrition affecting poor children in the Northern US — the rising price of heating oil meant that lower-class families were struggling to put food on the table. Hungry, low-weight children were unable to maintain their body temperature in chilly houses, and a vicious circle of illness, hunger and desperation ensued. Malnourished bellies began to be seen by pediatricians treating the urban poor in cold climates.[11] Food pantries reported enormous rises in demand and declines in donations because of rising transport costs and a growing economic crisis that reduced charitable giving and increased need.[12]

Shortages have long been a chronic problem in the poor world, but by early spring of 2008, they began to arrive in the rich world. Despite Japan's deep pockets, a shortage of butter and wheat reminded the rich world of its dependence on food imports.[13] Rising food prices meant that Japan's grain budget was exhausted months before it was expected to be renewed, causing them to call for emergency allocations. Many of the supply problems were due to climate change and energy issues, as Australian dairy farmers struggled with high grain prices and the extended drought that destroyed their pastures. In the winter of 2008/2009, a Reuters reporter witnessed elderly Parisian women fighting over discarded produce at an open market, where scavenging of food is apparently becoming widespread among a growing number of the hungry.[14]

Following anecdotal reports of limits at US bulk warehouse stores beginning in March,[15] rationing went official in late April of 2008. Many Costco stores were limiting purchases of flour, rice, cooking oil and other staples to avoid shortages — and the stores tracked purchases electronically to prevent customers from visiting other Costco stores.[16] In Alaska, near the end of the grain shipment lines, where many Americans are able to reach stores only infrequently, customers fought over bags of rice, and stores were unable to keep rice in stock.[17] One customer noted it was "just like the Philippines." Though no widespread food shortages were anticipated in most nations in the Global North, these incidents represented evidence that globalized supply chains were beginning to fray. Meanwhile, economist Jeff Rubin argued that globalization as a whole was being "reversed" by high transport costs, making it urgently necessary to begin growing and making things in the US again.[18]

The tightening of credit markets all over the globe also contributed to food insecurity. Most large US commodity farmers depend on bank credit to be able to plant. The estimate was that the US wheat crop might decline by as much as 4.4 percent, and Brazilian corn crops were expected to fall by nearly 20 percent because loans to buy fertilizers were no longer available.[19] In early 2009 it became clear that many farmers were unable to secure planting loans for the spring season.

In the early part of 2008, the US Federal Reserve shied away from acknowledging recession, and key inflation indexes actually fell, because the government doesn't include food or energy costs in the measures of inflation. This systematic mis-statement of inflation disguised that fact that many analysts estimated the real inflation levels to be at 10 percent or higher in the US.[20] Given that real wages had been falling in the US for almost 30 years, this meant that average Americans were overwhelmingly struggling to keep the bills paid and food on the table. Twenty-eight million Americans, one out of every 11, required food stamps to feed their families. In economically depressed areas like Michigan and Washington DC, it was one in seven. And as food prices rose and job losses increased to nearly half a million each month, families on food stamps struggled more and more to get enough to eat, even with the federal subsidy. As summer months approached, millions of poor families who could rely on their children receiving two free meals a day at school faced losing even that support, as summer food programs reach only 3 million of 31 million eligible poor school children.

By autumn 2008, the word *recession* was being replaced by fears of a new Great Depression, in large part fueled by the housing collapse, which was itself fueled in part by rising energy and food prices that were strapping homeowners. Banks and major financial institutions began failing under the pressure, while economic growth in booming nations like China and India was strangled by rising food and energy costs. Much of the developing world's middle class, the new consumers that had kept the economy growing, found themselves falling back into poverty.

The energy train, the money train and the food train were inextricably linked in a host of ways that were difficult to disentangle, and each crisis fed the other, until a near-inevitable crisis in the world economy is unfolding as we write this in the fall of 2008.

While the food crisis in the poor world made headlines, the energy crisis there went almost unnoticed. More and more poorer nations simply could not afford to import oil and other fossil fuels, and they began to slowly but steadily lose the benefits of fossil fuels. Nations suffered shortages of gas, electricity and coal.[21] Tajikistan, experiencing a record cold winter found itself with inadequate supplies of heating oil, food and in a humanitarian crisis.[22] South African coal supplies were so short that electricity generation dropped back to intermittency. In May, thousands of Indians rioted, protesting power shortages,[23] and it was revealed that nuclear power plants in India were experiencing uranium shortages and coal-fired generating plants were short of coal.[24] Indonesia's oil production fell so fast that it seceded from OPEC, and Mexico seems due to cease exporting oil by 2014.[25] Meanwhile aging energy transmission infrastructure in Britain and the US desperately needed updating, without funds to do so.

In the fall of 2008 a shocking report by the International Energy Agency (IEA) on the decline of the world's 400 largest oil fields was leaked to the *Financial Times*. It suggested that without massive investment in fossil fuel developments the annual depletion rate for oil was 9 percent per year,[26] more than triple the previous estimates. As funds to invest in new energy sources dried up rapidly and credit markets tightened, this meant a world facing rapidly depleting energy supplies with limited funds to develop either renewable or fossil-fueled replacements.

Routine air travel began to disappear, and airlines went bankrupt with astonishing rapidity. There simply was no way for airlines to absorb the volatile prices of fuel and the decline in tourist and business travel due to the economic downturn.[27] The cost of shipping fruit and other perishables from distant places, largely done by air, rose dramatically. New demand for energy-efficient vehicles in China and the US made diesel fuel short-ages a real possibility,[28] threatening the just-in-time delivery system most stores rely heavily on. Industrial agriculture, often described as "the process of turning oil into food," began to struggle to keep yields to match grow-ing demand. Yield increases, which had been at 6 percent annually from the 1960s through the 1990s fell to 1–2 percent, against rapidly rising de-mand. Trying to keep yields up demanded more and more investment of energy (and higher costs for farmers). Climate change threatened to fur-ther reduce yields in already stressed poor nations: Bangladesh struggled with repeated climate-change-linked flooding, the Sahelian African coun-tries and Australia with growing drought, China with desertification. The US Midwest suffered devastating flooding that reduced harvests and con-taminated water tables.

Meanwhile, a new form of wheat stem rust, named Ug-99, meant that a substantial percentage of the African wheat crop was expected to be lost. Ug-99, to which there is no resistance, had reportedly spread throughout the Middle East and into India and Pakistan, and scientists suggested it would not take more than a year to make it to China and then the US. Wheat provides 20 percent of the world's total calories, and it is estimated that it will take a decade of intensive agricultural research to find a Ug-99-resistant variety — at a time when research budgets are being cut.[29] Ninety percent of all commercial wheat strains world-wide are vulnerable to Ug-99.

All indications were that both food and energy supplies would fail to keep up with demand. Unchecked climate change (the only kind we've got so far) is expected to reduce rice yields by up to 30 percent by the end of the century, and food production in the already starving Sahel is expected to be reduced by half. Genetically modified organisms (GMOs), touted as a solution, have yet to produce even slightly higher yields. Arable land is disappearing under sprawling housing and development, and aquifers are heavily depleted. Thirty percent of the world's grain production comes from irrigated land that is expected to lose its water supply in the next de-cades. California, facing its worst drought in more than 30 years, is fast reaching the point in which it is more profitable for farmers to sell their water allotments than to grow food with them, and dramatic cuts in water for agriculture have been announced.[30] Australia has begun to buy out its farmers, encouraging them to leave the land and accept that some agricultural regions would never be able to support agriculture again, because of profound drought.

Meanwhile the costs of fossil-fueled agriculture skyrocketed, the cost of potash, a necessary fertilizer ingredient, rising by 300 percent in less than a year[31] and all fertilizers rising dramatically faster than other agricultural inputs. What should have been a boom for farmers, with demand so high, was actually the beginning of an increasingly precarious spiral of high prices, high indebtedness and market volatility. Agricultural indebtedness rose dramatically in the US. Rising prices for agriculture inputs began to reduce available food. In Tanzania farmers were unable to afford to plant additional land because of high fertilizer costs, and diesel costs made it prohibitive to transport food into the country; so a comparatively stable, prosperous African nation began to see rising hunger.[32]

American farmers began to see shortages of fertilizer.[33] While some American and Canadian farmers saw rising profits, others found their gains evaporating in the face of rising inputs. The only people who were getting rich were the multinational agricultural corporations like Monsanto, ADM, and Cargill, who posted record profits off of human suffering, their divisions of agricultural investment driving up prices for the world's poor and taking most of the gains in food costs.[34]

Meanwhile, the ability of nations to transport food supplies began to be called into question. Early trucker protests were intermittent and largely ineffective, but predictions of diesel shortages and a shortage of refining capacity made it a real possibility that all over the world food might not reach store shelves. In May of 2008 trucker protests brought a halt to much of European truck transport. After a difficult hurricane season in the fall of 2008, much of US oil-refining infrastructure experienced extended outages, and the Southeast, at the end of a segment of the Colonial pipeline and dependent on Gulf-coast refineries, began to suffer shortages of goods as local truckers struggled to get gasoline.

This analysis has not even included large chunks of the disaster unfolding before our eyes. By February 2009, the total committed funds for the US bailout alone stood at between 8 and 9.2 billion dollars, depending on who you asked. The housing collapse may reduce real wealth in the US by trillions of dollars, and at this writing, the world derivative markets are showing signs of trouble, which potentially puts at risk most of the world's financial wealth. The French bank Société Général recently advised its investors to take their assets out of Chinese banks, and Russia has suspended its markets on several occasions because of massive losses. Foreclosures are predicted to rise dramatically to as many as 3 million homes in 2008–2009, and total housing values may fall by as much as 5–80 percent over their peak. In May 2008 Princeton professor Kenneth Deffeyes noted that at oil prices of $130 barrel, energy costs exceed 6 percent of world GDP. His estimate is that 15 percent would essentially swamp the global economy.[35] With oil prices at time of writing around $40 per barrel, that seems unlikely; and yet, it is worth remembering that the oil price peak was only 8 months previous, and that price volatility is one of the features of our present crisis.

By the time you read this, the circumstances will almost certainly be very different. Whether the situation will continue progressing toward disaster or the crisis will be temporarily arrested is not clear. But an increasing number of analysts agree that our long-term projections suggest more such difficulties and a great deal of struggle. We are on a fast train, and it is coming off the rails. And at stake is our basic food security, justice and our hope for the future.

The Change

A revolution never come with a warning.
A revolution just arrive like the morning.
— Michael Franti —

This book begins from the simple premise that it is both possible and necessary to stop the harm that industrial agriculture is doing — resource depletion, global warming, global poverty, increased food insecurity and hunger, and unsafe, low-quality food — and that we can do so simply by choosing to change the nature of what we grow and what we eat. It is a call for more participation in the food system, 100 million new farmers and 200 million new cooks in the US, and more worldwide. It begins with the recognition that for a host of reasons, we simply have no choice but to radically alter our food system, to end its dependency on fossil fuels and to bring food security to the table as a central issue of our times.

We can almost hear your voices now: "Did they say *100 million* new *farmers*?" It sounds like madness if you grew up in an industrial society where there was always plenty of food in the stores and on the table, where too much food, rather than too little, was often the problem. Why on earth would we need millions of new farmers and cooks? Aren't we living in the richest country in the world, the land of milk and honey, the land where mothers don't have to let their babies grow up to be cowboys or farmers anymore? Even if you know that the food system is falling apart, it represents a huge psychological shift to say that this means that we must change our lives so radically that we must participate in the food system. After all, wasn't that what modernity was for — to free us from the endless drudgery of growing and cooking food?

Believe it or not, what we are describing is a call for a return to human norms and human community, to living in a way that is connected to our land and our food, much as all human societies before ours have. We argue that not only can we cease to do the harm that industrial agriculture does but we can replace it with something better — a better way of growing and preparing food and also a democracy of the sort that Thomas Jefferson imagined for his nation (more on this further on), a democracy that is not vulnerable to being stolen or sold, as our present one is.

Moreover, we think most of us have a rapidly growing sense of unease about our own security. More and more of us are struggling to put food on our tables. Food pantries are seeing more middle-class families show up at their doors. And most of us have the sneaking suspicion that there's no magical way of preventing the disaster from coming to us. So perhaps, just perhaps, it isn't quite so crazy to suggest that something about our food system is broken. Understanding this is essential — and we need to learn it quickly. Right now, we are seeing the confluence of multiple crises destabilizing both the economy and the food supply. We face the very real possibility that we and our children may be poorer and hungrier and less healthy than we were — and what parent or grandparent or anyone who cares about the future would not do everything necessary to prevent such a disaster?

So what are those problems? What is causing these shifts in the world we knew? We've touched a little on the immediate causes, but what is at the root of the difficulty? Does it really mean we cannot go on the way we are?

Peak Energy

*To alcohol — the cause of
and the solution to all of life's problems.*
— HOMER SIMPSON —

Brewing beer takes about 30 days. There's the malting and mashing and lautering and boiling, not to mention the hopping and the separation, the cooling and fermentation. Then most beer is filtered before being bottled. And let's not forget the drinking. Beer has been brewed since the seventh century BC, or perhaps even before, and will probably be brewed until humans no longer walk the face of this planet. As a Whistran Brewery sign says, "Beer: So much more than just a breakfast drink."

The above description makes it sound like an awfully complicated process. Really it's not. But the procedure does require adding specific ingredients, including heat, in just the right sequence so as to produce one of mankind's most beloved beverages. In this way brewing beer is not unlike the process of making oil. A long time ago a tremendous amount of oceanic plant material lived and died and sank to the bottom of the sea. There it built up into an enormous layer of biological material. Like brewing beer, this process required the combination of specific ingredients in the presence of heat. At lower temperatures it produced oil, and at relatively higher temperatures it produced natural gas. In certain locations the oil and natural gas became trapped in porous rock formations conducive to the containment of such materials. You can think of these formations as kegs of energy.

During previous millennia, before we discovered how to make use of these intense energy sources, the human population was relatively stable, never exceeding several hundred million. During our most recent experimentation with fossil fuels however, we've seen that number increase to just over 6.5 billion people. Even more important than the growth in population, lavish, consumptive lifestyles in the Global North have drawn on resources, so that inequity between rich and poor has grown. The average American consumes 30 times the resources of the average Kenyan.[36]

During the middle part of the 20th century, the United States was awash in oil. Germany, on the other hand, was so desperate for fuel that it was forced to take coal and press it into gasoline. Many historians point out that the Allied victory in World War II and subsequent rise in world power was made possible in part by our easy access to great quantities of oil and its abundant energy. Winston Churchill famously said, "Above all, petrol governed every movement."[37]

Following World War II, the United States was the world's most prolific producer of oil, and Americans were consuming ever-increasing amounts of it. This had a great deal to do with our remarkable prosperity. Writer and journalist James Howard Kunstler, author of *The Long Emergency*, describes the US's domestic use of fossil fuels this way:

> It is no exaggeration to state that reliable supplies of cheap oil and natural gas underlie everything we identify as the necessities of modern life — not to mention all of its comforts and luxuries: central heating, air conditioning, cars, airplanes, electric lights, inexpensive clothing, recorded music, movies, hip-replacement surgery, national defense — you name it.[38]

Most of us are familiar with regular gasoline fill-ups and the need to drive to and from work, the shopping mall, the elementary school. Cheap fuel made easy motoring typical of American life. And although that has begun to change with rising energy prices, we've barely begun a great shift. Imagine for a minute how hard most Americans would find living without a car. But aside from this most obvious of petroleum uses, there plenty of other ways we use oil in our everyday lives. Oil is so ubiquitous in our lives, we are barely aware of its centrality.

It is inevitable that when you fill up a mug with beer and begin to drink it that eventually you will reach a point at which your glass is half empty. If you go with friends to a bar, you are more likely to order a pitcher of beer to share. Now imagine that about the time that you have drunk half of it, someone announces that it is the last pitcher of beer in the whole world — that we're all very sorry, we thought we had more, but everyone in the universe has looked in their fridges, and the beer is all gone forever. So now you have half a pitcher of beer and that's it — no more. What do you do? Do you drink it fast, have one incredible party, and never drink again? Do you sell what is left to people who will pay you a lot for it? Do you hoard it, holding on to it at all costs? Do you ration it so that everyone gets a fair share? Fight over the rest of it?

It's likely that a lot of people will want that beer, and regardless of whether you share it out evenly or unevenly, people's desire for beer is going to be met with smaller and smaller supplies of beer. Now, it is possible that we could reduce desire — that if it gets inconvenient enough some beer drinkers will decide they like lemonade better anyhow. But no matter how many advertising campaigns praise the wonders of lemonade, quite a few of us are going to notice that it really isn't quite the same thing as beer, the wonder liquid.

Now, the nice thing about beer is that it is not required for human existence. (Okay, we know some people who will argue with us about this.) And in a purely technical sense, neither are oil and gas. But just about every part of our life here in the US is dependent upon oil and gas, both of which are most likely near the halfway point of availability. As we mentioned, oil doesn't just fuel our cars and heat our homes. Virtually everything we buy, from food and medicine to clothing and tools has petroleum as an ingredient. And everything we do has an energy cost. Much of that energy is supplied by oil and natural gas. And there are a lot of people who want what's left — even as it gets more expensive and harder to get out of the ground, and there is not enough to go around evenly.

No one really disputes that someday the pitcher will be half empty. When one examines the life of an oil well, it inevitably follows a pattern that looks like a bell curve. In the beginning, as an oil well starts to operate, it easily extracts oil, and production rises steadily. At a certain point in the life of the oil well, typically at about the halfway point, production peaks. All the easily extractable oil has been pumped out and the well is now working harder to extract oil that is tougher to get out of the ground. From this point on the oil is harder and harder to extract, so production slowly declines each subsequent year.

As individual regions and nations peak in oil production, the world as a whole gets closer and closer to the day when the global oil keg will reach halfway and then enter into an era of declining availability. Currently, 54 of the largest 65 oil producing nations are in decline.[39] Russia's production just declined for the first time, and at the peak of oil demand in the summer of 2008, Saudi Arabia, while strenuously denying it, seemed unable to meet demand. Large numbers of oil company executives have begun to admit we are at or near an oil peak. While tar sands, biofuels and rising prices that push the world's poor out of the market altogether have compensated to a degree, an emerging consensus suggests we are now at or very close to the world's oil peak.

Poor industry transparency makes it difficult to say for sure, but there is little doubt that for those of us not currently receiving senior citizen discounts, peak oil will happen during our lifetime, probably quite soon unless the current depression rapidly drops world demand enough to extend the oil plateau. It is possible that it is already past. This occurrence may turn out to be an event of even greater magnitude than the discovery of oil itself. In the US we have built an entire way of life on ever-increasing amounts of energy, especially oil, the liquid fossil fuel that powers 95 percent of transportation in this country.[40] It's not hard to see that peak oil will have an enormous impact on us as the global keg party winds down.

Natural gas is the other essential fossil fuel responsible for how we live our lives in the US these days. We use huge quantities of natural gas each year to heat our homes, cook our food and take hot showers. Six out of every ten homes in the US use natural gas as a heat source.[41] A natural gas well experiences a different sort of life cycle. Because it is a gas, natural gas flows out at a constant rate. When it is depleted, production drops off dramatically rather than following a curve, like oil. (Think chugging the pitcher.) In much the same way as with oil regions, natural gas regions reach a peak when the majority of the wells in that region reach their individual peaks. Right now the North American natural gas production appears to be approaching peak. Exxon's chief executive Lee Raymond was quoted in 2005 saying, "Gas production has peaked in North America."[42]

When will our global natural gas supply peak? That is one of the most urgent questions of our time and one to which the answer is not known. It's unlikely, however, that the global peak of natural gas production worldwide is very far off. Many analysts expect natural gas to peak about a decade after petroleum. It is important to understand that natural gas is much more difficult than oil to transport over long distances, so what matters most to Americans is the North American gas supply. US natural gas supplies peaked in 1973,[43] but the US has a NAFTA agreement that requires Canada to sell us much of its gas. All North American gas peaked in 2002, and soon that agreement may leave Canadians short of heating and cooking fuel.[44] Natural gas is the primary component of artificial nitrogen fertilizers and is a driving force in the rapid rise of fertilizer prices.

But aren't we making huge new discoveries every day? We hear about them in the news all the time! In fact, most of the discoveries we're making are very small in relation to world oil demand, and many of them will take a decade or more to develop. At this point, we're using six barrels of oil for every new one we discover,[45] and oil discoveries have been declining for 40 years. As Julian Darley told us in regard to the much hyped "Jack 2" discovery (which is beneath five miles of ocean), "We're digging around in the couch cushions for loose change now." [46] Even a very large find, of perhaps 30 billion barrels (the very outside estimates of the latest Brazilian offshore find), would delay the global oil peak only a year. And deep oil wells and Arctic energy finds are likely to be tremendously expensive and take years to develop — doing virtually nothing to reduce the cost of oil.

So it seems very likely that both our global pitchers of oil and natural gas are about half empty. What will that mean for us? A report commissioned by the US Department of Energy headed by Dr. Robert Hirsch states that, "the problem of the peaking of world conventional oil production is unlike any yet faced by modern industrial society." [47]

Richard Heinberg, author of *The Party's Over*, writes,

> Global oil production is peaking — for all practical purposes, now. In the past weeks [May, 2006], the *New York Times*, Bill Clinton, and the executive vice president of Ford Motor Company (among many others) have stated that world oil flow is at peak. We have even seen one of the major oil companies (Chevron) place ads in multiple magazines and newspapers in order — gently, perhaps, but insistently and conspicuously — to break the news to the American people that the era of cheap oil, and cheap energy in general, is finished, over, done, dead, and gone. And that era just happens to be the only one that Americans alive today have ever known. [48]

Saying "the era of cheap energy is over" may seem strange when crude oil prices hover around $40 per barrel, as they are at the time of this writing (early 2009), but one of the characteristics of deflation is the painful reality that prices decline — but buying power declines even faster. Even with oil down more than $50 per barrel over the previous year's prices, the number of unpaid oil bills increased over 2007.

The US Army Corps of Engineers put out a report in September of 2005 that stated, "World oil production is at or near its peak and current world demand exceeds the supply." [49] The above-mentioned Hirsch Report says that to deal with the coming peak in global oil production we would need 20 years of devoting virtually all of our national wealth and energies to developing alternative energies and building new infrastructure. The report stated that to do it in 20 years, we'd have to be devoting more of our time and energy than we did to fighting World War II. That is, most of our money, time and industry would have to be working together to make this giant change in 20 years. Otherwise, there could be major problems — a depression, huge changes in the economy, energy shortages, rationing, rolling blackouts and gas shortages poverty, even hunger. Especially hunger.

"So enough with the geology and beer analogies," you say. "I thought this book was about food." One of the most troubling ramifications of the coming peak in fossil fuels is the role that fossil energies play in how we get our food. Industrial agriculture is especially vulnerable to rising prices and declining availability of both natural gas and petroleum availability.

Petroleum has made possible the mechanization of much of the labor involved in agriculture. In 1900 roughly 38 percent of the population of the United States was actively involved in growing food. By 1950 that number had been reduced to just more than 12 percent.[50] Today less than 2 percent of the American population does that work. This shift in labor was made possible largely by the harnessing of fossil fuels, which were cheaper than human employees. Tractors and combines, among other machinery, replaced the human hand in the field. Pumps for irrigation rely on diesel fuel, as does the vast network of intercontinental trucking that hauls, on average, each item of food more than 1500 miles from where it is grown to where it is eaten. Fresh foods are made possible by refrigeration run by, you guessed it, fossil fuels.

Petroleum is also the feedstock for the pesticides used to support industrial agriculture and its vast fields of monoculture crops. Seemingly endless landscapes of corn, wheat and soybeans cover the Midwestern US and are protected with a combination of chemicals that kill the pests. When you grow a thousand acres of just one type of plant, the bugs that like to eat that plant are drawn to those fields in swarms. Without the ability to fight off enormous numbers of such pests, this system of monoculture probably wouldn't be possible.

Next there's the matter of all the nutrients needed to grow our food. We eat an incredible amount of corn in our country. A recent Corn Refiners Association study suggests corn is used as an ingredient in almost 4,000 products. This does not include the meat, dairy and eggs that are a derivative of corn used as feed or the many paper products that include corn.

Author Michael Pollan put it this way in a *Mother Jones* interview in February 2005:

> In addition to contributing to erosion, pollution, food poisoning, and the dead zone, corn requires huge amounts of fossil fuel — it takes a half gallon of fossil fuel to produce a bushel of corn. To grow the corn on which our current diet is largely based requires

providing it with an awful lot of one specific nutrient, nitrogen. The large amount of nitrogen fertilizer required to grow corn is currently created using the Haber-Bosch process of taking atmospheric nitrogen out of the air and putting into a solid state. And this process uses an inordinate amount of natural gas. But as we have already discussed, both natural gas and petroleum are finite resources beginning to enter into a stage of decreasing availability. The short-term effect is likely to be a rise in the cost of our food, especially processed food made from corn. The long-term effect will likely be failure of industrial agriculture to continue to feed the United States and the world.

All of us depend on long-haul trucking to get food to distribution centers and then to supermarkets. Most of us live some distance from our nearest stores, and we get our food by driving. Even if this problem could be overcome, household energy use amounts to 40 percent of total use, and large chunks of this come from our ovens, refrigerators, freezers and other food preparation and preservation appliances.

Taken in isolation, the idea that we'll prioritize energy for agriculture, or for any one thing or another, does make a lot of intuitive sense — as long as we are talking about some discrete, neatly isolated thing. It is easy to think that the reprioritization of resources will be both logical and inevitable — but the problem is that intuitive responses aren't always right. In actual working systems, there are a host of first priorities, all of them extremely difficult to triage.

The problem is that there are so many highest priorities in any society — do you cut back on police protection? Medicines? Ambulances? Heat for the freezing? Public transport? The transport of relief supplies? Military engagements? In times of radical shortage, prioritizing becomes the struggle of competing needs, political interests, black markets and a host of other factors, none of which ever quite get what they need. As costs rise, we can expect that we won't always respond in the most productive ways, and some energies will also be wasted.

What about renewable energies? Biofuels? Nuclear power? Hydrogen fuel cells? The truth is that none of these can replace the energy density of fossil fuels. Biofuels, for example, produce, at best, only 1.34 barrels of oil equivalent for every barrel of oil used to produce them.[51] That's not very impressive — oil gives you 30 to 100 barrels of oil for every barrel used to extract it. And it is possible that the energy return of biofuels is actually much less — that it actually consumes more fossil fuels than it replaces. And biofuels produce more greenhouse gasses, raise food prices, and essentially put cars in competition with people for basic foodstuffs. If we were to put every single acre of arable land in the US into ethanol production we could run cars for less than half a year. Biofuels have been a disaster for the environment, for the world's poor, and for the pocketbooks of ordinary Americans who suffer from high food prices.

Hydrogen is a technology that has been "just around the corner" for the past three decades, and which shows no signs of getting any closer. It is not, in fact, an energy source at all, but a medium for storing energy, and an inefficient one as well — it is four times less efficient to use electricity to generate hydrogen than it is to just use the electricity directly.[52]

Though we support growth in solar PV panels and wind production, the difficulty with both of these is that they are intermittent sources — solar cells produce energy only when the sun shines, wind turbines only when the wind blows. Thus, they both require large quantities of fossil-fueled backup capacity — up to 60 percent.[53] Add to this that both remain substantially more expensive than fossil fuels despite rising fossil energy prices, because the comparatively small technological improvements are overridden by the rising costs of the fossil fuels and metals used to make them.[54] We would love to see growth in renewable energy expand enough to meet our needs, but we have real doubts that this is feasible in the short time we have, particularly given the drying up of investment funds in the wake of the economic crisis.

Nuclear power is also dramatically more expensive than conventional electric power and requires an enormous investment in energy and infrastructure. The most compelling objection to nuclear power is that it requires that we be absolutely certain that our society will continue on precisely its present trajectory and that we will always have the knowledge, energy, wealth and technologies necessary to manage waste that will remain toxic for a hundred generations. Because we do not, at present, have a good way to manage radioactive wastes, nuclear power generally means passing the problem off to future generations, a strategy we consider unethical. The idea that our present comfort justifies putting our grandchildren at risk is ultimately wrong. As nuclear power advocate Alvin Weinberg admits,

> We nuclear people have made a Faustian bargain with society. On the one hand, we offer — in the catalytic nuclear burner — an inexhaustible source of energy....

But the price that we demand of society for this magical energy source is both a vigilance and a longevity of our social institutions that we are quite unaccustomed to....

We make two demands. The first, which I think is easier to manage, is that we exercise in nuclear technology the very best techniques and that we use people of high expertise and purpose....

The second demand is less clear, and I hope it may prove unnecessary. This is a demand for longevity in human institutions. We have relatively little problem dealing with wastes if we can assume always that there will be intelligent people around to cope with eventualities we have not though of. If the nuclear parks that I mention are permanent features of our civilization, then we presumably have the social apparatus, and possibly the sites, for dealing with our wastes indefinitely. But even our salt mine may require some surveillance if only to prevent men in the future from drilling holes into the burial grounds.

Eugene Wigner has drawn an analogy between this commitment to a permanent social order that may be implied in nuclear energy and our commitment to a stable, year-in and year-out social order when man moved from hunting and gathering to agriculture. Before agriculture, social institutions hardly required the long-lived stability that we now take so much for granted. And the commitment imposed by agriculture in a sense was forever; the land had to be tilled and irrigated every year in perpetuity; the expertise required to accomplish this task could not be allowed to perish or man would perish; his numbers could not be sustained by hunting and gathering. In the same sense, though on a much more highly sophisticated plane, the knowledge and care that goes into the proper building and operation of nuclear power plants and their subsystems is something we are committed to forever, so long as we find no other practical source of infinite extent.[55]

There are a host of reasons why we might not be able to pass on all the energy, money and technology needed to keep future generations safe from leaking nuclear waste and radiation exposure. Simple ethical principles should keep most of us from considering solutions that put others at risk. Weinberg goes on to acknowledge that nuclear power requires an enormous, technically sophisticated military presence in order to prevent the misuse of nuclear resources.

But that's probably not what will prevent a large-scale nuclear build out from occurring. Nuclear power is carbon and fossil-fuel intensive (not nearly as much as natural gas or coal, but researcher Mark Diesendorf estimates its total carbon production at about one-third that of a conventional coal plant, a proportion likely to rise as high-grade uranium is depleted by the building of new plants[56]) and takes decades to produce in quantity because of environmental and siting issues. Building plants is terribly expensive and must be heavily subsidized to compete with fossil fuel sources — and those costs will only rise as the cost of the fossil energies they depend on rise. Nuclear power is also tremendously water intensive, an issue that will increasingly come to the fore in the coming decades, as a worldwide water crisis strikes us. In the summer of 2007 the reduced water level of the Catawba River came within six inches of causing at least one nuclear reactor to shut down for safety reasons.[57] Though we probably will build some nuclear power plants, it seems clear that nuclear power cannot provide any sort of short-term, low-cost solution to our overarching problems, and that there are massive scalability issues that have not been overcome.

Although we will almost certainly build out some renewable energy sources, the reality is that our future involves using much less energy than we do now. We have no choice but to cut back radically. And a reasoned, careful, wise reduction will be more just and positive than a haphazard one done by necessity. As Transition Movement founder Rob Hopkins puts it, "small is inevitable."[58]

All of this makes it much more urgent that we get to work now if we are going to continue to feed ourselves and all the other human beings already on this planet without the help of fossil fuels. Yes, folks, the house lights are coming up as the party is winding down. It seems like we might want to sober up before trying to tackle the difficult question of just how best to deal with the problems of peak oil, chief among them fossil-fuel-based industrial agriculture.

We take it as a given in this book that whether or not it is wise to use oil to produce food, in the coming years we will have to create an agriculture that is far less dependent on fossil fuels and better adapted to the world we are going to be living in. At this center of this book is this presumption: we have no choice but to imagine and create a food system that is not fossil-fuel dependent.

A return to small-scale, sustainable agriculture with a focus on producing our food needs and wants locally would reduce our dependency on oil and natural gas in advance of their inevitable decline in availability. One obvious benefit will be the enormous amount of fuel saved by reducing the amount of food shipped all over the country. Fewer refrigerated tractor trailers crisscrossing the country means less oil needed as a nation.

Changes such as removing some of the mechanization from our agriculture and reducing or eliminating the use of synthetic pesticides and fertilizers will reduce our dependency on fossil fuels and on the foreign countries in possession of the majority of what fuels remain. Two-thirds of the world's remaining oil reserves are in the Middle East.[59] Much of the remaining natural gas is there too. If we needed a great deal less of their oil and natural gas to grow our own food, we would be less likely to get caught up in deadly conflicts that require huge amounts of money, energy and, worse yet, the lives of our men and women in military service. Imagine if we refocused the amount of money and human resources spent intervening in Iraq on learning how to grow our own food without Middle Eastern oil. We could disengage from a region that obviously isn't interested in our meddling.

Less oil involved in growing our food will also mean more oil available for precious commodities like medical equipment and necessary pharmaceuticals. Removing fossil fuels from our food could help us more gradually adjust to decreasing stocks of really important petroleum derivatives rather than face a drastic decline in their availability. Even more important, the health benefits of a more localized, nutritious diet might reduce our need for medical equipment and drugs.

Making this change now, rather than waiting until the peaking of fossil fuels creates more severe social disruptions, is important because it will take time to learn how to grow our own food without fossil fuel inputs. And it will take time to learn how to cook with whole ingredients and to adjust to a more seasonal diet. These changes will be much easier if we do them now while we have time to adjust rather than more abruptly in a time of crisis.

Climate Change

When the rain falls down, it don't fall on one man's house.
— Bob Marley —

In 2007, when the IPCC report on world climate change was released, billions of people began to realize just how serious climate change is. If there was any doubt left that the data shows that we are causing catastrophic global warming, that doubt has now been eliminated. Thousands of scientists agreed that we are facing ecological disaster.

Almost before the IPCC report was released, more data began to pour in, indicating that the IPCC had substantially underestimated the seriousness of climate change. For example, IPCC projections were based upon emissions data from the 1990s, but shortly after the report was released, it became evident that CO_2 emissions were rising three times faster than the IPCC had estimated.[60]

The IPCC report estimated that Arctic ice might disappear by the end of the century. But as data came in from the Arctic in the summer of 2007, it became clear that the Arctic might be ice free as early as 2013, 85 years earlier than projected just a few months before.[61]

One of the nightmare scenarios of climate change has always been the release of vast stores of methane from the Arctic seas into the atmosphere, because methane's global warming properties are 20 times greater than those of carbon dioxide. Huge quantities of methane are stored in the Arctic, and the last time Arctic seas melted, half the life on earth died off. In spring 2008 a report came out that methane was indeed bubbling up from Arctic seas.

> Since methane is a potent greenhouse gas, more worrisome than carbon dioxide, the result would be a drastic acceleration of global warming. Until now this idea was mostly academic; scientists had warned that such a thing could happen. Now it seems more likely that it will.[62]

New research released on October of 2008 found that methane levels in the atmosphere had risen dramatically in 2007 — and no one was entirely sure why.[63]

Meanwhile, reports from Carbon Equity and NASA's chief climate scientist, Dr. James Hansen, suggested that the world's climate sensitivity was about twice as great as previous estimates and that the IPCC numbers of 450 or 550 ppm were simply wrong. The crucial number is 300 or 350 ppm of carbon — and we're at about 390.[64] That is, we have to make rapid, deep cuts in emissions and, simultaneously, find ways to extract carbon from the atmosphere. We do not have time to wait for a major technical build out. We will have to rely on existing technologies and simply cease to produce fossil fuels. The estimated sustainable rate of carbon production is less than

1 ton per person, the same as the current carbon output of the average person in India.

Indeed, we are most likely already committed to a substantial worldwide temperature rise and the ensuing consequences, and we are thus facing massive extinctions, rising seas, increasingly violent storms, drought, floods and famine — nearly all the horsemen of the apocalypse. The planet will continue to warm for the next century, affecting our agriculture, our culture and our lives in dramatic ways no matter what we do. But there is a huge difference between what will happen if we fail to mitigate climate change and our future if we do cease to burn fossil fuels.

One of the most powerful tools we have to address climate change is our agriculture. Our food systems are also desperately endangered by unchecked climate change. As we did our research for this book, trying to determine whether and how the world could be fed, the biggest question mark we encountered was climate change. If we make radical changes in our pattern of carbon emissions very rapidly, there is every hope we might well not endure a massive worldwide famine. But if we do not, there is every reason to believe our grandchildren may go hungry.

A short survey of the potential consequences of climate change for food production worldwide gives a chilling picture. It is difficult to predict exactly what will happen where, but computer models offer some disquieting suggestions about the increase of drought. For example, a recent study suggests that Sydney, Australia, and the surrounding area will be in a permanent state of devastating drought by 2070.[65] In 2007, an extended drought destroyed much of the Australian grain harvest, helping to cause worldwide rises in the price of staples.

Elizabeth Kolbert documents in her book, *Field Notes from a Catastrophe,* that supercomputer models suggest that the probability of severe drought through much of the US becomes very high. She observes,

> In much the same way that wind velocity is measured using the Beaufort scale, water availability is measured using the Palmer Drought Severity Index.... When [David Rind, scientist for the GISS Climate Group] applied the index to the GISS model for doubled CO_2, it showed most of the continental United States would be suffering under severe drought conditions. When he applied the index to the GFDL model, the results were even more dire. Rind created two maps to illustrate these findings. Yellow represented a 40 to 60 percent chance of summertime drought, ochre

a 60 to 80 percent chance, and brown an 80 to 100 percent chance. In the first map, showing the GISS results, the Northeast was yellow, the Midwest was ochre, and the Rocky Mountain states and California were brown. In the second, showing the GFDL results, brown covered practically the entire country.

"I gave a talk based on these drought indices out in California to water-resource managers," Rind told me. "And they said, 'Well, if that happens, forget it.' There's just no way they could deal with that."[66]

Rind went on to tell Kolbert that there is no way to adapt to those levels of drought and that he "wouldn't be shocked to find out that by 2100 most things were destroyed." The doubling of atmospheric carbon that Rind fears is well within the present possibilities, sadly enough. No one can predict precisely how fast the rate of atmospheric carbon will rise, because carbon release is a snowball effect: higher temperatures melt permafrost, release methane from seas and make soils and water less able to absorb carbon. They destroy the rainforest's ability to sequester carbon and eventually cause them to catch fire, pushing more carbon into the atmosphere. There is no doubt whatever that without an enormous increase in mitigation and a reduction of emissions we will reach the critical doubling point by the middle of the century, and the survival of a large percentage of the human populace will be in serious doubt.

Currently, California is enduring extreme drought, while the Prairie states and parts of the Southwest are experiencing conditions that one commentator observed is "worse than the dustbowl." The American Midwest, our bread basket, and much of Africa, Australia, the Mediterranean and Central Asia too, can expect increased drought frequency; and when rain does come, there will be risks of intense flooding. Ethiopia is currently enduring a massive famine, probably in part due to climate-change-induced drought. It is impossible to identify any single weather event as caused by climate change — but there is no doubt that the frequency of droughts, cyclones and hurricanes such as the one that destroyed much of Burma in 2008 is increasing rapidly and will continue to increase.

Nearly half of the human population depends on rice harvests to keep them alive. The International Rice Research Institute in the Philippines has documented that with every degree of overnight temperature rise, rice yields fall by 15 percent.[67] The now-inevitable two-degree rise in world temperatures is likely, then, to seriously alter the food security of millions of people worldwide. The rise in temperature will also affect yields of other staples, including wheat and corn. Increasing ozone levels because of pollution suggest that total grain crop yields worldwide may fall by as much as 30 percent over the next 40 years.[68] And that doesn't take into account the impact of the aforementioned drought. Because the world population is predicted to increase by almost one-third before stabilizing, and the world is already eating its grain reserves, the consequences could be disastrous.

Rising seas are both a short-term threat — because storm surges and disasters disrupt food supplies, destroy harvests, create refugees, leave croplands covered with salt and destroy distribution infrastructure such as roads and trains — and a long-term one — because salt water from rising seas contaminates groundwater needed for irrigation, and rising sea levels make land uninhabitable and reduce snow pack that supplies water to dry regions. The more disasters we have to contend with, the less wealth we have for other necessary projects. Nearly half of the earth's population lives within 50 miles of the ocean, and many of those people will no longer be able to live where they do. Large pieces of the world's arable lands also lie along coasts. We can expect populations to be in motion — and in crisis — increasingly often, and can count on seeing regular disruptions in crops.

Only 17 percent of the world's agricultural land is currently irrigated, but that land produces between 30 and 40 percent of the world's staple cereal crops. Economists estimate that we could lose as much as 285 million tons of cereals each year because of reduction of water for irrigation.[69] Global warming represents an enormous threat to the water supplies of millions and to millions more who depend on irrigated land for food. The disappearance of glaciers means that millions who rely on melt-off for water supplies in places like Pakistan, Bolivia, western China and Ecuador will see their water disappear. Rising sea levels will contaminate fresh water needed for drinking and agriculture, and will salinate productive land in Britain, India, the Southern US, Thailand, Indonesia, Argentina and other nations. Water shortages will affect up to 600 million additional people directly, and another 300 million will see food availability fall and prices skyrocket.[70]

After all that deeply depressing news, however, there are some reasons for optimism. One of them is that the transition to organic, sustainable, small-scale agriculture by millions of people in the US and billions world wide could do an enormous amount to mitigate the consequences of climate change. Becoming a small farmer is not just a good idea for your own security, you might actually save the planet doing it. As agrarian activist Vandana Shiva has put it, all of our emphasis on lowering carbon fails to recognize that we need more carbon — in soils — and that the power of locally adapted agriculture is the "only adaption strategy that gives us any hope."[71]

There are a number of ways in which small-scale, relocalized, sustainable agriculture can help sequester carbon and prevent it from being put into the atmosphere to begin with. The first, and most obvious, aspect is that the transportation of food over long distance makes a tremendous contribution to burning carbon. Delicate produce is often shipped by air from Israel to the US or New Zealand to Britain. Air travel, besides emitting large quantities of carbon, creates contrails that increase the effects of global warming. When your kiwi fruit or grapes travel from overseas, it is as if someone drove them to you in a low-mileage Hummer with the windows open and the A/C on.

Whether flown or trucked, all industrial food has a heavy carbon impact. Food is fertilized with fossil fuels, including artificial nitrogen, which creates the potent greenhouse gas nitrous oxide. Pesticides are manufactured with and from petrochemicals. Soil amendments are trucked around the world, then added to soils with carbon-spewing tractors. The food is often harvested mechanically, packed into warehouses cooled with fossil fuels, and then trucked, shipped, refrigerated, processed in every way, each with its carbon impact, until the day you drive to the supermarket to buy it. Moving the food economy home eliminates many of those stages. The need for pesticides and chemical fertilizers is reduced or eliminated. There is no need for warehousing, shipping or energy intensive preservation techniques that allow the food to spend a week or ten days in transit from field to table. When you walk out your door or down the street to a neighbor to pick up your eggs and vegetables, you spare the earth tremendous consequences.

Industrial livestock farming is one of the largest contributors to global warming. Researchers at the University of Chicago have calculated that the impact of switching from a normal, American meat-eating diet to a vegan one would save significantly more carbon than converting our car fleet to hybrids. The climate-change effects of industrial meat production is enormous — both because animal feces is the largest source of methane (one of the most potent warming gases) in the US[72] and because it takes a great deal of grain to produce meat. It takes about 15 pounds of grain to produce 2 pounds of industrial beef, almost 9 pounds to produce the same amount of industrial pork, and 4.5 pounds of grain to produce 2 pounds of chicken. Add to that the shipping and transport costs of moving cows and chickens and meat around, of slaughterhouses and manure disposal, and it becomes clear that what we eat is destroying our children's future.

Reducing meat consumption is difficult for many people who are accustomed to lots of hamburgers. But a garden can be a good way of transitioning to a vegetarian or less meat-intensive diet. The sheer good taste of the food makes the flavors of meat less necessary. Moreover, livestock raised on pastures, eating the foods they are meant to eat, produce considerably less methane while also adding their manures to the soil and increasing the ability of pastures to sequester carbon. Less meat, raised sustainably in integrated agriculture is necessary to prevent runaway climate change.

Besides the many ways that becoming a nation of farmers can reduce our carbon output, the practice of sustainable agriculture can actually reduce existing carbon in the atmosphere by raising the levels of soil humus. We do this every time we add compost or mulch to our ground, every time we choose not to till or plow, and leave soil undisturbed. For large-scale grain farming, UC Davis Professor Johan Six estimates that 80 to 200 million tons of carbon could be pulled out of the atmosphere and sequestered in the soil by the use of conservation tillage, which reduces soil disturbance and requires fewer tractors and less oil and gas.[73] We could reduce carbon in the atmosphere at present by 5 percent or more simply by raising the level of humus in agricultural soils and reducing tillage. Doing so would also repair badly depleted farmland, damaged over the years by industrial agriculture.

More carbon still could be removed from the atmosphere if we were to raise the levels of humus in the millions of acres in the industrialized world that consist of back and front yards; public green spaces; office parks; church, synagogue and mosque grounds; and the White House lawn. The average residential home sits on slightly less than one quarter of an acre of land. By adding all the residential yards and commercial green spaces, public parks, etc., there are more than 7 million acres of green space in the US with soils that could be enriched to hold carbon.

In fact, this return of carbon to soil has even greater possibilities, as David Holmgren, co-originator of permaculture and author argues in *Permaculture: Principles and Pathways Beyond Sustainability*. Holmgren notes wisely,

Concern about the greenhouse effect has combined with the understanding that trees store carbon to produce a huge increase in research into "carbon sequestration" by trees. The interest in using trees as a "sink" to get rid of unwanted atmospheric carbon dioxide has increased awareness, as well as scientific knowledge, of the role of trees in storing carbon. From a permaculture perspective, the debate and activity is back-to-front; it focuses on the problem: carbon dioxide pollutions, rather than on carbon as a source of fuel for new life.[74]

Though it is not clear how much carbon is sequestered by trees in temperate climates, forests create soil humus naturally by dropping leaves and building soil that way. But Holmgren is right on target in that we need to think about ways that atmospheric carbon can be used to compensate for the agricultural losses of global warming. Recently, Gaia Theory creator James Lovelock argued that the only really viable remaining solution to climate change would be the transformation of our agriculture so the soil could hold more carbon. "It would mean farmers turning all their agricultural waste — which contains carbon that the plants have spent the summer sequestering — into non- biodegradable charcoal, and burying it in the soil. Then you can start shifting really hefty quantities of carbon out of the system and pull the CO_2 down quite fast."[75] In this model, our destructive agriculture is transformed into something fundamentally regenerative — and enormously helpful.

What is needed to do this is simply a commitment to return organic material to the soil and to cease rototilling and plowing to disturb it. Instead, we would return all of our spare organic material — leaves, food scraps, animal manures, waste hay and straw, weeds that have not gone to seed — to our soil in the form of sheet mulch (that is, lots of dry material like straw or leaves spread over the ground and nitrogen-rich materials like manures, food scraps, coffee grounds and grass clippings mixed in) or as compost. Instead of tilling, we would plant directly into mulched ground. This keeps the carbon sequestered. As levels of soil humus rise over the years, more atmospheric carbon would be removed.

Every one of us with any soil can do this — your tiny backyard or your giant farm can reduce the impact of global warming that we've already created. And by growing food and living locally, you can cease putting food-related greenhouse gasses into the atmosphere. Growing our own food may be the single most important way any of us can preserve the planet from climate change.

Economic Injustice and World Hunger

Them who's got, got out of town,
Them who ain't got left to drown.
Tell me how can a poor man stand such times and live?
— BRUCE SPRINGSTEEN AND "BLIND" ALFRED REED —

What is the most common cause of hunger in the world? Is it drought? Flood? Locusts? Crop diseases? Nope. In fact, most hunger in the world has absolutely nothing to do with food shortages. Overwhelmingly, hunger is caused by unequal access to food, land and wealth. We tend to assume that food shortage is associated only with famine, but most of the people who go to bed hungry, both in rich and poor countries, do so in places where markets are filled with food that they cannot have.

So much of the discourse about the present food crisis has focused on the necessity of raising yields with new technologies. Though it is true that we may need more food in coming years, it is also true that the world produces about twice as many calories of food as are needed for its entire population. The problem is food access, and any discussion must begin not from unproven technologies and fantasies of massive yield increases, but from the truth that the hunger of the poor is in part a choice of the rich.

A 1997 study found, for example, that 78 percent of all the malnourished children in the poor world live in countries with food surpluses.[76] Economist Amartya Sen has demonstrated that almost all cases of famine in the 20th century were caused not by food shortages but by inequity and politics that deprive the poor.[77] Because of destructive trade agreements, many nations regularly export food staples needed by their own populace. Brazil, for example, exported 20 billion dollars' worth of food in 2002, while 70 million people suffered hunger. During the massive famines in Ethiopia in the 1980s, which moved the world, Ethiopia was still exporting food.[78] Many of even the poorest nations in the world can feed themselves, or could in a society with fairer allocation of resources.

In much of Africa, which we think of as the land of famine, there are areas of high-quality crop land that are not being farmed. Frances Moore Lappé, Joseph Collins and Peter Rosset, in *World Hunger: Twelve Myths*, document the reasons for this, which include colonial land grabs, pressure from outside interests to invest in export crops and industrial agriculture rather than local small-scale farming, misguided policies that fail to connect with women, who are the major food producers of the region, and a whole host of reasons rarely presented along with the faces of hungry children. To a large degree, such poverty is a legacy of the impact that colonialism and Western society have had, and still are having, upon poorer nations. So there is little wonder that we fail to remediate the world poverty we help create and do not really understand. Indeed, there is compelling evidence that conflict and genocide in Somalia and Rwanda are linked to mandated shifts in agricultural policy that take food out of the mouths of people and send it abroad for export.[79]

It is hard for many of us to grasp the degree to which the Western lifestyle is implicated in the suffering of others. George Monbiot says this,

> The problem [of getting first worlders to make sacrifices for the benefit of others] is compounded by the fact that the connection between cause and effect seems so improbable. By turning on the lights, filling the kettle, taking the children to school, driving to the shops, we are condemning other people to death. We never chose to do this. We do not see ourselves as killers. We perform these acts without passion or intent.[80]

Although Monbiot is speaking specifically of climate change, we think his quote bears consideration precisely because it seems so unimaginable to most people to recognize the depth of the negative effect that some of our actions have on others, without ever wishing to do them harm. We don't realize that when we buy imported shrimp or coffee we are often literally taking food from poor people. We don't realize that we are doing harm by our economic system; in fact the economic system conspires to make it nearly impossible to figure out whether what we're doing is destructive or regenerative. We're not given the urgent information that we need in order to spend and buy and use less to preserve other lives. We're told the opposite: "Go Shopping" was the rallying cry after September 11. Never mind that, in part, the violence of terrorism was fueled by oil money, money we gave terrorists when we drove off to go shopping. We have been assured that "a rising tide lifts all boats" — that it is necessary for us to make rich people even richer, because that will, in turn, enrich the poor. But as we see now, the consequence of our globalization has been disastrous — for the planet as a whole and for the poor whose food systems have been disrupted and who never had a chance to be lifted by any tide.

And the fact that we do not realize this is no accident. We are told over and over again that things like our food choices and how we use energy at home are not "important" they are merely "personal" choices, without political implications. And yet, it turns out that the most ordinary acts of our lives are, in many cases, the ones with the greatest political impact. Sharon has written about this before. She says,

> The truth is that we have been sold a bill of goods by our society when we buy into the notion that we can choose between private and public solutions, rather than doing both. As long as loud voices cried out, "You go do the important work of manufacturing Business to Business Widget Distribution software, and leave the dull, unimportant stuff about dinner to ConAg and McDonalds" we did not look, we did not see, and we let a great deal of wealth and time and security be destroyed in the service of building corporate wealth.[81]

The recognition that we are fully implicated in poverty and human suffering is one of the most painful and difficult concepts imaginable for all of us. We want to be generous and giving, both to see ourselves that way and also to be that in truth. But it is also one of the most necessary transformations of thought. Because right now we fail to see that world poverty and hunger are in part created by the system that enables our lives and that this does not have to be so.

Jeremy Seabrook describes our efforts to eliminate poverty and hunger this way.

> It is now taken for granted that the relief of poverty is the chief objective of all politicians, international institutions, donors and charities. This dedication is revealed most clearly in a determination to preserve them. Like all great historical monuments, there should be a Society for the Preservation of the Poor; only, since it is written into the very structures of the global economy, no special arrangements are required. There is not the remotest chance that poverty will be abolished, but every chance that the poor themselves might perish.[82]

It is hard for many of us to recognize that the economy and the society we live in help create poverty, and that often our efforts to relieve it work to calcify the system and create more poverty. It is hard to come to believe that the way we in the West live creates poverty and insecurity for others, but it is true. We live in an economy entirely based on the endless mantra of economic growth. As Seabrook observes in *The No-Nonsense Guide to World Poverty*,

> Whichever way you look at it, extreme poverty persists while social injustice increases all the time. This has a powerful impact on discussions of poverty, since the model of improvement embodied in globalization is that *the poor will become a little less poor only if the rich become much richer.*"[83]

We are being told the lie that if the rich get richer, it makes other people less poor. Think about it for a moment — about how crazy that idea is. Wouldn't it make much more sense to directly enrich the poor, to help them get land and access to resources? But if we did that, of course, the rich would stop getting richer. As Pat Murphy puts it in *Plan C*,

> The second metaphor is the *trickle down theory*, which argues that if the rich get richer some percentage of their riches will trickle down to the less rich, making them better off than they were before. As we have seen, on a worldwide basis such trickling is minimal if it exists at all. But economists argue that life is still better for those with low pay because society has advanced to such an extent that even those in poverty are better off than they were in the past.... The poor have not generally subscribed to this argument.[84]

Most of what we do now is shift around the small percentage of wealth allotted to the 94 percent of us who are not among the world's most wealthy. For example, globalization has moved much of the wealth that used to be in the hands of blue-collar American families overseas to Asia. But in fact, the percentage of wealth that is shared in a globalized economy is smaller than it ever has been. Over the past 150 years, wealth in Europe, Japan and the US has increased 24 times, while in Africa it has grown barely at all, in Asia it has less than doubled, and in Latin America it has only just doubled.[85] In the US, 33.4% of all net worth is held by 1% of the population, and only 30% of the nation's total wealth is held by 90% of the population.[86] All that energy, all that money, and yet things have effectively stayed the same for many of the poor.

And in many ways, things have gotten worse. Historically, rural peoples have been quite poor but often, despite their poverty, could grow enough food to feed themselves. However, over recent decades, industrial agriculture and widespread industrialization have moved large chunks of the human population into cities, promising more wealth; but rising food and energy prices (rising because of this move and the new demands for energy and meat of this same urban population), have stripped people of land, leaving them unable to feed their families. As Peter Menzel and Faith D'Aluisio report, the same food companies have advertised their way into a large portion of the food budgets of the poor, using strategies that create dependencies:

> Food corporations have learned how to enter the developing world. Few of the families we met could afford a week's worth of a processed food item at one time, so the global food companies make their wares more affordable by offering them in single-serving packets. In Manila, individual portions of "foods" such as imitation-cheese spreads, chips and spiced rice dishes are much like the convenience packs sold in the United States. Highly processed foods are making inroads into the diets of the developing world, and with that comes dependence.
>
> Consider Alma Casales, who lives with her family outside Cuernavaca, Mexico. She was surprised to learn that the six gallons of Coca-Cola that she was buying for her family consists mostly of sugar water. Over time, the Casales family came to drink Coke at every meal, and in between. Casales's grocery list included a lot of fresh fruits and vegetables, as well as a lot of branded, packaged convenience foods. She could still quickly calculate the number of tortillas her family eats in a week (22 pounds' worth), but when it came time to tally up the snack foods and peripheral purchases, the numbers got fuzzier.
>
> We have visited hundreds of families in their kitchens and homes around the world over the last 15 years, and both here and abroad, we have seen a grand march toward unsustainability as some of us play catch up and the rest of us play keep up. Nearly everyone would love to have the wealth and choices that we enjoy in the United States. But that aspiration toward overflowing grocery aisles, with gas-guzzling trucks feeding a new appetite for imitation cheese spread, seems impossible to sustain. And it could lead to flour sacks full of nothing. [87]

Real alleviation of poverty and hunger means reallocating the resources of our world into the hands of people who need them most, and that means a little less for the richest folks out there. This is not only ethically the right thing to do, it is necessary. There is no hope that poorer, newly industrializing nations such as China and India will ever help us meet global warming targets if it means a great inequity between their population and that of the US. Indeed, Russia, India and China have all said so quite explicitly. The only alternative to the death of millions or billions in a game of global chicken is for everyone to accept that the world cannot afford rich people in any nation.

Industrial agriculture has worked to consolidate land ownership into the hands of smaller and smaller populations. First, rich nations dumped large quantities of cheap, subsidized grain on poor nations, competing with local farmers and, in many cases, driving them into cities. Local self-sufficiency was destroyed. Now, as the price of food has risen dramatically, those created dependencies on cheap grain that doesn't exist anymore mean that millions are in danger of starvation.

It is common to blame the problems on overpopulation. Reports from the field call the issue "Malthusian," after the 19th-century author who claimed that population growth would overwhelm food production and lead to starvation. But population growth was 1.6 percent from 2007 to 2008, while food inflation was more than ten times that — the numbers simply don't add up. We didn't suddenly gain billions of new people; what we gained were new consumers of meat and new owners of cars, which started to compete with people for food — and the cars of the rich world get to the table first.

Population is a problem, one we will discuss in great detail later in this book, and it will be difficult for many regions and the world as a whole to feed itself in the coming decades. But that makes it only more urgent that we recreate food sovereignties and that we change the way we eat and live so that there is enough to go around.

What is the best strategy of reallocation? Well, one such strategy would be to enable the world's farmers, who are often among the poorest and hungriest people in the world, to eat what they grow (that is, for those of us who live in nations where there is plenty of land and food to eat our own food rather than rely on the exports of poor nations) and to have sufficient land to feed themselves and their neighbors.

Peter Rosset notes that most of the world's poorest people are either urban slum dwellers or land-poor farmers without enough land to feed themselves. Most urban slum dwellers are displaced farmers — those who lost their land due to dumping or agricultural policies that moved them off their land. Both groups are increasing, in large degree because of global economic policies that prioritize food for export on the best land and that allow large quantities of land to be held in the hands of the richest. Rosset notes,

> The expansion of agricultural production for export, controlled by wealthy elites who own the best lands, continually displaces the poor to ever more marginal areas for farming. They are forced to fell forests located on poor soils, to farm this, easily eroded soils on steep slopes, and to try to eke out a living on desert margins and in rainforests. As they fall deeper into poverty, they are often accused of contributing to environmental degradation.[88]

In this system, poor people who depend on the land, and who best understand the urgency of preserving it, are forced by necessity to degrade and destroy it — and they, rather than we, are held responsible. But a large part of the responsibility rests on the way we eat. And this is an important point, because it acknowledges that there are things we in the wealthy nations can do to enable poorer people to eat better and to keep their lives. We can keep their blood off of our hands. This is desperately necessary in the face of the growing food crisis.

One way we can do this is simply to grow our own food, to rely not on foods grown thousands of miles away but on local farms and in our own gardens. We can concentrate on creating food sovereignty and enabling it in poor nations. We can cut back on globalized food trade, importing primarily high-value, fair-traded dry goods such as spices and coffee that take little energy to transport and place limits on food speculation, which drives up prices so that multinationals can get richer at the expense of the poor. Most of all, we can recognize that increasing our local food self-sufficiency is as urgent in the rich world as in the poor.

After all, globalization will come to an end anyway, as economist Jeff Rubin observes. The rising costs of transportation and the trade deficit in the US make it inevitable that we will be looking more locally to meet our basic needs. Globalization's demise is coming.

When we grow our own food, or buy it directly from local farmers, we take power and money away from multinational corporations and put it in the hands of our neighbors, many of whom, despite being from the industrialized world, are also the economic victims of globalization. In fact, we all know that hunger does not stem from famine, but from injustice, because we know that there are 30 million people in the United States who can't afford a basic, nutritious diet. More than 8 million children know hunger, and 20 million are in danger of it.[89] And yet, we live in the richest nation in the world, filled with the greatest variety of foods imaginable. In fact, it turns out that the things that make us poor — lack of education, lack of access to things like land and home, and the extractive power of the industrial economy — are precisely the things that make other people poor.

We can create both local and distant wealth by creating local food systems. We can enrich our neighbors, but also stop impoverishing our distant neighbors from other nations. When we stop buying food from multinational corporations, we do several things. We make it harder for multinationals to extract wealth and the best land of other nations. If we don't buy their products, they won't hold that land, often taken from local peasants in the first place. If they don't need that land, the local farmers may be able to use it for their own needs. If we grow more of our own food, we can perhaps afford to donate food and money to help the hungry, both near us and very far away.

Disappearing Farmers

One of the saddest, angriest and most eloquent pieces of writing we've ever read was written by Israeli farmer and writer Elaine Solowey. In it, she narrates the pain suffered by farmers around the world over the past 70 years of agricultural and political policies. She writes of the betrayal of farmers and the cost for them and societies:

> For the last 100 years there has been a world-wide effort to get rid of farmers.... Some were eliminated for political reasons the way that Stalin starved the Ukrainians to death and shipped the kulaks off to Siberia. Some were driven off their land by the vast illegal enclosure actions of wealthy landowners in South American nations. The Nazis in WWII swept up the farming inhabitants of Russian and Polish and Jewish villages and worked them to death in the factories that fed their war machine. Millions of farmers were displaced by dams financed by the World Bank. Millions more were removed from agriculture by the policies of the WTO.

Some had their farms taxed out from under them and the land turned over to developers who built cheap houses and strip malls on it. And more were eliminated by agricultural globalization, the belief that every farmer should specialize and produce as much of their single product as possible (to the neglect of everything else) — then we would all merrily cross — ship these things to each other for ever.

Still others were "sanitized" out of business. The small dairies and animal husbandry operations could not afford the large and expensive machines needed to raise animals and process milk and meat under the rules of "modern" hygiene. These small operations were declared to be inefficient and dirty, never mind the fact that modern "hygienic" production units for meat and milk are night-marishly cruel, filthy, and squalid. (Indeed, a backyard pigpen or chicken coop is a relative paradise compared the confining "crush" pens of the modern pig farm or the cage batteries of the modern poultry house.) So farmers were eliminated, one after another, by murder, displacement, bankruptcy, by taxes that would not let land be passed from generation, by on-farm prices that left farmers un-able to feed their own families, by subsidies that favored farms be-yond human scale. Many studies over the years showed that the small farm produced much more food with less environmental damage than the larger "economic" models. But the "economic" models produced more of their one product and looked good on paper, never mind the cost to the locale, the water or the soil or the people who lived in the area.

Get big, said the US secretary of agriculture. Or get out. So we got out.[90]

She goes on to conclude that now it is not just farmers who are suffering from this loss, but the rest of the world as well. She argues that just when the world is hungry, as food riots break out all over, when the call is for more food production worldwide, there's "not a bibbed overall in sight." That is, the farmers are gone, are aging (the average age of American farm-ers is nearly 60 years old) or are starving, displaced by neoliberal economic policies that drive them to cities where they can no longer afford to eat.

We imagine that many of our readers find it hard to imagine that the lack of farmers is a crisis on the scale of economic inequity, climate change, and peak energy. But we want you to try and grasp that the destruction of farmers and farming communities all over the US and the world is, in fact, a terrible danger to the world at large, potentially a major contributor to food insecurity both among the world's poor and in the US. We believe our future may well hinge upon whether we are able to create new farmers.

It is easy in our vast agricultural system to imagine that someone will always produce what is needed and make sure we can get it. But as we've seen, that system has already begun to fall apart. However, we have become so disconnected from agriculture that most Americans simply don't fully grasp the relationship between farming and food in any meaningful sense. Writer and nutritionist Joan Dye Gussow describes the gap in this understanding by even well-intentioned people in her book *The Organic Life*.

> The extent to which I'm not self-sufficient reminds me constantly that I depend, as we all do, on neighbors — increasingly remote neighbors — to carry on for us the demanding work of food production. Because farmers keep planting and harvesting, tending trees and vines and caring for animals and birds, none of us is required to survive on our own production capacity.
>
> Consequently, the invisibility of these people as the *source* of our food never ceases to alarm me; witness a commentary by David Hage recently published in *The Nation* asking why taxpayers should be rescuing farmers who are once again in financial trouble. The first answer, the author says, is because Congress always responds to the farm lobby. "A second answer is that a government should cushion its people against the cruelties of the market." I'm waiting here for him to mention the fact that farmers grow our food and we'd starve without them, but he says, "Finally, farmers give the nation a certain economic and social diversity. They provide a counterweight to the grain and meat-packing giants that control our food production, and they undergird a rural culture that millions of families still find preferable to suburbanized America." I'm certain that this writer knows that we need farms to produce food, because he's located in the middle of farming country, but he seems to feel no necessity to point out that these providers of economic and social diversity, these undergirders of rural culture, feed us. [91]

The essay Gussow cites seems to share a widespread perception that farmers don't matter — that food will always be delivered from somewhere.

And that has been the overwhelming message of our society as a whole —
that in a globalized world there is always someone to provide food. In fact,
however, there's evidence that suggests that a world with too few farmers
may well be a complete and utter disaster for some societies.

We would guess that most Americans, raised on the narrative of US
victory over Communism, never imagined that the Soviet Union may have
collapsed in large part because of lack of farmers. And yet, that's precisely
the claim made by former acting Prime Minister Yegor Gaidar in his recent
book, *Collapse of an Empire: Lessons for Modern Russia*. His claim is that
the Soviet Union's collapse came because of its policy of moving farmers
into factories and cities, and buying cheap grain on the world market. [92]

When energy prices and thus the economy collapsed, the Soviet Union
could no longer buy sufficient grain to feed the population or afford to
run the heavy mechanized machinery it depended on for food. Without
enough farmers on the land to increase domestic production, the people
went hungry, and the government fell apart. Gaidar notes that the move to
world grain markets seemed entirely rational — as long as there was plenty
of money to buy wheat. Without stable access to bread, the Soviet era came
rapidly to an end. Starvation was narrowly averted in Russia, mostly by the
re-creation of kitchen gardens and vacant lot urban farming. At one point,
10 percent of the land supported 90 percent of the population.[93] As the
example of the Soviet Union shows, the number of farmers you have can
determine the stability of governments and whether a population goes
hungry.

Now, it is common for Americans to argue that examples from communist countries do not apply to them — that any seeming similarities are
overwhelmed by the differences in economic structure. But Dmitry Orlov,
author of *Reinventing Collapse*, argues otherwise. He observes that despite
our disinclination to consider them, the similarities are greater than our
differences. Orlov argues,

> In spite of the monumental failures of Soviet agriculture, the over-
> all structure of Soviet-style food delivery proved to be paradoxi-
> cally resilient in the face of economic collapse and disruption. The
> combination of local food stockpiles administered by politicians
> conditioned to treat bread riots as career-ending calamities, the
> prevalence of government institutions that attended to the suste-
> nance of their employees and plenty of kitchen gardens, meant that

there was no starvation and very little malnutrition. But will fate be as kind to the United States?

In the United States, most people get their food from a supermarket, which is supplied from far away using refrigerated diesel trucks, making them entirely dependent on the widespread availability of transportation fuels and the continued maintenance of the interstate highway system. In an energy-scarce world, neither of these is a given. Most supermarket chains have just a few days' worth of food in their inventory, relying on advanced logistical planning and just-in-time delivery to meet demand. Thus, in many places, food supply problems are almost guaranteed to develop. When they do, no local authority is in a position to exercise control over the situation and the problem is handed over to federal emergency management authorities. Based on their performance after Hurricane Katrina, these authorities are not only manifestly incompetent, but also appear to be ruled by the ethos that it is better for the government to deny services than provide them, to avoid creating a population that is dependent on government help.

Many people in the United States don't even bother to shop and just eat fast food. The drive to maximize profit while minimizing costs has resulted in a product that manipulates the senses into accepting as edible something that is mainly a waste product. Under strict process control procedures, agro-industrial wastes, sugar, fat and salt are combined into an appealing presentation, packaged, and reinforced by vigorous advertising. Once accepted, it beguiles the senses by its reliable consistency, creating a lifelong addiction to bad food. The chemical industry obliges with an array of deodorants to mask the sickly body odor such a diet produces. Immersed for a lifetime in a field of artificial sensory perceptions, dominated by chemical, man-made tastes and smells, people recoil in shock when confronted with something natural, be it a simple piece of boiled chicken liver or the smell of a healthy human body. Perversely, they do not mind car exhaust and actually like the carcinogenic "new car smell" of vinyl upholstery.[94]

In agriculture, the similarities between the Soviet Union and the US are striking. Both pursued policies of massive industrialization of agriculture, and both displaced farmers at a striking pace. The US, more industrialized, displaced more farmers, ultimately leaving less than 2 percent of the American population to feed the other 98 percent.

The similarities may be closer than we have been permitted to understand in the past, when both nations endured famine in large part due to mismanagement within the lifetimes of our grandparents. In 2008, Russian researcher Boris Borisov produced an article in which he used US Census data to estimate that 7 million Americans died of famine during the Great Depression.[95] There are questions of methodology and the degree to which Borisov was motivated by ideology, but there is no doubt that many people did die of hunger and hunger-related illness during the Great Depression. In fact death rates during the Depression were higher than during the years of World War II.[96] Herbert Hoover famously spoke the words "At least no one has starved," only to be confronted with newspaper reports of the starving, such as this one:

> Middletown, NY., December 24, 1931: …The couple, Mr. and Mrs. Wilfred Wild of New York, had been unemployed since their formerly wealthy employer lost his money, and several days ago, they invested all they had, except 25 cents for food, in bus fare to this region in search of work. Finding none, the went into the cottage, preferring to starve rather than beg. They said they had resigned themselves to dying together."[97]

Meanwhile, photographer Dorothea Lange was taking pictures of whole families who had had nothing to eat in days or weeks. Historian David Shannon quotes the director of a relief agency in Philadelphia on the question of starvation:

> Another family did not have food for two days. Then the husband went out and gathered dandelions and the family lived on them.
>
> Still another family thinking to get as much as possible with their last food order bought potatoes and for 11 days lived only on them.…
>
> I should also like to say that when we talk to people who ask about unemployment they say, "Well, people manage to get along somehow or other, don't they? You do not have very many people who really drop dead of starvation?" That is perfectly true. Actually, death from starvation is not a frequent occurrence. You do not often hear about casualties of that sort. This is because people live in just the way that I have described. They live on inadequacies, and

because they live on inadequacies, they die of disease. The thing does not become dramatic and we do not hear about it. Yet the cost in human suffering is just as great as if they starved to death overnight.[98]

In fact, most of the 24,000 people who die each day of hunger worldwide don't actually die of starvation, but of diseases that they would have shaken off had they not been starving. Which makes it all the more disturbing that in 1932, Senator Copeland of New York reported a rash of cases of starvation appearing in New York Hospitals. Thus, we begin to see how the US has steadfastly avoided calling the depression a period of "famine" — and we are forced, we think, to reconsider our faith in the idea that we do not have to make plans to provision ourselves.

Social worker Lillian Wald speaks of the rise of hunger-related disease even before the stock market crash,

> The nurses' daily records are delicate barometers of conditions. This was brought home to me once as I watched our statistician sticking her pins in the map that shows the current cases of pneumonia.... I was told that the children of the kimono workers then on strike were probably getting less milk and good nourishment and hence their resistance was lowered.[99]

We have somehow accepted on faith that none of these people died, that the safety nets available to most Americans even then protected them from tragedy. That is almost certainly not true. And if it was not true then, it is quite possible that, facing a new depression, more deaths will ensue if we do not protect ourselves. It is also not unlikely that we will not know the true scope of the disaster as we attempt to preserve the idea that the US always protects its own.

The hunger endured in the US during the previous Depression was tied to market orthodoxy that caused food that could not be sold to be destroyed rather than distributed to the hungry. Oscar Emeringer, testifying before a Congressional subcommittee in 1932, described the paradox of "appalling overconsumption on one side and the staggering underconsumption on the other side..." and described wheat in Montana left unharvested because of low prices, thousands of bushels of apples rotting beside the road in Oregon, an Illinois farmer who killed 3,000 of his sheep and threw their bodies into a canyon because the cost of shipping the sheep was greater than the cost of sale. In Chicago, men picked through garbage cans for rotting meat scraps. He went on to add,

> The farmers are being pauperized by the poverty of industrial population and the industrial populations are being pauperized by the poverty of the farmers. Neither has the money to buy the product of the other, hence we have overproduction and underconsumption at the same time and in the same country.[100]

The systematic removal of more than a million farming families from their land during the Depression resulted in both a new class of the desperately poor and hungry and in the disruption of links between local regions and food supplies. In the absence of money and energy to transport food long distances to markets, people starved. And the process of dispossessing farmers meant that even in the Depression, when there were vastly more farmers than there are today, the links between food-producing areas and urban consuming ones were broken.

Again, we begin to see how essential it is to maintain a healthy agricultural population, but more than that, how urgent it is to keep the relationships between city and country, suburb and field tied together in hard times. We are already seeing signs of such difficulties, as food pantries report that they can't afford the gas to transport edible food discards to hungry people.

It is also worth noting, however, that as Americans have been moved away from agriculture, farmers in the poor world have been used to take up the slack. Thus Brazilian farmers have been pressed into growing soybeans for export markets to be fed to US livestock, Ecuadorians into banana production and Kenyans into coffee growing. That is, the numbers we use for US farmers are misleading — far more of the world's farmers are employed in feeding us than we realize. How many? It is almost impossible to tell. Our society erases many of the farmers who raise our food, not counting either the hundreds of thousands or millions of farmers who grow food for export into the US or the immigrant laborers who do the picking. The US is now the world's single largest net importer of food, and though we currently produce enough grains to feed our populace and for large-scale export, our misguided biofuels policy is leading us to put almost a third of the US grain harvest into cars.

This is already causing a crisis in the US, as school children experience reductions in nutritional level of school lunches because of rising costs, and the poor increasingly depend on food pantries and food stamps to get by. But bad as this is, is it really possible to imagine that our present course could lead to a United States unable to feed its populace? We would argue yes, if the US, struggling in a depression, becomes reliant on the one thing it still has to export — grain. Because of our insatiable demand for oil, we risk becoming enchained as an agricultural colony, forced to trade our increasingly tight food supplies for energy resources. We no longer manufacture many goods, and our financial system is falling apart, so we are in danger of shifting, as other nations have, to exporting our food, even if there isn't enough to feed everyone.

Meanwhile, other nations are now entering the agricultural colonialism business across the world. China has announced new policies that encourage the purchase of land in South America and Africa to be farmed exclusively to meet the growing needs of China, which has 40 percent of the world's farmers but only 9 percent of the world's agricultural land.

> "China must 'go out' because our land resources are limited," said Jiang Wenlai, of the China Agricultural Science Institute. "It will be a win-win solution that will benefit both parties by making the maximum use of the advantages of both sides."[101]

Meanwhile, oil-rich but dry Saudi Arabia recently announced that it would stop growing its staple crop, wheat, altogether because of acute water shortages. Saudis are now in negotiation with African countries to grow grains for them, relying on their oil supplies to ensure their ability to outbid other nations to feed their populace.[102]

The world is entering an increasingly acute struggle to meet all the needs that is has created — meat for a growing middle class in the Global South, ethanol for the cars of the North and for a new middle class, and a vastly expanding world population. Lester Brown, president of the Earth Policy Institute and author of *Plan B 2.0,* observes that China will shortly require wheat imports equivalent to the entire Canadian wheat harvest to meet projected demands. And Cornell agricultural researcher David Pimentel notes that by 2020, the US will have to stop exporting grain to meet the needs of its growing population.[103]

In the face of food crisis, more and more exporting nations are closing down exports. India has proposed to end all futures contracts on grains, cooking oils, sweeteners and other staple foods. More and more nations are reserving their grains for themselves, while those who don't have sufficient are desperately seeking large quantities of grains to stabilize prices. Already the reverberations are being felt in the rich world, as wholesalers struggle to find imports and to fill the gaps in supply created by the sudden shut down of exports by various nations.[104] So far there are no absolute food shortages in the US or most other rich world nations — but this is early days yet.

In fact, one of the most striking things about this is that a food crisis that many thinkers, including Brown and Pimentel, have been predicting would occur has begun at least a decade before either imagined it would become acute. This should be a powerful warning to all of us.

As Jeffrey Brown, originator of the "Export Land Model" for oil points out, it is a bad time to be an importer of both food and energy, as the US is.[105] And the situation is exacerbated by decades of economic policies that emphasized trade created in times of cheap and abundant fossil fuels. If oil and gas are cheap and most people are unaware of the dangers of climate change, there is no difficulty transporting large quantities of food around the globe. It was perfectly possible to grow soybeans in Brazil to be transported to feedlots in the US for consumption in the era of cheap oil. The cost of transport is comparatively low and it is easy to ignore the consequences of climate change. But things have changed — energy prices are reverberating throughout the system.

The simple truth is that our food system is enormously fragile, dependent on cheap energy and on an increasingly complex system that does not work anymore. And so food security and sovereignty — the idea that the people who live on the land have a right to access the food that the land produces, may have to be central to a new understanding of the world.

An Interview with Richard Heinberg: Spring 2008

Richard Heinberg has done more to bring awareness of peak energy to the world than almost anyone else. He is the author of four books, including the widely acclaimed *The Party's Over* which first brought energy depletion to the consciousness of millions, and *Peak Everything*, which includes the essay "50 Million Farmers." He travels and teaches about energy and ecological issues all over the world. We were very lucky to catch up with him.

ANOF: When people hear about the rise in the price of oil, they immediately think about the cost of gasoline and how much they're paying at the pump. But it seems we are experiencing a host of other rising costs, including most notably a rise in the cost of food. Could food end up being the way we come to terms with the changes needed to address how much oil is really left?

RICHARD: Interesting way of framing it. I don't think everyone really understands yet the connection between higher food prices and higher oil costs. Higher oil prices mean higher production and transportation costs in the agricultural sector. But of course that also bleeds through into just about every other sector of the economy too, where transportation is a factor. Farmers are having a tough time affording diesel fuel for their tractors, and the fact that the average food item on an American plate travels 1,500 miles to get there means that transport costs are driving up food costs too. Then there's the factor of higher demand for biofuels. As the price of oil goes up, that creates more incentive to produce biofuels rather than food, and so an ever-larger percentage of corn and soybean crops is going to biofuel production rather than food production. And of course that pushes food prices up too. And this is happening by no means just in the United States, but also in places like Africa and India.

Then, on the more remote linkage between food and fuel, it really doesn't have to do much with price at all, it's simply the fact that as we burn more fossil fuels, we're destabilizing the global climate. And that means more desertification and more flooding, both of which are reducing yields. So as a result of all of this and more, we're seeing crop yields declining in many cases, and in others, failing to keep up with rising demand.

So there are the linkages. But are they going to cause people to wake up to fossil-fuel depletion any faster? Frankly, I doubt it. I think that most people are unlikely to follow those chains of causality. If anything is going to make them wake up to peak oil, it's just the cost of gasoline at the pump.

ANOF: You mentioned food insecurity in other parts of the world. How much of a security issue is this for the United States, as people all over the world, and maybe eventually in this country, find themselves with not enough to eat, and that becomes the tipping point for insurrection or even revolution?

RICHARD: Well, it's a huge security issue, and you're right to say that this could be a domestic problem at some point. Right now, of course, there is still a huge surplus of food for people who can afford it, which is an interesting way of putting it, because there are increasing numbers of people who are being priced out of the food system. If we produced food just a little differently, a little less meat and more grains, if we distributed food a little differently, there would still be plenty for everyone.

However, as time goes on, that's going to be less and less the case, because the curve of declining food being produced on a per capita basis is pretty relentless. There are, in fact, voices being raised now, warning of potential famines, even within the next year or two if we don't have record harvests of grain this year and next year. There are warnings of famine, but only in the poorest countries.

The real problem for Americans, of course, is what happens when the food system breaks down domestically. What happens when the truckers can't get diesel fuel? Well, the average supermarket carries only about three days' worth of food on its shelves, and if those shelves aren't being replenished on a regular basis, then famine could hit here just as easily as China or Bangladesh.

So the problem is a systemic problem. It is not just a problem of declining crop yields, it's really the whole way we are producing and distributing food, all of it based on depleting fossil fuels.

ANOF: There are some studies that suggest that small-scale, sustainable agriculture — largely organic agriculture — is actually more productive per square foot than industrial agriculture. The United Nations has various human population models, but most of them show us in a range of 9 to 11 billion people on this planet later this century and then leveling out after that. Setting aside the idea of whether or not it's a good idea to have more people than we do now, can we feed 10 billion people on this planet, even with the higher yields that look possible through small-scale sustainable agriculture?

RICHARD: The answer is, it's probably theoretically possible. It's one of those "if I were king of the world" questions. If global agriculture could be made as efficient as possible, if all of the world's officials who have anything to do with the food system could agree on a policy to make the transition to small-scale sustainable agriculture in the most efficient way, and if the world's wealthy people could agree to eat less meat, then I think, yeah, we probably could feed 9, 10, maybe even 11 billion people. Not sustainably. I don't think there's any way of producing that much food that doesn't degrade natural ecosystems over time.

Over the long run, I think, you know, we're going to see a much smaller human population, probably ultimately in the range of a billion or less, but how we get there, of course, is the big question. Do we get there through famine and die-off or do we get there through some kind of rational policy? Realistically, the best-case scenario is probably some combination of the two. I think the fact that we're already seeing soaring food prices and the threat of famine with the population at 6.7 billion should be worrisome to those who think, you know, that we're going to have to feed 9 to 11 billion by mid-century. What all of this means is we have to think both about reforming the food system and also about population policy.

ANOF: You've specifically mentioned a target number for new farmers in the US, using a model other than industrial agriculture, and you've said 50 million. And I wondered if you would just talk for a moment about that specific number and how you came to that number.

RICHARD: Well, how I came to that number was by looking at how Cuba reformed its food system in response to an oil famine. And they did so by increasing the number of farmers, by growing more food within the city, creating incentives for urban gardens, rooftop gardens, by training more farmers, adding agricultural courses in every college, making sure that everyone who graduates with a degree in medicine or law or whatever knows how to grow food. And then I took those numbers and applied them in a very rough way to the much larger US population and came up with the result that, in a post-fossil-fuel food system, the US would need something like 50 million farmers.

But of course those wouldn't be farmers like we have now necessarily. Probably for a long time, it's going to make sense to grow grains on a large scale, perhaps even using field machinery. But just about everything else, fruit, nuts, vegetables, potatoes, you name it, will be able to be produced much more effectively and efficiently without fossil fuels but using much more human labor.

So that could be seen as a huge opportunity. Here's an occupation for millions of American young people. And if we use the kinds of new knowledge-intensive as well as labor-intensive methods that have been pioneered in permaculture, biointensive [agriculture], biodynamics and so on, that occupation could in fact be very fulfilling, much more so than what a lot of young people are doing today for income. If we see it that way, if we plan for it, if we create policies to revitalize farming culture, especially in rural communities, then I think, in fact, the result could be a very happy one for all concerned. We could see, for example, the realization of Thomas Jefferson's ideal of an agrarian democracy. And we could have a revitalization of American family life as a result of this transition.

So when I talk about 50 million farmers, in a sense it's a somewhat arbitrary figure, but it's pointing in the direction, I think, of what's inevitable, which is that we will need more human labor in agriculture than we have now. It's a reversal of the historic trend. During the 19th century, something like 70 to 90 percent of Americans were involved in food production at some level, whether it was backyard gardening or farming. Over the course of the 20th century, the number of full-time farmers fell to about 2 percent of the population. And now, in the 21st century, that trend is going to reverse, one way or another.

That would include a lot of people who would just be growing on a subsistence basis for themselves. And we have to remember that that's [been] the normal condition of human life for the past several thousand lives. My father grew up on a farm that was basically a subsistence farm, and that was a normal situation for rural people throughout much of the US during even the early part of the 20th century. The fact that we've gotten away from that pattern of life, I think, should be some cause for concern. We've gotten ourselves out on a pretty thin ecological limb here, where so few produce all the food for so many. And that has consequences all the way down the line, for human psychology, for the economy, for the fragility of the food system.

Sometimes those of us who pay attention to environmental issues wonder, how could people possibly ignore the fact that songbirds are disappearing, that we're overfishing the oceans, that the topsoil is eroding and depleting and so on? Well, the answer is, they can ignore it because they're not right up against it. Farmers have to pay attention because that's where their livelihood comes from. They have to pay attention to water and topsoil and pollinators and so on, and everyone else can afford to just look the other way because they don't get their food from the land; they get it from the store. So the fact that fewer and fewer of us are on the land and working the land means that fewer of us are paying attention to the environment as we degrade it.

ANOF: I hear a lot of energy-descent and climate-change activists describe how difficult it is for them to simultaneously make changes in their own lives and spend a considerable amount of time talking about and writing about change. You are especially busy with your efforts toward spreading information about our future. Could you talk a little bit about the changes that you've made in your own life?

RICHARD: Sure. Well, I see the two things going hand in hand, because if one isn't doing anything in one's personal life, then it's pretty hard to preach to others. And on the other hand, if you are doing something in your own life, then, you know, you do have something to share, and what you say has more of a ring of authenticity to it. My wife and I live on a quarter-acre suburban lot in a small, old, ranch-style house. We converted the house for energy efficiency when we bought the place about eight years ago — put up solar photovoltaic panels, insulated the walls, did all those sorts of things. And then we killed the lawn. There was nothing but Bermuda grass when we bought it and two big shade trees. So we killed the Bermuda grass, not with chemicals, with sheet mulching. And, sadly, we had to take down the shade trees. Then we put in a couple of dozen garden beds and about 25 fruit and nut trees, all sorts of varieties.

And it's been a wonderful experiment every step of the way since then, learning what varieties grow well together, what crop varieties are more productive and so on. It's been a real ongoing thrill to see our fruit and nut trees mature and start to produce. At this point we're just about self-sufficient in fruit and nuts and self-sufficient in vegetables for several months of the year. We still have to buy grains and whatever processed foods we use and animal products. We don't have chickens yet, but we're planning to add maybe three or four chickens over the next year or so. There are still things that we haven't done that we've had on the plan for a long time, like solar hot water.

But in doing all of this, we've learned first of all that it's possible, that it is a lot of work. You can't just set out to do this kind of thing and hope to have it all accomplished in one season or one year or two years; it's really an ongoing process, and it does take a lot of time. But it's tremendously fulfilling and it's also an educational process. We've had I don't know how many people here on our little quarter acre — students, journalists, all sorts of folks, just, you know, wanting to see what we're doing. And they come here and they get ideas about what they can do in their own backyard. And also, I should mention that we garden not just in our backyard but the front yard as well, and that's a way of letting our neighbors know what we're doing and what's possible.

RECIPES

Kale Chips   *by Lynn Jones of the Ottawa Valley Food Co-op*

These are amazingly good, light, crispy and delicious. Everyone I have served them to likes them a lot. Kale is a nutritional dynamo and a garden miracle for those of us in northern gardens. Easy to grow, it is extremely hardy, harvestable after several hard frosts and even after being covered in deep snow for several months. The chips are really quick and easy to make.

Ingredients
- Kale
- Seasonings (e.g., sea salt and olive oil). We like a sprinkle of cayenne and sometimes garlic. Some folks include a sprinkle of vinegar. My daughter claims to prefer these made without oil, and they are quite good, but I definitely prefer them drizzled with a bit of olive oil. Presumably other vegetable oils would work too.

Directions
1. Pick the kale and wash if necessary.
2. Cut out the stems and cut the leaf part into chip-sized pieces.
3. Season to taste. Just a little. It's easy to overdo it.
4. Spread on cookie sheets. (Avoid overlapping pieces for quickest drying.)
5. Bake for 20 minutes at 250°F or dehydrate for several hours. I imagine a solar oven would work too though I don't have one yet.

Crock Pot Black Bean Stew   *by Aaron*

This recipe can also easily be made in a solar oven, with a slightly longer cooking time. It makes a terrific quick dinner, served with cornbread or tortillas.

Ingredients
- 2 cups of dried black beans soaked overnight
- 1 cup of corn cut from the cob
- 4 chopped green onions
- 1 tsp cumin
- 2 cups of chopped tomatoes
- ½ cup green chili peppers
- 1 tsp dried and chopped chili

Directions
Cook in crock pot on medium for about 5–6 hours.

CHAPTER 2

Hands on the Wheel

What We Should Be Getting from Our Food System

I looked to the stars
Tried all of the bars
And I've nearly gone up in smoke
Now my hand's on the wheel
Of something that's real
And I feel like I'm going home.

— WILLIE NELSON —

SHARON: Today is my oldest son Eli's eighth birthday. Yesterday we had a day full of kids, balloons, sugary junk the kids aren't normally allowed and other special Eli pleasures. Today is quieter but just as happy — at least, as long as I ignore the financial and environmental crisis unfolding around me.

For my own eighth birthday I received my first pocketknife. It was a prize that stunned me — because it had never occurred to me that I was old enough to have something as adult as my own knife. Tools were for grownups. I had never expected to have my own.

I wish I could say that I still own it, but it disappeared into the world of lost things that is childhood long ago. I do still have the scar on my right hand from where I ignored my father's command to always cut away from yourself when whittling — and a strong memory of the flash of recognition I felt when I suddenly realized that grownups actually have reasons for some of the things they say. But most of all, I kept the memory of how suddenly taller and older I felt because of the confidence my parents had in me. I think that was the first time I suddenly really grasped that someday, I too would be an adult, and that I was on a journey in that direction.

As Eli approached eight I somehow realized that some secret part of me believed that my sons would also receive pocketknives at the same age. But, of course, for Eli, this is unrealistic — he's autistic, and although he progresses steadily, he doesn't yet have the ability to use a knife safely. (Of course, the scar suggests neither did I.) Every child is different, of course, and what one child can handle at six, another can't until ten.

Still, my husband needed a replacement for a lost pocketknife, and as long as I was ordering one knife, I lingered over knives suitable for children. I hesitated a while, and then I ordered not one but four pocketknives suitable for young boys. And I put them away in a corner to wait for the day when my sons are each of them ready — or perhaps, as I was, almost ready — to take that step toward adulthood.

With Eli, part of this is gesture of faith. I hope and trust that the day will come that he is ready for this. It doesn't matter that much when it comes — I'm not in a hurry — just that it does. But, of course, any time we invest in our children's future, we are investing our hope and trust that they will grow up safe and secure and become good and honorable people. For me, this small investment in my children's future competence — a competence that will be, I think, increasingly important in a depleted world — ensures me that when the day comes that each boy is ready, he will get that moment of feeling ten feet tall because his parents think he is grown enough to have a knife.

They come to us as babies or small children, and we look and try to find the men and the women they will be. And bit by bit, we see them appear; we enable them to appear. The kind of men and women we create depends in part on our vision of the future. We push them back, we pull them forward, we risk our precious kids for the sake of the grown people we trust they will become, people we do not yet know but must imagine. These are the future men and women on whose powers our better hopes must rest. This thing I do not know but must believe — that my children have a future, both rich and strange to me.

I bought the pocket knives because I don't know where the dollar is going and I don't know where my husband's job will be in a year or two. I bought them because even if money is tight, this gift I want to give. I bought them because I do believe that one day, I will see my oldest son take out his pocketknife in the pursuit of some ordinary bit of competence. I bought them because no matter what the future is, my children will be men in it, and our children, men and women alike, will need good tools and the skills to use them. I bought them because I trust that even if I do not know where I am going, the journey into the future has promise and reason for hope.

Grace: Universal Thanksgivings

In efficacious grace we are not merely passive, nor yet does God
do some and we do the rest. But God does all, and we do all.
God produces all, we act all. For that is what produces, viz. our own acts.
God is the only proper author and fountain; we only are the proper actors.
We are in different respects, wholly passive and wholly active.

— Jonathan Edwards —

Why is it so very hard for most of us to imagine living in an entirely different food system? Why is it so viscerally difficult for many of us to imagine growing what we eat, eating what we grow, living primarily on things we cook from scratch? As authors, we don't think there is any point in denying that we are asking our readers to make a massive and potentially difficult psychological transformation, because the whole of our society tells us "Food isn't important. Business is important. Politics is important. But food — that doesn't really matter."

We became aware of how important it was to articulate that a different food system is possible partly in response to another writer's work. Michael Pollan's wonderful book *The Omnivore's Dilemma: A Natural History of Four Meals* documents, among other things, the important distinctions between industrial food production (gigantic combines, petroleum, greenhouse gases, BST and pesticides) and industrial organic agriculture (the stuff you get at Whole Foods is pretty much the same, except for the BST and pesticides, and its labor practices are often even worse), and then compares those dinners with two meals, one produced by small farmers and the other produced by Pollan himself by hunting, foraging and growing his own. His was an enormously important and eye-opening book for many Americans.

Pollan's otherwise terrific book concludes with the troubling assessment that the homegrown and sustainably farmed foods are niche foods. He determines that ultimately, it cannot be possible for everyone, rich and poor, to enjoy the best, safest, sustainably produced food grown in their own gardens, harvested from their own wild places, or from nearby farmers. He says,

> Perhaps the perfect meal is one that's been fully paid for, that leaves no debt outstanding. This is almost impossible to do, which is why I said there was nothing very realistic or applicable about this meal. But as a sometimes thing, as a kind of ritual, a meal that is eaten in full consciousness of what it took to make it is worth preparing every now and again, if only as a way to remind us of the true costs of the things we take for granted. The reason I didn't open a can of stock was because stock doesn't come from a can; it comes from the bones of animals. And the yeast that leavens our bread comes not from a packet but from the air we breathe. The meal was more ritual than realistic because it dwelled on such things, reminding us how very much nature offers to the omnivore, the forests as much as the fields, the oceans as much as the meadows. If I had to give this dinner a name, it would have to be the Omnivore's Thanksgiving.[106]

Reading this, we became angry, not at Pollan, who had revealed so many remarkable things about the disaster of the industrial food system, but at the Big Lie that convinced even Pollan that it is impossible for all of us to eat like this every day. And if Pollan, an expert on our food system, does not believe that ordinary sustainable eating is possible, why would ordinary people recognize that it is?

Why should it be impossible for every one of us to eat simple meals, meals that are also meaningful and sustainable and good and even fully paid for? In fact, is it not necessary that we find some way to do so? It is true that we can't always eat hand-hunted wild boar, but there is no reason most of our dinners cannot consist of omelets from our hens, vegetables from our gardens and the wild edibles that already grow in our yards, and bread we made by hand from wheat grown near us.

Thus, this book starts from the simple assumption that there is a way to create a universal Omnivore's Thanksgiving. That there is a way for people, rich and poor, all over the world, to have a reason to give thanks for sufficient honest food that is fully paid for. We believe that there is a way also to address the terrible threats to our larger society created by peak energy, climate change, inequity and agricultural ignorance and lack of farmers.

How to get there, though, from where we are? Perhaps we might start by thinking further about Pollan's idea of *thanksgiving* — because the term contains written into it the idea of gratitude, of a reflective pause in which we calculate the cost of our meal and ensure that gratitude goes to the originators.

This is "grace" in its broadest sense — the prayers and expressions of thanks given by all indigenous (and by this we simply mean "tied to place and shaped by it") populations. Thus native peoples gave thanks to the animals they took for meat. Christian farmers thanked God for good harvests and the strength to do their work. South Indian farmers celebrated their cattle for their contribution to the harvest. All graces before meals are an imperfect attempt to articulate the debts of food production, to establish to whom payment is due.

It is impossible to say a complete grace for the global meals we eat now — to articulate and thank (and it is not always clear that thanks should be our reaction) all the participants in the complex, oil-drenched, depleting food system we have now. Do we express gratitude to the impoverished Brazilian farmer who cleared rainforest to grow the soybeans? He may have had little choice, but are we grateful? To the wealthy landowner who profits most from the farmer's work? Do we thank the shipping company that brought the soybeans across the world to the port? Do we express our gratitude to the feedlot owner who confines the cow, keeping it in miserable conditions and dosing it liberally with antibiotics? The underpaid slaughterhouse workers, many of whom are seriously injured while killing hundreds of cows a day? The multinational corporation that then ships the meat off to a processing facility, and may also have owned the land in Brazil, the feedlot, the slaughterhouse and the trucking company? The immigrant workers who operate the machinery that transforms the meat into convenient patties and encases them in plastic? The trucker who hauls the refrigerated truck to the supermarket? Gratitude is a product of understanding; appreciation is a recognition that we owe a debt. But not only does the current food system conceal and erase the people in the system we might be grateful to, many of whom do difficult, unpleasant jobs so that we don't have to, but it also produces a product that we are hard put to be grateful for.

A world in which most meals looked like the Omnivore's Thanksgiving would have to have vastly simplified supply chains and a much more profound connection between each of us and the sources of our food. That is, we would have to live and eat like people did for most of human history. We would have to return to the work that most people in the world today include as part of their lives. We would have to return to ordinary human norms — in which provisioning is ordinary human work and the saying of a grace before meals is not the arcane remnant of an older mysticism but the recognition that there are debts to be paid and that not all of them are fully explicable or articulable, but for that, are none the less real.

The Omnivore's Thanksgiving is possible — because it was the way people ate for most of human history. It is only in the past 75 years we have lost our recognition that, as Wendell Berry puts it, "Eating is an agricultural act." And perhaps it starts with a grace before meals, a moment of grace, in which we simplify and clarify and recognize that what we once had, we can have, with a bit of effort, once again.

Getting Back to the Victory Garden

Professional standards, the standards of ambition and selfishness, are always sliding downward toward expense, ostentation, and mediocrity. They tend always to narrow the ground of judgment. But amateur standards, the standards of love, are always straining upward toward the humble and the best. They enlarge the ground of judgment. The context of love is the world.
— Wendell Berry —

What would a nation of farmers and home cooks look like? Many of us are so far removed from food production that imagining that world seems like a return to the dark ages. In fact, we only have to look back two generations, to the US in 1945, at the end of World War II. In 1943, 44 percent of all the vegetables eaten in the US were produced in home Victory Gardens, and 20 million American families worked in gardens, in addition to the one-fifth of the population living on farms. Americans fed themselves and were proud of their ability to meet their own needs. A popular war poster read, "Guts…and sweat…that's the stuff victory is made of! We're fighting this war to WIN…and every mother's son of us is doing his job.… Who said the US is soft? PRODUCE FOR VICTORY!" We tend to think of growing and cooking our own food as unimaginably arduous, but even were that true (and it isn't — more on this shortly), have we gone soft? Are we really incapable of guts and sweat any more?

Envision this. During the First World War, the town of Marian, Indiana, for example, had a population of 29,000 and more than 14,000

Victory Gardens. In Dallas, Texas, during the same period, there were 20,000 Victory Gardens.[107] During World War II, the total quantity of vegetables produced in Victory Gardens was equal to the total output of produce from all US farms combined. Think about that — Americans produced in their yards and in vacant lots as many vegetables as all of the farms in the US. That, we think, gives us a sense of the scope of possibilities.

A society in which many of us cooked dinner every night and got our food from our own gardens and the farms and gardens of our neighbors would look very much like the World War II era. Only this time, we'd all be fighting our war from home, rather than sending sons and husbands off to battle. A nation of farmers and cooks is one that needs less oil and is less vulnerable to terrorism — and thus needs to fight fewer wars. Instead of a war on two fronts, all of us would be working together on a single victory — a victory at home.

The problems articulated in the previous chapter have been described as each *individually* requiring a national build up and commitment on the same scale that was required to succeed in World War II. Joseph Romm, former assistant secretary of energy, argues that climate change alone will demand such an effort of us: "This national (and global) reindustrialization effort would be on the scale of what we did during World War II, except it would last far longer."[108] We have already mentioned the Hirsch Report. The report assesses that in order to address peak oil and avoid massive economic and energy crises, two full decades of full-scale, crash-program mitigation work would be required. The report refers repeatedly to World War II levels of production, but then says what would be required to avoid a worldwide recession is "unprecedented" — that is *more* national effort and unity than World War II required.

Lester Brown, director of the Earth Policy Institute, notes in *Plan B 2.0* that we are now in the situation that many people were in at the beginning of World War II — that much must be asked of us if we are to have a future.[109] And, of course, we've been told by our leaders that the war on terrorism is our generation's World War II. Whether you believe that last statement or not, it is almost certainly true that our security depends on our ability to meet our sovereign needs for basics such as energy, food, clothing, and shelter. Right now, the US is dependent in part or in whole on foreign sources for all of the above. We have, in only 60 years, gone from being people who could supply our own needs to being the most dependent people in American history. A single act of terrorism — a bomb in a shipping container that closed ports or the closing of the Straits of Hormuz — could cut off our supply lines and energy resources. We begin from a position that is in many ways weaker and more vulnerable than we were in World War II, and it will require a matching level of commitment to free us from our dependency.

If climate change alone, and peak oil alone and soil depletion and falling food supplies alone each require an effort on the scale of World War II, what will they ask of us together? The answer may well be "As much courage and passion and commitment as has ever been asked of any people in human history." Addressing these crises will demand that we cease to be dependent and step forward and take responsibility for ourselves and our future. We believe this is something we can accomplish with grace, courage and dignity, but we must begin soon. We may already be too late to avoid a global tipping point in climate change; we certainly have far less than 20 years to begin preparing for a global energy peak; and our degree of dependence on foreign sources and multinational companies for everything from water to food to shelter increases daily.

You will notice that most of our political leaders have not called for radical change — and do not always even admit there is a serious problem. Some are just waking to the realities of climate change and have yet to acknowledge peak oil. In part this is because doing so would be political suicide, or so our leaders believe. They have bought the Big Lie; they believe that the people of the wealthy West will never give up their comforts and take up plowshares and defend their nation and their future. Most (there are a few important exceptions) fear to be the ones to tell unpopular truths.

We cannot expect leadership from those who call themselves leaders until we make it clear that as a nation we value our future security more than any short-term pleasures, that we care more about a livable world than trivialities. They think we are cowards, and they think we are shortsighted and willing to sacrifice our own children for short-term comfort. But they slander us. We must show them otherwise — that we are people of courage, people of strength, people who want the best for the US and are willing to sacrifice to get it.

If our leaders will not lead us there, then we will lead them. In truth, that's what democracy is — the people leading. The people deciding. We ordinary people have the power to change the world, and we invite you to do so. We need to go forward into something like the recent past, in which ordinary people did more than buy things; they made things, tended their places and helped them grow, prosper and their land bloom. We need to reinvoke the best parts of the history we've inherited, while not duplicating the mistakes that we made before. We need to become a nation that can meet its needs without consuming more than a just share of the planet's resources.

Food production is a remarkably democratic exercise. The original war gardens of World War I were founded not as an institutionalized national product but by home gardeners and garden clubs as a way to ensure a stable food supply. All over the world, when nations fail their people, small-scale home agriculture, led by the people, arises to fill the gaps. For example, in Kampala, Uganda, after that country's civil war, urban farmers and gardeners fed the city, keeping most of its populace alive.[110] In Cuba, when a large percentage of oil imports were lost and the nation starved under the embargo, ordinary Cubans led the way in feeding their nation. Eventually, governments claimed the work of ordinary people, but feeding people in hard times is generally a grassroots project, one that individuals and communities are remarkably well qualified to lead.

The first step to compensating for the limitations of our government is a new Victory Farm and Garden movement. This alone has the power to mitigate many of the ills in front of us and address the most urgent needs we have. A nation of farmers can ensure enough food and water for all and can soften the blows of the coming crises.

Becoming victory farmers will reduce the amount of climate-warming gasses released into the air each year, create stronger local economies, reserve resources for the world's poor, reduce the amount of fossil fuels our nation is dependent upon, improve soil and water quality everywhere and give us all access to better, healthier, safer food in our own communities. It will improve our communities and our relationships with our neighbors, improve our health and well-being, strengthen our democracy and make our air cleaner and our homes more beautiful. How often does something so simple have so much power? How often can a small piece of dirt and a little effort change the world?

We are calling for 100 million new farmers and victory gardeners — up to one out of every three men, women and children in the country. We are also calling for 200 million people to take their places in the kitchen and begin cooking and eating sustainably. And when that many people act together, how can millions of small pieces of dirt and effort fail to change the world?

We should say that in the course of the book we will speak mostly about the US — American history, present-day American practice, and how Americans can make change. We in no way mean to exclude other people. In fact, we believe strongly that the other rich nations must begin to grow their own victory farms and gardens as well. But the US has had a particularly powerful role in shaping the present-day Western lifestyle and has been a disproportionate contributor to all of the problems that we are seeking solutions to. To some degree, global warming and peak oil are American problems: we created and modeled the lifestyle that so many others now dream of, and we are the largest single contributors to global warming and the largest consumers on earth. As others have pointed out, to a large degree, where Americans go, others will follow. And so we believe that we must focus on our own nation, not just exhorting Americans to act, but tracing through our own history the strains of uniquely American thought that could enable us not only to do less harm but to repair what we have done. We believe that not only will the US be better off but so will the world if we succeed.

The Problem of History

No working farmer or shopkeeper helped write the constitution.
— SHELDON WOLIN —

We cannot but be aware that there are significant structural problems to the invocation of any history. When we invoke Jefferson, we necessarily raise the issue of the ties of agriculture to slavery; when we invoke World War II, we invoke militarism. It is not possible to tie our work to history without finding ourselves caught up in complicated questions of whose history and what kind of history we are calling upon.

There are enormous tensions between histories, between narratives that emphasize populism, resistance and the power of ordinary people and those that emphasize power, states and the people who have power. Howard Zinn, in his superb book *The People's History of the United States* which narrates the history of ordinary Americans articulates this tension this way:

> My viewpoint in telling the history of the United States is differ-
> ent: that we must not accept the memory of states as our own. Na-
> tions are not communities and never have been. This history of
> any country; presented as a the history of a family; conceals fierce
> conflicts of interest (sometimes exploding, most often repressed)

between conquerors and conquered, masters and slaves, capitalists and workers, dominators and dominated in race and sex. And in such a world of conflict, a world of victims and executioners, it is the job of thinking people, as Albert Camus suggests, not to be on the sides of the executioners.[111]

If we invoke Jefferson, are we on the side of the executioners? Certainly Jefferson stands on the side of slave owners as well as the democratizers. It is not sufficient, as many writers about him do, to sanitize him to use his admitted ambivalence about slave-holding to erase the ambiguity of Jefferson's actions. On the other hand, our establishment as a nation does bear his hand — and the contrary hands of those who finally overruled the powerful founding fathers to eliminate slavery and allow women to vote. And yet, we believe there is some power in his idea that the best possible citizens for a democracy were those who, by virtue of their self-sufficiency, could offer an independent democratic voice. We believe it is true that being beholden to multinational corporations for every bite in our mouths makes us powerless — and that Jefferson, despite the evils of his slaveholding, may have had a small piece of the answer.

The simple truth is that glorification of our past makes us believe lies. Glorification of our state makes us accept unacceptable things. And yet, there is a United States worth believing in — moments in history in which competing forces of powerful and weak met and created something decent, something worth treasuring and admiring. It never happened without resistance, but neither was the story always a narrative of good people and evil leaders — it is far more complicated than that.

All of us were taught a state- and hero-centered history that erased too many ordinary contributions and focused our national pride on the wrong things. But we did have that teaching; we did learn that nationalism. Perhaps a large part of our project is the unlearning of the untruths, but smashing idols isn't enough — we need to give people who love their country a place to put that love, give those who derive hope and comfort from their sense of the past a past to attach themselves too.

We could easily have left this section and the discussion of agrarian democracy out of our book — we considered it. We're not sure we know the right answers to how to deal with this dilemma. We recognize that history is a hard territory to navigate and that some readers will find us too critical of our country, others not critical enough. We do recognize that there is, as Sojourner Truth put it, "a little weasel" in the narrative we have been given:

Now I hears talkin' about de Constitution and de rights of man. I
comes up and I takes hold of dis Constitution. It looks might big,
and I feels for my rights, but der aint any dare. Den I says, "God,
what ails dis Constitution?" He says to me, "Sojurner, dere is a little
weasel in it." [112]

And yet we cannot help feeling that the tension between what we as a
people have done badly and what we have done well is important. That is,
sorting out the merits of what is good seems like worthy work in a complex
narrative. Most of us were raised to a kind of nationalism, a belief in our
country — a belief often built partly upon falsehoods and uncritical historical glorification but resting on a bit of solid ground as well. This book
is filled with shattered idols — technologies and visions of the future. We
think that simple iconoclasm is insufficient if we are to create a uniquely
American agrarian narrative.

We also recognize that the language of Jefferson and the way an alliance of power and people pulled together during World War II is important to creating a new patriotism (as opposed to nationalism), one that
rests on the literal *patria*, the land we live on, rather than the false histories of our state. The truth is that there have been moments in history when
we did better than we are doing now and that, though there is no golden
age, those moments are worth memorializing. Thus, we imperfectly walk a
fine line, invoking what we value but hopefully never forgetting that real
change comes primarily from the work of ordinary people like all of us and
that our hope for the future not only doesn't rest primarily on our leadership — and that it never really has.

Organic Industrial Won't Cut It

*Love and business and family and religion and art and patriotism
are nothing but shadows of words when a man's starving.*
— O. HENRY —

The first change we need to make is to reduce the scale of agriculture. This
may seem counter-intuitive, particularly if you have been listening to the
largely unchallenged claim of industrial agriculture that bigger is better,
that biotechnology is the solution to world hunger, and that we must invest
in biotechnology research to "feed the world." Over the past few decades,

however, evidence has mounted steadily that the counter-intuitive claim is true, that small-scale agriculture works better than large — not just occasionally but almost universally. Small-scale polyculture (lots of plants and animals grown together, rather than one endless field of corn) is higher yielding, protects soil and water better, is less dangerous to the climate, less toxic and, if done locally everywhere that people live and need to eat, produces more secure food systems.

The word "small" here is the operative one. We have tried as a society to create sustainable industrial agriculture, and we have failed miserably. As Michael Pollan documents, industrial organic agriculture, even when begun from the best of intentions, has failed to reduce fossil fuel use, failed to treat animals more humanely, failed to treat human beings more humanely, failed to create local systems and support local economies, and most of all, is the product of vested corporate interests rather than the interests of people who want to eat well and sustainably. As Pollan observes,

> Yet while the struggle with the government over the meaning of organic was making headlines in 1997, another equally important struggle was underway within the USDA between Big and Little Organic — or, put another way, between the organic industry and the organic movement — and here the outcome was decidedly more ambiguous. Could a factory farm be organic? Was an organic dairy cow entitled to graze on pasture? Did food additives and synthetic chemicals have a place in processed organic food? If the answers to these questions seem like no-brainers, then you too are stuck in an outdated pastoral view of organic. Big organic won all three arguments.[113]

The questions of the use of fossil fuels and just labor practices didn't even make it to the table in those discussions. In many cases, industrial organic labor practices are worse than the labor practices of conventional industrial agriculture — because hand picking and other repetitive activities use migrant labor instead of pesticides. Though it does result in a reduction in chemical deaths and exposures, few farmers can afford to pay well for the labor they use.

In small-scale polyculture, however, farmers often own their land, use vacant or unvalued land, or rent it cheaply and work it with family members or a little hired labor. Instead of picking tomatoes for ten hours in the hot sun, they might pick tomatoes for several hours and then clean the chicken house, repair fences and do other work. They work largely for themselves, in their own interest, and have incentives to vary their tasks and conserve their strength and health. Industrial farms employing hundreds of migrant laborers have no such incentives.

As for fossil fuels, there is debate, but a recent British study showed that industrial organic agriculture may be more fossil-fuel intensive than conventional industrial agriculture — and both are contributing to the warming of the planet. Agriculture produces 8 percent of all climate-change gasses. According to Dale Allen Pfeiffer's *Eating Fossil Fuels*, all sources of agriculture combined require 400 gallons of oil for every man, woman and child in the US. Thirty-six percent of that is used for pesticides and artificial fertilizers, and since most large organic farms do not grow even a significant portion of their own fertility by raising cover crops or high-carbon compostable crops, fossil fuels are needed to generate and transport things like livestock manures and soil amendments.[114] At the very best, organic industrial agriculture uses three-fifths or more of the fossil fuels that conventional agriculture does — and in order to stabilize climate change and deal with oil depletion we must cut our use by much, much more.

A lot of us have been kidding ourselves and imagining that we can somehow purchase our way out of the problems of climate change and peak oil and the rest of the environmental damage our habits of consumption have created. We go shopping at Whole Foods and read the labels and believe we have done enough. We imagine that becoming a green consumer is all that is needed.

But more is going to be asked of all of us than that — we need to get used to the fact that all of us must do more, as well as purchase better. So if we are to create a non-toxic, humane, just, human-scaled, non-industrial agriculture, many, many more people are going to have to begin to farm. This is simple demographics — a huge industrial farm of 3,000 acres might require only two people and an enormous body of fossil-fueled machinery. Small-scale polyculture on 1000 three-acre farms might require 4 to 6,000 human beings, managing, growing, planting, harvesting. This will mean an enormous shift in our economic and social structures — but a necessary one. There is no empirical reason why farmers must be paid worse than software engineers — it is a reflection of our cultural priorities and can be amended if our priorities change.

How we buy does have a powerful role here — and simply shopping at Whole Foods or in the organic aisle of Walmart is insufficient. Instead, we need to get the vast majority of our food from friends and neighbors who farm. We are also going to have to cook this food, which comes to us in its natural state, and to make delicious meals from things that can be grown locally. Every one of us is going to have to participate if we want a better world and a secure food supply. This is especially difficult if we are poor. Because smaller farmers do not get significant economies of scale or receive tacit permission to externalize their pollutants, they must charge more. Which means that the poor struggle to find sustainable food that can feed them — and the only solution is for those who have more income to subsidize the creation of a system large enough and robust enough to feed everyone. Indeed, to create this system, we will almost certainly also need to shift government agricultural subsidies to small farmers.

The truth is that if we remain a nation of consumers who trust that someone else will take care of providing our most basic needs, we will have the food system we deserve — the one we have now, with all its environmental consequences, and then, when that falters because of lack of fossil fuels, we will have no system at all. We cannot do this without you. The good news is that what you are being asked to do is not as arduous, difficult or strange as it sounds — we promise.

We're sure some of you are panicking right now, thinking, "I can't be a farmer — I've got a job. I don't have the time. I don't have the energy. It sounds hard. I can't handle the physical work. My dog ate my straw hat. I'm allergic to llamas. I don't live in Iowa. And I have no freakin' idea what millet is!"

Don't worry. This only sounds scary. You can begin from where you are, in the job and the place you are.

A Nation of Farmers

Bring out your social remedies.
They will fail, they will fail, every one,
until each man has his feet somewhere upon the soil.
— DAVID GRAYSON —

Chances are, the last time you thought of becoming a farmer you were a child at play. Farmers, like doctors, teachers and firefighters, are among those clearly delineated jobs that even very small children understand completely. There is no puzzling over what it is a farmer actually does, in the ways that there are for jobs that many daddies and mommies actually do, like B-to-B software engineer, waste removal technician, retail assistant or tax lawyer. So the odds are good that once upon a time, long ago, most of us imagined ourselves as farmers, if only for a moment.

If you can remember so far, you probably didn't imagine yourself de-beaking chickens, building a hog manure lagoon, or riding in a giant trac-tor while spraying Roundup. What you dreamed of, if you were anything like most children, is the kind of small, mixed farm that hardly exists any-more. It would have some animals, a big garden, pasture, orchard and fields. This is the farm of children's books, the farm of stories, and 75 years ago, this was the farm of reality. But gradually, as we all grew older, such farms disappeared from the landscape.

And as each of us grew older, we put away our childish dreams and imagined other things. Some of us imagined those other things because we wanted to, and others because we had no choice — we had already watched the farms in our own family fail, or we were told in a thousand ways that farming was not suitable work for us. We watched the farm of our child-hood dreams change into something else — 2,000 acres of monocropped corn, suburban houses or 400 cows who never leave their barn. Whether we consciously chose otherwise or not, for most of us the farm became an impossible dream, a childish thing.

Or perhaps you did become a farmer, are one now, and have watched over the years as the rural populations dwindled. Perhaps you are one of the aging farmers whose children don't wish to do the work because it is hard and there's little return except in selling land to developers. Or per-haps you are one of the children who did continue and are trying to make your land survive in a world that values your contribution less and less. Ei-ther way, though your views of the farm were probably less romantic than those of many of us, in most cases, you lost something too when the land-scape and the vision changed.

It turns out that the old sort of farm, the one we dreamed of as chil-dren, really is the best way to feed the world. Small-scale polyculture that mixes animals and multiple plant crops together is vastly more productive than industrial row crops. Organic methods alone can match and exceed the yields of chemical fertilizers, and polyculture and intensive techniques are more effective still. Peter Rosset documents that small farms are be-tween 4 and 100 times more productive in total output per acre than in-dustrial farms.[115] Meanwhile, the System of Rice Intensification (SRI), a technique for hand production of rice, shows significant increases in rice production in many areas, while reducing costs for seeds, fertilizers and other inputs.[116]

Gardening is more productive still, because the more attention you give your crops, and the more carefully you manage them, the better your results. As the old saying goes, the best fertilizer is the gardener's shadow. On a garden scale, John Jeavons and Ecology Action have documented that a human being can feed himself for an entire year on as little as 700 square feet. Most of us would rather use a little more land and eat a more diverse diet, but we should be aware that the average half-acre suburban lot could fairly easily provide much of what a family eats for a whole year.

Becoming a victory farmer or gardener doesn't mean moving to Iowa or Montana. In fact, the places we most urgently need people to grow food are the places where people live now — in downtown Manhattan and suburban Atlanta, along the I95 corridor and in Detroit housing projects, in the Hollywood Hills and south central LA, in cities and suburbs where populations are most concentrated. It is perfectly possible for many of those places to grow a large percentage of what they eat. Though New Yorkers will never grow everything they eat, Hong Kong, one of the most densely packed and modern cities in the world produces two-thirds of its poultry, half its vegetables and one-sixth of the pork eaten in the city.[117] Most of us could get most of our vegetables and some of our staples locally.

In fact, as we will explore later in this book, most of the farmers we are talking about will be farming near population centers simply because that is where good farmland already exists, now subdivided into suburban houses and made into public parks. And, of course, that is where many of you live. We are now at the point of using most of the world's best arable land — the land that rich-world denizens have transformed into housing. And it is there we have our best hope of raising yields. As Nobel Prize-winning economist Gary Becker puts it,

> The first is that only a small fraction of potential arable land is used for farming because the growth of cities and suburbia has led to mass conversions to other purposes of land formerly used to grow foods. Persistent high and climbing prices of grains and other foods will induce conversion of some of this land back to farming.[118]

That is, even economists are starting to recognize that to feed ourselves, we need to reclaim the suburbs. So what we are speaking of is not "going out" to farm, but coming home to it.

What Happened to Happiness?

I don't know what your destiny will be,
but one thing I do know:
the only ones among you who will be really happy
are those who have sought and found how to serve.
— Albert Schweitzer —

If industrial agriculture isn't the best or most efficient way to feed ourselves, is it possible that we are simply happier and better off without having to do the miserable work of growing food ourselves? Why would we want to go back to digging the dirt when McDonalds and Taco Bell are both open past midnight and happy to feed us? Didn't our grandparents struggle to get off the farm and away from the land?

It may well be true that a few generations back when nearly everyone was a farmer, the bright lights of the city looked awfully good, compared to milking at 5 AM. But in fact, we didn't get any happier when we traded our hoes for ten hours a day in front of a computer screen or double shifts at a fast food restaurant. In fact, it turns out that the time we spend in front of computers is among the least satisfying time in our lives. In *Deep Economy* Bill McKibben documents the steady decline in the happiness of Americans over the past 60 years,

> All that material progress — and all the billions of barrels of oil
> and millions of acres of trees that it took to create it — seems not
> to have moved the satisfaction meter an inch. In 1946, the United
> States was the happiest country among four advanced economies;
> thirty years later, it was eighth among eleven advanced countries;
> a decade after that it ranked tenth among twenty-three nations,
> many of them from the third world.... The proportion of respon-
> dents saying they were very happy peaked sometimes in the 1950s
> and has slid slowly but steadily in the years since. Between 1970 and
> 1994, for instance, it dropped five full percentage points, dipping
> below the mark where one-third of Americans were able to count
> themselves as very happy.... As one reporter summarized the find-
> ings, "There's more misery in people's lives today." [119]

It may be pure coincidence that this drop in our happiness came at the same time that corporate power over us was increasing and we saw a steady loss of connection with the land we live on. More people than ever before consider themselves depressed or take medications to deal with anxiety, stress and depression. Even adjusted for increases in diagnosis, we're much less happy than we were in the past, when we had less and did more work outside, ate more of what we grew and lived outside. We have tested, as McKibben points out, the question of whether more stuff makes happier, and the answer is a resounding no. I would also argue that we have tested whether being "freed" from homemade dinners, collecting eggs and growing Victory Gardens makes us happier — and the answer is also a no.

Nor are we working less. As Juliet Schor documents in *The Overworked American*, the total hours spent working on tasks that we consider "work" have risen from back in the days when we were growing our own food. We're working longer hours — with less quiet, less rest, less autonomy — than we did back when we had those vegetable gardens and farms. We got more money and more stuff, but we also traded working for ourselves in our own gardens for working for other people under their discipline. Instead of growing our dinners, we get to put our kids in daycare, put on the neckties or pantyhose, and go someplace where our boss times our bathroom breaks and reads our personal e-mails. It may be necessary, but some of us could work less and have more time — the one thing we say we desperately want — if only we were to put those Victory Gardens back on our lawns and grow some of our own food. Some of us might enjoy the work of professional agriculture if it paid enough to keep us going.

And it might improve our happiness and our children's happiness as well. In *Last Child in the Woods*, Richard Louv documents the consequences of disconnection from nature in children. He argues that many cases of Attention Deficit Hyperactivity Disorder may come from children spending increasing amounts of time inside rather than out playing. He cites studies that demonstrate that the chance of being diagnosed with ADHD rises by 10 percent with each hour a child spends watching television. Some cases of ADHD may represent misdiagnoses, children who would have seemed entirely normal in a world where they

> …would have been directing their energy and physicality in constructive ways: doing farm chores, baling hay, splashing in the swimming hole, climbing trees, racing to the sandlot for a game of baseball. Their unregimented play would have been steeped in nature.[120]

Louv also cites studies that show that the average child today experiences more anxiety than the average child *under psychiatric care* in the

1950s. It seems clear that our children are not happier with us working more hours and letting them hang out in front of the Sega system. Meanwhile, recent studies have shown that children have fewer allergies and stronger immune systems when they spend time around farm animals and playing in the dirt and that dirt actually contains a chemical that may help make us happy.

Whether or not we could solve the ADHD crisis with more exercise and time outdoors, there is no doubt whatsoever that the average American would be much, much healthier if they spent part of their time outside in the garden. Gardening provides both aerobic and weight-bearing exercise and the food you grow is documentably better for us than the processed diets we've been eating. Ill health is a major contributor to personal unhappiness; 70 percent of people who suffer from chronic illnesses rate themselves as unhappy. And the economic cost of those illnesses is enormous — billions of dollars in an increasingly underinsured population. In a very real sense, gardening could make us happier, physically healthier and more secure economically and physically. It could give us both longer lives and better ones.

Servicing the Economy

The recession started upon my arrival. It could have been — some say February, some say March, some speculate maybe earlier it started — but nevertheless, it happened as we showed up here. The attacks on our country affected our economy. Corporate scandals affected the confidence of people and therefore affected the economy. My decision on Iraq, this kind of march to war, affected the economy.
— GEORGE W. BUSH —

So we're asking you — if we aren't happier, and we aren't doing less drudgery, and we aren't growing food more efficiently, what exactly is the justification for industrial agriculture? And a deafening silence is the only answer we receive. Or at best, someone mutters something about the economy.

Well, the notion that it is our job to serve the economy is another one of those big lies. We as a people do not exist as servants to the industrial economy — our economy is supposed to serve us. That is, it is supposed to help us get what we want. But it manifestly is not doing so. Marketplaces, going back to the very first open markets in villages and wandering traders, are about the exchange of things people want — if you want good food and I want enough money to pay my taxes, we're in luck. The notion that we all have to keep Walmart going in the interest of serving the mythical economy is nonsense. Just as the economy adapted just fine going from an agricultural society to an industrial one, it will adapt just fine to a degree of deindustrialization. Right now, many of us are seeing just how vulnerable our service to the economy has made us, as the recession builds.

What will be harmed by this policy is corporate power. I'm afraid if you weep for the heirs of Sam Walton whose steady income of billions will be negatively affected, we cannot dry your tears. Creating a vibrant local economy of people who make and produce food is likely to be bad for Walmart, Monsanto and McDonalds. That it will be good for us — that we will be healthier and happier, and more secure, with a healthier environment and less dependency on things like foreign oil — will have to console us. And for those of us who feel that rich, powerful corporations haven't been a good influence on our society, it might just be that our lives and our democracies are improved by taking power and wealth out of the hands of corporations and putting it back into the hands of ordinary people. It might be that if we stop giving our cash to ADM and start giving a little bit of it to our neighbor, our neighbor's life might be vastly improved, rather than making ADM just a little bit richer.

Usually, the casualties of a great economic change are regular people — people whose jobs were off-shored, mechanized or downsized. This time, the casualties will be corporations, and we need not weep for them. In fact, deindustrializing agriculture can create better markets. The current model is one in which maximizing profit is the only real consideration — environmental damage and disruption of people's lives be damned. As Maria Mies and Veronika Bennholdt-Thomsen argue in *The Subsistence Perspective*, however, markets can and do exist that are relational — that encourage relationships between people and derive some of their value from them. That is, it isn't inherently necessary to have a "Screw you, I want to get the most for my cash no matter what" economy. It is possible to have an economy in which people matter. Mies and Bennholdt-Thomsen argue,

> The claim that the market operates according to inherent abstract laws helps politicians, managers and bankers — and not only them — to protest their complete innocence; it allows individuals to wash their hands of responsibility for their everyday economic activities. Men and women declare themselves to have no power in

relation to the market, thereby legitimizing their own consumer-
ism, their own environmental and market behaviour.... The market sphere itself is not perceived as a site of responsible behavior. It
no longer occurs to anyone in our part of the world that traders and
customers might have some obligations to one another.[121]

This lack of responsibility, the absence of mutual obligation and awareness is not inherent; it is a product of a consciously created economy that is
structured to work that way. The economy is designed to create the maximum disconnect between people so that they will be as little aware of the
consequences of their actions as possible, and as little concerned about
them as possible. This is why a universal thanksgiving is not possible in an
industrial food system.

As Rob Hopkins notes, without fossil energies we'd be accomplishing
about one-seventieth of what we are now — or less.[122] Now, all fossil fuels
aren't going away, but we need to cut emissions by more than 90 percent
while dramatically increasing the ability of the planet to absorb carbon. So
even if we had fossil energies aplenty, we'd need to cut back dramatically
on their usage. And that means an end to endless economic growth and a
picking and choosing of what we can accomplish. Saying that we could accomplish much less without fossil fuels is terrifying if we imagine our cuts
coming across the board, taking away from everything that matters to us;
but in fact, there is so much waste in our system that we have enough energy for what actually matters to most of us.

If we look at our economic output in those terms, thinking about what
matters to us, it becomes rapidly clear that we need food, clothing, tools,
and other basic goods, and that we don't need Barbie dolls, Hummers, flat-
screen televisions, plastic shopping bags and a host of other things. If we
look at what a lower-energy life must look it, it is one that is stripped down
to essentials. Hopkins argues the merits of relocalization of economies
this way:

> I would argue that we need to be building the capability to produce
> locally those things that we can produce locally. It is, of course, easy
> to attack this idea by pointing out that some things, such as com-
> puters and frying-pans, can't be made at a local level. However,
> there are a lot of things we could produce locally: a wide range of
> seasonal fruits and vegetables, fresh fish, timber, mushrooms, dyes,
> many medicines, furniture, ceramics, insulation materials, soap,

bread, glass, dairy products, wool and leather products, paper, building materials, perfumes and fresh flowers — to name but a few. We aren't looking create a "nothing in, nothing out" economy but rather to close economic loops where possible and to produce locally what we can.[123]

A more local, direct economy disrupts the industrial paradigm. When your neighbor's well-being is tied to yours, you both have an incentive to ensure that the other comes away happy. When you enjoy going next door to chat with your neighbor and pick up some eggs, the pleasure of the exchange justifies the extra quarter you may pay. And knowing that your elderly neighbor who bakes for you has enough money to live on has value as well — just as knowing that your supply of food is secure even if something stops trucks from running has value to you. We need to give up the notion that all value can be represented in cash and that we have no obligations to one another.

Farmer or Gardener?

The seed of God is in us. Given an intelligent and hard-working farmer, it will thrive and grow up to God, whose seed it is; and accordingly its fruits will be God-nature. Pear seeds grow into pear trees, nut seeds into nut trees, and God-seed into God.

— Meister Eckhart —

Honestly, the terminology only sort of matters. You can call yourself whatever you want, but words do shape how we think, and perhaps it would be worth asking how the name we use shapes us. *Garden* derives from an old Germanic word that means yard or enclosure — so a gardener is someone who manages a specific space. There's nothing wrong with that term, but we believe that the sense of limitation contained in the word may not be the one we most want to convey now.

The word *farmer* however, derives from the same root as *form* — from a word for creation, and in old Anglo-French it meant to strengthen, to mend. And right now we truly need to be creators rather than consumers, and people whose work is the repair of the world. In this sense, *farmer* is preferable to *gardener*.

The other reason to use the term *farmer* is that it is the traditional term for what you are doing, because it isn't such an outrageous leap to imagine yourself as a farmer. We have a very powerful image of what a farmer is in our heads, but this too, has been shaped by industrialization. It turns out that only in our highly commodified culture, which values only large-scale agriculture (and even that not much), is a farmer defined as a big man with a big red tractor who grows a thousand acres of corn and votes republican. Now don't get us wrong, we need those guys too! But farmer, well, that's a bigger idea than just "professional commodity farmer."

In reality, despite our perception, the farmer's not a "he" at all — the average farmer, worldwide, is a woman. Even in the US, the only really fast-growing segment of agriculture is that of independent women farmers. The average farmer in the world is a non-white woman, farming about 4 acres, growing 15 different crops on them. They own no tractors and do most of their labor by hand, and their household has at least one outside source of income. (That last part is the only thing that is true of most professional farmers as well — 70 percent of them must either hold a second job or have a spouse work outside the home to support the household.)

And the average farmer world-wide doesn't look all that different from what American farmers used to look like. The average first settlers in the US farmed only seven acres, and by the time Thomas Jefferson was rhapsodizing about the democratic possibilities of a nation of farmers, the average farmer only had 11 acres.[124] It turns out that small farmers are the real farmers in most places — millions of people farm on plots of land no larger than the lot of a suburban house. Only we have stopped calling the ordinary people who grow food for sale or their own use (subsistence farmers) farmers.

And I don't think that's an accident. Americans are very rich by world standards, but often that wealth doesn't do us as much good as we think it does. We've already talked about how it doesn't make us happier, and it doesn't necessarily make us healthier either. And because the costs of living in a rich society are so high and we judge ourselves not by the world average but by our neighbors and what we see around us, including what we see on TV, we never really feel rich.

In fact, many of us are extremely vulnerable to hunger and poverty. One extended job loss, disability or pension disaster can mean the difference between security and hunger, between a home and homelessness, between health care and no medical care at all. But everything in our industrial culture tells us over and over again that we're nothing like those poor people in other places. We see peasants and ordinary people in other nations and we don't think of them as our potential allies, as people with the same vulnerabilities we have.

But what if we in the rich nations saw ourselves as subsistence farmers, if we looked at our own gardens that feed us and saw in them a connection to Thai rice farmers and Guatemalan peasants? Might we have to change our thinking about what kind of actions are acceptable in the world, if we looked at them and saw ourselves? If we looked at small farmers all over the world and recognized the same basic needs — good, safe food, basic shelter, enough security — what kind of political and economic changes might we create in our world? What movements might arise from a united world movement of people who are connected to the land and the future?

Thomas Jefferson believed that independent farmers were the key to democracy. He felt that only those who were truly self-sufficient, and thus not beholden to others for their basic needs, could create a true democracy. In fact, we've seen the truth of this in our own society — when politicians take political contributions, we know their judgments cannot be fully trusted. When we are economically dependent on corporations to feed and clothe and house us, we are not free to judge them.

What we are talking about, then, is a return to democratic society in the sense that the founding fathers intended it. Most of us will be subsistence farmers, growing only for ourselves along with doing our other jobs — the ones that pay the bills (now smaller because we need less) — with perhaps with a little extra to trade, sell or give away. Some will grow a bit more on small farms and in large gardens or specialize in a few crops, and some will be larger-scale farmers, producing grains, vegetables, fiber, fertility and animals on farms of ten to a few hundred acres.

To a large degree, what we are imagining is an economy and culture of subsistence. But that's a word that, like *farmer*, has come to mean something other than what its origins and history would suggest. When we speak of subsistence agriculture, or a subsistence perspective, many of us imagine a life of terrible poverty and suffering, unending drudgery. But subsistence means having enough, being sufficient. The word derives from a theological term, used in the *Book of Common Prayer*, to mean having a real presence in the world. In its most literal sense, a subsistence society is a real one, one concerned with real needs, rather than abstracted wants.

Perhaps most importantly, a subsistence economy does not require eternal growth or expansionist political and military policies. It does not require there to be vast differences between rich and poor. Its wealth lies in communal resources — the aid of neighbors, the pleasure of community, social and cultural wealth, good food, comfortable clothing, shelter, enough surplus for basic security, and a strong identification with one's local community. And thus, the community, rather than external programs provide support for those who can no longer support themselves. And, at the same time, those who participate in the subsistence economy have a measure of autonomy unknown to us who are so terribly dependent upon outside resources and political and economic forces we can't control.

Americans like to think of ourselves as independent — we want to think for ourselves, and we are proud of our history of demanding independence. But right now, we are as dependent upon the whims of others as any serf in history ever has been. Our food, shelter, water, clothing, security — all of them rely on outside resources and energies, many of them limited resources that others compete over. As long as we depend for food on trucks that come from far away, and oil that comes from further, we are not truly independent. We saw in Hurricane Katrina how quickly people who ordinarily do for themselves can go to having nothing and waiting for a handout that might not come in time. Truly independent people do everything they can to rely on themselves and their neighbors, not on the government and not the goodwill of outside sources.

Who Shall Farm?

What is — "Paradise"–
Who live there —
Are they "Farmers" —
Do they "hoe"
Do they know that this is "Amherst" —
And that I — am coming — too —
— EMILY DICKINSON —

If we are to define ourselves as farmers, we need to erase some of the baggage that comes with that word. First of all, we have to stop imagining that growing our food is so physically demanding that it can be undertaken only by the young and healthy. Sharon's family has grown an enormous amount of food, mostly with their own muscles, and she has run a community-supported agriculture (CSA) program well into late pregnancy, growing not only her family's food but food for dozens of other people in her ninth month. We know many elderly people and people with disabilities who garden — Sharon's great aunt announced a few years ago that she (at 94) had "finally had to give up the big garden and go down to just growing thirty tomato plants." Our friend Pat and her husband are both disabled and over 60 and they grow virtually all of their own produce in containers around their small home. The writer Ruth Stout described her low-effort gardening method as making gardening feasible for those "between 70 and 90."

We have been taught to see agriculture as intolerably arduous, when in fact, on a small scale it is merely a good workout, and can be adapted to most levels of physical ability. In many pre-industrial agricultural societies, people had considerably more leisure than we do. In pre-conquest Britain, for example, the average peasant worked only 174 days per year. It says something about the bill of goods we've been sold by growth capitalism that many of us have fewer days off and less free time than 11th-century serfs.

And we need to rid ourselves of the assumption that mechanization is necessary for farms of an acre or two. When you raise children, you can do terrible damage to their capacity for self-sufficiency by always following them around and sparing them any struggle or inconvenience, telling them that things are "too hard" and being right there to ease their labors. The same thing is true with most labor-saving devices — in many cases, their very proximity convinces us that we cannot do without them, that our lives without tractors and tillers must be unendurably exhausting. But although machines have their place, not only can we not afford to choose them as a first option, but we harm our own sense of competence and ability to know what our bodies can accomplish. The shovel and the hoe are ancient tools, and much can be accomplished with them. Even more can be accomplished by minimizing their use, using mulches and natural system farming.

Equally urgently, we need to stop conceiving of the farmer as a white person living in a largely or wholly white community. Some of our cultural nostalgia for agriculture is, I think, a fantasy of a world of perfect whiteness. But, in fact, our nation of farmers was built on Native American land with the sweat of slaves, and our nation of consumers now lives on produce harvested by Latino farm workers.

Though African Americans have been productive small farmers for many generations, they are losing their land and livelihood at a much higher rate than farmers in general. We can assume that as poverty rises and hunger haunts us, African Americans will, as usual, be the first and most deeply harmed. To build sustainable, local food systems that serve African American communities will be a task of the utmost urgency, and the members of those communities are the only ones who can tell us what they need and how best to get it. We need to stop sending young African Americans to war and to prison, and give them access to the land, knowledge and power they have every right to.

Nor can we afford to mistreat and disdain the people who mostly grow our food right now. We call them migrant workers, or farm workers, instead of their proper name — farmers, as though the person who owns the land has done the essential work of farming simply by owning it, while these unskilled "workers" have merely planted the seeds, weeded the ground, watered, fertilized, tended and harvested the food we eat. What we deem our "immigration problem" would look very different if we realized that the greatest wealth of agricultural knowledge and skill in our nation is in the bodies of those we think of as primarily "illegal." We depend on these workers, and instead of including them in our thanksgivings, we dismiss them. But as Jonathan Bloom, who blogs about food waste (current statistics suggest we waste more than a quarter of all food, but Bloom estimates it higher, closer to half), observes, orchards and fields go unharvested and large quantities of food are wasted, driving prices up, when immigrant labor is prohibited.[125]

The other exploited group whose needs have to be addressed are present-day industrial farmers. That may seem like a counter-intuitive point, but we as a nation have done more harm to ourselves by the destruction of our existing agricultural communities than we can possibly imagine. Wendell Berry points out that what we've done to our rural communities over the past 100 years is a form of colonialism. Colonialism, as we all know, is the subjugation of a people for the purpose of extracting their wealth from them. And the very first project of colonialism, as Edward Said observes, is to devalue everything the colonized person knows and believes, and to replace it with the culture of the colonizer, so that when you debase and humiliate and destroy the colonized person, rape the land and take its riches, they'll believe you are doing it for their own good.

Could there be a better way of describing what has happened to millions of farmers over the past 100 years? They've been told they were hicks and rednecks, that their profound knowledge of their craft and their place was less valuable than professionalized knowledge coming out of agricultural colleges and cities, and their children were encouraged to have contempt for their parents' knowledge and to leave for the cities as soon as possible. We told the children of farmers that what people in cities had was knowledge, and what they had was ignorance. Their forests were logged, their minerals mined, their soil stripped, their economies destroyed, families broken apart and towns converted into bedroom suburbs.

And if you don't think the people who grew out of farming communities all over the country are mad as hell about it and want to strike back at the people who disdained them and took away their sense of place, of competence, and their culture, look at the 2000 and 2004 elections, the deep division between the places where farmers are and the places where they mostly are not. Farmers are not inherently politically conservative (in the 1920s, Kansas and Oklahoma were hotbeds of Marxism and labor radicalism); nor are they fools. But we stripped farmers of what they had and what they knew, and left them willing to give over power to anyone who seemed to show them the respect they so deeply deserve.

It should shock us realize that the Kansas farm where Dorothy walked the pigpen fence in *The Wizard of Oz* is now nearly as mythical and lost a place as Oz is. We spent decades pursuing the wrong programs, and we now must reverse course. If we're to avoid the worst prices of our ignorance, we must act now; we must today stop buying supermarket food and start growing it for ourselves and our neighbors.

The American Dream is a phrase so trite and misused as to be meaningless in most contexts, but not, perhaps in this one. Because the original American Dream was simply this: land, autonomy, peace and plenty. What was suburbia but a failed means of stripping the agriculture and labor away from the dream of a small green space? We teach our children about the farm from birth — one of the very first things most children learn about the world is that cows say moo. The dream of the farm — the real farm, not the suburban fake — is so deeply ingrained in us that it would not be hard to bring it back. So many people tell me that they'd love to do what I do — and they can, not in some distant place, but where they are now, with a hen and a tomato and a hoe. It was, after all, a garden we were cast out of.

For the purposes of this book, we will call ourselves "farmers" and "victory gardeners" interchangeably. Because both are true. We are creators, sustainers, strengtheners, but also those who enclose a small space and nurture it in order to bring about the greatest victory of all — the preservation of the future and the repair of the world.

Without Slaves?

As I would not be a slave, so I would not be a master.
This expresses my idea of democracy.
— ABRAHAM LINCOLN —

Writing a book called *A Nation of Farmers* and arguing for Jeffersonian democracy brings you, sooner or later, bang hard up against the question of slavery. It is not possible to address that issue by eliding the problem of slavery, as many of Thomas Jefferson's advocates do. Nor can slavery be addressed by claiming, as many anti-agrarians do, that Jefferson's slave-holding makes the whole question of agrarian society so irrevocably tainted that it cannot be useful to us any longer. Our opinion is that the only answer we can come up with is to address this vexatious question full steam ahead.

Jefferson made quite a number of statements arguing that independent farmers were the best candidates for democracy. He claimed in *Notes on the State of Virginia*, "Those who labor in the earth are the chosen people of God, if ever He had a chosen people, whose breasts He has made His peculiar deposit for substantial and genuine virtue."

Speaking slightly less effusively, he went on to say in a 1785 letter to John Jay, "Cultivators of the earth are the most valuable citizens. They are the most vigorous, the most independent, the most virtuous, & they are tied to their country & wedded to its liberty & interests by the most lasting bands."

His opposition to Alexander Hamilton's plan to create large, state-supported financial institutions and move toward industrialization represents one of the great philosophical battles at the founding of our nation. Henry Cabot Lodge famously called it the founding debate of our society.[126] And it would be easy for agrarians to see Hamilton, and Hamiltonianism, as the bad guy; that is, Hamilton supported the notion of concentrating wealth in the hands of an elite and moving the nation toward trade and manufacturing.

But the undercurrent of their debate, less popularly considered, was slavery. Hamilton was an abolitionist who regularly attended New York Abolition Society meetings. He believed that manufacturing was the only alternative to an agrarian slave society. Wage labor, he felt, would end slavery. Jefferson, of course, was a plantation owner and slave holder. That he was ambivalent about slavery and at times worked for its overturn does not erase that at times he also supported it and had no desire, as Hamilton did, to see African-Americans working in America in independent agriculture or factories. Jefferson imagined that freed slaves would be sent to Africa or Haiti, rather than they would grow independently alongside white people.

Roger Kennedy, in his Book *Mr. Jefferson's Lost Cause*, argues that in fact, Jefferson's agrarianism struggled with two conflicting impulses and ultimately operated to reinforce slavery in our society. Jefferson's agrarianism, he argues, wasn't quite what it seemed to be. While independent, largely self-sufficient farmers with good educations and a great deal of civic engagement were a norm in the North, the South was largely divided between white, wealthy plantation owners and small backwoods farmers, who Jefferson regarded with a great deal of distaste.

Kennedy makes a compelling case that Jefferson's vision of agrarianism, which included the slave plantations, enabled westward expansion and the subjugation of the Native population. He does a fascinating analysis of the rate at which plantation owners destroyed their soils — at almost three times the rate of non-slave holding southern farmers and five times the rate of northern farmers — and argues that Jefferson's rhetoric and the Louisiana Purchase were predicated on a notion of ever-expanding slavery as a way of expanding the depletion of the other natural resources, such as soil, in newly acquired regions.[127]

This is a compelling critique, and to Kennedy's enormous credit, it is a nuanced critique. He does not claim that Jefferson cynically manipulated the plantation-owner vote so much as argue that Jefferson both believed in the notion of independent farmers and was unable to bring about the society he imagined.

Here, I think, is the beginning, not of a rehabilitation of Jefferson but of a way of thinking about agrarianism and slavery. Because it would be foolish to argue, as Thom Hartmann does in his book *What Would Jefferson Do?*, that Jefferson figures largely as a helpless opponent to slavery.

Hartmann, whose arguments are otherwise well taken, seems to belong to the category of Jeffersonianism advocates who rehabilitate him only by looking at the anti-slavery writings. But to do so is to ignore the fact that Jefferson's legacy to us was more than just his principled objections — it was his practices.

No. To find a way toward Jeffersonianism, we must not erase slavery but face it. However, one of Hartmann's own arguments directs us usefully to the urgent larger question. That is, Hartmann argues that instead of eliminating slavery, the US merely moved it elsewhere. He wrongly uses it to defend Jefferson saying,

> Yet how many of us would willingly free our slaves? I'm typing these words on a computer containing many parts made in countries where laborers are held with less freedom and in conditions worse than those of Jefferson's slaves.[128]

Hartmann has a point, but not in defense of Jefferson. In that sense, his language is a rationalization — Jefferson did more than simply hold slaves, he enabled slavery on a large, public scale. And although today most of us don't actually own slaves, we too foster their forced labor. If we are to imagine, as Hamilton did, as many anti-agrarians have since, that the debate between industrialization and agrarianism can come down to the question of slavery, we need to ask, how good has industrial society been at freeing its slaves? That is, do we have fewer slaves right now than we did in an agrarian society? How many slaves are there in the world today?

When you add up the numbers, the results are surprising. At present, according to the UN (and this is a conservative estimate), the world has 27 million literal slaves — that is, people who are held as slaves, owned as objects, and treated like them.[129] Add to that 158 million child laborers, which UNICEF documents are almost always forced laborers.[130] Then add 100 million adult women prostitutes (the child prostitutes are included in the previous number) who, according to the UN committees on human trafficking, can be said to lack control over their lives, bodies and earnings,[131] and the minimum of 400 million poor workers who live in conditions of effective slavery, either in debt to the company store or given a choice between starvation and working in unsafe, dangerous conditions for virtually no money,[132] and we end up with between one-third and one-half a billion people on this planet in slavery or effective slavery. That means that one out of every 25 people on the earth is enslaved or as near as to make no difference.

This figure is almost certainly too low, however; these are estimates, and low estimates in many cases. For example, at least 200 million women worldwide engage in prostitution of one sort or another, and it stretches the imagination to conceive that the 100 million that the UN does not consider to be effectively enslaved are all fully willing participants who simply chose prostitution as their career. Nor does this figure include involuntary military conscripts all over the globe, many of whom (including a substantial number of children), are used for forced labor or cannon fodder.

The child labor figures are hotly disputed. For example, the International Textile, Garment and Leather Worker's Union estimates that 250 million children, more than half of them under the age of 14, are at work in clothing and textile manufacture alone.[133] Because these constitute only about half of the UNICEF figures, that would raise the estimate up dramatically, toward one-half billion people in slavery, at least one-third of them children. Far more than half are female. Because women are often poorer than men, less well educated and more likely to be encumbered by children, they are disproportionately likely to end up in sweatshops, domestic service or the sex trade from lack of other options.

Some may protest that adults who are not literally enslaved shouldn't be included here — adult sweatshop workers, for example. We'll concede that their conditions aren't quite the same as slavery. But *res ipsa loquitor* — the thing speaks for itself. This is testimony taken from a single sneaker plant producing Nikes and Adidas in 1998 in El Salvador:

> …12 hour days in hot, unventilated conditions. Workers are given backless wooden benches from which to work. Cushions are not allowed. Supervision is brutal, with constant verbal abuse against those who do not keep up the required pace, physical violence and sexual harassment. Permission is required to drink water or use the bathroom. The drinking water is not purified and comes from the cistern into which the toilet empties. No toilet paper is available and the toilets are filthy. Male supervisors come into the women's toilets regularly to harass the women back to work. Talking is not allowed. Workers leaving the plant are subject to humiliating body searches. Workers are expected to work when they are sick. One or two days pay is deducted for any visit to the clinic. Women are made to undergo monthly pregnancy tests which they have to pay for themselves. Pregnant workers are fired instantly. In some plants supervisors give depo-provera contraceptive injections to women who are told they are getting anti-tetanus jabs.[134]

Both effective and literal slaves have little control of their own lives. They are subject, in the literal sense of the word, to the whims of their

masters. They experience physical violence and control of the full range of
their lives, including sexual activity. They are subject to degradation and
told that they deserve their conditions. They are not free to leave or to stop
their work, and they often do their work under the terror that their families will be harmed or their children will starve to death.

As historian Kenneth Stampp, writing of American slavery points out,
"the predominant and overpowering emotion…in the majority of slaves
was neither love nor hate, but fear." [135] Those who live in constant fear of
their bosses or masters are always slaves.

And who are they enslaved to? Well, directly speaking, they are enslaved to pimps, factory owners, industrial farmers, large companies, mining corporations, private entrepreneurs, local warlords, private slaveholders
in countries that largely turn a blind eye to this sort of thing (including our
own — there have been a number of high-profile liberations of effectively
enslaved immigrants in domestic service, garment factories and agriculture
in the US, and that's almost certainly only the tip of the iceberg).

But who motivates these slave owners to enslave people? Their work
and its proceeds move up the economic food chain, and the people who
profit are us. That is, the appetites of people rich enough to travel around
the world seeking out prostitutes are fulfilled often by slaves, but so are the
appetites of people who want cheap coffee and bananas, the appetites of
people who want cheap T-shirts, diamonds, energy and oriental rugs.

Most of the work we enslave people to do is work that the rich world
directly or indirectly benefits from. Our cheap bananas come from the
Ecuadorian plantation where whole families, including children, are so in-
debted to the "company store" that they can never hope to do anything
else. And you and I eat their bananas and support this system. We wear the
fancy sneakers, put the diamonds on our fingers, burn the Nigerian oil in
our cars and decorate our homes with the labor of small children. We do
not benefit from every slave, and responsibility exists all down the line, but
it is also true that the economic function of slavery is to make masters rich
and our riches cannot be separated from those holding the whip.

Still, we might overall say we're doing pretty well with abolitionism,
if we compare ourselves to the past. After all, the best guess is that maybe
1 in 25 people are enslaved, but in ancient Athens, it was almost 1:1, and in
the American South, in most plantation regions, slaves outnumbered free
white people by between 2:1 and 10:1. But if you look at the society as a
whole, ancient Greece at the height of its slaveholding had about four free

people to every slave, and the US in 1860 had about 4 million slaves and just over 23 million people.[136] At present there are certainly more enslaved people than ever in history. How many of us have said to ourselves that certainly had we lived in the mid-1800s we would have spoken out against slavery? And yet here we are, and for the most part, we are silent.

We have not so much abolished slavery as offshored it. So one answer to the question of whether agrarianism is irretrievably bound up in slavery would be to say yes — but no more so than industrialism. Both are slave societies. In one, we see our slaves; in another, we hide them so that we can feel righteous and not be confronted with their suffering.

Looked at in this light, Jeffersonian agrarianism is no better — and no worse — than industrialism, which of course, depends on colonialism and enslaved labor. So the question becomes, how would we get out of slavery altogether, in either system? That is, which system can best be adapted to be truly slave free?

First though there's one kind of slavery we haven't included, but probably should — our energy slaves. These slaves aren't people, of course, but they have enabled most of us to live like masters. Fossil fuels have enabled most rich world denizens to live their lives as though they have slaves — not just far-away slaves making their clothing and growing their coffee, but in-house slaves to do things like wash their dishes, carry them places they want to go, and cook their food. The term "energy slaves" is a useful way of thinking about our lives now — denizens of the rich world are living like slave owners of prior days, dependent on fossil fuels and a good bit of globalized distance to separate us from the consequences of our actions.

It is certainly true that we shouldn't look on energy slaves with the same degree of horror as we look on human slavery. But it is also the case that we might look on a lifestyle that requires human slaves and the equivalent amount of non-renewable energy with the same level of disturbance one might look at the lives of southern plantation owners. Because when the non-renewable energy runs out, we'll have created a generation of people who lack the essential skills, the physical fitness and the mindset to do their own work. The future of people trained only to be masters is not bright — either they remain rich and do evil by enslaving more people to compensate for their diminishing resources, or they do quite badly indeed when they first have to pick up the work they have so long avoided.

Which brings us, of course, to the real question. Is it possible for human beings to imagine a society in which no one is enslaved to anyone else and we also don't burn fossil fuels? In which human beings cannot be com-modified? Is it possible to imagine a low-input world in which there are no slaves and no masters?

To some degree, of course, we can build renewable energies that allow us (and in an ideal world, more of the world's populace) to retain some of our energy slaves. But the larger issue of abolitionism must take center stage as we do this. It is not enough to say "When we have all the power we need, we'll free our slaves" because, of course, that day never comes. The only choice is the choice of abolitionism itself, to acknowledge that it will cost us something to give up such a profoundly immoral structure, and that we will do it anyway, because it is right.

The idea of going back to a slave society in the absence of fossil fuels is a thought that haunts many of us trying to envision a world with fewer fossil fuels. It is true that we still live in a slave society, and that we have to undo both evils — both fix the broken infrastructure in a society that can't imag-ine life without infinite cheap energy and also eliminate our slaves. But this answer is woefully insufficient. How, after all, do we disengage from slav-ery? How do we face a future with less energy that doesn't lead to a perma-nent, huge, underclass?

Neither capitalism (which institutionalizes the disparities that en-courage slavery and depends on reducing the value of human labor and re-sources, ideally to nil) nor communism (which outright controls humans and their labor) can provide us with an economic model for slave-free so-ciety. Fortunately, these are hardly our only choices. But it should remind us again that we are often presented with false dichotomies, in this case be-tween Marx and Smith. That both our "choices" lead to the enslavement of peoples should, I think, be sufficient to dismiss them.

Gandhi's *Swaraj,* or "self-rule," movement offers one piece of the puzzle for a life without slavery. The notion that self-rule contained elements of political, economic and social theory meant that the system did not com-partmentalize labor in ways that enabled slavery. It is a difficult system, be-cause it places enormous faith in the independent good will of individuals, for, as Gandhi put it,

> In such a state [where Swaraj is achieved] everyone is his own ruler.
> He rules himself in such a manner that he is never a hindrance to
> his neighbour.[137]

And yet, all deeply democratic systems depend on precisely that faith, that trust that ordinary people can and should hold in their hands the most essential details of our lives. It is Utopian, of course, but in the best sense. As Gandhi himself said,

> It may be taunted with the retort that this is all Utopian and, therefore not worth a single thought.… Let India live for the true picture, though never realizable in its completeness. We must have a proper picture of what we want before we can have something approaching it.[138]

The idea that democracy can be separated from the way we earn our livings or treat our soils is false, and Jefferson was right in articulating this. The idea that we can also separate our agrarian ideology from its history of racism and slavery is also false — we cannot erase the inconvenient parts of our history or minimize them. But what we can do is create our own sort of *Swaraj* and take the complex legacy of our agrarianism and make it into something else.

How might this come about? Well, a nation made up not of plantation owners but of true small farmers might be able to do so. A distributist model, a la Chesterton, in which most of the land is held by small farmers, is a potential beginning.

As we have noted, we have already done much of the inconvenient work of chopping up land and putting small houses on it — we call it suburbia. And most suburban lots come with a piece of land, perhaps not quite sufficient to sustain a family, but often enough to render them independent of a host of created needs and able, because of that independence, to make their choices based not on their fears and dependencies on corporate entities but from a dispassionate consideration of what is best for the society as a whole. Small suburban farmers cannot need slaves — their land is too small to require them. Larger farmers who are paid well for their produce can afford to pay workers or can afford to share a tractor or have horses. Intensive agricultural techniques mean that small lots can come close to supporting a family. It isn't necessary to take seriously the distributist's focus on biological family units here. We can create these "family" structures in other ways, in imagine cooperative ownerships that work in concert with distributism.

The question, of course, is how larger agriculture will be enacted over time. Reallocation of fossil fuels means that part of our job is to create such a loathing for notion of holding either immediate or distant slaves that we would no more consider it than we would consider eating human flesh.

200 Million Home Cooks

*What my mother believed about cooking was
that if you worked hard and prospered someone else would do it for you.*
— NORA EPHRON —

The idea that a large portion of the population should be involved in growing food is a truly radical one by Western standards. In contrast, the suggestion that we should all begin cooking the food grown in our various
Victory Gardens and farms seems positively ordinary. But in fact, a call for
200 million new home cooks is indeed a call to arms, because Americans,
for the most part, do not cook much. Rich or poor, urban or rural, Americans across every class, racial and cultural line do little or nothing to prepare a large proportion of food they consume. Laura Schenone, author of
*A Thousand Years Over a Hot Stove: A History of American Women Told
Though Food, Recipes and Remembrances* observes,

> The inability to find time to cook seems to cut across class. The work-
> ing poor may choose the cheapest and least-healthy options; fast
> food burgers and pizza. The wealthier may eat "gourmet" frozen din-
> ners, organic mesclun salad out of a bag, or Asian take-out food.[139]

In order for us to talk about the issue of cooking, how we cook now and
how we should cook in the future, we must talk about the population who
has done most of the cooking through most of human history — women.
But we wish to be absolutely clear that despite our focus on women at the
outset of this section, this is not a call for women to return to the kitchen
by themselves — this is a call for whole families, men and women, children
and elders to go into the kitchen and foment revolution by cooking. To ask
why we are not cooking now, we have to talk about women — and to talk
about women, we have to talk about men as well. But rather than assigning
blame, let us begin anew with this mantra — dinner is everyone's job!

Why is it we cannot cook for ourselves? Some of it is probably lack of
time and energy, for as women entered the workforce, they had less time
for domestic labor. In a recent article in *The Nation*, Ruth Rosen argued
that women in the US are experiencing a "care crisis" in which their obligations to their jobs, aging family members, their children, etc., have rendered them burdened and exhausted. There is some real truth to this.[140]
That is, it should be taken as a given that women cannot do the work of creating our new society on their own. Meals come three times a day, and it is
simply unfair to ask women alone to take on the burden of cooking.

That said, however, we think that Rosen's contention should not be taken entirely at face value. Though the argument that women simply don't have enough time to cook might hold for the poorest 21 million households in the US, many of whom are headed by overburdened and impoverished single mothers, it is not at all clear that this is true for millions of other middle class women who outsource the care of children and elderly family members to still lower-income employees.

It is certainly true that women entered the workforce en masse over a period of several decades, and almost certainly true that the woman of the 1980s, who worked an eight-hour day and then came home to cook and clean, was more burdened than her mother, who in the '50s had only the cooking and cleaning — at least if her mother was a fortunate, middle class woman. However, Sharon and her husband Eric each had two grandmothers who had no choice but to work in the 1950s — one was divorced from an abusive husband; another was a widow. Eric's paternal grandmother was a war refugee in an impoverished family and sold Fuller brushes door to door before coming home to clean and cook; his maternal grandmother worked both to make money to send her daughter to college and because she enjoyed it. Long before the feminist revolution, women were making their way into the working world; in 1960, more women worked than had at the height of the "Rosie the Riveter" years of World War II.

But more importantly, we would be making a mistake if we viewed the abnormal experience of the 1950s generation as the reality of women in our past. Let's count back another generation. Compare the woman of the 1980s with her own grandmother, the depression-era farmwife. True, Grandma didn't commute to a job. Yet I have my doubts that the average working woman in the 1980s truly worked much harder than their grandmothers who walked miles to the store, cooked on a wood stove, milked cows, tended the garden and boiled the laundry on the stove, while raising large families and tending elders.

Our history of our own exhaustion, in which we are the most burdened generation in history, is a strangely short one. We do work long hours. And despite that, we also squander enormous amounts of time and social surplus on shopping, television and other activities. We have chosen the '50s housewife to examine ourselves in opposition to, even though she was an anomaly. Historically speaking, it has always been possible to both do a great deal of work and feed oneself.

Poor women in our past and in other nations today often cook their own food in addition to household and outside work. If they do not go out to work (and many, many women throughout history have done so) they do economic work at home in their fields and gardens; they do small-scale manufacturing or textile work at home with their children present. A poor woman in Guatemala who raises food in her field, weaves textiles and takes them to market does not have more free time than a middle-manager in New Jersey who commutes into the city. We're not trying to criticize American and Western women for not cooking — they are overburdened and exhausted — but we do think the claim that we work too hard to make lunch bears some consideration.

Part of the problem is the failure of husbands, partners, sons and brothers to help. Part is the loss of the extended family and the strong local community, in which one could rely upon others to offer aid. Part of the problem is that both women and men are working longer and longer hours at jobs without more pay and with less job security. But a significant part of the difficulty is lack of skill; another is the manufactured perceptions of what constitutes work and what constitutes rest.

For example, the time it takes most suburbanites to pack all the kids into a car and drive to Taco Bell and back is the time in which a simple meal of stir-fried chicken, rice and salad could be prepared. The time we spend watching TV is often time that we could either be cooking or sleeping — that is, the four hours each day that the average American spends watching television after work is cutting into either their ability to feed their family good food or their sense of being rested, which affects basic health considerations and contributes to how overwhelmed they are by the need to make breakfast for everyone the next morning.

It is worth asking why it is that time in our cars seems less stressful than cooking, and why it is that we have such a deep need for "mindless" time in which even the simple activities of stirring a pot or kneading dough are too burdensome? Is it that cooking is so intolerably onerous, or because our culture itself is onerous?

We think it is important to distinguish between the purely psychological sense that cooking is time-consuming drudgery and the reality of our ability to do the work. The truth is that many of us do have the time in our lives to cook and garden — but to do so would mean prioritizing food growing and preparation over other things we have come to believe are essential. Both of us, for example, have done this reprioritization and find that though it comes with challenges, we can grow food while working full time, raising small children and doing community work.

Many of us could have more time for these activities if we needed less money; and though this is something of an oversimplification (we will talk more about economics later in the book), broadly speaking, one of the ways we could need less money — and thus fewer hours at work — would be to grow food and cook from scratch and thus spend less money purchasing food, particularly prepared food.

So why are women (and men) so tired and overwhelmed by the idea of producing dinner? There are several reasons. The first is that we are less skillful at doing so than prior generations. Despite the proliferation of cookbooks and the increasing percentage of people who say they cook as a hobby, many of us have little practice at the ordinary work of making food. Skill levels have dropped dramatically in the kitchen. In *Made from Scratch*, Jean Zimmerman documents,

> Half of all meals are now prepared outside the home. In the 1970s, 80 percent of women prepared at least one meal a day in their home kitchens, but in the 1980s the number of home cooks had dropped to 74 percent and in 1998 fell to 68 percent. Even when we do prepare our meals in our own kitchens, what we're doing is more often assembling pre-packaged ingredients — only 56 percent of all meals made in North America include one or more homemade items.[141]

She goes on to observe that women, whether working or not, are not cooking. Meal preparation dropped to twenty minutes *total* per day in 1998 — and we're overwhelmed by spending those twenty minutes in the kitchen. Zimmerman cites the NPD Group, a tracker of food trends, and observes that in 1999, six percent of all homes had no frying pan, and only 57 owned a roasting pan. Not only do we lack skill, we lack the basic tools of meal construction.[142]

It seems logical then, to observe that nobody, male or female, is cooking enough to get good at it. Like all activities, cooking takes practice before it can be done easily and without being stressful.

The second reason is that we have been told that cooking is difficult drudgery that requires a great deal of specialized knowledge and equipment so long that we have come to believe it. Food-related advertising almost always refers to kitchen work as drudgery, something to be escaped from, and belittles the value of the work done there. We learn that jarred sauces and frozen lasagna are better than what your Italian grandmother can make and show Grandma, mad as hell, having to admit it. That

Grandma's lasagna contained no Xanthan gum, benzoates or red dye #12 and didn't taste like cardboard is considered hardly relevant — pissed off Grandmas are funny.

This message that cooking is too hard, that one must rely on others for even something as basic as dinner, has been the constant narrative of advertising for the simple reason that processed and premade foods offer more profit than whole foods; the more that corporations can convince us cooking is drudgery, the more we will turn the work over to them. And the more we turn the work over to them, the richer they get. There is only so much money one can make on plain potatoes straight from the earth — frozen dinners are so much more profitable. To an enormous degree, what we want is manipulated not by our needs but by the creation of wants by advertising.

Cooking can be difficult or easy, complicated or simple, time consuming or not. It is not the work of cooking (or gardening for that matter) itself that is the problem, but the fact that we are unpracticed, that we have been misled into believing that buckling the kids into their car seats and making them behave while you pick up the take out is easier than preparing a home-cooked meal. When women came out of the kitchen through feminism, no one went back in — corporations took over. And this is both environmentally unsustainable and also costly for families. The kitchen, we are told, is a place to renovate, clean and microwave, but not to cook, and certainly not to enjoy time with your family in shared work.

The truth is that three meals a day do not have to be a great burden — but only if we know how, if the work is shared among family or friends, if we have communities to help out when someone is sick or tired or unable, if we have ways to share resources.

Shared work and shared pleasure are the only way we can make this happen. If only women are put back into the kitchens, they will shortly come back out complaining, rightly, that they have too much else to do and are stuck with the dirty dishes. Everyone cooks. Everyone helps clean up. The good thing is that this is pleasurable work. Food is fun. It is sensual quite literally — a pleasure for all five senses. Working with food need not be drudgery, particularly if we do it together, in our homes, with our families instead of watching TV or playing video games. It takes some practice, and ideally, any mass movement will involve collective learning. In World War II, community groups got together and traded recipes, practiced new techniques and worked together. Not only should food be social within families, but within communities — neighbors can take turns sharing meals and get together for larger projects like bread making and canning. But we must do it. If we don't, no matter how many Victory Gardens we create, we will fail.

The Informal Economy

Reality is that which, when you stop believing in it, does not go away.
— PHILIP K. DICK —

Perhaps the most compelling argument against growing and cooking our own food is our lack of time. And that seems an insurmountable barrier for most of us — because our time is increasingly taken up with the very basic work of earning a living. How do we find time to garden, to cook from scratch, to preserve food during harvest season for the coming winter? We have already seen that industrial society steals our time away from us. How on earth do we even begin to get it back?

The only way to get our time back is to take it. This is difficult, increasingly so as our budgets are stretched tighter and tighter meeting basic needs. Which is all the more reason that many of us have to find ways to cut our dependency on the grocery store and gas station supply lines. As simply getting to work and buying basic foodstuffs eat up more and more of our earnings, at some point, we have to ask the questions, Is it worth it? Is there a better way?

And for those whose families have two middle-class incomes, there often is: the savings from having a member of the family stay home, not driving, growing food on a lawn or in a community garden, cooking from scratch, practicing thrift and giving up the working wardrobe. Not only will your family often save money in the net, but the environmental advantages will be enormous.

What about the poor, the single parents, and those who need a second income to provide health insurance? Only you know your circumstances, but in many cases lower-income households are beginning to struggle with whether they can afford to go to work at all. Families with young children, for example, often find that childcare costs, combined with food and energy costs, mean that they are deeper in the hole every month. The truth is that independent separate homes for every household may be a short-lived phenomenon. So most of us who are struggling may need to double up. And if that's the case, many of us will find that we need fewer formal-economy incomes to enable a household to survive.

What's the informal economy? It is the value of all the things you do that that aren't calculated into GDP. It includes the criminal economy (15–20 percent of the world's total), unpaid domestic labor, volunteer labor, under-the-table exchanges, barter between neighbors and everything else. The formal economy (that of taxes and salaries and GDP statements) is about one-quarter of the world's total economic output, while the informal economy makes up three-quarters of the economy. Peasant economist Teodor Shanin observes that for a long time economists couldn't understand how poor people in many nations got along, as they didn't seem to fit into the formal economy. The answer was that they were meeting their basic needs in the informal economy.

So putting a foot into the informal economy — doing more subsistence labor (that is, growing food and making things you need), not needing things (the gas to get to work, the clothing and makeup), the use of the time you gain to practice thrift for the things you do need (making use of ordinarily wasted materials, finding the cheapest source for things) and perhaps starting to make some money either officially or unofficially (selling produce, building furniture, repairing clothes and shoes or something else) — combined with sharing resources with family and friends can keep us from getting into the direst economic straits. This is, again, how people once lived.

Now, the tax people don't accept honey and it can be hard to barter for health insurance, so our contention is not that everyone can live in the informal economy but that to the extent we can put a foot there, this offers us a measure of security in difficult times that the formal economy doesn't. That's one of the potential powers of Victory Gardens and small home farms.

We Need Big Farms Too — and Land Reform

The only difference between a pigeon and the American farmer today is that a pigeon can still make a deposit on a John Deere.
— JIM HIGHTOWER —

Land Institute scientist Stan Cox recently wrote an essay arguing that gardens alone can't fix the food crisis. He makes the point that our primary staple foods are grains, and those are going to be grown on the land most suitable to them, so that to have a deep influence on food systems we have to change the practices that we use on those acres as well. Cox writes in his essay "It Will Take a Lot More than Gardening to Fix Our Food System,"

> But most of the world is utterly dependent on grains. The desperate people we saw on the evening news earlier this year, filling the streets in dozens of countries, were calling for bread or rice, not cucumbers and pomegranates.[143]

We agree with Cox that if we don't focus on how we grow and use grains, the result will be mostly an exercise in feeling good, that our gardens and small farms will be secondary to a larger industrial system. As Cox argues, central to this project is land reform — and it is needed just as badly in the US as in any other country. We don't just need millions of suburban farmers, we need larger-scale farmers willing to produce staple foods in more sustainable and wiser ways. And we need to get corporate land into more hands if we are to end the destruction created by industrial agriculture.

Where we differ with Cox is in emphasis — Cox spends a good bit of time in his essay implying that the gardens and small farms one can create in urban, suburban and exurban areas don't really make a difference in the food economy, because what we mostly eat are grains. We think that is untrue — or rather, it could be untrue. It is certainly the case that an uncritical lyricism of the garden won't end the power of industrial agriculture, although it could certainly cause some economic harm to companies that now sell produce. It could certainly end some of the exploitation of migrant laborers who pick produce now. But the gardens in and of themselves, are not entire solutions.

The gardens can be the beginning of something, however, as we'll discuss in Chapter 4. Among other things, they can be the beginning of a shift to a vegetable-centered agriculture. Cox notes that ancient Greeks ate the same quantity of grains we do; but if we were to shift our view to Ireland in the 18th century, or to Peru or to West Africa, we'd find populations that thrived not just on grains but on root crops. And most of those root crops grow extremely well in home gardens. Will they obviate bread and tortillas on our tables? No, but potatoes can cut our appetite for grains somewhat.

Moreover, home polycultures that include animals can dramatically reduce our dependence on grains — three chickens in a backyard, times 10 million households make 30 million fewer battery hens, and 300 fewer battery operations, and each hen will produce 150 to 200 eggs a year, mostly on grass and food scraps. Does that fix the problem of grain-fed animal products? No, of course not. Does it make a dent in the problem — and the pocketbooks — of the people in question? Might we be able to gradually shift our diets just a little, along with reducing our desire for grains in cows and gas tanks? The truth is that the large farms are linked more closely to the small gardens than most of us realize.

But perhaps most importantly, we have to ask where — if we can implement land reform — all these new grain farmers are going to come from? We're going to need them no matter what system we work under. The average American farmer is in his 50s, and in many families there's no one to come after him. If we were able to implement land reform to, say, discourage corporate-owned farms and incentivize small family farms and large ones that practiced organic no till and polycultures, where would the new farmers come from? Some of them would come from rural communities, the children of farmers who didn't want the job when it meant endless work and endless poverty and then losing the land anyway. But we'll need more than that, particularly if we were to create incentives to keep farms small and thus more productive and diverse.

The old systems for raising and training young farmers and enabling them to get land are as damaged by industrial agriculture as any other system. So the new farmers, small and large, are going to have to come out of the gardens. As Gene Logsdon writes, the garden is the "proving ground" for the farm. Logsdon was talking about testing agricultural techniques, but it is also true of new farmers. Without gardens in cities and suburbs all over the world, young people will never get the message that food is important. Without first stepping out into the garden world and finding competence there, they will never take the next step to the internship or work on a larger farm, never begin the process of moving toward land of their own. The garden truly will be the proving ground for the new agriculture.

What Do We Get Back?

That is the mystery of grace: it never comes too late.
— FRANÇOIS MAURIAC —

After reading the litany of looming disasters that small-scale agriculture can at least partially forestall, we wouldn't blame you if you believed that we grow food to save the world. But you'd be wrong. We became farmers because it was the right thing to do, of course, but mostly we do it for the food. Both of us like to eat well, and when we bought the freshest food, everything tasted wonderful. So the biggest reason both of us became home growers was because we really wanted to eat well.

Even if you aren't worried about peak oil, terrorism, climate change, currency collapse and marauding bands of crazed weasels, even if you don't care about the soil, aquifers, and hungry children, and you think both of us are tree-hugging lunatics, you should still be a farmer, because the food is really, really fabulous. Think "best meal you ever ate in your life" — every day. Think "much less effort to cook, because it all tastes so good with simple preparations or just eaten straight." Think "saving a lot of money, while eating better and being healthier." Think "all the raspberries you can put away every day for a month, not just the teeny little basket you pay five bucks for at the store." Think, "corn so sweet you don't have to cook it, you just strip back the husk and gnaw on an ear." Think "tomatoes that drip down your chin with perfect juice, and peas that pop out of their pods and taste more like candy than vegetables." Think "the scent of fresh basil and rosemary hitting you from 10 feet away, and cucumbers that you don't have peel and that smell of fresh melon." Think, "chard so crisp and sweet that your three- and five-year-olds (if they are anything like Sharon's three- and five-year-olds) will fight for the first bite." Think "watermelons that are crisper and more luscious than anything you've ever eaten."

Think we're exaggerating? We're not. Until you've grown your own, you can have no idea what a sungold tomato, picked from the plant and popped into your mouth, tastes like — savory, sugary, tangy, vaguely tropical. You can't imagine how different almost every vegetable is when you grow it — a potato has a richness and buttery texture that bears no resemblance to the supermarket options. A parsnip or a carrot after a frost is a confection, not a vegetable. The humble turnip is something entirely other, a vegetable no one could help but adore. Asparagus can be eaten raw, straight off the ground.

In many cases, this is food money literally cannot buy. Because the most spectacular flavors are reserved for those who are there when the food is picked. If you join a CSA or go to a local farmers' market, you can get close, but it will never be quite the same as setting the water to boil and then going to pick the corn, or tasting the vegetables as the sun pours down on the field. But this is a luxury that isn't available for cash. And it is an awfully cheap luxury. You can save yourself hundreds or thousands of dollars by growing your own food, maybe even make some money too.

The food is sensuous, luxurious, beautiful, lush. It will make you happy, feed every sense as well as your hunger. Growing it and picking it with your family will give you a sense of warmth, security, happiness and joy. It will improve your health, improve your diet, improve your sex life.

Wait a minute. Did they just say "sex life?" Yup. Food is sensuous. We all know that. Ever read *Like Water for Chocolate* or see the movie *Tampopo*? Ever feed each other strawberries or enjoy the taste of coffee on a lover's lips? Well growing food is the ultimate sensual experience. The range of tastes and textures, the pleasure of the sun on your shoulders, or the warm rain on your back, the smells of herbs, flowers and warm earth, the rich colors and silky textures… Whether you wait until bedtime or fall down and take one another in the garden, the taste of mint or blueberries still fresh on your tongues, gardening together and cooking together improves your sex life. It awakens your awareness of one another, warms up your muscles and gets your juices flowing.

Despite its innate sensuousness, gardening is also an excellent family activity, if, by some chance, you should be so swept away that you lie down among the eggplants and plant a human being. If, in the pleasure of generation you decide to do some generatin' yourself, rest assured that gardening is one of the best things you can do for your family. It gets you all outside. When children help grow food, they are more likely to eat it. They can play in the garden and learn to help at an early age, pulling weeds and planting seeds. Children are naturally attracted to the garden, and it nurtures them, helps them develop a sense of place and an appreciation for their environment. It is good for their bodies and good for their souls to be out in the garden, especially with Mommy and Daddy, working and playing together, watching the sky and the butterflies and nibbling at the strawberries. This is what childhood should be.

It is good for your whole family. Teenagers often disdain family activities, but gardens are excellent places for teenagers to experiment with autonomy. They can make money, deride your choices of food and your slowness with a shovel, and show off their physical skills. They may tell you how boring and stupid they find the garden, but they will also, in their time of turmoil, be secretly nurtured by it. Teens who will not speak to you in your house, suddenly allow you glimpses into their thoughts when you work side by side. And rebellion against the garden is perhaps the pleasantest form of adolescent rebellion humanly possible. The teenager who shouts angrily, "I'm not going to help you raise those stupid beets anymore" is probably a teenager who may not need more radical forms of rebellion. In fact, their rebellion may take the form of becoming a radical vegetarian ecological activist. Try not to smile.

Many of us do not get enough exercise, as we all know. Garden and farm work are among the best forms of exercise for children and adults; because they are both aerobic and weight bearing, they accomplish something (unlike all those treadmill miles) and can be adapted to any level of health and activity. With our weight causing real consequences to our health, it may be that the better nutrition and exercise we get from our gardens may help us survive in a direct, literal sense, regardless of whether we are ever short of food.

When and if there comes a time that older members of the family can no longer get down on the ground and garden, there are still containers, raised beds and, if nothing else, a place among the flowers and herbs for an older person to sit and enjoy the sun.

Gardening can also give you a better, happier life. If you did not have to buy food for your family, or not much, would you need to work so much? Might someone in your family be able to stay home and pursue a garden, a small farm and spend more time with children or friends? Perhaps you could even make a little extra cash selling produce to neighbors or creating a tiny CSA. Or you might make your garden and farm your work, and turn it into a family business. Perhaps you and/or your partner could work less and be home more. Would your life not have more leisure for the joys of family, sex, exercise, music, hobbies, art and love if you could enjoy the fruits of your garden? Would you not be freer, less stressed, more able to do what you want when you want? Might you be happier? Might your wife or husband, children, family and friends be happier, both because you are happier and because they spend more time with you? Might you find yourself doing exactly what you will look back on in old age and think "Those were the days when I did what was worth living for"? And what more can anyone ask than more of those sorts of days?

You can become a farmer for all sorts of reasons — to save the world, to save yourself, for the food, for the sex, for the years it can add to your life, for your children's sake, for your health, for the love of the earth, for the sheer joy of it, or simply because you can. But you can have all of those things at once as well. And there are few pursuits about which that might be said.

What do we get back? Ultimately, we get back what we began with — grace. A world in which we have some way of measuring the costs of our appetites, in which we have some way of compensating for our needs. We get back a world in which we know who to thank. We get back the Omnivore's Thanksgiving, and we get it back each and every day.

An Interview with Bob Waldrop: Spring 2008

Bob Waldrop founded the Oscar Romera Catholic Workers House in Oklahoma City and delivers thousands of pounds of food to the poor weekly. He is the president and founder of the Oklahoma City Food Coop, bringing local foods to city residents. He has run for mayor of Oklahoma City, served migrant and refugee communities and otherwise worked to improve access to food and justice for people all over the nation and to help others find ways to duplicate his work. He's one of our heros. The full text of this interview can be viewed at http://henandharvest.com/?p=107.

ANOF: Is it correct to characterize your work with local food as a social justice issue?
BOB: Well, that's true. During a lot of my life I've just been really poor, and so there was a time in my life where the only reason that I had bread was that I had wheat and I had a grinder and I was able to grind my own flour to make bread. And the only reason that I had tomatoes is because I had tomato plants in my yard. And the only way that I had a meal at all was that I was willing to cook meals from basic ingredients. So I actually come at this not from a position of affluence but from a place of experience with scarcity and having to figure out how to feed eight people with a quarter pound of sausage and a cup of milk.

ANOF: As the cost of food is rising in this country, we're hearing that people are making poor nutritional choices — the idea being that if they can't afford to buy better food, fresh food or organic food and they're forced to buy processed foods, then they're basically eating ramen noodles every evening for dinner. Are you saying that they can have nutritionally adequate diets?
BOB: Well, you can take ramen noodles and you can make something better, more healthy out of them also. I've eaten a lot of ramen noodles in my

day, and ramen noodles are actually kind of an interesting substrate for many different kinds of stirfries. People aren't changing their food choices so that they're buying, say, pork neck bones and whole wheat flour — or even white flour for that matter — they're just buying the cheaper processed foods, the corn dogs and the cheap pizzas and hot dogs and mystery meats like that.

There's been an almost complete loss of cultural information from generation to generation in a lot of poverty communities. A lot of strategies of their parents and grandparents, the younger generation simply isn't aware of. Just one example is lambs quarters. It grows pretty prolifically in every poor neighborhood on the street, and very few people pick them and eat them. And they're very tasty — I call them Oklahoma spinach. They're very tasty and a good source of vitamin C and other things that you get in green vegetables, but people just don't recognize that as food; they think of it as a weed, and so they don't take advantage of the fact that they can get it for free, basically, just by picking it.

ANOF: How does the lack of transportation affect people's access to food?

BOB: Well, that's a very significant thing. Someone asked me one time why all these little convenience stores all over the place, besides the typical convenience store things that you think of like cigarettes and beer and candy and soda pop, also sold the basic selection of basic groceries — canned foods, things like that. I said, the reason for that is that some people don't have transportation and they just can't get to a supermarket and that's where they do their grocery shopping. And they were just horrified by that thought because it's very expensive and the selection isn't very much. And part of the reason is that Oklahoma City has very poor public transportation, so people without cars aren't able to access larger stores. One thing that I have noticed happening, however, in the lower-income neighborhoods that are mostly African-American is that there is a whole group of vegetable tenders that buy from rural farmers and then bring produce to street corners in low-income neighborhoods.

ANOF: What sort of plants do you have growing at your house?

BOB: Well, we grow over 100 different types of plants in our former lawn, and two thirds of those are perennials. We have peach trees and apple trees and elderberries, boysenberries, blackberries, dewberries, raspberries, blueberries, mulberries. We have plums; we have apricots; we have a persimmon tree that hasn't grown anything yet. We have bush cherries; we have clove currants and sand cherries; we have a Siberian pea shrub; we have Nanking cherries; we have chokecherries, and we usually have several varieties of each of these. We have roses, which we grow for the rose hips — and also the rose petals are edible. We have comfrey, which is medicinal, and we have prickly pear cactus, which is edible.

For annuals, we tend to concentrate on things that we can't get easily from other local sources or organic sources, or where we want a lot of something, more than we want to spend money on. So we grow a lot of paste tomatoes because I like to make my own tomato sauce. We grow a lot of alliums. We grow multiplying onions and shallots and various kinds of chives and garlic, and we grow cooking greens like chard and collards. Actually, this year we aren't growing any collard greens, we're growing mostly chard. And then I grow a few carrots and potatoes, but we don't have enough room to grow a lot of those. This year I'm going to experiment with some container growing. I've tried growing potatoes in a bucket. We grow hot peppers. We grow a lot of haberneros, sachwanas, cayennes, and jalepenos.

ANOF: From a big-picture perspective, Bob, what concerns you most, going forward, about the future of food or, in a more general sense, the future of human existence going into the 21st century? Is there a particular problem that most concerns you?

BOB: Well, I just think we're coming to a perfect storm with the whole peak oil, the climate change, and general ecological devastation. And I think we're more dependent than we've ever been on highly centralized systems of distribution, just-in-time inventory systems. That's all just a lot weaker than most people think, and it puts us truly at risk. I think we also have lost a lot of cultural information. My grandfather used to be known throughout his county for the ability to cure hams and make sausage. But those recipes — he didn't teach my father how to do that, and my father didn't teach me, and so those are all lost. And my dad remembers that it was very good, he said it was the best-tasting sausage that he'd ever had. But the recipe was never written down; it was just in his head, and so it was just lost.

—— *RECIPES* ————————————————————

Ramen Scramble *by Bob Waldrop*

This is a great way to make one egg and a little bit of breakfast meat serve more than one person.

Ingredients
- 1 egg
- 1 package of ramen noodles
- whatever small bits of meat or soy you've got around
- onion and hot pepper if you've got them

Directions
1. Break uncooked ramen into smaller pieces. Add the flavor packet to the ramen cooking water and cook the ramen to package instructions.
2. Meanwhile, fry some bacon bits or sausage. You can add chopped onions and hot peppers too if you like them.
3. Drain the ramen and add to the cooked meat.
4. Add one egg, scrambled. Stir in pan until the egg is cooked and serve.

Gallos Pintos *by Shaunta Alburger, who blogs at shauntagrimes.com*

This is the national dish of Costa Rica, and is a family favorite here. We like to add some salsa to the pan and stir it in. My kids like it in a tortilla like a burrito. I like to eat it in a bowl topped with cheese and cabbage.

   It reheats beautifully.

Ingredients
- 1 chopped white onion
- 1 cup corn kernels
- chili powder
- 3 cups cooked black beans, drained
- 3 cups cooked rice (white or brown)
- optional toppings can include cabbage, cheese, tomatoes, or fresh onions
- 1 tbsp olive oil
- salt and pepper
- Salsa (optional)

Directions
1. Heat the oil in a large pan. Cook the onion until translucent but not browned.
2. Add the beans (if you're using canned beans, use two 15-ounce cans, drained) and corn (one can if using canned, also drained).
3. Cook, stirring often, until the beans start to dry and break up, 5 to 10 minutes. Season to taste. Add the rice. Adjust seasoning if necessary.

Mee Pad (Thai Drunken Noodles)   *by Sharon*

This is one of the recipes most frequently requested by guests after we serve it to them. We got the recipe from the chef at Viet Thai, one of our favorite restaurants in Lowell, Massachusetts, by promising that we were moving far away and wouldn't try and set up in competition. It can be made with meat, but we prefer a vegetarian version with tofu. It makes a large batch.

Ingredients
- 3 pounds dried or fresh rice noodles (you could make this with linguine too, or homemade pasta, although the taste and texture will change)
- a lot of scallions, chopped finely (garlic chives or onion are okay too)
- 2 pounds Chinese broccoli or other greens of your choice, chopped coarsely
- 1–2 pounds tofu, fried until golden, or meat of your choice
- canned or fresh bamboo shoots, or sliced sautéed fresh daikon (optional)
- small amount of oil for stir-frying
- ¼ cup oyster sauce (you can substitute vegetarian mushroom sauce)
- ¼ cup sweet soy sauce (also called by its Malay name, *kecap manis*)
- 1 tsp chopped fresh chiles or Asian-style chili sauce
- some basil — more is better (Thai basil is more authentic, but it can be made with any basil)

Directions
1. If using dried noodles, set several quarts of water to boil in a large pot, and boil the noodles until beginning to soften but still firm.
2. If using fresh tofu, press out all of the excess water and then fry it in oil until crispy and golden brown on the outside.
3. Stir-fry the scallions and greens in oil in a large skillet until the greens are cooked. Add the tofu and bamboo shoots, along with about half of the oyster sauce, sweet soy sauce, and chili sauce. You can adjust the amounts of the sauce ingredients to taste. Add the basil and transfer everything to a large stockpot.
4. Now stir-fry the noodles in some additional oil, along with the remaining sauce ingredients (again adjusting amounts to taste). Cook until the noodles are slightly translucent. Then add the noodles to the rest of the ingredients, stir together, and serve.

CHAPTER 3

Ring the Bell

It Starts with How We Eat

Everyone addicted to the same nicotine
Everyone addicted to the same gasoline
Everyone addicted to a technicolour screen
Everybody trying to get their hands on same green

— MICHAEL FRANTI —

SHARON: There are tiny green apricots on my two apricot trees. I'm sure those of you from more southerly places are thinking, "So?" But this is upstate New York. I live at 1,400 feet, effectively zone 4, and no one grows apricots here. Whenever I mention my apricot trees, people look at me strangely, as though I'm mad to even attempt it. And I'm pretty awed myself. The first thing we did after moving here was to plant two apricot trees, which hung around looking pretty but producing nothing for a couple of years and then died in an especially cold winter. So although the appearance of apricots isn't a miracle, it is perhaps the next step down — something extraordinary that gives you, if not evidence of transcendence, a tiny, tasty hint of its possibility.

But to understand the apricots, you have to know about the two gardens that came before this one. The first one was in Paramus, New Jersey, perhaps the most archetypical suburb I've ever visited, the kind of place that makes James Kunstler moan with pain. It was also Eric's grandparents' home for 20 years. They lived in a 1950s style suburban brick ranch house in one of those places where lawn mowers are going at 7 in the morning and you can't walk to anything useful.

But that's only part of the story. It was also another kind of sub-urb — one where Inge and Cyril were friends with their neigh-bors and the neighbors' kids. They tutored the Russian immigrants down the road in English, shared holiday dinners with the or-thodox Jewish family across the street, babysat for the Pakistani neighbors. As they got older and less physically able, their neigh-bors looked out for them, came and helped them out with chores, brought over meals — as they had for neighbors before. The sub-urbs may have been a mad dream, but the mad dreamers came, and some of them brought their love for a place and a house and a space, and they loved it into something beautiful.

And it was where their garden was. All my best memories of them are of their garden. If the weather was at all warm enough, that's where one went — out to lie in the lounge chairs or play games on the grass. It was lush, green, enclosed, and miraculously peaceful. Both of them worked long hours in their garden. Cyril was the architect, and I remember him, at 92 or 93, slowly but surely planting out begonias and saving me seeds from his lovely blue columbine. It was their paradise, their pride and their delight. It literally gave them life; I suspect that Grandpa lived at least a year longer than he would have if he had not had his garden to get him out of his chair and into the world.

It is easy to mock suburbia. Whatever the value of the idea of suburbia, its execution had its troubling parts but also its pecu-liar virtues and beauties as well. It is easy to forget the latter as we sit judgment of what we ought to have done. But I think a limited view of the suburbs is probably a mistake. At least, I can't have one, because I remember the tremendous beauty and generosity of a host of suburban gardens and the neighborhood they fostered. Be-cause if you can love even a 1950s brick ranch house and a suburban neighborhood into beauty, you can love and transform anything in the world.

When it came time for Inge and Cyril to come live with us, one of the things they desperately wanted was a garden. By that time, Cyril was too ill and Inge too exhausted from caring for him to want to maintain anything. They simple wanted a beautiful space to rest in. And they were a little overwhelmed by the sheer size of our open rural landscape. After all those years in suburbia it felt isolated. They wanted a garden to bring back what they knew and loved.

So we made one. We helped them hire a landscape designer. And he made them a suburban garden in miniature, a truly beautiful one, lending shape to our landscape. The addition they lived in had its main entrance in an area enclosed on three sides by the house and the attached garage, making it a sheltered area far warmer than the fields and woods around it. It faced south, and the landscape designer hauled in far more fertile topsoil than any that came with the farm and filled it in with beautiful shrubs and low-care perennials. I planted the scarlet runner beans and columbines they'd had since Cyril was a boy in Wales, and they rested in their garden.

Until only a month or two before he died, Cyril was the garden designer. He said would say, "Sharon, darling, would you get me that grass seed in the garage." And, of course, I would oblige. "What do you want to do with it, Grandpa?" I asked. "Well, I'd like to plant it, but I'm afraid I'm not up to it. Have you any thoughts about how it might get planted?" He was a clever man, and not much limited by his physical constraints.

Sadly, Eric's grandparents lived with us only a short time. Cyril died a few weeks before his 95th birthday, and Inge couldn't live without him; she lived only four months longer. For the first year without them, we were simply too sad to do anything with the garden but look at it and miss them.

In the springtime after their deaths, I had a dream. I dreamt that a grapevine and a rosebush in their garden grew all the way up to the second floor of the house and burst in through our window one morning, blooming and scattering lush petals and fruit across the floor. When I woke, I looked at their garden and, for the very first time, thought that perhaps the garden could continue to be their memorial — and perhaps a better memorial if I changed it a little and made their garden bring forth not just beauty, but fruit, so that their great-grandchildren could enjoy not just the shaded beauty but the taste of the space and gift they'd left us.

The first year I dug out a rhododendron and a couple of viburnums and replaced them with two apricot trees and two quinces. I didn't do much else, but that itself was enormous. At first it looked like I'd defaced their garden, removing beautiful, productive shrubs and placing little sticks in their place; but they are glorious trees and grew rapidly, and the beauty came back. The next year I took out a few more plants, added some raspberries and blackberries, comfrey, sweet woodruff, some pennyroyal as a ground cover, and a row of alpine strawberries to edge it.

This year, I started out cautiously, afraid that if I took out the weigela and spirea I'd have stripped their garden altogether. But I really looked at the garden and saw how beautiful it was — no less, and perhaps more — and I got brave. I bought blueberries to replace the evergreen shrubs (they are being moved off to another part of the garden, don't worry), hazels to go where the weigela was, and two peach trees to replace the forsythia. I planted lupins in around the blueberries, mixed in yarrows, and I've got two wolfberries waiting to be planted. And I bought some grapevines — I'm going to see if I can train them all the way up to the second floor.

The apricots bloomed for the first time this year and, in our protected, south-facing microclimate, their blossoms even survived a hard late frost. I was afraid they hadn't been adequately pollinated, but yesterday the boys came running in to tell me that there were dozens of small green apricots on the tree. As I said, it isn't quite a miracle — just a grand unlikelihood brought to fruition.

The garden is a fusion. The blue columbine seed brought from New Jersey, an echo of flowers from a garden in Wales, still come back every year. A few of the shrubs they picked out are still in that part of the garden. The scarlet runner beans race up the trellis every year, and my boys pick and eat them, calling them "Grampy's beans." The fruit and nut plants are mine and my idea, but Eric and the boys do all the planting this year while I write this book. And the dream, well, who knows where that came from?

All gardens are fusions, hybrids, mixes of memories from our childhoods and dreams of future bounty. They are mixes of ideas we pick up, the gifts of friends who bring chives and new thoughts, the love of people who taught you, and the kindness of strangers who lived here before. They contain histories so long and vast we cannot track them back — who first domesticated the potato? Who first bred this tomato, this flower? Who carried this seed across water, and how did it change when it reached these shores? What wild meadow and ancient apple combined to create this fruit? And how is it now different, in my place, in my garden?

This garden of mine is the fusion of dreams and memories, of people we loved and love still, no less that they are less proximate. It is the fusion of desires — of the suburban landscape and the food-producing one. It is the linking of past and present, with the futures that run about me, nibbling and dancing. And sure as God made little green apricots, it will change some more under future hands, and continue changing without end.

What Will We Have For Dinner?

*I am worried about the decline
of farming communities of all kinds
because I think that among the practical consequences
of that decline will sooner or later be hunger.*
— WENDELL BERRY —

What shall we have for dinner tonight? What shall we eat? How shall we cook it? And how will the meal make you feel? How will your dinner affect you and the world at large?

These are all big questions to ask of one's dinner plate, particularly given that many of us haven't the faintest idea what we're going to eat, and are dreading the moment that we have to confront the issue. It is also an overwhelming set of questions because, after all, we all eat three times a day, every single day. There's a lot of potential trouble involved in reconsidering an act that is unavoidable and sometimes already a source of anxiety and stress.

But, of course, it turns out that our most ordinary acts are the ones that require us to ask the hardest questions. The everyday things that six and a half billion people do all the time are the ones that poison the atmosphere and change the climate, and they are the ones that must change in a world of evolving scarcity and increasing injustice. This is an easy point to miss, but an important one.

But there are also other good reasons to ask these questions about your meals. Our goal here is not to send you into a frenzy of panic that your dinner is the source of disaster but to consider what it is that food should do for us and we for it. Perhaps there are ways in which our meals might improve our lives and reduce our stress levels, while also improving the lives of others, if only we ask the right questions of and about them.

This is a book about some very dark and difficult problems and the potential solutions to them. In it, we are talking about frightening things like hunger and suffering. And it would be very easy to begin thinking of the project of feeding ourselves and the world only in the context of a dam against a flood of disaster. But the transformation of food into merely something to keep us alive and hold back misery would be a failure. No joyless way of life will ever succeed. We will never transform our nation and our culture, never even succeed at forestalling disaster in the long term, unless we remember that producing food and eating are sources of joy, the origin of most rituals of human connection, and the expression of human generosity and love.

At the root of our project lies this very basic truth. A life in which we cook more and eat better, grow our own food and are more able to provision our own needs is a better life, a happier one, a more delicious and luxurious one, a more sensuous, more loving and more peaceful life. We present this not merely as a way to forestall disaster but as a way to create something greater and better.

Let us be absolutely clear, however. We are not claiming that every meal can be an unadulterated joy; nor are we poster children for the perfect life and perfect meals. Just like you, some days we do better than others about getting food on the table or choosing wisely. Like you, we compromise, we get frustrated, we get tired, and sometimes we look on food preparation as a burden we wish we didn't have to attend to. So let us be clear that we are not sitting in judgment of you but offering up ideas for improving all of our futures.

What we eat and how we cook is at the root of everything. Because, before we can be a nation of farmers, we must be a nation of people who eat quite differently than we do. If you believe, as we do, that industrial agriculture is both immoral and tragic for our nation, as well as completely unsustainable, we know that the answer lies in bringing more of us into food production. But a nation of farmers can exist only if it feeds a nation of people who want to cook and eat what farmers grow, who are willing to eat locally and sustainably.

Right now, we are mostly people who desperately want to eat well and find a way back to a kind of joyous meal sharing, but who have no time and no energy, and do not have the training or the gift of eating straight out of our gardens or our neighbors' gardens. We once knew how to do this, but a century of turning food production and preservation over to others has eroded our skills, and that erosion has had further consequences, causing, in part, the erosion of our very democracy.

Does that last bit sound a little bit over the top? Perhaps, but only because we are accustomed to separating out politics and dinner, when, in fact, they are tightly intertwined. Our ability to resist the powers that have overcome us is precisely related to how dependent we are on those powers. The more we need Kraft and Phillip Morris and ADM to feed us, the more we need the government to regulate and control what we can have for dinner; and the less certainty we have that what we eat is clean and safe and was grown in a way we would choose, the less powerful we are.

We cannot be free of the powerful influences that do not have our interests at heart as long as we do not know how to make a good loaf of bread, or as long as we believe we cannot provision ourselves and grow and make a meal our kids will eat. As long as we think Lunchables and purchased baby food are necessities for our children, and that factory-farmed meat and bagged salad are required for a healthy dinner, despite the ironies, we will be to some degree powerless against the forces that try to control the messages our children receive. As long as getting dinner on the table is a burden that we'd like the larger economy to free us from, we will never be free from the oppressive qualities of that economy. And as long as we give our money to fast food and large industrial food corporations, they will have power over us. Ultimately, where we put our dollars has a greater impact than what we say we believe. If we cannot eat without the things we deplore, who are we?

And that alone justifies changing the way we eat. But we also have the capacity to become people who take earth and clay and transform it into something more, something greater, something that is filled with an essence that exceeds its component parts. That is what cooking is. That is what growing food is. We take dirt and seed, oil and fire, and from it comes an eggplant or a tomato, an apple or a bunch of basil. And from that comes a meal and a memory and an act of love.

We cannot create a just society without creating a new (or perhaps old) way to eat and cook. And we cannot change the world unless each of us is able to craft a meal out of the things that grow in our own earth, on our own victory farms and in the gardens and farms of our neighbors. We cannot even begin to speak of agriculture unless we answer the question, What shall we have for dinner?

Eating is an Agricultural Act

One of the delights of life is eating with friends, second to that
is talking about eating. And, for an unsurpassed double whammy,
there is talking about eating while you are eating with friends.
— LAURIE COLWIN —

Much of the discussion of our agriculture has focused on changing the way we grow food. And though this is absolutely necessary, it is also the case that transforming our agriculture begins at our tables. We do not think it is overstating things to say that how we grow food will always be secondary to how we cook and eat. If we are to thrive after the coming crisis, a surprising amount of it will depend on our ability to adapt our diet — and that will depend on our ability to cook and eat differently.

To many people it seems a small thing to talk about cooking, self-evident that when different things are in the stores or our gardens, we will eat differently. But further consideration will show that it doesn't work that way. Consider the dual problem of hunger and poor nutrition in the US. Overwhelmingly, these are problems of poverty, as you would suspect. But also, these are overwhelmingly cooking problems.

That is, a number of people have shown that it is perfectly possible to eat nutritiously and cheaply — for example, that a whole-grain, vegetarian, even organic and local diet is possible on a food-stamps budget. No one in their right mind would rather see their kids go hungry than eat this way. And yet, 12.5 percent of Americans do experience hunger, do struggle to make the money and meals meet the end of the month.

So why is hunger so endemic in the US? There are many factors, including time and experience, but a part of the problem is simply not knowing how to cook inexpensive foods. For example, the director of a local food pantry observed that flour is one of the last things to leave their shelves — because few of their patrons know how to make their own bread or baked goods. When dried beans are given out, they must come with instructions, and often people don't seem to follow them. The nation's poor aren't any worse at cooking than the average American — but average Americans no longer know how to provision themselves from ingredients as we have discussed.

Now, many of the nation's poor suffer difficult conditions that make it hard for cooking lessons to alleviate their problems. They work two or three jobs, and meals for children are often made by other children, older siblings caring for kids in the absence of hardworking parents. Many of the nation's poor live in housing with minimal cooking facilities. Our intent is not to suggest that the poor are poor because of their ignorance of food preparation — but it is also true that this ignorance, which exists across class lines, can especially exacerbate poverty. And many middle class Americans, equally incapable of cooking for themselves, are closer than they realize to a similar kind of poverty.

The truth is that Americans do, in part, go hungry because they cannot cook. We think it is important to note how significant that is. No one likes being hungry. And yet, Americans do suffer hunger because they lack the skills to use inexpensive staple foods effectively. We do not commonly recognize inability to "cook from scratch" as a cause of hunger — but it is.

It is also a cause of poor nutrition. A study released in 2007 found that in most nations, better nutrition is making people steadily taller; average heights are rising across Europe and Asia. But they are not rising in the US; in fact, Americans have pretty much stopped getting taller.[144] Another medical study reported that women in many of the poorest regions of the US are seeing their lifespans get shorter, reversing a trend toward longer lives that has been going forward for 100 years.[145] The authors of both these studies attribute the changes to widespread nutritional deficits, particularly in children, who are eating more and more processed and fast food. That is, we are literally stunting our children's growth and shortening their lives with an inferior diet — in part, because we do not know how to give them a better one.

Even those of us who do cook often and well usually rely upon a set of assumptions — created by wealth and cheap energy — that our present life will continue as it has been. That is, we assume that we will always have access to all the ingredients we want, and with reasonable freshness. So if I look up a recipe for pork loin with orange pepper salsa or double-chocolate blueberry fudge cake, I can wander into any supermarket and leave with all the components, no matter what time of year. Oh, the blueberries might be pricey in February, but blueberries I can have if I want to and can afford it.

But the system that provides all the blueberries you want in February is showing real signs of falling apart on a host of levels. First, of course, there's the energy and carbon costs of those blueberries. Getting them to your table from, say, Ecuador requires an enormous amount of fossil-fuel energy. All that energy produces all that carbon — and it is a wasteful use of our declining energy stocks. Unless the berries say "organic" (in which case they'll cost twice as much), they were probably sprayed with a host of carcinogens — maybe even some that are illegal in the US. And if they do say "organic" well, can it really be organic if it took 200 kilocalories of oil to get every calorie of blueberries to you? If the grocery store refrigerator truck produced exhaust that made your kid's asthma worse, and if the produce was grown by poor workers who were essentially enslaved? What is "organic" in this situation, anyway?

Meanwhile, most of us are seeing our food budgets stretched to the maximum. The *New York Times* reported in late April that people were beginning to go on "recession diets,"

> Home prices are sliding, wages are stagnant, job losses are growing and the Standard & Poor's 500-stock index, a broad measure of stock performance, is down 6 percent in the last year. So consumers are going on a recession diet.
>
> Burt Flickinger, a longtime retail consultant, said the last time he saw such significant changes in consumer buying patterns was the late 1970s, when runaway inflation prompted Americans to "switch from red meat to pork to poultry to pasta — then to peanut butter and jelly."
>
> "It hasn't gotten to human food mixed with pet food yet," he said, "but it is certainly headed in that direction." [146]

People are eating less red meat, buying fewer name brands, and are still struggling to make ends meet. Those blueberries aren't looking so good — but how to eat more cheaply still? A neighbor of Sharon's joked that she was "going to give up food for Lent." But this is serious — the recipes most of us know, if we know any, are for the foods of good times. What do we eat now?

We need new recipes — first of all, a new recipe for how to go forward, but also literally new recipes for how to eat in the food system that replaces it. How do you deal with a glut of pea pods from your garden? How do you replace local honey for sugar, or kale for cabbage in that stuffed greens recipe? We need to adapt ourselves to shortages of things and to seasonality — to recognize that all foods, including things we've never thought of as seasonal, such as milk, meat and eggs, have seasonal cycles. We need to store and preserve food, buying what is inexpensive and in season, and putting it up for times when it is scarce and pricey.

And to do all this, we have to learn to cook again. The fact is that as a nation we don't cook, and we don't know very much about how food is grown, how it is produced, harvested, preserved, prepared. We are unprepared for this new diet of ours. And we are unprepared for the time it will take to learn and make use of these skills.

Time, of course, is the master resource here. Over the years, advertising has convinced most of us that we simply don't have time to cook from scratch or to grow and preserve our own food. Someone once observed that you can tell what decade you are in by how long the "quick and easy" meals take. In the 1970s, a good portion of quick meals took as much as an hour. By the '80s and early '90s, 30 minutes was it. Amazon now counts 23 cookbooks advertising meals in 20 minutes or 15 minutes or less, and a number of them are best sellers.

Now, there are 15-minute meals in sustainable, from-scratch cooking that don't rely on commercially prepared ingredients. They are called "salads" or — if you don't count the time spent to make cheese, can jam or bake bread — maybe a sandwich. That's not to say that cooking from scratch is all that onerous. Most of the time, the food preparation isn't consuming of your time so much as you thought — it might take several hours to bake bread, but the bread does all the work of rising without your attention. It might need only five minutes of your time to mix the bread dough before bedtime, leaving it to rise overnight. But you do have to think and work that five minutes into your life. With some effort, it is perfectly possible to produce a pot of soup, a loaf of bread and a salad in 20 minutes over the stove — but with a couple of hours' notice.

This kind of time can be easily integrated into the lives of even people who work — a pot of soup with 20 servings is no harder and only slightly more time consuming to make than a pot with two servings, and thus, lunch is in the freezer for a number of meals. But because we are unaccustomed to thinking this way, we struggle.

It isn't that there is no such thing as sustainable, quick food — there are a lot of options there. But there is no such thing as sustainable, *thoughtless* food — that is, meals we don't think about until five minutes before we eat them. Either we think about them far, far ahead, when we stock up on pasta and can tomato sauce so that we can have five-minute spaghetti come winter, or we think about them that day, when we soak the bulgur, harvest the parsley and tomatoes, dig out the lemon juice we froze when organic lemons were on sale, and sort out a sweet onion for the tabbouleh.

It seems beyond self-evident to say that the ability to cook is tied to our ability to eat, but it has not been so in the first world. That is, most of us, except for the 12 percent of Americans who go hungry, have had the money to buy the processed bags of baby carrots, the premade yogurt, the restaurant meals, the canned beans. Now we may not have that money, or we may not be able to get that produce, or we may not be able to afford the harm that shipping them around does to the planet. And we have now raised several generations of people who do not cook.

If we do not learn to cook the foods that are local to us, if we do not learn to cook the foods that can be grown with minimal contributions to climate change, if we do not learn to cook what is inexpensive and available, if we do not learn to cook well with what we have, we too may go hungry.

Thus, we take as central to our understanding of what has to change that we have to learn to cook — that the 200 million cooks may be, in many ways, more essential than the millions of new farmers.

What To Eat

We may live without friends; we may live without books
But civilized men cannot live without cooks.
— Owen Meredith —

Enough philosophy, you cry out! I don't want my dinner to save the world, I just want to eat, and reasonably humanely. What do I eat for dinner? How do I cook it? And how do I do that and live my life as well? I have planted my garden, begun my farm, and there are rows of things to eat, but how do I get dinner from them? When I look at recipes, they often call for ingredients I don't have and often look long and complicated. How do I simply grow what we will eat, and eat what we can grow?

This is a big and serious question. One of the things that we have noticed is that the connection between garden and table is not one that many people fully understand how to navigate. In many ways it is easier to grow the peas than to figure out what to do with them day after day, how to use them every day they are available, and preserve some for later eating, and then do without them until the next season or the next crop. We're accustomed to recipe cooking, to accepting combinations of ingredients based not upon our region or our season but upon an endless, seasonless availability, fueled by oil and chemicals. This is different, and at first it is hard.

Seasonal eating does require a different set of skills than the conventional ones we use to get dinner on the table. And since we as a nation are not huge or diverse vegetable eaters, and much of what grows in a garden is vegetal, it can be awfully difficult to figure out what to grow, and once grown, how to eat.

One of the first questions worth asking is why we don't cook this way already? That is, why aren't we used to enjoying the very best fresh produce in its season, cooked simply and well? Why don't we have the skills to cook a wide range of the things that are easy to grow? Why don't we eat the way nutritionists tell us we're supposed to, with lots of whole grains and fresh vegetables and fruits and much less of everything else? Why don't we know what a fresh kohlrabi or a bowl of just-picked gooseberries taste like, and why don't we look forward to them as much as we do a bowl of barbecue chips?

It is worth asking these questions because none of these things are accidents. We eat what we do for complicated reasons, and those reasons matter. We need to address those reasons, and find new ones to eat a different way. Unless we understand what we are doing, and the ways in which our choices are manipulated, our decision to transform ourselves is likely to fail.

We need to be aware that our preferences have been consciously, intentionally and maliciously manipulated, often as bluntly as a recent president of McDonalds Japan did when he claimed that "the reason Japanese people are so short and have yellow skin is because they have eaten nothing but rice and fish for two thousand years.... [I]f we eat McDonalds hamburgers and potatoes for 1,000 years, we will become taller, our skin white and our hair blonde." Americans too have been sold a collection of lies, telling us that we will be healthier, happier and have more free time if we only turn food and cooking over to others. As we will see, none of the above is true.

Staple Foods

Lord, to those who have hunger, give bread.
And to those who have bread,
give the hunger for justice.
— LATIN AMERICAN PRAYER —

The first question that needs answering is perhaps the most complicated one. If I grow my own food, what will I be eating? And the answer is complicated by all sorts of factors, including regional adaptations, climate, water access and your personal tastes and ethnic origins. We cannot give you a complete answer, but we might begin by talking about the distinction between vegetables and staple starches.

Staple starches and proteins are the basic elements of every human diet, except perhaps the unhealthy Western one we eat. Staple foods are calorie-dense foods that, usually in combination, supply carbohydrates, complete proteins and other nutrients. They are usually easily stored, with no special technology. The starch itself varies based on a number of factors — on what the person in question can afford, what their customs and family staples are (that is, do you come from bread-eating or rice-eating or corn-eating people) and what is available at the time. But throughout human history, every single cuisine has had a staple starch (or several) attached to it. Some of these are grains, such as rice, rye, wheat and corn, and others are vegetable starches such as potatoes, breadfruit and manioc. But in most places in human history, there are one or two basic foods that are eaten in some form every day, and often multiple times per day. This might be wheat, eaten as porridge or pudding at breakfast and as bread at lunch and dinner, or it might be rice, eaten with fish for one meal and vegetables for the next. It could be corn, in the form of tortillas, or fried potatoes for breakfast and mashed ones for dinner.

Because staple starches tend not to have sufficient protein for an entire diet, they are combined with a staple protein food — usually beans or legumes, sometimes fish, meat or dairy products — to create complete proteins and a balanced diet. This combination is usually sufficient to sustain life with some greens and other foods.

From our Western point of view it would be easy to imagine that eating rice or bread at every meal was a step down from the diversity and wonder of our own habits, where we can have take-out Thai for lunch, Mexican for dinner and oatmeal for breakfast, but that is not the case. Most people love their staple foods, find them comforting and pleasurable, and come to believe that a meal without them is not a meal. For example, in several Asian cultures the question, "Have you eaten?" actually means "Have you had rice?" In many parts of Africa, the word for "food" refers only to staple foods, rather than snacks and luxury items. As Margaret Visser points out,

> Rice eaters are intensely knowledgeable about varieties of flavour and aroma in their favourite food; they may be used to eating little, but they care a great deal whether that little is good.[147]

The same is true of any people with staple foods. Varieties of bread are debated and preserved and recipes passed down among those who rely on wheat. Sourdough eaters preserve their starters; those accustomed to dark ryes search the earth for them when they travel; and at holidays everyone enjoys their sweetened celebratory breads. Those whose traditions involve corn preserve ancient varieties, such as traditional Mexican and Hopi varieties for making tortillas, because of the remarkable flavors involved. They know a thousand ways to use cornmeal — as breads, porridges and desserts — and never seem to tire of them. And anyone who has ever eaten a buttery, yellow Yukon gold potato and a waxy carola potato know how different they can be, how much a "meat and potatoes person" finds a meal without potatoes an empty thing indeed.

In fact, you might turn Visser's statement around and point out that the only people who don't care about the quality of their food are us, the people who have so much of it that we don't know what to do with it. We have allowed our tastes for salt and fat and sugar to override the natural, profound liking for a staple whole grain and its natural partners, and we can no longer taste the subtleties of their pleasures. Or perhaps because we rely on the supermarket, we simply don't know how very diverse these flavors can be. We imagine ourselves as having a tremendously interesting diet, but is it really better to eat increasingly scarce lobster and factory farmed chicken and pork in one week than to enjoy sourdough, black rye, honey-wheat and salt-rising bread?

I want to emphasize that when we call for a return to staple-starch-based diets, we are not calling for a return to the bland, the boring, the unbalanced or the unpleasant. We have become accustomed to another kind of diet, one that is tremendously energy and carbon intensive and often very boring — in the sense that everything tastes strongly of salt and fat. Becoming a nation of home cooks means, in part, developing a new, but not at all inferior diet. It involves opening ourselves to new tastes and reconsidering what constitutes novelty and good food.

We imagine ourselves as eating a variety of foods, but in fact, if we eat from the typical supermarket, much of our diet is derived from a single ingredient. As Michael Pollan points out in *The Omnivore's Dilemma*, corn is a central ingredient in virtually everything Americans eat. We are not aware of how dependent we are upon zea mays (corn), but we are, as Pollan observes, rather like Koala bears that eat only one sort of plant. He says,

Corn is what feeds the steer that becomes the steak. Corn feeds the chickens and the pig, the turkey and the lamb, the catfish and the tilapia and, increasingly, even the salmon, a carnivore by nature that fish farmers are reengineering to tolerate corn. The eggs are made of corn. The milk and cheese and yogurt, which once came from the dairy cows that grazed on grass, now typically come from Holsteins that spend their working lives indoors tethered to machines, eating corn.

Head over to the processed foods and you find ever more intricate manifestations of corn. A chicken nugget, for example, piles corn upon corn: what chicken it contains consists of corn, of course, but so do most of the nugget's other constituents, including the modified corn starch that glues the thing together, the corn flour in the batter that coats it, and the corn oil in which it gets fried. Much less obviously, the leavenings and lecithin, the mono-, and di-, and triglycerides, the attractive golden coloring, and even the citric acid that keeps the nugget "fresh" can all be derived from corn.

To wash down your chicken nuggets with virtually any soft drink in the supermarket is to have some corn with your corn. Since the 1980s virtually all the sodas and most of the fruit drinks sold in the supermarket have been sweetened with high-fructose corn syrup (HFCS) — after water, corn sweetener is their principle ingredient. Grab a beer for your beverage instead and you'd still be drinking corn in the form of alcohol fermented from glucose refined from corn.[148]

Wow, doesn't that sound yummy! It turns out that our diet isn't nearly as diverse as we'd like to think it is, and changing to devote ourselves primarily to a few staple foods might actually be an expansion, rather than a contraction, of our experience and our palates.

There are powerful reasons to wish for all of us to eat a diet primarily based upon food staples. Whole grains and legumes are far better for us than the meats and processed foods we are accustomed to placing at the center of our diets. But also, eating grains, roots, vegetables and legumes is a diet that keeps human food feeding humans and reduces world hunger. Our hunger for large quantities of meats fed on grains that could feed people, and for processed foods that extract non-nutritious elements from whole grains, has reduced other people's access to food.

We would encourage people to think about what is likely to be their own natural staple food, and how to provision themselves with it, to learn to cook it well and in multiple ways, and to enjoy it. That does not mean this is the only food you will eat, but it may be the basis for many of your meals. For many people farming on small lots, growing a lot of grain is probably not feasible, although you certainly can grow a surprisingly large amount with intensive methods. Most of the world's rice is grown on plots of less than five acres, for example.[149] There are good reasons to grow some staple grains and vegetables. One of them is as a hedge against famine in hard times. It is also a means of creating complete local food systems. If the basis of your diet has to come from far away, there are limits to how food secure your community can ever be or how free you can ever be from corporations.

It is probably true that much grain growing will still take place on a field scale, on larger farms, and those of you who plan to take up farming on a larger scale than in the backyard should consider, perhaps, creating CSGs — something like the traditional CSA (more on this in the next chapters), but with staple grains (thus the "G") at the center of the thing. You might provide several subscribers with their year's supply of wheat or rice or barley and beans. But even those of us who get most of our grains from larger farmers should try to grow a little of our own staple foods, so that we can get to know them and develop an intimacy and understanding of what it takes to produce these things that give us life. Doing so also means that if our sources ever dry up, we are still able to provision ourselves.

Corn, Potatoes, Wheat, Rice, Roots

Humble is the grass in the field, yet it has noble relations.
All the bread grains are grass — wheat and rye, barley, sorghum and rice;
maize, the great staple of America; millet, oats and sugar cane.
Other things have their season but the grass is of all seasons…
the common background on which the affairs of nature and man
are conditioned and displayed.
— LIBERTY HYDE BAILEY —

Corn is the native American staple. We are most familiar with corn in its fresh "green" phase, as sweet corn, and extracted into corn sweeteners and starches. But what we're talking about here are flour and dent varieties that can be ground for cornmeal. Some of these, like Black Aztec are good in their green stage as well. If corn is central to your diet, you will need to nixtamalize it; that is, cook or soak the corn with something alkaline, such as baking soda, wood ashes or lime, to unlock the niacin. Without nixtamalization, people who eat corn as a major staple of their diets often develop pellagra or kwashiorkor. The discovery of nixtamalization was an enormous revelation for the early peoples of the Americas.

Corn does have the disadvantage of being extremely nitrogen intensive and cannot be grown over and over on the same ground. To grow corn, you must have enough land to rotate your crops and allow the soil to recover from the heavy requirements of corn. In the US we have taken to growing "continuous corn" — that is, corn grown over and over on the same fields, made possible with heavy use of nitrogen fertilizers and pesticides. This has been an ecological disaster. So those of us who are "corn eaters" must be especially careful of how we treat the land and of what kind of diet we have. It may be that we cannot be corn people every year but will have to choose less hungry foods, such as wheat, rice or potatoes to fill our bellies in the years in which we rest our soil. Fortunately, dry corn lasts a very long time, so we may not need to grow it every year in our gardens, if it is integrated with other staples.

In ancient Native American cultures (and some present ones) corn was not just necessary to live, corn actually was life in many faiths. One prayed to the Corn Mother and told stories of the birth of the world through scattered corn seeds. This reverence for a staple food as the basis and source of all life is duplicated in almost every culture in the world. In many Asian cultures, the Rice Mother is the origin of all human life. In ancient Judaism, the central religious ritual, the Sabbath, is based upon prayers for the bread given forth from the earth. In British folk music one can hear the story of "John Barleycorn" and the spilling of his life in order to enable the lives of others in the form of beer and bread. In folk stories the world over, those who throw away their beans or grains are impoverished and those who preserve and love them are enriched. All over the world, staple foods are the thing that gives us life, enables us to go on, creates and sustains the world. That we in the industrial culture have lost the notion of the sustaining staple should be an indicator of our failure to remain connected to the roots of our humanity.

Corn was ordinarily eaten with beans, and for many of us in the world the combination of beans, or other legumes, and grains will most likely be our staple protein sources. Meat production is energy, carbon, land, water and labor intensive, and most of us will be eating less of it over the coming years. So when we think about staples, we should be thinking of things we can easily grow in our own backyards and on our small farms. Grain and bean dishes are often quite delicious, whether they appear as chili and cornbread in the Southwest, Cuban yellow rice and beans, brown rice and spicy garlic tofu from China, Boston brown bread and sweet baked beans, British-style Split pea soup with whole grain breads, or even peanut butter and jelly sandwiches (peanuts are a legume).

For those of us who live in the northern half of the US, potatoes are likely to be our staple starch rather than corn. We can grow corn too, but cool summers sometimes prevent good maturation. The good thing about relying on potatoes is that they are amazingly easy to grow, even on land that won't grow much of anything else. They are sometimes subject to potato blight, the disease that caused the famous Irish potato famine. But there are disease- and insect-resistant varieties. Most cultures that rely on potatoes have historically mixed them with peas, which also like cool weather, or with milk and sometimes fish. That is because potatoes thrive in cool, wet climates, such as are often found in northern coastal areas, and are easily grown on land too steep and rocky to grow other crops or land too cold for hot-weather crops like many dry beans. The other best use of such land is grazing for dairy animals or growing cold-weather crops such as dry peas and fava beans, so the combinations are natural ones.

We natural potato eaters might enjoy them as lefske, a classic Scandinavian potato pancake, or Colcannon, a mixture of mashed potatoes, milk and greens. We can eat them fried for breakfast or baked with cheese for dinner. We can boil or steam or bake or fry them. Potatoes are high yielders and easily grown on almost any soils, producing much more than a comparative amount of grain. Our families enjoy mashed potato cakes, scalloped and roasted potatoes, vichyssoise (potato leek soup), potato frittata (potato omelet), hashes (potatoes mixed with a small amount of meat or fish or even mushrooms), latkes (classic potato pancakes eaten among Jews particularly at Chanukah) and a host of other ways.

Besides potatoes, there are other vegetable crops that are dense in calories, highly nutritious and keep well in many climates with a minimum of food preservation. John Jeavons, author of several books, including *How To Grow More Vegetables Than You Ever Thought Possible...* and perhaps the world's greatest expert on how to grow an entire human diet on very small amounts of land, and his foundation, Ecology Action, have created a system of sustainable farming that allows people to be food secure on as little as 700 square feet of land for a single adult. (If you have trouble visualizing, 700 square feet is about the size of a basketball court.) He suggests a division of 60 percent carbon crops (such as many grains whose straw can be used to improve soil), which produce some food but mostly are returned to the soil to maintain fertility, 30 percent calorie crops, most of which are roots such as beets, sweet potatoes, Irish potatoes, and parsnips, and 10 percent flavoring crops. Though many of us have more land than this, some do not, and it is worth knowing how to feed yourself a balanced and secure diet this way. There are very few fats and not an enormous amount of protein, but you will live and be full. Ecology Action has had quite a few volunteers live for extended periods on these diets, and regular medical checkups document that they are healthy.

Other roots, including burdock (bet you didn't know you could eat it), turnips, beets, rutabagas (swedes), parsley root, parsnips, carrots and daikon (among others) are also significant sources of nutrition and calories and are also quite delicious. Most Americans have never eaten a turnip, carrot or parsnip kept in the ground after a frost and have no idea how sweet these vegetables can be. It is worth noting that in much of Europe during the middle ages, humans and animals survived winters to a large degree on root crops. Many of these can be cooked in much the same ways potatoes can. If you live in the south, sweet potatoes are almost as easy to grow as potatoes and are even more nutritious.

If you derive from bread- and pasta-eating European cultures, the thought of relying on another staple food can be overwhelming. It is certainly possible to grow patches of wheat, rye, barley and oats on the home farm. In fact, in an Ecology-Action-style system, some straw plants must be grown, and in many cases the grain can be harvested and the straw returned to the soil. Harvesting and threshing most grains (except buckwheat, amaranth and quinoa) is considerably more work than growing root crops or corn, but it is worth remembering that millions of people throughout human history lived on their own grain crops. It does take some land to do. Gene Logsdon, whose *Small-Scale Grain Raising* is the definitive work on human-scale grain production, notes that the amount of space required to grow a bushel of wheat is about 10 feet by 109 feet, and a bushel of wheat will make 40 loaves of bread. A space 10 by 200 (approximately $\frac{1}{20}$ of an acre) will give you bread to eat every week of the year, and a little leftover for cookies and piecrust.[150] And wheat is a grass, so it is comparatively easy to sow and raise.

It is not merely in our sayings that bread is "the staff of life," which means that it holds us up and keeps us going. In bread-eating cultures, life is organized to a large degree around the growing of wheat, much as rice cultures and corn cultures organize around the needs of their basic crops. Wheat is less nitrogen intensive than corn and has the additional benefit of being (in many cases) a fall-sown crop, so it helps keep soil stable over winter. Wheat does require threshing, winnowing and grinding, as well as harvesting, but much of this work can be put off until cold weather and done in the shelter of a barn or shed during quieter times of year.

Good bread is made from good wheat, and home-grown and home-ground wheat makes flour that is as different from what you buy in the supermarket as the tomato you grow in your garden is from the one in the supermarket. Good bread does not taste like the pasty white stuff that many of us have.

Simple meals that center on bread include soups with bread for dipping, sandwiches made from whatever is ripe in the garden along with sweet or spicy condiments like onion-garlic jam or pickled hot peppers, bread with jam and homemade peanut butter, bread puddings, summer puddings, all made with old bread, tomato and bread salads, and, of course pizzas and the polycultural items wrapped in bread, from empanadas to Russian cabbage pie and English meat pies.

Other grains make traditional breads of other cultures. Teff makes injera bread, without which Ethiopian food would never be the same. Oat breads and oatcakes define Scottish cuisine. Buckwheat pancakes are typically Russian, and spelt and other breads were the food of the ancient Middle East. Rice flour buns are common in Asian cooking.

Rice is typically grown in wet, warm, humid areas, and could be grown in much of the deep south. Aaron has grown some rice in his small city yard, and Sharon has made several attempts to grow rice in upstate NY, with little success. But it is worth remembering that rice is the staple food in Korea and Northern Japan, so it is probable that rice could be more widely grown than it is at present. Rice is well adapted to small-scale agriculture and can be combined with fish production if it is grown in a paddy system. There are dryland rices as well.

Rice is a demanding crop, one that requires a great deal of attention and water throughout the growing season. But it has many virtues — it is delicious and nutritious. It is virtually impossible for people to be allergic to or sensitive to rice, so if digestive difficulties run in your family, rice is an excellent crop. When rice comes off the plant, it needs to be hulled before being eaten. Brown rice has had only the outer hull removed; white rice has had the germ and most of the nutrition polished off. Once rice is hulled, brown rice lasts only a few months, so white rice, despite its lower nutrition, is better for long-term storage, although unhulled rice stores best of all, and allows you to enjoy the nutty taste of brown rice after hulling. There are plans on the Internet that allow you to make a rice huller out of a simple grain mill.

Rice comes in a tremendous variety of types and flavors. Sticky rice has a slightly sweet taste and a glutinous texture that is wonderfully filling and tasty. Short-grained rices, such as are used for risotto, sushi and other foods, absorb a lot of liquid and have a smooth, creamy texture. Most Americans are familiar only with long-grained rices. The best of these are jasmine or basmati or other fragrant varieties. And there are red rices and black rices, all with their traditional flavors and uses. Wild rice is native to North America. It can be used in many of the same ways as domestic rice or cooked into porridges, fried as pancakes and used as a stuffing for vegetables.

Our families love rice in every form. We eat it as risotto in the spring with fresh new greens and cheese, as rice and pigeon peas with hot Jamaican sauce, stuffed in grape leaves, as paella, in Iranian-style stuffed vegetables, for dessert in lemon rice pudding, in Indian style pulaos, or as kheer, a rice pudding flavored with cardamom and ground nuts, as fried rice both Chinese and Indonesian style, and in vegetable sushi.

Regardless of what staple food or foods you are most likely to have in your life, it only makes sense to begin to delight in the bounty of a comforting food staple. Get used to your staple foods. Experiment with them. Try different varieties, different tastes, different cuisines. Think of them as most traditional people have — as the origin of our well-being, something to be honored and eaten with gratitude. The ground that we grow these foods on is sacred, no matter what our beliefs, and deserves nurturance and attention, and our staple food deserves space and attention in our gardens. Thus, we ensure both food security and maximum pleasure.

Changing Our Staples — The Possibilities of Vegeculture

What I say is that, if a fellow really likes potatoes,
he must be a pretty decent sort of fellow.
— A. A. Milne —

In his book *African-American Gardens and Yards in the Rural South*, Richard Westmacott notes that a good bit of southern African American agricultural practice derives from West African and Caribbean practices of "vegeculture" as opposed to European style-seed agriculture.[151] The term, coined by D. B. Grigg in his classic *Agricultural Systems of the World*, applies to agriculture based primarily on root crops, including manioc, sweet potatoes, yams, taro, arrowroot and, in cooler climates, adapted to potatoes as well. Root crops were integrated with tree crops.[152]

Vegeculture has several advantages over grain culture for small-scale growers. For example, you don't have to till a lot of ground at once, as these crops are adapted to "patch" culture. They often can be stored in the ground and dug up as needed, and can tolerate being integrated with perennial tree plantings. The West African tradition of planting in patches and leaving ground fallow to restore fertility translated well to slave gardens in the US and Caribbean islands because such gardens often had to be hidden. Often slaves, and later share-croppers, had only hilly or otherwise difficult-to-use land, which is best served by being kept in perennial or semi-perennial root crops. Because slaves and tenant farmers had very little time to work their land, they needed high-yielding crops that could provide nutrition and caloric density together.

In her essay "They have Saturdays and Sundays to Feed Themselves: Slave Gardens in the Caribbean," Lydia Pulsipher observes that there is considerable evidence that islands that included many slave gardens didn't suffer the classic malnutrition of slavery. In fact, the available data on the history of produce selling by slaves (who sold their surpluses to both white and black customers) suggests that white people were considerably healthier on islands that had large numbers of slave gardens. The implication seems to be that the starchy, vegetable-poor diet of Europeans on these islands was significantly inferior to the vegetable-rich, nutrient-rich diet of the slaves, and the influence of slave gardens improved the European seed diet enormously (probably to the less-than-total delight of the slaves themselves).[153]

Only 2.5 percent of American agricultural land currently produces vegetables, fruits and nuts for consumption. The other 97.5 percent is largely devoted to the production of grains and seeds for things like feeding livestock, feeding cars (ethanol and biodiesel) and transformation into processed food.[154]

What struck us about this is how small an impact we would have on the industrial agricultural juggernaut even if we were able to replace every single vegetable, fruit and nut we eat with locally, sustainably produced produce. That is, if we are looking to home production to help end the tragic power of industrial food production with its heavy greenhouse gas outputs, water consumption and soil degradation, we need to start thinking in terms of producing more of our total calories at home. Growing our lettuce and tomatoes is a good start, but the next step is a return to home production of calorically dense foods, and to that, we are more and more convinced that vegeculture is part of the answer.

Between desertification, a rising population and the transformation of agricultural lands to housing, by 2050 there will be less than half as much arable land available to feed each person in the US — a total of 0.6 acres, one-third of what is used now. We cannot hope to continue deriving many of our calories from "shadow" acres in other nations, in part because it would be unethical and in part because it is likely that China, which is right on the cusp of being unable to feed itself, will be able to outbid us. So while we may have the luxury of a considerable amount of land per person, our children will not. It would be unconscionable, however, for us not to begin to transition to living on a fair share.

Traditional West African gardeners, growing food in hot, dry areas of comparatively low fertility, emphasized perennial and annual root crops as their staple foods, as have many Latin American farmers. Indeed, despite the tendency to rely on grain crops, even Northern Europe made much of its agricultural prosperity on the turnip, and later, the potato. Large-scale root cultivation enabled the milk culture of Northern Europe, and there is archaeological evidence that in areas where turnips were cultivated people grew taller and healthier than in areas where wheat and barley were emphasized. Root crops were higher yielding than grain crops, particularly when grown on a small scale. Hot-weather root crops such as sweet potatoes were tremendously drought tolerant and could be grown on ground of low fertility.

A few centuries later, John Jeavons at Ecology Action would pioneer an intensively grown diet for a human being based largely on calorie- and nutrient-dense root crops. In his book *One Circle*, David Duhon documents his life on a diet that could be produced on an average of less than 700 square feet; it is heavily based on parsnips, potatoes and sweet potatoes. By eating these in place of grains, one could get virtually all the nutrition needed, keep full and healthy and feed four people on a single yard.

Meanwhile in Cuba, as grain imports fell, Cubans were raising more vegetables and replacing rice and beans with sweet potatoes. In Russia, as wheat imports ceased and no one could figure out why the Russian people weren't starving to death, beets and potatoes provided the primary food sources to keep people alive.

What the Heck is a Kohlrabi and What Do I Do With It Anyway?

The greatest service which can be rendered any country is to add a useful plant to its culture.
— Thomas Jefferson —

When you asked us what to grow and eat, you probably were not thinking about rice and wheat so much as about the typical foods that most people grow in their vegetable gardens. You are thinking of tomatoes and eggplant, greens and carrots, rather than grains and potatoes. And those are also important foods in our diet. If the grains and vegetable protein foods are the basis of our diet, vegetables and fruits should be its centerpiece. Unfortunately, in the US, they rarely are.

Peter Menzel and Faith D'Aluisio's book, *Hungry Planet: What the World Eats,* contains some of the most fascinating images we've ever seen. Families of all shapes and sizes sit with an entire week's worth of food for them. In some cases, as in the US, there is hardly room for all the packages and boxes of things; they pile up on the counters, and pizzas overflow onto people's laps. In another case, a very poor Malian extended family sits before a mat on which sit a few sacks of grain and other staples, fewer varieties of food than there are members of the family. Besides the shocking visual disparities between rich and poor nations, there is another, equally shocking impoverishment, but in this case one that affects almost equally the very richest and very poorest nations — the shortage of truly fresh produce.

For the family in Mali mentioned above, 15 adults and children share only a few pounds of tomatoes, okra and onions to go with their rice and millet. In a refugee camp near Darfur, a family of six refugees shares, in their weekly rations, five limes and less than two pounds of garlic and onions. To someone like me, accustomed to eating vegetables at every meal, theirs is poverty indeed. And yet, among wealthy and privileged Americans, too, the variety of vegetables and fruits is poor. A family in California eats mostly bananas, apples and grapes, with just a few carrots and some broccoli added in. In California in April, fresh greens and strawberries and other precious new things abound, but the family is eating apples stored for many months and bananas from further south, rather than the food of their time and season. In Texas and North Carolina, the quantities are greater than for the deeply impoverished people of Mali and Chad, but still there are only stingy quantities of unprocessed fruits and vegetables.

Except in nations with climates inhospitable to agriculture and the ones experiencing dire poverty, most of the people living in poorer nations than ours eat a much more varied, fresher diet. In rural China, for example, a family eats nearly 20 pounds each of two kinds of melon, another 20 pounds of other fruit, and 30 or more pounds of fresh vegetables. But a prosperous urban Chinese family eats more packaged foods and fewer vegetables, although they still eat more than 20 pounds of fruit among them each week. In Cuba, again, nearly 30 pounds of melon, another 20 pounds of additional fruit, and a dozen pounds of vegetables. Extremely impoverished families in Bhutan and Guatemala still enjoy more produce, and more varieties of produce, than do Americans or many Europeans. We should be troubled that all our wealth has created a kind of voluntary impoverishment of diet.[155]

The average American doesn't eat very many vegetables or fruits at all, and what we do eat is resolutely the product of industrial agriculture. For example, one quarter of the vegetables American children eat come in the form of French fries, and three out of four Americans get less than five servings of vegetables per day — many much less. And many of the servings we do get are processed, homogenized, canned or frozen, drenched in fat, sugar and salt in the forms of frying, dressings, etc. Even the fresh vegetables we eat aren't really fresh — our salad greens are packaged in plastic with nitrogen gas to keep them from wilting. Our apples have been sitting, gassed with ethylene and chilled, for weeks or months, not hours. Marion Nestle documents the process of getting our "fresh" produce to our tables, a system that is similar even for many chains that specialize in organic ingredients,

For a large supermarket chain with its own distribution system, that broccoli undergoes a journey like this: farm, local warehouse, regional distribution center, refrigerated truck, regional distribution center at destination, another truck, local supermarket, backroom stocking area, floor, and finally, shelf. All this can take a week, but ten days would not be unusual. Even if the broccoli is kept cold throughout this odyssey (something hardly likely with all those transfers in and out of trucks and warehouses), it isn't going to be my idea of fresh by the time I buy it, and it will be even less so by the time I actually get around to eating it.[156]

The natural sugars in most vegetables begin turning to starches almost instantly after being picked. So after 10 days on trucks and in warehouses, much of the fresh crisp flavor, the natural sweetness, the texture and smell and simple lush, ripe pleasure will be gone. In addition, most industrially produced vegetable varieties are selected not for flavor, scent or texture, but because they pack and ship well. No wonder we don't like to eat our veggies! No wonder George H. W. Bush announced that he had always hated broccoli — he's probably never tasted any that bears a resemblance to real broccoli, picked on a cool fall morning from the garden and nibbled on the way into the house to steam or sauté it.

Many of the foods we are going to be eating in the future are unfamiliar to us or eaten only occasionally in our present diet. For example, in northern climates, people have historically eaten root vegetables through the winter. Of the major root foods, only carrots, potatoes and onions are a regular part of our diet. We need to come to familiarity with things like beets (yes, we know many of you think you hate beets — but you might be surprised), parsnips, celery root, salsify, daikon and more. In spring and fall in cold climates, greens are among the first and last things standing in our gardens, but other than in salad, most Western folk eat few, if any fresh greens. American southerners do eat them, but almost universally cooked with meat, and cooked for long periods. We need to learn how to eat and enjoy greens, and how to make vegetables the centerpiece of our meals. That means that many of us will have to begin trying new things.

This can only be good for our health. Our bodies are generally designed to eat a balance of seed plants and vegetables, but as we have gotten richer, we are eating more and more grains in the forms of processed foods and meat, and fewer vegetables and greens, with predictable consequence to our health. And we have been implicitly taught that these foods are not as good as those laden with fat and sugar, that they are not as flavorful, that they are not a treat. We need to begin looking upon them as a pleasure and a luxury, not a penance.

The best way to do this is to expand your seed orders each year and add fruiting perennials and trees. You can find space for these by replacing decorative plants with food plants that are both ornamental and edible — blueberries, for example, are unbelievably nutritious and quite beautiful. They are more decorative than many shrubs. We can edge borders with strawberries, replace landscape trees with fruit trees. Those who live in truly warm climates have done this for decades — there are few yards without their avocado or orange trees. Here in colder places, we need to get used to adding edibles to our yards as well. And try new things from the farmers' market, ask your farming neighbors to grow new vegetables and expand your repertoire and your palate.

For most Americans, a diet flush with vegetables would be a very strange thing indeed. And part of the problem is that we don't do much with our vegetables. We tend to overcook them and toss a few on the edge of the plate, where one eats them because one feels one should. Or at best, we have salad with bland lettuces or the ubiquitous, E. coli-laced bagged spinach, a soggy winter tomato and a bland cucumber. But when we garden, or get our food from local sources, the world of flavor opens up to us.

Salads can contain 5 or 10 or 20 delicious greens. In the early spring they might have spicy arugula (also known as rocket), bitter dandelions (and don't get all wussy on us when you hear the word "bitter" — you drink coffee, right? That's bitter too. Bitter, mixed with sweet and tangy is a pleasure, not a pain), garlicky-tasting garlic chives, lemony sorrel and fresh spinach. Add a few new radishes, some sweet peas dumped out of the pod, and a little cheese or a few cooked chickpeas and you have created a lunch that has a hundred different tastes and textures in it. It needs only a dressing of vinegar, a little oil, and a touch of honey, with a few scallions or chives tossed in.

If you don't know what to do with a kohlrabi or an edible chrysanthemum, a rutabaga or a bunch of fresh kale, turnip greens or long beans, now is the time to explore. Look up recipes. Visit the farmers' market. Try your vegetables in many forms. Raw first, of course, and if necessary dipped in something you like. But also steamed and baked and souped and stir fried. Almost everything tastes good steamed until tender and served with lemon and olive oil or added to vegetable soup. Try and center you meal around a grain with many vegetable foods, perhaps flavored with some meat or fish, dairy or eggs.

We are people who find it very hard to change our food preferences. We often are so certain we do not like some food that we cannot experience it with an open mind. Add to that the fact that we have been deprived of good food for a long time, and this is not an immediate transition. That is why we must change our diet now, today. Because the day will come when the change will be urgently necessary, and there is no reason to face hard times in a misery because our conventional diets are over. Better we learn pleasure in the new ones. And there is a great deal of pleasure to be had.

How To Cook

This was after stew, but so is everything.
When the first man first clambered from the slime
and made his first home on land, what he had that first night was stew.
— WILLIAM GOLDMAN, *THE PRINCESS BRIDE* —

You almost certainly have strong opinions on this subject, even if you don't cook. But at a minimum, we would suggest you master five different basic styles of cooking: soup/stew, salad, stir fry, pie/dumpling and casserole/one pot. These are ways you can cook almost any vegetable and grain combination, and make them taste good. They do not depend on specific combinations being available all the time, they just assume that you can combine what you have until it pleases you.

1. Soup/Stew. This is one of the easiest things to do. Heat up some liquid. Water will do, but if you have time to make a vegetable stock by simmering some peelings or if you have meat or fish bones and scraps lying about, that will only improve it. You need not follow recipes for stock. Throw whatever you've got — whether it be carrot peelings and onion skins or chicken bones, dried mushrooms or miso — into a good-sized pot of water. As part of your liquid you can also use vegetable juices (such as the water that drains off tomatoes held in a colander overnight for making sauces), the liquids in which you have cooked things like beans or steamed vegetables, wine, or diluted yogurt or milk. How much liquid you add will determine whether this is a soup (more) or stew (less).

After you have made your liquid, add the vegetables you like. You will probably prefer not to add greens until the very end, since they tend to overcook easily; likewise eggplant, cucumbers or squash, or fruit, generally speaking, although you should feel free to experiment. For roots, cook longer. Do not let milk or yogurt soups come to a boil — cook them over low heat. Add dry herbs, onions, garlic, ginger or any other flavoring that appeals. Cook on low heat until all the vegetables are tender. If you like, add some rice or barley, beans or pasta (not usually to milky soups). Puree or not. Season to taste.

Congratulations — you have soup. With variations, you can have cream of cucumber soup with fresh mint (milk or yogurt, cucumbers, mint, salt) or carrot-barley soup (carrots, broth, a bit of wine, salt, dill, barley), or tomato-vegetable soup (tomato juice, water, carrots, potatoes, onions, beans, garlic, basil, sage, thyme, parsnips), or cream of eggplant soup (water, eggplant, rice, milk, cumin, garlic, tomato), or sorrel soup (water, sorrel, garlic, salt). There are few ways to screw this up. At the worst, it will be bland. Add more flavorings. If you cook green vegetables too long, they may be bland and taste odd. But the pot of soup will rarely be unsalvageable with a little soy sauce, vinegar or other flavorings. The beauty of soup is that it can be stretched to feed many people — just add more barley or more potatoes, a little more milk or even more water. In the hardest of times, soup feeds everyone and warms us to our bones.

Soups can be set on the back of the woodstove when we're heating the house anyhow, made in the solar oven on sunny days, or cooked rapidly in a pressure cooker to conserve energy. Cold summer soups often need little or no cooking at all. We need to be conscious of the energy costs of our meals, but soup making need not consume very much energy — or very much time. It is simple to combine ingredients and let the cooking do the work of melding flavors and making something far greater than the sum of its parts.

2. Salad: We have already discussed salads, but it should go without saying that salad can be made of anything — cooked vegetables, dried vegetables (rehydrated or not), cold leftover greens or beans, wild foods such as nuts and mushrooms. It can be dressed with oil and lemon, vinegar and a little honey, pureed herbs mixed with a bit of wine or vinegar or even water to thin them, or fancier things like green mayonnaise (herbs mixed with mayo and vinegar) or chipotle-raspberry sauce (hot chilies mixed with mashed fruit and a bit of oil). Whenever you have a bit of this and that, salad or soup should be your first thought. Think "stretching your fats, proteins and energy foods" with lots of delicious, flavorful greens and grains. One egg is not much among three people, but crumbled and tossed atop a salad of greens, bulgur, tomatoes and onion, it is sufficient. Much of our future may involve stretching expensive foods with easily grown, highly nutritious, easy-to-come-by ones. Many salad greens grow wild in our yards as weeds — instead of trying to get rid of them, we can enjoy them and their intense nutritional value.

Salads have the special virtue of using uncooked or leftover cooked foods very well. If we are short on fuel or taking care to preserve the environment, salad is the perfect food for us. And so many of the things we grow in our gardens are at their best tasting a few minutes out of the ground, uncooked and lightly dressed.

3. **Stir-fry**: Many people have a hard time making a good stir-fry. One reason is that they use woks, which don't work terribly well on conventional stoves. Stir fried foods were invented in areas where cooking fuel was scarce — they cut food up before cooking and then cooked very quickly on hot fires. Woks work beautifully on these fires, but conventional electric stoves, and even many gas ranges, don't get hot enough to cook food in a wok, particularly if you want to make stir-fry for more than two people. And why wouldn't you — it is one of the quickest, tastiest meals you can serve to a guest. We recommend that instead of trying to use a wok, you use a cast iron, flat-bottomed frying pan. This heats up well and retains heat well, is safe (many woks are covered with toxic non-stick materials), and can be used for many purposes. The old reasons for stir frying are good ones for doing it now. Among other things, it requires very little fat, and fat is one of the harder things to come by in poor societies.

Stir-fries are made, as mentioned above, by chopping things up finely and cooking very quickly on high heat. Sauces reduce rapidly in stir frying and should not be watery. They need not resemble the heavy, sweet, corn-starchy glutinousness we are used to in poor-quality restaurants. A simple stir-fry might include, of course, the classic tofu, pea pods, peppers and broccoli, but equally likely could contain carrots or daikon, fresh shell beans or green soybeans, tomatoes, wild or cultivated greens, pickled greens, fresh cabbage, and almost anything else that can be cooked quickly. Add tofu, or meat, fermented black beans, or perhaps peanuts or tree nuts for a bit of protein, and serve it over a cooked grain. Rice is traditional, but stir-fries are delicious over steamed quinoa, or buckwheat groats, barley, bulgur or with a sweet steamed Chinese-style wheat bun.

4. Pie/dumpling: The dumpling and the savory (not to mention sweet) pie have something in common — they represent a way to stretch flavorful fillings with starches. The wonton, the knish, the pot sticker, the apple dumpling, the empanada, the meat pie, the perogy, bao, the world is full of sweet or salty insides wrapped inside a starch. Because there are so many kinds, we cannot hope to explain them all, but we will offer some recipes and some broad rules.

Fillings should be highly seasoned, nicely textured and have strong flavors. A meat pie, for example, might contain less than an ounce of meat, stretched with potatoes, onions and garlic, and fresh herbs, and yet it tastes rich and meaty. A vegetarian dumpling could be delicate, rice paper wrapped around the sweetest of pea tendrils, but more often is filled with meat or fish or chopped, spiced vegetables.

A traditional pie crust is made with some kind of cold fat, water, flour and salt — nothing else. The trick is to touch it as little as possible, to quickly mix ingredients and roll it out. We've included some recipes. If fat is in short supply, you can use more liquid or an egg, and create something with a slightly different texture. Remember, good pastry making is something of an art, but much can be compensated for by a good flavored filling. Fill the pie with whatever looks good, is fresh and tastes good. Spanakopita uses fresh greens, a little cheese and egg; you could leave out the egg if need be and try it with only the cheese. Empanadas often use meat or vegetables and dried fruit, all cooked together with spices. Traditional English pies use meat or potatoes. The knish also represents the ultimate triumph of the staple food — dough with seasoned potatoes or buckwheat inside.

Russian pies were often filled with fish or cabbage — it is hard to describe how delicious a filling of cabbage, cooked in butter with garlic and dill, can be inside dough. It sounds so plebian. The same is true of Indian samosas, made with mashed potatoes and peas cooked with mustard seeds and tumeric until they glow.

5. Casserole/one-pot: The casserole/one pot meal is really not all that different than soup or stew, with the difference that many soups and stews cook the grain separately. You bake the bread or cook the rice that the stew will be served over in one pot, and cook the soup or stew in another. This is not always the case, but often enough to generalize. But the advantage of the one pot meal, in which all the ingredients are combined or layered with spices and seasonings, is that everything tastes equally good and there are few dishes to wash. For this, one takes a large, heavy pot and often sautés the flavoring ingredients together — onions, garlic, ginger, spices, meat or tofu, other vegetables improved by a bit of sautéing. Then, in the same pot, add the grains, beans and vegetables. They can be mixed up or layered. For example, whole wheat noodles might be layered with tomatoes, eggplant, basic and garlic, and a bit of cheese to make a layered noodle casserole or lasagna. Or, you might mix beans, rice, garlic, onion, pepper and greens together with some sausage or seafood to make a jambalaya (which literally means mixed up). The idea, as in stew, soup and salad, is that the combined ingredients be greater than the sum of its parts.

Cooking this way requires practice and experimentation. After a time you begin to know what you can expect if you add, say, ginger or wine to a pot, and you can predict how to balance flavors. This is much more art than following a recipe. But it also gives you the gift of being able to make and serve good food even if a particular ingredient is absent or if one day you must combine unfamiliar things to make something warming, comforting — ultimately a new source of familiarity.

Stretching Dinner and Sharing It

All suffering is bearable
if it is seen as part of a story.
— Isak Dinesen —

The most urgently needed skills of the future will almost certainly not be esoteric but basic, and the most basic will be these: making dinner extend to all the people who need it, making the food last until the next payday or the garden is ready to harvest, making the money meet the end of the month, welcoming the extra mouth to dinner, being able to offer a helping hand to the hungry.

It has been a long time since our culture at large has valued frugal cooking, even though we have taken frugal peasant cooking from many places and called it high cuisine. This should give the lie to anyone who says that frugal cooking means bad or bland food — quite the contrary, we have elevated the cuisine of the frugal peasant housewife and served it in fancy restaurants. If only we had elevated the housewives themselves, we might be better off. There is an art to making a little food go a long way and taste delicious in the course of it, much more art than taking fancy ingredients and making something of them.

There are quite a number of ways of extending meals to include more hungry mouths or make more leftovers. One of the most obvious ways is to substitute "extenders" for the expensive ingredients in a meal. For example, grated zucchini, of which we all have a great deal most years, can be used to extend ground beef in soup. Soy flour can be used to substitute for most of the eggs in baked goods, and extend the baking season when the hens are not laying or local eggs are expensive.

Most of us are accustomed to eating a lot of meat, and one of the best ways to getting used to eating less is to simply cut it down in the recipes we use — make your beef stew with half or ⅓ the meat and more potatoes, onions and carrots.

Things that we are accustomed to buying can be made from scratch — yogurt, tofu, soy sauce, bread, cheese, butter, salad dressings, granola, spice mixtures, any mix of any kind — all these things can be made (usually better) at home and should be. Learning to make our own tofu was a revelation — why had we been paying all that money for that bland stuff when I could have this instead? It does take some practice to get good at making all of these things, but the experimental results are well worth it.

We can and should use parts of our vegetables that we are not accustomed to eating. Broccoli stalks are delicious peeled and can certainly be cut up and added to soups, steamed and frittered, etc. The outer leaves of cabbage, broccoli and Brussels sprouts are just as edible as the main parts, and can be used like cabbage leaves, or they can be dehydrated, ground up and added to flour to stretch it and add vitamins. Carrot greens are more nutritious than the roots, as are turnip and beet greens — these can be used in salads, or dehydrated, or even canned or frozen, but if we do not waste them, if we look at every edible thing in our gardens as something that can keep us from hunger, we will have that much more.

Eggshells should not be wasted. They can be baked and ground up and give to the chickens for calcium, so as to get more eggs, or ground very finely and added 1 part to 10 parts flour to add calcium to our baked goods.

Fats can be reused, carefully. If they are contaminated with bits of burnt material, etc., they can be put on a stove in a pot of water and the clean fat skimmed off for reuse. If fats are in short supply and expensive, one can use one's cooking fats several times for frying and frittering, and, when they start to taste bad, they can be turned into soap.

It was famously said of southern cooks that they used every part of the pig but the squeal. *Little House in the Big Woods* describes butchering time and all the uses the slaughtered pig was put to. If we eat meat, we owe it to the animals to make the best possible use, and no waste, of their sacrifice. That means eating not just the steaks but organs (these can also be used for feeding pets, but they really are quite delicious properly prepared), bones, fats, skin, and everything else we can make use of. Chicken feet make the best soup. We are accustomed to using giblets in gravy or in stuffing, but giblet stuffing with no bird is a fine main course indeed.

Frugality is an art form, a dance, a balance beam on which you are doing cartwheels. You must simultaneously make things beautiful, delicious and artful, and equally, make it seem effortless — that there is always enough.

While we are speaking of frugality, it might be a good time to speak of generosity. They are related to one another — frugality enables generosity. The careful husbanding of your resources on one day enables you to feast on the holiday or celebratory occasion. Good, frugal cooking means you will be able to welcome guests with an open hand, rather than fear that there will not be enough.

One of the obvious, immediate reactions to fear of the future is to protect one's own. But poor cultures generally speaking are far more generous than we are. They recognize that ultimately, you cannot be wholly self-sufficient, cannot depend only on yourself and your resources. The only way for communities to survive in a world where people are regularly short of food is for them to share within the community. Thus, one person's bad luck does not result in disaster.

In *Extending the Table: A World Community Cookbook*, a friend of the author recounts the story of walking in a rural village in Lesotho. She visits a friend, 'Me Malebohang. The woman is cutting up pumpkins and expressing regret over the poor pumpkin harvest, which has left them only eight of this staple vegetable to last the winter. When the author's friend rises to leave, 'Me Malebohang chooses one of the largest pumpkins, and gives it to her. Over the friend's protest, 'Me Malebohang explains, "We Basotho know that this is the way to do it. Next year I may have nothing in my field, and if I don't share with you now, who will share with me than?"[157]

This is how the world of poverty works — within one's community, generosity is an imperative. It is no accident that every faith in the world makes hospitality to the guest and generosity to the poor a central tenet, and that fairy tales reward the generous and punish the greedy. It is no accident that every faith and culture tells the story of the stranger who comes in disguise to receive hospitality and turns out to be a god or king who rewards the good. And these stories arose in a time when everyone had less security than we do. We must learn to think in terms of collective well-being, shake off some of our natural fear and be generous, so that generosity will someday return to us.

Food Storage

The jelly — the jam and the marmalade,
And the cherry-and quince-"preserves" she made!
And the sweet-sour pickles of peach and pear,
With cinnamon in 'em, and all things rare! —
And the more we ate was the more to spare.
— JAMES WHITCOMB RILEY —

It is disturbing to realize that the responsibility for feeding ourselves in a disaster will be ours — we saw this in Hurricane Katrina. We now know that we cannot rely on the government in a crisis. And as many communities have little in the way of preparations, everything you do not only makes it more possible for you to protect yourself and your family from hunger, but also makes it more likely that you will have something to share with your neighbors.

The US government relies on us to store food and be prepared. At a minimum, FEMA and the American Red Cross expect every household to have an emergency evacuation kit, a two-week supply of stored food and water, and ideally, a three-month supply of stored foods and medications for every member of the household. Did you know that? We find that most Americans don't have any idea that the government expects us to be able to rely upon ourselves. If they do, vaguely, remember this from the post 9/11 days, most people ignore it.

That's just foolish. Food storage could do a great deal to ameliorate private hardship or a public disaster. You don't need a massive collapse of infrastructure to be grateful for food storage — just a job loss or a long-term

illness. In fact, you don't even need those things — in an inflationary economy, the food you buy or grow today is worth more tomorrow and can save
you money in the long term.

All of us need to store food and water for hard times. And a solid reserve makes us better able to help the poor and our neighbors, who may
not have been so prescient. It makes us less dependent on handouts from
others and the government. It can enable us to keep our pride intact or reserve resources for those who are even more needy. It can be the difference
between healthy children and hungry ones, between standing in line and
standing on our feet, between not having anything to share and having
enough to give.

Most food storage programs involve buying a lot of food from industrial producers — things such as surplus meals ready to eat (MREs) and
tons of tuna from chain stores. But when we do that, we are voting with
our dollars in support of the industries that operate most against our best
interest and undermining our own Victory Gardens and the new economy
that accompanies them. So we need to think about ways to build food storage that also reinforce our basic values.

So how do we store food sustainably? How do we make our desire be
prepared for the lean years match up with our ethics? Most centrally, we
focus on local food sources, the extras we can grow, and on local farmers
whenever possible. If we are going to buy foods from far away, they should
be long-storing grains and beans, bought from organic farmers, rather than
pre-processed food. Our families' storage is heavy on things bought at our
local food co-op and from local farmers (beans, grains, herbs, spices), the
food we put up from our garden, and a few things (powdered milk, oils
and seasonings) that we cannot provision locally. But it is important to remember that a long enough period of unemployment, illness or crisis will
overwhelm any food storage — there is no way to store enough for the rest
of your life. So food storage is something that works in concert with your
community (because your security depends on everyone having food) and
also with your own practices of replacing what you use — food storage
comes from your garden, which replenishes your stores.

Those of us who live in climates without a year-round growing season need to get used to putting up food in the same ways that our grandparents and their grandparents did. That includes storing dry things dry
(beans, grains); storing fresh foods in cool places (potatoes, onions, garlic, apples, pears, pumpkins, squash, sweet potatoes, beets, daikon, carrots,

parsnips, burdock, cabbage); using season-extension techniques so that we can keep growing during the cold or dry season (cold frames, pit gardens, hoop houses, sunny windowsills, shade gardens); dehydrating, either by solar or low-energy usage (berries, many fruits, many vegetables, fruit leathers, jerky, dried meat and fish); lacto fermenting, which means allowing vegetables to ferment naturally and then putting them in a cool place like a cellar or in the ground (pickles of all sorts, sauerkraut, many kinds of kimchi, pickled greens); and the more traditional canning and freezing, if the power for these methods is there.

Squash, pumpkins, sweet potatoes all can live at reasonably cool human temperatures. They are best stored in closets and under beds in our houses. We can design our houses to have a cool place that will not freeze in the winter to store our food. And we should make sure that we find room in a spare closet or guest room to store enough food to last us for a while in hard times.

As the world food crisis has grown, there has been an attempt to describe those who simply store food prudently as "hoarders" and to suggest that this is unpatriotic. If you will forgive our descent into the vernacular, this is complete and utter bullshit. All locations and cultures have a dry or hot or cold season in which many foods are not available, and all cultures in human history have responded to this by storing some foods, whether for short or long periods. The idea that one of the most ordinary acts in human history should be stigmatized is deeply troubling.

Meat or No Meat?

*Centuries ago, sailors on long voyages used to
leave a pair of pigs on every deserted island.
Or they'd leave a pair of goats.
Either way, on any future visit,
the island would be a source of meat.
These islands, they were pristine. These were home to breeds
of birds with no natural predators. Breeds of birds that
lived nowhere else on earth. The plants there, without enemies
they evolved without thorns or poisons. Without predators
and enemies, these islands, they were paradise.
The sailors, the next time they visited these islands,*

the only things still there would be herds of goats or pigs....
Does this remind you of anything?
Maybe the ol' Adam and Eve story?....
You ever wonder when God's coming back
with a lot of barbecue sauce?
— CHUCK PALAHANIUK —

Aaron is a vegetarian and Sharon is not, although her family eats meat only once or twice a week, and only meat they raise or that is produced locally. Both of us believe strongly that we will all be eating less meat in the future. The environmental impact of factory-farmed meat is disastrous. A University of Chicago study recently demonstrated that an average household would reduce their carbon emissions and energy consumption more by giving up eating an animal-product based diet than by buying a hybrid.[158] Most of the grains grown in the US currently go to feeding livestock. The two biggest stresses on the world's food supply are meat eating and the demand for biofuels. That is, we have enough food to go around, but we are using it inequitably, producing lots of meat for the wealthy in the Global North and starving the poor of the south.

Whatever we eat in the future, it will not look like the present. No one, save the Inuit, will live on anything resembling the Atkins diet. Most of us will simply eat fewer animal products as a whole. There simply are not enough resources to go around — if just the Chinese were to eat meat in the same quantities we do, they would use two-thirds of the world's grain harvest, leaving billions of people starving.

All of us must cease eating factory-farmed meat, milk and eggs immediately — that is a non-negotiable. The environmental and ethical costs are simply too great. The cheap meat that has enabled us to add more and more animal products to our diet comes at a cost to future generations, other people and the planet that is simply unacceptable. If this troubles you — get over it. There is no way around the fact that all of us must eat less meat, and from better sources.

If all that is true, however, why isn't Sharon a vegetarian? The reason is this — animals are too useful to us to be left out of sustainable polyculture. And all meat production was not created equal. The animals we raise in our backyard, or hunt sustainably and carefully in the wild, or that farmers raise on grass on land that is otherwise too rocky or steep to grow vegetables on, is of a great deal of utility. And because those of us growing much of our food in the cold part of the US and Canada are likely to experience some difficulty growing enough easily produced fats, it makes a great deal of sense to use butter and animal fats — in limited quantities. A recent Cornell University study found that the state of New York could feed a larger percentage of its population if we added small amounts of meat, milk and eggs to maximize our use of land.[159]

Even small gardens can make some use of chickens or rabbits to eat weeds and scraps of food that humans would not. Meat is likely to be an occasional, festive treat, much enjoyed, much appreciated, but rarely eaten, and mostly as a flavoring. If you eat meat and are not eating this way now, it is time to begin.

Vegetarianism is one way to ensure that grains grown go to human uses, not animal ones. So is eating small amounts of homegrown or locally grown, grass-fed meat. Animals are good at turning things like grass, which we cannot eat, into food we can, and as long as we treat them humanely and kill them carefully, feeding them mostly food that human beings would not be able to eat anyway, neither Aaron nor I believe that it is ethically wrong to eat animals. After all, domestic livestock would not exist at all without us. Sharon believes it is better that her hens have life, have their two years in the sun scratching around the yard, and then be rapidly and peacefully killed and respectfully eaten than that they do not live at all. Aaron's hens will live out their full lives laying eggs if they can continue to successfully forage from his yard and he can continue to provide enough scraps from the garden and the kitchen to adequately feed them.

On the other hand, neither do we wish to give the impression that vegetarianism is not a wise choice. As long as we eat eggs or milk, we do not need any other animal products at all. Vegans require small quantities of vitamins, which may be difficult to acquire if supplements are not readily available, but which are abundant now. But whether we choose not to eat animals at all or to eat them occasionally, we must take real responsibility for the harm our diets do to others. Vegetarian diets often do much less harm than those of meat eaters.

If we are going to eat meat, or eat at all, we need to know where the food we're consuming comes from and take responsibility for the life and death of the animals we eat. This can be very hard — many of us are squeamish about killing — but most of us aren't so squeamish we won't eat meat. We're just too squeamish to kill our own. Ultimately this means many of us settle for industrial meat which is bad for everyone, especially small people.

We are willing to put up with industrial meat that is incredibly toxic and inhumane, inferior and sometimes contaminated simply to avoid having to kill a chicken. If we choose to eat meat, what we eat must reflect a just set of priorities. In the end, we should be willing to do our harm in our own neighborhoods. We must ameliorate and limit that harm as much as possible and find a way back to a relationship with and responsibility for both the life we create and the deaths we create.

The Really Local Diet

Until you do what you believe in,
you don't know whether you believe it or not.
— TOLSTOY —

For the most part, even those of us who try and eat 100 Mile Diets have diets that look a lot like everyone else's 100 Mile Diets. Farmers are mostly growing the same crops, during the same seasons, that everyone else does. And this was fine as the beginning of local eating, but we can't base either a true local cuisine or a low-energy, low-carbon society on diets that aren't local to their soils, their climate, their agriculture.

For example, Sharon lives in the cold, rocky, rainy, northeast, on land that gets more than 50 inches of rain per year and has fewer than 10 days over 90 degrees most years. Even in the hottest weather, most nights are in the 60s, and temperatures often fall into the 40s even in high summer. Hills are steep and often can't grow vegetables or grains without significant terracing. The soils have heavy leaching of nutrients and are acidic, which means that some plants grow better than others. There are better soils in the valleys and river plateaus nearby, including naturally high-lime soils good for growing things like alfalfa.

So what would her local diet look like? It would probably be low in heat-loving plants that go dormant when night temperatures fall below 50, such as hot peppers, okra and sweet potatoes. It isn't that she can't grow them — Sharon can — but they wouldn't be staples of her diet. Instead, potatoes, short-season corns, oats, rye and roots such as parsnips, beets and carrots would probably act as her family's staples.

Because Sharon has a lot of land too hilly to till, it would make the most sense to graze animals on it, and eat the animals or drink their milk when the grass is lush. Because the land tends to be wet, livestock breeds that tolerate wet conditions well makes sense, along with ones adapted to cold places. Romney, Icelandic, Soay or other sheep might well fit the bill, as would Scottish Highland or Dexter cattle. Right now, Sharon has Nigerian Dwarf goats that have adapted well to her location. Milk would be a good summer crop — cows and goats that can produce enough milk on grass alone make sense here because ample rain means that the pasture rarely goes dormant.

Instead of soybeans, this area would grow New England-bred bean varieties such as Jacob's Cattle and Maine Yellow Eye. Favas and peas also do well. But beans like limas, black beans and pintos are simply high-effort crops to grow on a field scale in Sharon's region, so she would eat fewer of them.

For oils, butter would probably make the most sense, given the abundant pastures. And farmers in the region might experiment with oilseed pumpkins and sunflowers to replace olive oil. The area can certainly grow mustard in the summers, and mustard seed oil is quite delicious.

Sharon can grow leafy greens easily all summer — she doesn't have problems with bolting in her climate. The same is true for cole crops and almost all roots. And she needs roots because they store so well over the winter. Onions are particularly well suited to the sulfuric soils of the area — they grow well, store well, and add a lot of flavor to food, as does garlic.

Apples, hazelnuts, black walnuts, hickory nuts, sunflower seeds, pumpkin seeds, quinces, plums, pears, raspberries, strawberries, and many indigenous cold-climate fruits such as lingonberries and sea buckthorn would probably become the primary fruits, nuts and seeds along with many others. Wild mushrooms, wild greens and other wild foods would be daily additions.

Aaron's local diet would be completely different — although delicious in its own right. The traditional foods of the Southeast are corn, sweet potatoes, heat-tolerant greens and beans. And the residue of that traditional diet still exists in Southern culture, in the form of sweet potato pie, collards and cornbread, just as Northeastern culture uses things like baked beans and potatoes. In some senses, we will be returning to the diets of the people who lived in places before us.

Aaron's area is hot, with a year-round growing season and summer temperatures that can make it difficult to grow through the months of July and August. His summers will be abundant in watermelons, hot peppers, tomatoes and okra, crops that Sharon struggles to grow. Meanwhile Aaron will eat lettuce salads only in spring, fall and winter, as summer greens bolt instantly and refuse to grow. Where Sharon struggles to replace nutrients leached away in the rain, Aaron must husband his water, as the drought in the Southeast stresses the region.

Aaron's diet will look different than Sharon's — he'll eat more fresh foods in the winter and store more foods for the summer hot season. He'll grow when there is rain and use different flavorings. He might have milk to drink in spring, fall and winter but none when grasses are dry in the summer. As his region gets warmer, Aaron may grow more and more tropical plants and be able to derive more and more of his food from perennial plantings with low tolerances for cold — eating homegrown olive oil or hardy bananas.

Their foods will be shaped by the seasons, the soil, the climate, the culture in ways that are hard to imagine in these days of supermarket mono-diets. And that will be the beginnings of their new cuisines, shaped by past and future. The truth is that all our diets are about to become truly local.

And a Fair Share

We learn from our gardens
to deal with the most urgent question of the time:
How much is enough?
— WENDELL BERRY —

Sharon doesn't really enjoy admitting this, but she has been carrying around more than a few extra pounds (Aaron is practically an elf and doesn't have this issue), and this is one of those little things that we don't talk a whole lot about in discussions of equity. That is, when we talk about equal food for everyone, we very rarely own up to our own deficiencies in the "eating only a fair share" department.

As we write this it is Thanksgiving. Heading into the winter holidays is a terrible, terrible time to start a diet, and since we pretty much make it a firm policy not to advise anyone to do anything we're not prepared to do, Sharon wants us to be absolutely clear — clear we don't want anyone to start one. She's not giving up her pumpkin pie.

And that's appropriate — feasting is a good thing. It is important — there should be times in our lives when we live lushly, when we rejoice in full larders and the pleasures of excess. We may be into energy-related austerity, but we're also all for sensual pleasures and the delights of communal festivity. There should be times when the food and the wine flow without restraint.

The problem is that in the wealthy Global North we are always in feast mode, almost always without restraint. We can eat what was once a month's work of luxury foods in a single meal at a chain restaurant; we can have whatever we want, whenever we want. We live in a culture where it is hard to tell feast days apart from ordinary ones — except, perhaps that in many homes Thanksgiving is the one time in a year anyone eats a root vegetable that isn't a french fry and the one time a year anyone cooks from scratch.

So, far be it from us to discourage any of us from feasting. But the thing that Sharon is trying to bring herself to remember is this: just as seasonal eating represents an increase in pure sensual delight, a newfound pleasure in eating things when they are at their peak, and only then, so would greater restraint make our moments of feasting more pleasurable. That is, we could enjoy our feasts without the slightest hint of discomfort if we ate less the rest of the time, if our current meals were a bit more austere.

And doing so would be both just and fiscally sound — the reality is that many of us eat more than we need to and more of the rich, luxurious fats and sweets that are supposed to be an occasional treat. Our goals, as we come out of the feasting season, and into the quieter, leaner times of winter, should not be so much to lose weight (although that would be good) or eat less, but to derive more pleasure from what we do eat — that is, to feast thoroughly and fully with great pleasure and no discomfort, and then, in the ordinary days in between, to take as much pleasure from lighter and simpler things as we did from our feasts. We should be seeking to eat less and appreciate more the beauty and simplicity of food and the way that simpler meals with less fat and sweet and salt, more vegetables, greens, beans and grains, are both delightful in themselves, and a way of heightening the pleasure of our feasting days.

An Interview with Thomas Princen: Spring 2008

Thomas Princen is the author of *The Logic of Sufficiency*, which explores the possibilities of an ethic of "sufficiency" rather than "efficiency" as a driving force for our way of life. He's a professor of natural resources and

environmental policy at University of Michigan and one of the most brilliant minds exploring the complex questions of how we shall go on in our
changing future.

ANOF: You describe material security as being not necessarily in opposition to the idea of ecological integrity and diversity but that in fact the opposite is true — that if we pay attention to the integrity of the environment
and we protect its diversity we actually ensure the material security of our
systems. Am I describing that accurately?

THOMAS: Or maybe put it in the negative: without ecological integrity
we cannot have material security.

ANOF: So what would you say is driving the difference between the way
our culture regards its environment and the relationships of other cultures
with their environments? And I'm thinking here more of previous cultures
that have been more respectful and more in tune with the limits of their
environment. Why is it that we seemed to have tossed that wisdom out the
window?

THOMAS: That's a big question: what all the drivers are. In some sense,
the whole project of modernity is behind us…. If we look at the way our
current economy is structured, that comes out of an era with a long history
where resource abundance was the norm. And if abundance could not be
found in one's locality, there was always another locality, another frontier
to extract from. I think that [is one reason] in combination with scientific
revolution and technological advance and the seeming ability to always
squeeze out more goods from a given resource, whether its land or water or
genetic diversity; it always seems like there is more. And in some sense there
has been for a long time. Like I said, there's just always another frontier.

And at the same time, hunger and famine were the norm. I think that's
very hard for us — Americans in the last half-century — to really understand how pervasive that was for so much of human history. And so the
project was one of production — producing more goods, because obviously goods are good and more goods are better. And not only was there an
abundance of resources, there was an abundance of waste sinks. So I think
in a nutshell, it has only been in the last 20 years or so that we've gotten to
this point in human history that we're bumping up against an ecological
wall where we've filled the waste sinks and now the costs are coming back
to haunt us.

ANOF: For those who aren't familiar with your book *The Logic of Sufficiency*, could you contrast the thinking of today that focuses on efficiency with the idea that you proposed: the idea of sufficiency?

THOMAS: Okay. Well, first of all, efficiency is a perfectly good idea. We all know that for a given amount of effort, if we can figure out how to get a little more benefit for that effort, we're all better off. Or similarly, for a given benefit, if we can use less effort, less toil, less energy, less drudgery and less wear and tear on our bodies and so forth, we know that we're better off. Moreover, from a biological perspective, it's more reasonable that those organisms that got more bang for the buck were more likely to reproduce and pass on their traits to their progeny. Efficiency is, in some sense, built into our biological being and the biological being of other organisms, so it's very natural in that sense. But the way it has become, in the last century or so, the way the term itself has evolved linguistically and rhetorically, it has moved from being a perfectly good idea, a perfectly natural, normal idea to one that in the first instance was highly useful for industrialization, for making machines more efficient, or more effective I should say.... for making people's interactions with machines more effective. (We call that efficient.) And if the terms had stayed in those usages — whether it was the biological or the strictly mechanistic or the human and the mechanistic — it would probably not be a problem.

But it has really seeped out of the factory floor, if you will, and has permeated all of society. So it's become not just a good idea but a broad social organizing principle that's so pervasive, so commonplace, that it's the water in which we swim. We don't examine it; we don't think about it; we don't stop to question what exactly the efficiency is, what is the ratio of good to the effort we expend. And so, because efficiencies necessarily are ambiguous in what they express, they open political space for manipulation, and we've gotten to the point now where we can have leaders say that we will improve the efficiency, the pollution intensity of our economy to deal with global warming, which appears to mean that we will reduce emissions, but in fact we increase emissions. That's when the concept of efficiency shifts from a very useful term to a maladaptive term.

ANOF: When examining industrial agriculture, it seems that the idea of efficiency can be focused on any number of inputs. Industrial agriculture has been largely about making the practice of growing food more efficient in terms of human labor, but it's done so to the detriment of the natural world and the natural systems that could more sustainably provide food. In other words, we've minimized the number of people it takes to grow food, but we've done so at a great cost to a number of the other systems it takes to grow food. It sounds as if sufficiency is a principle that would address efficiency in agriculture in terms of human labor at the expense of soils, water degradation and the fossil fuel energy, etc., and think about agriculture more holistically.

THOMAS: Well, I think so. I think [we need] to apply a rich, or deep, notion of sufficiency, which is more than "just enough," "good enough;" rather it's "the best, given the aim of" any number of aims beyond that which could be reduced to a simple metric like bushels per acre per man-hour. I think what the potential is (and I think you're right with the term holistic) of concepts like sufficiency and that sort of stuff is that…it enables one to be very precise about what exactly the objective is. So in industrial agriculture, as I read it, the immediate objective might be bushels per acre, but the larger goal, I think, if you pushed its proponents a little bit, it is to feed people, generate wealth, grow the economy, provide jobs and a whole bunch of other things. So in a sense, they actually do have a somewhat holistic view. But it's one that presumes there's abundant resources, endlessly renewing topsoil, fresh water and waste sinks and so forth. And I think what the non-industrial, alternative agriculture necessarily says is we've got to get a much larger piece, both on the biophysical side and on the social side.

ANOF: A lot of politicians are saying that if we do more to protect the environment, it's going to hurt us economically. What's your response to that sort of thinking?

THOMAS: Well, the first thing is that with the kinds of changes that are now occurring…I think the burden is increasingly shifting to those that are advocates of business as usual, albeit with a bit of greening and more efficiencies; the burden is shifting to them to show that pursuing business as usual, degrading ecosystems, filling waste sinks, increasing the gap between the rich and the poor, depriving people of basic needs and so forth, somehow that will not destroy the economy. Because all the evidence, it seems to me, from the food crisis to the fuel crisis to the financial crisis that we're experiencing right now in April 2008, even though no one can prove that the entire system is in crisis, I think the weight of evidence all points in that direction. So those who wish to somehow divide the material world between the ecological, as if that were just a luxury or an externality, and economics, as if that was the real thing — the burden is on them to prove that they can keep on doing it and not destroy the planet.

ANOF: Currently people seem to be focusing largely on supply-side fixes. In other words, other resources that we can turn to in order to keep the larger machine of industrialism and modernity going. If we run out of gas, no problem, we can make ethanol. It seems to me that the camp splits between those who are continuing to say we'll have more supply, and those who are interested in reducing demand. I'm wondering about your thoughts concerning how we might best address resource depletion in terms of demand-side responses and supply-side responses.

THOMAS: Let me see if I can just take a couple of points on it. One is to get a society on a sustainable path. I think it's ultimately unhelpful to separate [the economic question] into supply and demand, production and consumption. There's obviously some utility in that, but [to include] the overarching principles, such as no waste, we have to have an economy that has no waste. That is a fundamental, biophysical, ecological principle, and it has to be a social principle. And that doesn't divide neatly between production and consumption. So that's just one example. And I think it's sufficient....

Sufficiency, I would like to think, is more of an integrating concept across production and consumption.... There's a twin rhetorical device — on the one hand there are those who say we just need to get new supplies, and on the other hand, well, consumers need to work on the demand side. I think those actually go together, not into two different camps, because what they both do is deflect attention from the real nature of the problem, in many cases filling up waste sinks. And [those on] the demand side [say] the consumers need to buy better, buy greener; that deflects not just attention but responsibility from those who are proceeding to fill the atmosphere with greenhouse gases and extracting hydrocarbons at ever-increasing rates and so forth. To shift attention, to shift the burden in a sense, to the individual consumer is to shift the responsibility away from those not just who are producing but those who are writing the rules of the game, those who are creating a system that makes it not just possible but virtually imperative to keep this whole fossil-fuel-based economy roaring ahead as if we could do it forever. I think there's a little bit in the book about how constructing a consumer as a role, and elevating it, deflects attention from those who are really responsible for the current and unsustainable system.

ANOF: I'm asking you to solve one of the world's biggest problems!
THOMAS: I'll give you a big, grand answer too. It is to change the norms. And that's very much a purpose of this work on overconsumption and sufficiency — to make normal that which seems either superfluous or trivial or fringe in a hard-charging, fast-paced industrial consumeristic society. And part of making it normal is telling good stories, and part of it is also finding the language.

I just came across a quote recently that hit home. This is from Richard Rorty, the philosopher. To paraphrase it, it was something like, "Fundamental social transformation occurs when people learn to speak differently, not argue well." And so I think much of the environmental movement and back to the land and so forth has been about arguing well, and we have to learn how to speak differently. So much of what we've talked about already this morning I think is of that sort, is rejecting the producer/consumer dichotomy, rejecting the idea that people respond primarily to prices and the force of government. Well, we know that's not true, so let's speak as if it's not true, and find the language to do so.

— RECIPES —

Ginger Spice Tea   *by Tom Princen*

Time
Preparation: 10 minutes; 1½ hours of simmering

Ingredients
- 2 pinches anise seed
- 2 cloves
- 6 fresh ginger pieces, sliced thin, each about the size of a quarter
- 1 pinch cayenne pepper powder
- 1 date

Directions
1. Lightly simmer all ingredients for at least an hour in three quarts water. Adjust water and cayenne to taste.
2. If the tea is to be stored for more than a day, withhold the date and add sweetener at time of use.
3. For added anti-inflammatory, anti-oxidant effect (or so a nutritionist with Aryuvedic leanings once told me), put a quarter teaspoon of turmeric in a mug and pour in hot ginger tea to steep for 15 minutes. Don't boil the turmeric as

that presumably destroys the anti-oxidant effect (and yet is required of the ginger to extract its essences — why the difference, I don't know).

What-the-Heck-Am-I-Going-to-Do-With-All-of-These-Cherries Crisp   *by Gina Mendolo*

For when you have more than a sufficiency of cherries. This can be adapted to take advantage of gluts of any fruit.

Note: this recipe is soy-free and egg-free. It can be made vegan by substituting margarine or any oil for the butter and it can be made gluten free by substituting more almond meal for the all-purpose flour.

Ingredients
- ¾ cup butter, melted
- ½ cup flour
- ¼ tsp almond extract
- pinch nutmeg
- 1 cup oats, uncooked
- ¼ cup white sugar
- ⅛ tsp cinnamon
- 3 cups cherries, pitted
- ½ cup almond meal (or finely ground almonds — other nuts will work too)
- 1 cup brown sugar (honey or maple syrup can be substituted)

Directions
1. Preheat oven to 350 degrees.
2. Grease a 9-inch baking dish.
3. Combine all ingredients except cherries in a bowl.
4. Press half of the flour and sugar mixture into the bottom of the pan to form a crust.
5. Pour cherries over the crust.
6. Sprinkle the remaining and sugar mixture over the cherries.
7. Bake for 30 minutes. Can be baked in a solar oven.

Homemade Granola Bars   *by Sharon*

Every house with kids (and maybe every house) needs treats. This is one of my kids' favorites — and mine, because it really is no trouble to adapt this recipe to what you have. Flavor it with anything you want; just keep the rough proportions of wet to dry the same. We like them with dried apricots and strawberries in them, and I once let my kids dip them in chocolate but that's not going to win me any awards either for environmentalism or healthy parenting, so we'll skip over the details. And we'll leave out how many of them I ate.

Ingredients
- 3 cups rolled oats (old fashioned or instant)
- ¼ cup amaranth or coconut

- 1 cup peanut, almond or cashew butter
- ¼ cup sesame seeds, poppy seeds, sunflower seeds or pepitos (pumpkin seeds)
- ½ cup wheat germ or bulgur
- ½ cup slivered almonds or chopped hazelnuts
- 4 tablespoons butter or oil
- 3 tbsp brown sugar
- ¼ cup honey, molasses or sorghum
- 1 cup raisins, dried cranberries or other dried fruit (chopped to raisin size if bigger)
- 2 teaspoons vanilla extract
- 1 tsp cinnamon
- (You can leave things out or make substitutions if ingredients don't suit or aren't available.)

Directions

1. Bake the oats, coconut/amaranth, sunflower/sesame seeds, wheat germ/bulgur and nuts on a 9-by-12-inch baking sheet for 20 minutes, starting as you preheat your oven to 300 degrees.
2. Heat the butter, brown sugar, nut butter and honey in a small saucepan, simmering while the dried ingredients are baking. (I leave the out sugar if the peanut butter is already sweetened.)
3. Add the raisins/dried fruit to the toasted mix as soon as it's removed from the oven.
4. Remove the saucepan from the heat, mix in the vanilla extract and pour the liquid mix over the oat mixture, stirring until all the dried mixture is coated.
5. Press the granola firmly into the bottom of a greased 8-by-8-inch pan and place the pan in the still-warm oven to bake (at 300°) for 20 minutes. You can cut the batch into bars after the granola has cooled slightly, but wait to take the bars out of the pan until they're completely cool.

CHAPTER 4

God's Away on Business

What Are Our Choices?

The ship is sinking, the ship is sinking
There's a leak, there's a leak,
in the boiler room,
The poor, the lame, the blind,
Who are the ones who are kept in charge?
Killers, thieves and lawyers.
God's away, God's away,
God's away on business.

— TOM WAITS —

AARON: Fifty miles outside of a big city might not seem like all that far, but my parents live in a convincingly rural redneck area of the woods, about that distance from Charlotte. The last stretch of the journey to their home was paved only a few years ago. In this part of North Carolina farming is still alive and well — if largely industrialized — with cropland interspersed between logging clear cuts and commuter cul-de-sac communities servicing the big city some distance away. Still, there are long stretches of country road where the view is just what you might expect from the rolling foothills of the Appalachian Mountains. It is beautiful country.

My stepfather grew up not too far away, and after years of moving around, he and my mother settled again in a home we built as a family. The house is 60 feet from the Yadkin River, just a day's upstream paddle from Uwharrie National Forest. Theirs is a home in the woods.

A few years back my parents bought an additional three acres up the street from their address. It was mostly cleared, and they purchased it as an investment. Still unsure as to when and if they would build a house for sale on this parcel, my stepfather decided to farm it. "I'm going to buy a tractor," he informed me one sunny summer afternoon. He never quite got to mentioning growing food, but I gathered that was the gist of it.

My stepfather has a history of renovating old contraptions. He was planning to buy an old tractor, a classic red Massey Ferguson long associated with the small- to medium-sized farms throughout our area, and when he talked about "fixing it up," I knew he meant completely restoring the old red iron horse.

When I went to visit he would have parts and pieces laid out all over the garage floor, and he would be full of explanations about who he had lined up to repaint the old body parts or retool some of the key piece of his mechanized agricultural puzzle. He was plainly delighted by the challenge.

For Christmas that year I offered him a gift certificate to Seeds of Change, one of my favorite seed companies, so he could purchase his spring seeds, and a copy of John Jeavons' biointensive handbook, *How to Grow More Vegetables*. Jeavons' book is about the power of small-scale hand agriculture to maximize food production. It became clear that my stepfather and I were seeing his project very differently.

It's important for me to say that one my first experiences in farming was not dissimilar to my stepfather's. I didn't have a tractor, but had my city lot been bigger, I might have purchased one. I was born into the tractor era, and that's how I thought about growing food. A tractor turns the soil. A tractor prepares the furrows. A person (or sometimes a tractor) plants the seed in rows. And a combination of tractor and human with hoe hold back the onslaught of unwanted weeds while water is provided by irrigation.

My first garden was in raised beds, but it was row planted in bare soil, carrots in one bed, beans in another. Far be it from me to suggest that it is easy to overcome what we've been taught about late-20th-century agriculture. And those messages have been part of my stepfather's life far longer than they were part of mine. The mental picture of industrial agriculture has engulfed us all.

Our collective image of farming has become a field plowed by red tractors, and this restored iconic piece of farm machinery became admirable, powerful, even beautiful. It was, dare I say, parade ready.

But the tractor allowed him to turn over more square footage than was necessary. It meant a clean slate for not only the crops he grew in straight rows across more than an acre of his land but also for the weeds that inevitably dogged the garden, awakened by disturbed soil. Bugs and other pests were drawn to the large patches of single crops. The heat and the sun baked the red clay that surrounded each plant and helped to dry the soil, which would shun the first of any rain as the nutrient-rich clay ran off to enter into the small creek nearby. The remaining soil waited in vain for the input of organic matter and the interaction of microorganisms that would follow and colonize to create the densely populated ecosystem that is the topsoil of our world. The restoration of a vibrant web of life on many such sites still waits.

My parents produced lots of food from that garden. Subsequent years have seen a smaller effort. Their lives are busy, a problem as acute for me as for them, as I type this story in the spring of 2008 — inside my home instead of out in the garden.

We Americans have arranged our lives in such a way that the idea of spending more time in the garden is a dream that requires the dismantling of other preconceived notions; ideas about how we could live differently require us to rewrite the meeting of our needs and indeed the very definition of need.

But I also believe my parents stopped gardening in part because of the time it took to cultivate such a large tract of land in a way that worked against the helping hand of nature. Americans think big — we take on too much and we want to approach such undertakings in familiar ways. But too much and too close a fixation on our tools can keep us from realizing the potential of others' ways of accomplishing our goals. Weeds can be largely eliminated if mulch is used after planting. This helps to hold in precious moisture and to slow down the runoff of rain before the earth can begin to accept the water.

Planting many different crops together and in specific combinations can help avoid offering the all-you-can-eat monocrop buffet to insects that would like to devour all that is planted. Growing cover crops specifically to hold soil, choke out weeds, and to feed the soil can help build soil fertility, add carbon (and remove it from the atmosphere) and provide the basis for a community of micro-organisms crucial to the long-term fruitfulness of the soil.

A tractor is overkill for many small gardeners and farmers. We have to look beyond it — but we can't do so unless we approach our food systems with fresh eyes and open minds. All of us can partici-pate, even, and perhaps especially, without a tractor.

It Was the Best of Times, It Was the End of Times

In the future, airplanes will be flown by a dog and a pilot.
And the dog's job will be to make sure that if the pilot
tries to touch any of the buttons, the dog bites him.
— Scott Adams —

Growing up in the past half century, most of us spent a lot of time exposed to imagined visions of our future. We encountered them in science fiction novels, comic books, or on TV, and we've spent much of the past hun-dred years with our necks craned as far as possible, trying to see into the future. And the future, as portrayed in almost every one of these visions, is progressive, moving forward, solving problems and making things better. Think about it — from the Jetsons (where's my flying car?) to *Star Trek*, where all problems except the Klingons have essentially been conquered. Medical and technological journals made projections that describe how magic technologies will fix everything, and economists and their reporters saw us moving toward a perfect, globalized world, united in capitalism. All the visions of the future with which we are familiar entail going forward as we are but becoming better through advancements that make us more ho-mogenized, more technologically advanced, to the logical culmination of our perfection.

Or, they don't. In the same genre, there's *Battlestar Galactica*, in which the remnants of a decimated population have to seek a new world after an apocalypse. There is an entire film genre dedicated to the imagined after-math of human cvilization gone wrong, from the low-budget 1975 clas-sic *A Boy and His Dog* and the *Mad Max* movies of the early '80s to the time twisted *Terminator* series in which people of a devasted future go so far as to send heroes back in time to try and prevent an apocalypse. For every novel that imagines us enjoying our leisure with robots that do all our work, there's a reciprocal novel like Cormac Mc Carthy's apocalyptic *The Road,* which imagines us wandering hopelessly in an utter wasteland.

Ever since we realized, in the 1940s, that nuclear weapons meant that we really could destroy the entire world, we've been fascinated by this flip side of our progress — the ability to utterly annihilate ourselves, the logical contrast to the idea that we can become the perfect species, *Homo technologicus,* roaming the galaxy in our faster-than-light spaceships, civilizing other peoples on other planets.

Thus, it is perhaps no great surprise that if you ask most people about the problems discussed in the previous chapter, you will find that most of us place a great deal of faith in growth-market solutions and new technologies, and a smaller, but equally certain group feels that we are bound for complete and utter self destruction. After all, those are the choices that our culture has given us. Virtually everyone living in Western society grew up with those choices presented to them as starkly as possible.

But as we discussed before, market and technological solutions are beginning to fail and show no signs of being able to solve our problems. Does that mean we're bound for an inevitable disaster, an absolute and utter apocalypse? Some people think so. For example, Gaia-hypothesis creator, scientist James Lovelock, imagines that within a hundred years human beings will be limited to "a few breeding pairs at the poles." No wonder most people prefer to believe that something — the market, scientific solutions, divine intervention, extraterrestrial technologies — will fix our problems. After all, what is the point of contemplating the absolute and utter destruction of everything? Why not deny that there are problems at all, or perhaps place our hopes on the assumption that anyone who says they can develop another technology if just given enough money? Moreover, what possible incentive could any of us ever have for overcoming our trained faith in capitalism and technology if the best alternative we can be offered is a chance to hole up in a bunker with some Spam and an automatic weapon?

But like all dichotomies, the choice to "rely on technology and growth to perfect us" or "accept the end of the world" is a false one. There are other options, but we have not been taught to see them. We have been told for so long that all we have is to go forward as we are or accept absolute annihilation that we have come to believe that we cannot change our course and move in some new and different way. But this is not true, and the first step in recognizing this is to learn to see false dichotomy for what it is. Then we can begin to look around at alternatives.

Writer and activist Maria Mies writes in her seminal book (written with Veronika Bennholdt-Thomsen), *The Subsistence Perspective,* about the fixity with which many people believe that these are the only choices. She talks about attending a panel in Germany with a number of scientists prognosticating an absolutely bleak future for the world, and then goes on to answer them by observing,

> I looked at the audience: all young people with worried faces. They had come on this Sunday morning to get some orientation from these famous speakers for their own future. But they only painted an apocalyptic picture gloom and hopelessness. The gist of their presentations was that there was no alternative, that we could do nothing. I could not tolerate this pessimism any longer and said, "Please, don't forget where we are. We are in Trier, in the midst of the ruins of what once was one of the capitals of the Roman empire. An empire whose collapse people then thought would mean the end of the world. But the world did not come to an end with the end of Rome. The plough of my father, a peasant in the Eifel, used to hit the stones of the Roman road that connected Trier with Cologne. On this road where the Roman legions had marched, grass had gown, and now we grew our potatoes on that road." I wanted to say that even the collapse of big empires does not mean the end of the world; rather, people then begin to understand what is important in life, namely our subsistence.... The image of my father behind the plough on the old Roman road stands for another philosophy, another logic. For most...scientists this subsistence logic is difficult to grasp. It is neither expressed in the slogan that "life will go on by itself" (nature will regenerate herself, grass will grow by itself) nor by the attitude that we humans can control nature and repair all damage done by our master technology. The difference between a subsistence orientation and scientific omnipotence mania is the understanding that life neither simply regenerates itself, nor is it an invention of engineers; rather, we as natural beings, have to cooperate with nature if we want life to continue.[160]

Here Mies begins to articulate the possibility of something in between apocalypse and progress, a new way of thinking. She and Bennholdt-

Thomsen call this "the subsistence perspective," but it might also be described as a return to cyclical, rather than linear, thinking and living. What she describes is the idea of our integration into history and nature, rather than a choice between our mastery over both forces or our utter destruction at their hands.

Our culture has been dominated by the linear thinking. We have been trained to believe that we are at the "end of history," as neoconservative thinker Francis Fukuyama puts it. But the history of our thoughts and lives also contains a powerful undercurrent of the subsistence perspective. That is, there's an existing, permanent tension between two ways of thinking, but in the past century, the progressive narrative, in which we are headed to perfection or doom, has overtaken the cyclical one.

Viewing our thought as caught in a tension between two ways of understanding the world might also help us navigate the question of our ability to change — because, of course, the Big Lie, as we've named it, says that we can't change course, and while we have plentiful examples of people doing so, it is also true that we are handicapped by enormous inertia. But if we imagine ourselves as always caught between two urges — moving toward a more natural and equitable society while simultaneously being driven away from that goal — we can perhaps begin to see that it is possible that we could alter our course and also recognize the difficulties in doing so. Thus, as we discussed in Chapter 2, it is possible to have multiple simultaneous histories — the histories of ordinary resistance and the histories of the powerful's attempts to remain powerful.

It might be useful here to explore the differences between species of thought that are linear and climactic and those that are cyclical. There are alternative ways of thinking to those that imagine that history ends in a vast denouement, or as the end of the fairytale suggests, that "they lived happily ever after." There are cyclical patterns of thinking that imagine instead a steady state of life that strives not for dominance or submission but for a continued balance.

Linear models include modern growth capitalist/globalization orthodoxy. *New York Times* columnist Thomas Friedman offers one example. Friedman, in his book *The Lexus and the Olive Tree,* claims that there simply are no alternatives to the present model, likening the economic choices to ice cream flavors, saying, "There is no more mint chocolate chip, there is no more strawberry swirl, there is no more lemon-lime. Today there is only plain vanilla and North Korea."[161] That is, Friedman claims that the only

economic choices are the worst kind of dictatorship or free market glo-
balism. Besides being factually inaccurate (there are many other economic
models out there), his own paradigm is articulated as a loss of choice and a
loss of freedom, with no chance of interesting variation and pleasure.

Moreover, if we were to take Friedman seriously, we'd be throwing good
energies after bad. For the past 50 years, the notion that if we just make very
rich people richer some of that money will trickle down to the poor and
make them less poor has been the standard orthodoxy. And for 50 years,
that has simply been untrue. Some nations, notably China and India, have
redistributed wealth, but many economists have argued that this redistribution was essentially taking money from the American working class and
redistributing it to the people of India and China. The concentration of
wealth in the hands of the very wealthy has radically increased in the past
decades.

That is, instead of taking money from the tiny percentage of the world's
truly rich and making many more of the world's truly poor more prosperous, we moved our manufacturing work to other nations, put many Americans out of work or into jobs with less pay, lower benefits and reduced
security, got rid of pensions and health insurance for working-class Americans, and transferred much working-class money to China. We engaged in
a massive program of reallocation of wealth — from the lower middle class
to the poor, instead of actually moving wealth from the rich to the poor.

Wealth inequities, and the concentration of wealth in private hands,
has increased — 60 percent of China's new wealth went to 1 percent of the
population. The world's richest got steadily richer, while "real wages" have
been declining even in the rich world for decades. The idea that we should
address the current ecological and economic crisis, which was created by a
set of practices that have failed in every stated altruistic goal and succeeded
only in concentrating wealth, by continuing the same practices is patently
ridiculous.

The idea that technological progress will fix everything is also a kind
of linear thinking, one that leads us to a series of additional problems. The
simple truth is that all of our major present problems have been caused by
our technological solutions to other problems. That is, global warming and
peak oil are both products of all the ways we've used fossil fuels to abate
other problems.

We have thus succeeded in creating problems that are actually worse
than the ones we were trying to combat in many cases, creating a system

with eternally diminishing returns. Joseph Tainter argues in his classic book, *The Collapse of Complex Societies*, that the more we invest in complex solutions of mitigation, the lower the total returns and the greater the danger that the system will fall apart. Tainter notes,

> Investment in sociopolitical complexity as a problem-solving response often reaches a point of declining marginal returns…. This process has been illustrated for recent history in such areas as agriculture and resource production, information processing, sociopolitical control and specialization and overall economic productivity. In each of these spheres it has been shown that industrial societies are experiencing declining marginal returns for increased expenditures.[162]

Roughly translated, Tainter is saying that we are investing more time and energy into solving problems with increasingly complex and energy intensive strategies, and getting less and less back for our investment. We are nearing the point at which the returns become negative, especially in systems like biofuels, which offer a very minimal return, if any, on the energy investment. That we are so deeply invested in these destructive, barely functional systems should be a solid indication that we cannot fix our problems with more of the same in yet greater complexity.

In his book *Collapse: How Societies Choose to Fail or Succeed*, Jared Diamond observes that technological solutions cannot address most of the problems we are facing now. In response to those who say that "technology will solve our problems," he says (and this lengthy quote is included because it is a superb description of the limitations of technological linear models),

> This is an expression of faith about the future, and therefore based upon a supposed track record of technology having solved more problems than it created in the recent past. Underlying this expression of faith is the implicit assumption that, from tomorrow on-wards, technology will function primarily to solve existing problems and will cease to create new problems. Those with such faith also assume that the new technologies now under discussion will succeed, and that they will do so quickly enough to make a big difference soon…. But actual experience is the opposite of this assumed track record. Some dreamed-of new technologies succeed, while others don't. Those that do succeed typically take

a few decades to develop and phase in widely: think of gas heating, electric lighting, cars and airplanes, television, computers and
so on. New technologies, whether or not they succeed in solving
the problem that they were designed to solve, regularly create unanticipated new problems. Technological solutions to environmental
problems are routinely far more expensive than preventative measures to avoid creating the problem in the first place: for example,
the billions of dollars of damages.... Most of all advances in technology just increase our ability to do things, which may be either
for the better or for the worse. All of our current problems are un-
intended negative consequences of our existing technology. The
rapid advances in technology during the 20th century have been
creating difficult new problems faster than they have been solving
old problems: that's why we're in the situation in which we now
find ourselves. What makes you think that, as of January 1, 2006,
for the first time in human history, technology will miraculously
stop causing unanticipated problems while it just solves the problems that it previously produced?[163]

These are questions that we almost never address in our rush to technological solutions, but as our resources become more limited, they are questions that must be answered.

The "end of the world as we know it" model is also linear. Maria Mies
observes that those who have invested themselves enormously in the present system are most vulnerable to the notion that the end of the world is at
hand if the current systems collapse. She speaks of those who "at the end of
their lives, are horrified when they look at themselves and their works, and
when they realize that the God to whom they have devoted their whole
life — scientific progress — is a Moloch who eats his children." That is,
when people become aware of the limits of the technological/growth capi-
talist model, the overthrowing of the intellectual model that has served as
their basis for understanding reality is so total that it is as destructive as the
catastrophe they imagine. They remake the world in the image of their own
destruction.

Of course, not all "end of the world" scenarios are based on faith in
science and market forces. Some of them are based upon religious faith.
Here we get into murky territory, because religious belief can be either linear or cyclical in nature. Many, perhaps most, of the world's faithful adhere

to the cyclical origins of their faiths. Christians, Jews, Muslims, Hindus, Buddhists — all come from faiths that are deeply tied to the land and to the seasons.

But many religions also include forms of fundamentalism, from ultra-orthodox Judaism to fundamentalist Islam and Christianity that are finally climactic in origin. Though all the world's major religions originally evolved in cyclical, agrarian societies, today many have extreme forms that focus on a more linear view of human ontogeny and future events.

Besides the apocalyptic streaks of fundamentalism, another form of linear faith would be extremely secularized visions of religion such as those associated with the Christian notion of "prosperity gospel" — the perversion of the Christian faith that teaches that Jesus (who was enormously critical of personal wealth) wants Christians to become ever more rich. Though this particular strain of Christianity may be said to be particularly extreme, there are strains in almost all faiths that essentially treat religion as a subset of contemporary consumer culture, which is, of course, why many critics have noted that the US's dominant religion seems to be not any particular faith but worship of free market economies. Thus, again, we come cyclically around to the linear as we examine how this change in thinking has become so pervasive in our Western world.

It may initially seem counter-intuitive that Christians waiting for the rapture, people who dream of colonizing space as a solution to our problems, those who sing the praises of a completely globalized economy and those who tell us we're doomed to environmental disaster are all of an intellectual piece, and yet their similarities exceed their differences.

You may well be wondering what is left, after we've scrapped these visions of technological progress and apocalypse. We will explore this a bit further in a moment. First, we need to see where the linear model has gotten us. But it is worth noting that there is one overarching characteristic to a cyclical society. This is a profound awareness of future generations — that is, our current system has made most of its gains by using up resources that our children and grandchildren will also need, by stealing from future generations. Most cyclical societies recognize that short-term gains are short term, that human beings do die, and that our chance at immortality lies not in perfect comfort and consumption now, in dying with the most toys, but in what we leave to those who will follow us.

The enormous tension between linear and cyclical in our society can be seen in the fact that most of us do want better for our children than we have, most of us do believe passionately in creating good for future generations — and yet, most of us live our lives as though we don't care about them, taking more than a just share. Both ways of thinking have deep roots in our minds, and until we gently separate them out, sort out what we really value and what we're simply accustomed to, we cannot make our lives fit our beliefs.

Thinking Straight — and Wrongly — about Food

Dig deeply in most social, economical or environmental problems and you will find connections to farming and food issues.
— INTERNATIONAL FORUM ON GLOBALIZATION —

Agriculture also can be either linear or cyclical — it can steal from the future and leave devastation in its path, or it can renew and restore. One of the assumptions of the linear structure of agriculture is the idea that new technologies will create endless quantities of food. We should be suspicious of this because, as we will show, it is not absolute quantities of food that are primarily at issue. But this fantasy of endless production, we are told, will thus free us from ever having to worry about issues of equity, population or whether our economic system is wise or just. The claims are, of course, overstated, and again, the problem is that the continued extension of our current agricultural strategies — the strategies that caused our present problems — will not fix the problems they created.

The idea that the same system that depleted aquifers, created the dead zone in the Gulf of Mexico and enabled the transmission of mad cow disease will magically cease causing problems and merely create solutions is nonsense, and yet we are accustomed to believing it. It requires a belief in a linear, climactic vision of humanity, in which we are perfected by technology; but, of course, we have been trained in that vision, so we find it immediately accessible. And because those forms of perfection are all that we have been offered, the instinctive reaction of many people who are told they cannot fix our problems is to assume that nothing can — the precisely parallel linear response.

The policy of eternal expansion is unlikely to solve our agricultural problems. As we have noted, most agricultural growth of the last 50 years has involved stealing food from future generations by rendering land and water unusable to them. The food we eat now comes out of the mouths of our children. Any solution is going to have to find a way to reduce the factors that diminish returns, while also improving on the present model. That would mean a complete reconsideration of our approach to agriculture or, as Guilhem Calvo, an adviser with UNESCO's ecological and earth sciences division, recently called for, "a paradigm change" in the way we grow food. That paradigm change involved primarily the removal of fossil fuels from agriculture and greater equity.

The short-term gains of linear systems are incredibly intoxicating. Given the power of previously stored energy released into agriculture during the past half century, it is not surprising that we've blown away our soil and vaporized our aquifers as we've used the power of fossil fuel inputs to boost production while reducing the number of people working the land. As if drunk and playing with fire, we have settled into a way of growing food that requires enormous inputs of limited resources and burned away the age-old practices that not only fed human beings for thousands of years but also sustained the soil in which crops grow and nurtured the streams and waterways that give the gift of water and nutrients.

Linear agriculture isn't just an invention of the 20th century. History is replete with examples of civilizations past that pushed the ecological boundaries of the systems on which they were dependant for food as we are doing. As Diamond points out, the Anasazi, the Mayans and the population of Easter Island all put too much pressure on their surrounding environments to the extent that they ended up unable to feed themselves. The difference now, however, is the scale of the potential consequences of our environmental destruction. It was once the case that a society could destroy only itself and its near neighbors. Industrial agriculture is the first near-global attempt by humans to undermine their ability to feed themselves as a species. Thus, the UNESCO report mentioned above brought together hundreds of scientists and ultimately argued that there was no choice but to end industrial, chemical agriculture if we were to feed the world in the future.

Was there ever an agriculture that wasn't destructive, that allowed people to survive and thrive over long periods? F. H. King's book *Farmers of Forty Centuries: Organic Farming in China, Korea and Japan* suggests that there have been societies that have managed their limits extremely well, successfully farming the same regions for long periods. And in Indonesia Sharon visited rice terraces on steep hillsides that have been farmed for more than a thousand years and still provide steady yields. So although agriculture has a mixed history, there is no doubt that it is possible to minimize damage and even regenerate the capacity of land to feed us. We would have to go a long way to find an agricultural system as destructive as the present one.

The development of the Green Revolution fostered a shift from growing food largely for the subsistence of the farmers, their families and their neighbors to an industry focused on wealth accumulation. Initially started as a project by Rockefeller Foundation working in Mexico, the Green Revolution began as an attempt to avert famine by using synthetic pesticides, artificial fertilizers and irrigation techniques to boost the yields of staple foods. In the rush to alleviate short-term hunger, however, sufficient attention was not paid to the long-term consequences of these practices. Where other successful and sustainable forms of agriculture, persistent in places like China for thousands of years, sought to always protect and nurture the entire ecological systems that made food production possible, this new strategy of agriculture focused too narrowly on the short term. It valued an increase in near-term yields over the extension of those yields into the indefinite future.

These increases in output were enormously profitable, and as such, agriculture shifted from a skill of sustenance and sharing to a business primarily focused on wealth aggregation. Soon the artificial inputs themselves became big business, with the agrochemical companies earning fantastic wealth through ever-increasing control over the world's food harvest.

Today the commodification of agriculture has expanded far more than food production ever did. In the face of the food emergency we're experiencing, we risk becoming more and more dependent on the multinational companies that commodify agriculture. We've given up long-term thinking in our concern for the hungry — and it is true, they need food now. But the problems of high prices and inputs will remain threats to the lives of the poor, including the new American poor, unless we alter the system that creates them. The longer we invest in the strategies that underpin our current way of growing food, the harder it gets to change. Any successful strategy aimed at changing the way we grow food and eat it will have to address both the needs of people now and a successful way of transitioning away from our failed strategies of agriculture.

Because of this and the other enormous challenges associated with making changes to our current model of agriculture — returning it to a more steady-state, cyclical system of growing food — it's worth examining in a bit more detail the failures of industrial agriculture. It's worth examining because the hole we are in is so deep and because we have not yet stopped digging.

Soil

The soil requires a duty of man which he has been slow to recognize.
— HENRY A. WALLACE —

It's fair to say that we're picking on industrial agriculture here when poor practices of resource management have occurred throughout the history agriculture. What makes our most recent failure to manage our natural resources so scary is the scale at which we are failing. Hugh H. Bennett and W. C. Lowdermilk said, "Soil erosion is as old as agriculture. It began when the first heavy rain struck the first furrow turned by a crude implement of tillage in the hands of prehistoric man. It has been going on ever since, wherever man's culture of the earth has bared the soil to rain and wind." But soil loss and degradation are now happening at an alarming rate and they're happening most dramatically here at home. Each year in the US we lose more than 1 million acres due to soil degradation, not to mention the 2 million more lost to land development.[164]

When examined more closely, the phrase "land development" seems to be a contradiction in terms — the development of land often results in the destruction of its capacity to produce food. Francis Moore Lappé et al. point out in *World Hunger 12 Myths*, that it is not in the underdeveloped global South where soil is being lost at the greatest rate. North America is now the continent with the most severe desertification problem. Since widespread farming began in the United States in the 18th century, an estimated 30 percent of total farmland has been abandoned because of erosion, salinization, and waterlogging. Fully one-third of the topsoil in the United States has been lost. Today about 90 percent of US cropland is losing soil faster than it can rebuild, and more than half of US pastureland is overgrazed and subject to high rates of erosion.[165]

In this country we are losing soil 17 times faster than it can be replaced.[166] In fact more than half of the incredibly rich Midwestern prairie soils that underlie the bread basket of the US, and indeed the world, have been lost to wind and water erosion during the past 100 hundred years.[167] And now that this soil has been swept out to sea by the rivers and the streams of our nation, it will never be available to us for farming. How long will it take to wash away the other half?

It seems we've become very careless with our treatment of the soil here in the US, and sadly, the same is true of the treatment of our soils worldwide. Almost sixty million tons of topsoil are lost each day. And this shouldn't surprise us. Citizens in overdeveloped nations have supported the transformation of countless acres of poor-world subsistence farms and sustainably managed ecosystems into industrial farmland for the production of commodities for export. This means that many more people in the underdeveloped world find themselves unable to provide food and fuel for themselves. A feedback loop has been created whereby hungry people, in order to feed their families, destroy the soil that kept them from starvation. In other parts of the world, biomass, including trees, shrubs and other perennial plants, is stripped from large areas and massive amounts of soil are lost because of a shift in agricultural management practices, overgrazing and cutting for fuel to heat and cook.

This need for food and fuel, coupled with distorted economic priorities, which are often at odds with long-term security, results in massive soil loss in the developing world. Pressures from the developed world bear down to increase the destruction. Every year thousands of square miles of rainforest are cleared, much of it at the order of fast food companies like McDonalds (and by extension anyone who eats there) who need land overseas for cheap beef production. As Dr. M. E. Ensminger, former chair of the Department of Animal Science at Washington State University, says in *Animal Science*,

> Is a quarter pound of hamburger worth a half ton of Brazil's rainforest? Is 67 square feet of rainforest — an area about the size of one small kitchen — too much to pay for one hamburger? Should we form cattle pastures to produce hamburgers in the Amazon, or should we retain the rainforest and the natural environment? These and other similar questions are being asked too little and too late to preserve much of the great tropical rainforest of the Amazon and its environment. It took nature thousands of years to form the rainforest, but it took a mere 25 years for people to destroy much of it. And when a rainforest is gone, it's gone forever.[168]

This is true all over the world as large land owners employ dubious land use tactics to displace small local land owners. In this case, those who recognize the value of soil and its potential to provide for those who know how to care for it are no longer in charge of the stewardship of this resource, having been replaced by multinational corporations with economic goals that supersede the care of this precious resource.

One might think the economic impact associated with soil loss might get their attention. The global loss of more than 75 billion tons of soil each year is worth $400 billion annually. US agricultural losses due to the need for irrigation and nutrient replacement associated with soil loss are estimated at $28 billion alone.[169] And there are other costs too, described by Dale Allen Pfeiffer as,

> the offsite costs of soil erosion: roadway, sewer, and basement siltation; drainage disruption; foundation and pavement undermining; gullying of roads; earth dam failures; eutrophication of waterways; siltation of harbors and channels; loss of reservoir storage, loss of wildlife habitat and disruption of stream ecology; damage to public health; and increased water costs.[170]

But what makes this enormous loss of soil so alarming is just how long it took to create this precious resource. It takes more than 500 years in nature to build one inch of healthy topsoil,[171] and it takes a minimum of six inches of soil to grow food.[172] Much more is definitely desirable. That's at least 3,000 years' worth of natural soil building for the start to finish in an agriculturally productive land base. As Franklin Delano Roosevelt declared, "A nation that destroys its soil, destroys itself."[173]

In recent years, chemical fertilizers and pesticides have in part compensated for the loss of soil humus, and we have been able to overlook lost soil productivity. As the feedstock for such chemicals becomes more costly and scarce, however, it is likely that we will experience the true extent of the damage we've done to ourselves through damage to our soils.

So what is the alternative? What cyclical model is available to us? Well, there is some good news. Though the process by which soils build up by breaking down organic material and eventually stabilize that material into what we call humus is naturally a slow one, it can proceed much more rapidly with active human participation. Historically most successful older societies have managed not only to avoid degrading their soils, but have helped build them up.

We work against nature by not returning organic material to the soil and we do worse with our practices that strip vegetation from the ground and cause erosion and with the poisonous chemicals we spray on our crops. We can, however, reverse this damage with healthy soil management practices and begin to build soil. Pesticides and concentrated chemical fertilizers damage healthy soil by destroying the microscopic life that makes up the soil; what soil is left after it is blown and washed away through poor cultivation techniques. So the first step is clearly to stop these practices, to add organic matter, to end tillage, not by pouring on more Round Up but by making use of organic strategies for sustainable planting.

This means cultivating small plots of land with a much more hands-on approach. Turning under thousands of acres at a time with enormous earth-churning machines should give way to increasing the amount of food we grow with practices of reduced tillage or no-till strategies. By this we do not mean the drenching of soil with herbicides and planting resistance crops into the ground — that is what many people mean when they speak of zero-tillage. But as the Rodale Institute has found, organic no-till agriculture can outyield both conventional chemical no-till and conventional tilled organic practices.[174]

The healthy soil of a carefully managed quarter-acre Victory Garden can be administered easily with a shovel and a hoe. Water and wind erosion can be almost eliminated, and organic material in the form of compost and manure can be used to maintain soil health and fertility. For larger farms, the use of crimper and other tractor or horse attachments can minimize erosion, and the returning of manures to soil can improve humus levels. Using other strategies like compost teas and manure teas can result is a bloom of micro fauna that helps to repopulate barren soil with its natural inhabitants and fertilize it in a more natural way.

We have wasted much that nature can do to aid us in food production in chemical agriculture. Pesticides and chemical fertilizers destroy the community of living soil. The top six inches of soil is the most densely populated ecosystem on the planet. It is a mysterious world of micro and macro fauna that recycles the dead and provides for the living. It is this subterranean community that we all depend on for our survival. Permaculturalist Scott A. Meister points out, "In fact, there is more life below the surface of the earth, than above it." He says of healthy soil,

> It's important to have soil biota such as microflora and fauna (bacteria, fungi, actinomycetes, and algae) micro, meso and macrofauna such as centipedes, worms and termites. These soil biota are the managers, or underground stewards of the earth. Some serve as

highway makers, others as transporters, others act like the underground internet. Termites and ants are the earthmovers, as well as digesters and soil makers. Worms, specifically, break down organic material into smaller forms that can be digested by the smaller beings such as bacteria and fungi, in order that the minerals can be more easily taken up by plants. Worm castings (worm poop) are nature's best fertilizer, and worms can create 60 tons of worm cast per acre per year.[175]

We must regain respect for the well-being of this community and foster its health if we are to return to a sensible way of growing food.

Beyond fixing soil is the more basic task of maintaining the fertility of the soil that remains and fully returning to the practice of sustainable soil management. John Jeavons, author of *How To Grow More Vegetables* and the man largely responsible for popularizing the form of French intensive gardening in this country, suggests that to farm sustainably in a biointensive manner — a manner that produces a lot of food in a relatively small amount of space — requires that 60 percent of all gardened areas be devoted to growing compostable crops. These crops, which include grains, also produce food, but much of their value is in the fertility they provide — this means a new way of looking at our food crops. In other words, he says that more than half of all the plants we actively grow under such a system should be put back into the ground in an effort to feed the soil. It is possible to work with nature to speed up the process of soil formation through processes like growing crops for compost and recycling the carbon and nitrogen in fallen leaves and other discarded plant material, as well as food waste, in an effort to increase the amount of healthy soil available for agricultural production.

However, our ability to foster healthy soils will go beyond the support of sustainable agricultural practices. Not only will we need rich soils to feed the growing population of people on this planet but soil building might also become a major tool in our effort to stabilize atmospheric levels of carbon and combat the climate change associated with global warming.

Francisco de Orellana, a Spanish conquistador who explored the Amazon River basin in the 16th century, spoke of a vastly populated region thought by most modern historians to have supported only sparse numbers of humans. The reason for this was that it was assumed that because tropical rainforest have notoriously poor soils it was unlikely that such soils could have supported high numbers of humans.

Recently however, archeologists have made a discovery that might support Orellana's report. It appears that coexisting groups of Amazon inhabitants from 400 to 1200 AD utilized a soil-building technique that resulted in *terra preta* or "black earth" — a type of soil made up of plant and animal remains mixed with charcoal. The result was an astoundingly fertile soil that could have supported many more inhabitants through increased agricultural yields than the sparse population in the Amazon basin previously estimated by researchers. Michael Tennesen, writing for *Discover*, goes on to explain,

> As thrilling as this evidence is to archaeologists, it may also have very practical importance as a modern weapon against some of our most urgent ecological problems. Soil scientist Johannes Lehmann of Cornell University believes that the mysterious dark earth holds clues to creating sustainable farming practices and even to combating global warming…. First, because the enriched soil remains fertile for a long time, its use would discourage farmers from moving on and burning more forest to open up new fields. Second, because of the added charcoal, terra preta holds up to 10 times as much carbon as unaltered soils. The late Wim Sombroek — a legendary soil scientist whose long interest in terra preta earned him the epithet "the godfather of dark earth" — began to wonder if dark earth could be used to sequester carbon. Lehmann's studies have shown that it can: Fifty percent of the original carbon in plants and trees used to make biochar remains in the terra preta soils after the conversion.[176]

So it appears that a low-tech alternative such as adding charcoal to our soil could work not only to repair depleted soils but also help with some of the much needed work of sequestering carbon. That is, there are ways in which we can revitalize the soil and thus avoid the false choice of making it temporarily productive with hydro-chemical concoctions or simply stopping such fertilization efforts and starving to death.

And there is more good news about how our ability to help recreate healthy topsoil and sequester carbon can further help. Joel Salatin operates Polyface Farm a "family owned, multi-generational, pasture-based, beyond organic, local-market farm and informational outreach in Virginia's Shenandoah Valley." His strategy of pasturing animals relies on perennial grasses in a rotating system. The grasses feed cows, who then move on to other pastures. Chickens are then allowed to follow the cows to pick through the manure and graze on the grass not eaten by the cows. The combination of cow and chicken manure fertilizes the grasses, which are then allowed to regrow before the pasturing cycle is repeated. The fields are never tilled. This might sound like a simple, unimportant description of farm animals being raised for meat, but it isn't.

Peter Bane, editor of *Permaculture Activist,* describes the possibility in an article entitled, "Storing Carbon in Soil: The Possibilities of a New American Agriculture." After hearing Salatin describe his 500-acre farm in the Shenandoah Valley in Virginia and its soil-stewardship practices, Bane was moved to do some math. Salatin said that in 1961, when his family first arrived on their current plot of land, soil testing revealed 1.5 percent organic matter. A subsequent test in 2007 revealed 8 percent.

> In 46 years of rotational grazing without the addition of any fertilizers except composted manures from the animals' winter bedding (supplemented with woodchips and other carbon from local sources, but minus the animals that leave the land), Polyface has built up 6.5% additional carbon in their pasture soils while taking a profitable return from the sale of meat. They use essentially no toxic inputs, and need very little machinery…. An acre of soil covers 43,560 square feet. The top six inches, which is where most of the carbon is stored, weigh about 1900 tons per acre. The annual increment of increase in soil carbon at Polyface is 0.14%, about 2.7 tons per year…. A [more?] reasonable estimate of land [agricultural land in the US] with more than 30 inches of rainfall per year (the average in the Shenandoah Valley is 32" per year) is 800 million acres. That's about ⅔ of the area east of the Dakotas, roughly from Omaha and Topeka east to the Atlantic and south to the Gulf of Mexico. It's mostly growing corn and soybeans now, and they are mostly going to animal feed or industrial uses: paint and ink ethanol, fizzy drinks, and junk food, none of which is good either for people or livestock. If that land were farmed as the Salatins farm Polyface in Virginia, it could sequester 2.2 billion tons (2 billion metric tonnes) of carbon per year. That's equal to present gross US atmospheric releases, not counting the net reduction from carbon sinks of existing forests and soils.[177]

Bane goes further to suggest that if carbon is traded at $50 per ton, such a shift represents a $100 billion boon for American agriculture. "Who needs subsidies from Washington?" he adds.

Feeding the Soil

If a healthy soil is full of death,
it is also full of life:
worms, fungi, microorganisms of all kinds....
Given only the health of the soil,
nothing that dies is dead for very long.
— WENDELL BERRY —

One of our hobbies here in the United States is the hyper-distillation of ideas. We're trying to perfect the sound bite, a pursuit made necessary by a mainstream media that consists of a handful of news tycoons trying, in a fair and balanced fashion, to offer us only two perspectives of exactly 150 seconds per idea. Never mind that some of these complex ideas have to be dumbed down immensely to fit into this short window; the complex versions are really important to the lives of the citizens of our nation. It's as if what really matters is whether the nightly news can afford to fit in a quick story about the state of American health care between commercials for burger joints and drug companies.

A good example of our oversimplification can be seen in our whole approach to the question of plant nutrition (well, human too, but that's another discussion). NPK stands for nitrogen, phosphorus (phosphorus pentoxide) and potassium (potash or potassium oxide). K is the atomic symbol for potassium. P was already taken and the Latin for potassium is *kalium*, so that's how we get K. See how complicated this is getting already? But stay with me here, this is important. This acronym NPK describes three major plant nutrients and helps to describe the ratio of each as a percentage of weight in any particular synthetic fertilizer. For instance, a bag of fertilizer labeled 20-7-10 has 20 percent nitrogen, 7 percent phosphorus and 10 percent potassium. The remaining 63 percent is ballast, or stuff not necessarily useful to the plant.

NPK represents only three of the six plant macronutrients. That is, these are things that the plants need to survive. The other three are calcium, magnesium and sulfur. In addition, plants need varying amounts of micronutrients including iron, manganese, boron, copper, molybdenum, nickel, lithium, chlorine, zinc, selenium and others. But ask someone who sells fertilizer about how to choose which fertilizer to use in your garden and they will rarely get past NPK, any more than politicians get past the sound bite. And not only do we have a hard time getting past those three nutrients, we almost never get to the delivery system of these nutrients, which is just as essential.

Most people think in terms of plants absorbing needed nutrients through their roots. The truth is much more complicated. In fact plants feed themselves through a host of symbiotic relationships between the plants and other microorganisms in the soil. The plants in turn feed the microorganisms sugars. In some cases the connection is a physical one. Sometimes the roots of plants are penetrated by microrhiza; other times the plants are fed by nearby neighbors. The soil is a community of living organisms that makes up one of the most densely populated ecosystems on the planet.

Try to imagine billions of living organisms in one cubic centimeter. It is this community on which all of us who eat plants — or eat animals that eat plants — are dependant, which is to say it's much more complicated than a three-letter abbreviation. Forget the idea that plants eat first. Microorganisms are at the head of the table.

It is true that nitrogen, phosphorus and potassium are very important for the successful growth of plants. It's just silly to say that the right combination of these three alone can continue to provide enough food to feed us. The very reason we need to add N, P and K to our farm fields is that we've stripped off much of the topsoil in which the healthy ecosystem of soil microbes lived. In many cases the remaining microbial communities were then killed by applications of synthetic fertilizers and pesticides. The topsoil of many industrial farming operations is rightly described as a lifeless sponge onto which chemicals are poured in order to make up for this community that once nourished the plants without such inputs.

And perhaps if this was a simple trade, the life of the soil traded for better living through chemistry, it might be a trade we would be willing to make. But as we have discussed elsewhere in this book, these chemicals have negative effects on human beings as well as destroying entire ecosystems such as our waterways. The cost in terms of human health and in terms of ecological health are two strong reasons for imagining a different way of growing food. Another is the economic cost.

Frank Deen of ICL Performance Products says the price of Merchant Grade Acid (MGA) used to process phosphate rock into phosphorus fertilizers rose between 25 and 30 percent in 2007, while "fertilizer phosphates, which use MGA as a feedstock, have increased by as much as 70% to 100%."[178] That means some fertilizer phosphates have nearly doubled in price in only a year. Meanwhile, the price for potash rose by 230 percent in April 2008, and potash production is increasingly concentrated among only a few companies.[179]

No projections include a drop in demand for food or for the fertilizers currently used in their industrial production. In fact it is precisely the opposite. "World fertilizer demand has grown by 14% in the last five years — Equivalent to a new US market," said Deen. Phosphorus and its uptake by plants is a somewhat complicated matter, but the practice of mining rock phosphates from the other side of world and shipping them to the US for use as fertilizers is likely not a practice that will increase in the future. While a worldwide economic crisis may reduce consumption of energy, it is unlikely to dramatically reduce the desire for food.

Meanwhile, synthetic nitrogen fertilizers are extracted using natural gas (NG), which is itself a finite resource, one likely to decline in production during the next decade or two. Already we've witnessed fertilizer companies moving oversees to parts of the world where NG is more abundant. This is another way that we face increasing reliance on faraway places that don't have our interests at heart. It is not just that dumping massive amounts of synthetic nitrogen fertilizers is bad for our health and bad for the environment; doing so is fast becoming prohibitively expensive and further increasing our reliance on parts of the world where we aren't popular.

And natural gas isn't the only fertilizer macronutrient potentially in short supply. Researcher Patrick Dery has concluded that the world is facing a peak in phosphorus production.[180] Industrial agriculture strips phosphorus rapidly from the soil, and we are mining rock phosphates rapidly. This means that the price will rise and the ability of the world's lower-income people to buy fertilizers to grow food is in real danger. In the longer term, we must address the problem of phosphorus availability in order to ensure a reliable food supply for our grandchildren.

But is there an alternative? The short answer is yes. The long answer is more complicated than a three-letter initialism but is not beyond the understanding of those who study soil and understand how the microbial community therein can help in a world in which we can't afford the costs of synthetic fertilizers. There are more than 100 microorganisms, including rhizobia and several yeasts, that fix nitrogen from the atmosphere and make it available to plants.[181] These microorganisms provide plants with nitrogen on demand — far more useful and complex than simply pouring on the fertilizer. That is, if the plant is in need of nitrogen, the microorganisms make it available. If the plant no longer needs more nitrogen, the microbes stop making it available. Nitrogen doesn't have the opportunity to build up to toxic levels in the soil or run off into nearby waterways. Microorganisms also make available other nutrients, macro and micro alike, and are the key to developing a sustainable soil structure for supporting permanent agriculture.

Ever wonder why forests don't need to be fertilized, how towering oak trees came to be without someone applying the right combination of NPK? Microorganisms break down carbon and leach weak acids that break down minerals, making them available to plants. Those oak trees and the other plants in the forest rely on the nutrient recycling undertaken by the microbial community naturally occurring in the soil. We can mimic this process. We can establish healthy soil communities and provide nutrients for recycling. We can sequester carbon, a necessary part of this soil recycling program, helping to offset carbon emissions while we build soil. (More on this later.) The typical NPK approach to providing the nutrients necessary for useful industrial agriculture needs to be turned on its head. The answer isn't an initialism. It's fostering natural soil systems and the communities of beneficial microorganisms that make up those systems and protecting them at all costs.

That doesn't mean we won't have to fertilize soils if we continue removing agricultural products from them — we will. But we can do so with largely organic materials. Indeed, it is a basic premise of this book that we will probably have no choice but to shift toward organic agriculture — not out of some elitist preference but because we simply can't feed the world any other way. Reliance on distant macronutrients and fossil fuels is a recipe for disaster as those things rise in price and availability. Many people have assumed that if we cannot get these things we are doomed to starvation. But this is not true.

Not only can we make nature work for us but we also have an enormously valuable resource that we largely waste — human manures and human urine. On a planet with 6.7 billion people, the one thing we have in abundance is human outputs. These outputs can indefinitely recycle the phosphorous and nitrogen we've been using all along, keeping world food yields high.

To do so, we will have to shift our relationship to our own manures. Historically in many places there was a tie between city and country. We will talk more about recreating the ties between urban and rural cultures, but one way we will probably have to do this is by the return of human bio-solids to agricultural fields. In rural areas, we will have to take up the com-posting of human manures and the collection of human urine.

We tend to be very squeamish about these issues, but we will have to face these subjects head on in order to keep up our food supply. Our food supply depends on our ability not to treat these complexities as sound bite issues, but to truly understand the ways in which we can transform our li-abilities into assets.

Poison in the Well

When the well's dry,
we know the worth of water.
— Benjamin Franklin —

If you live in a part of the US with a municipal water system, then you might be one of the people who pay annually for an average of 13,000 gal-lons of water to be pumped from lakes and rivers, then be purified to drink-ing water standards so that you can pee and poop into it.[182] Yes, as a nation we literally flush more than 6.8 billion gallons of drinkable water down our toilets each day.[183] Depending on how many people live upstream from you, this fact might raise other questions, but we'll leave those for you to explore.

We are indeed as careless with our waterways and aquifers as our soil. And this is foolish, because the rivers and aquifers that have slaked our thirst and made our deserts bloom will be even more urgently needed by future generations in a warmer, dryer future. The Colorado River no lon-ger reaches the Pacific Ocean,[184] and we continue pumping water out of it at an alarming rate. "With the population we have now, we are more than capable of pumping out the supply faster than it can be recharged," said Rita Pearson, director of the Arizona Department of Water Resources.

And while Arizona might seem like a particularly thirsty place, the rate of ground water depletion in other parts of the country to service irriga-tion needs is a growing problem. The result is a short-term gain in agri-cultural land that without irrigation would be unusable, at the expense of long-term access to water for domestic use. The citizens of Arizona might have enough to drink today, but if their source of ground water runs out they'll join the more than 1 billion people worldwide who don't have access to clean drinking water.[185] Each day almost 10,000 children under the age of five in poor world countries die as a result of illnesses contracted by use of impure water.

More than 70 percent of the Earth's surface is covered with water. When you more closely examine the water on our planet, though, you find that most of it isn't drinkable. There are a million trillion gallons of water on earth, 97.5 percent of which is salinated and makes up the seas and oceans. It is possible to strip the salt and other compounds out of this salt water, but the process is energy intensive, not to mention costly. Seventy percent of the remaining 2.5 percent of water considered fresh and directly useful to land plants and animals is locked up in polar ice caps (for now — soon it could join the saline water of the seas and oceans as global warming melts the ice caps). Take into account inaccessible water such as that found in the very deep underground, and only 0.007 percent is considerable clean enough to drink.[186] Perhaps you are beginning to understand why one might consider the use of more than 6.8 billions of gallons of water each day to flush American toilets troubling.

Industrial agriculture causes enormous pollution of our world's fresh water. Though only 17 percent of worldwide agricultural operations are irrigated, those fields produce 40 percent of our harvest.[187] Industrial agriculture concentrates pesticides and fertilizer run-offs in the groundwater that irrigates our most productive land, leading to even more intense levels of contamination. Managing water resources will become even more important in a warming world. It's likely that climate change will mean not just gradually rising temperatures but increasingly unpredictable weather. Periods of prolonged drought are likely to become more common, making us more dependent on irrigation for adequate food, just as sources of water begin to run out.

The washed-away topsoil we discussed before is one of the largest pollutants in streams and rivers. It disrupts river life by clogging the biological systems of plants and animals and shuts out light normally available to aquatic life. Soil in our waterways also collects behind dams. These deposits of silt gradually build until eventually the affected hydroelectric power plants will have to be abandoned or dredged at enormous expense.

Low levels in rivers of the Southeast in 2007 caused the shutdown of at least one nuclear plant in Alabama[188] while others came within inches of a similar fate. "Water is the nuclear industry's Achilles' heel," said the executive director of North Carolina Waste Awareness and Reduction Network, Jim Warren. "You need a lot of water to operate nuclear plants," he said in the summer of 2007, and this "is becoming a crisis." All forms of electrical generation depend heavily on water access, and experts have raised the specter of power failures because of insufficient water supplies on the Canadian plains, in parts of Australia and in the US Southwest.

And while the water troubles of the West and more recently in South have come under close scrutiny by the media, the National Climatic Data Center, in its October 2007 report noted,

> By month's end, the U.S. Drought Monitor had parts of western and northern New York and southwestern West Virginia under Severe Drought conditions. Adjacent to those areas as well as parts of central Connecticut, south central Massachusetts, southern New Jersey, and most of Maryland and Delaware were moderately or abnormally dry. According to the USGS, streamflow was much below normal from eastern Massachusetts to the Washington, DC metro area.[189]

All of this while chances of a Midwestern drought that could severely affect corn and wheat harvests are up. "There is a significant chance of drought," says Elwynn Taylor, an agricultural meteorologist at Iowa State. Concentration of the production of grains in certain areas continues to foster increased susceptibility to regional water shortages made worse by bad water management policies. This comes as agricultural scientists warn us that the food crisis could expand into worldwide famine if any major harvests were lost.

And then there's the pollution. The runoff from factory hog farms represents some of the worst water pollution coming out of industrial agriculture. It includes lots of really nasty stuff like chemical fertilizers, carcinogenic pesticides and the waste water from beef, dairy, pork and poultry plants. Environmental Defense characterized a recent disaster related to industrial meat production this way,

> Many North Carolinians will never forget the overflow of waste after the torrential rains and flooding caused by Hurricane Floyd in 1999 or the disastrous lagoon overflow at Ocean View Farms in Onslow County in 1995, which dumped more that 20 million gallons of hog waste into the New River, causing massive fish kills and contaminating drinking water.[190]

All of this creates a toxic cocktail, greatly damaging aquatic ecosystems in many ways. Chief among them is the introduction of massive amounts of specific nutrients, often large quantities of nitrogen, which produce massive algae blooms that that choke the life out of streams and rivers. The Mississippi River is so polluted by industrial agriculture that at its mouth lies a lifeless area roughly the size of New Jersey — the aforementioned dead zone.

And it isn't just our above-ground sources of water that we are over extending. The Ogallala Aquifer is a prime example of the unsustainable use of ground water. A mainstay of access to water for residential, industrial and agricultural needs, this aquifer of the south central United States is being overdrawn at 130 to 106 percent of its recharge rate.[191] It's unlikely that the American Midwest could continue to serve as the breadbasket of the US without this water source, and yet it is being drained in a manner likely to cause water disruption to this vast agricultural area in the future.

The human population itself is increasingly in contest with agriculture for available fresh water resources. As our population grows, more people use more water for drinking, bathing, cooking and cleaning. Our affluence encourages us to overconsume and waste water, as well as other resources. In the future of a warming world with increasingly volatile and unfamiliar weather patterns, water conservation will be increasingly important.

A return to small-scale sustainable agriculture and eating locally would go a long way toward changing our patterns of destructive water use and the need for massive amount of water to be used to irrigate farm fields. Small-scale farming techniques include better stewardship of available water resources. Much less is lost to the practice of overhead irrigation. Practices like sheet mulch and adding organic material utilize water more efficiently. The practice of completely draining our rivers and aquifers to support industrial agriculture in arid regions of our country and all over the world could be slowed, stopped or even reversed.

Reducing our meat consumption or switching to meat raised on small local farms that don't require fecal lagoons could help avoid disasters like the 1999 North Carolina hog waste spill. Hogs raised as part of a sustainable polyculture system of food production serve to turn waste material into fertilizer, help to prepare planting beds by cultivating them and provide a healthy source of meat. Almost any such system utilizing animals as soil improvers will help to keep waste out of our waterways.

Other practices such as dryland agriculture techniques, like the ones recommended by The Wyler Department of Dryland Agriculture at The

Ben-Gurion University of the Negev, include ways to conserve water in an attempt to grow food in places where it is scarce. They include using,

- local runoff water and brackish ground water to grow firewood, agricultural produce and livestock fodder
- runoff catchments to collect runoff water, in a variety of sizes and shapes on slopes, in channels and valleys
- natural, desertified and restored rangeland for livestock grazing

Such practices can be used not only in extremely arid parts on the world but also in areas with only marginal expectations of annual rainfall. These ways of conserving water could be important in many more places if drought becomes a more regular visitor as the effects of climate change begin to be felt.

Two's a Crowd

Insight, I believe, refers to the depth
of understanding that comes by setting experiences,
yours and mine, familiar and exotic,
new and old, side by side,
learning by letting them speak to one another.
— Mary Catherine Bateson —

Linear systems tend to assume that anything that cannot be economically exploited has no value at all. Thus, biodiversity and millions of animal and plant species have been discarded and destroyed by industrial agriculture and the society that demanded it. Modern agriculture has selected a slim number of food crops to support exclusively. The practice of monoculture, or the growing of one particular crop to the exclusion of many other possible crops, has led us to practices that further degrade our environement and threaten even our own health and well-being

It is important to recognize that most present-day societies and all past ones have had a very different relationship to edible plants than we currently have — one in which we routinely waste them. Monoculture has never been normal. As garden writer Robin Wheeler notes,

Like most people visiting Asia, I have experienced the constant dripping of a rain of epiphanies during my stays. One of these occurred on a trip to Northern Thailand, as I was standing on the edge of a new friend's yard. I admired the grove of towering bamboo that edged her garden boundary, in a row so straight I could have marked it off with a piece of thread, with not a single trace of bamboo growing out into the road.

"How do you do that?" I asked her. "How do you keep the bamboo from growing all over the place, outside of your yard?"

"Well, that's easy," she replied. "Everyone knows how good bamboo shoots are in their dinner. The minute one shows its head outside of my garden, someone takes it home."

"Oh," I said, "In Canada we hack down the bamboo and throw it in the bushes and buy bamboo shoots in a can at the store."

But that is what North America is all about. We have been trained that if it is right in front of our face (e.g., free, accessible) it is somehow inferior, and that the only really good stuff is at the store. The more abundantly and freely something grows, the more reviled it should be.[192]

Why this is so bears some exploring. Archaeologist Martin Jones has written *Feast: Why Humans Share Food*, a remarkable book about how very strange our relationship to our food really is. In one section, Jones explores the custom of choosing *not* to eat, to render taboo commonly available foods. For example, he explores bone piles from coastal British tribal populations that show no sign of including fish bones, even in periods where there are signs of famine and protein shortage.[193] This suggests that the cultural taboos against eating fish were powerful enough to affect even the starving. It may well be that the cultural habit of not seeing things as food made them effectively invisible to the hungry.

And, of course, we know that this is true from our own experience. Despite the fact that one recent report showed more Americans going hungry than in decades, how many hungry Americans know how to go out in the parks near them and dig up burdock roots? How many know that we can eat grasshoppers? And how many Americans can overcome their aversion, the profound idea that something is not "food"?

The ability to take some edibles and call them taboo is an important way that cultures differentiate themselves from one another — what we eat is who we are. And that's no less true now than it was in any other society. Of course, some of this is simply wastefulness as Wheeler describes, but part of our practice is also the cultural sense that we are identified by our ability not to recognize these things as food — this is our way of differentiating ourselves from our agrarian prior culture.

How many ethnic narratives describe being embarrassed by a parent or grandparent harvesting a wild plant from a public place or by agrarian food traditions? It isn't just that we're wasteful — it is that we're still sending out the cultural message "We're different from our agrarian parents," even though that's become painfully obvious, and many of the agrarian parents and grandparents are gone. That is, we are constituting ourselves as fundamentally different from what came before us, as a new people, even though for most of us, what came before is long, long gone. The difficulty, of course, is that we may need to be rather more like the old people we can no longer locate, the people we are busily denying our connection to.

One of the ways we are abandoning our agrarian roots is by disdaining wild foods. That may seem like an odd claim, given our tendency to think of the world as historically divided into highly discrete hunter-gatherers vs. agrarians, but in fact, the archaeological record suggests that most agrarian societies relied quite heavily on wild plant foraging, and that the line between gathering and agriculture probably predates any solid archaeological evidence. For example, Laura Schenone, author of *A Thousand Years Over a Hot Stove*, observes about our perceptions of gatherers and their connection to the origins of agriculture,

> Let's have a look at her again, a woman moving light-footedly through brambles, gathering berries. To our modern perception, the image seems somehow innocent and trivial. In fact, the ancient gatherer women were nothing short of botanists with extensive knowledge far beyond the scope of berries for dessert. This knowledge could only be built up over generations through careful judgement, skill and yes, even some poisonous trial and error along the way. By the time the Europeans came, Indians from coast to coast were gathering almost 2 thousand types of edible roots, nuts, vegetable plants, greens, fruits, and herbs, as well as insects and shellfish....
>
> Spend one week (even one day) in the wilderness with no food, and you'll quickly realize that without know-how, you'll starve or poison yourself. And it's not just knowing what you can eat, but where to find it and when it will be ripe or available. If you get to

the nut trees or fruits even a few days late, more enterprising animals will have beat you to them, or you'll find yourself left with the taste of overripe or rotten fruit in your mouth, opportunity so closely missed....

While we can never be sure, many experts believe that women "discovered" horticulture and were probably America's first farmers. The rise of farming was a gradual process. Perhaps one woman decided to help along the wild plants she liked best. First, she began to weed away competing plants or give water to her favorites. Maybe she noticed that a basket of dropped seeds had sprouted in the loosened soil where she'd built an earthen oven.[194]

When European scholars arrived in Africa to study African gardening, they were stunned by how small the cultivated patches of roots were in African house gardens. The assumption of early thinkers was that Africans were simply bad farmers — it was only decades later that it became clear that large patches of jungle near villages were actually cultivated patches of food crops.

And the line between gathering and agriculture has remained fine through most of agrarian history. Martin Jones argues in *Feast* that in fact, "the cultivated field was more unusual to our modern eyes.... We could envisage instead plots of land that were certainly sown from a particular stock of seed corn, often a maslin mixture to hedge against poorer years. After these plots had been tended and brought to maturity, quite possibly everything in them was treated as a resource, not just the progeny of what was sown."[195]

He backs this up with evidence from bodies excavated from peat bogs, many of which contained mixtures of both wild and cultivated plants in their bellies. He notes that as recently as the early 20th century, Danish farmers were still eating wild brome grass seeds, a grass that flourished when the rye harvests were poor and so were allowed to coexist in fields to ensure a secure harvest.

Jones also argues that farmers in most societies had every incentive to diversify their diets because agricultural taxes have usually been based on single, monocropped analyses (and we still count food this way). That is, farmers were forced to pay based on single-crop food webs — on how much corn or rice or wheat they grew. Secondary and marginal crops had no fixed value on the markets, and thus were often ignored. The way to minimize taxation and retain the most for your family's diet, then, was to vary one's crops as much as possible and rely on fields and forests to have as diverse a food web and harvest as possible.

There are still modern rural populations that make full use of the food around them. One of the revelations of Dmitry Orlov's superb book *Reinventing Collapse* is that most Soviet families fed themselves on extremely small gardens, much smaller than most of us would expect. But this was heavily supplemented by the foraging of wild foods, particularly berries and mushrooms.

What does all of this have to do with food taboos? Well, on the one hand it is worth reminding ourselves that strong identifications of ourselves by what we don't eat do have a purpose. They aren't just wastefulness; they help us identify ourselves as part of particular community. It suggests that in our agricultural shift, we may first have to change how we identify ourselves.

And since food taboos are part of most cultures, the first priority must be to change our set of taboo foods, to render "dirty" the processed foods we now rely on. And this is happening already because these are increasingly dirty and dangerous — toxic to us in many cases and often contaminated. Since 2006 the US has been rocked by the discovery that there is deadly E. coli in bagged greens, melamine in pet food and Asian infant formulas, botulism in canned chili and a host of other toxic dangers in our globalized, industrialized food system. More and more, Americans are starting to recognize that food they've been raised to think of as "dirty" is actually cleaner than the food we were taught to trust.

Even more, however, it suggests that we need to be working not only on our gardens but on our integration of our home and small-farm agriculture into the farmer-hunter-gatherer paradigm. That is, most of us will feed ourselves not simply through horticulture (smaller-scale agriculture that includes tree culture) or agriculture but as mostly fixed human beings have for thousands of years — with the integration of all of the above skills.

It isn't simply a matter of replacing one kind of agriculture (big, industrial) with another kind of equally linear food production system (small, not industrial); it is something more complex. Think of the role of farmer-hunter-gatherer in a community as the integration of the margins into the whole. That is, our job is not just to cultivate as much earth as we can, but also to familiarize ourselves with what is out there and make the absolute best use of it we can.

In some cases, this will mean traditional hunting and foraging. But that also means recreating the ability to *see* what is around you — to make use of sidewalk margins as growing space or to view the weeds that compete with our crops as potential hedges against crop failure. It involves the recreation of a deeply intimate and profound knowledge of place. This will take time and practice, and a new crop of home botanists with the eyes to see and the courage to cook.

In order to do this, we must stop contaminating the biosphere and destroying biodiversity — otherwise, there will be nothing to harvest, or what there is will be so toxic that we dare not eat it. Right now our roadsides are covered with wild plants we dare not eat because of accumulated lead and pesticides.

Pesticides kill unwanted plants, animals, bacteria and fungi, and function as an unnatural way of limiting many species to support a select few. It is a practice characterized by dramatically diminishing returns. Each year in the US the agriculture industry uses 1.2 billion pounds of pesticides. That's five pounds per person.[196]

In the past two decades, the use of hydrocarbon-based pesticides in the US has increased *thirty-three* fold, and yet each year we lose more crops to pests.[197] Even while the toxicity of commercial pesticides has increased tenfold, over the past 50 years, insect-related crop loss has doubled.[198] That is, as we use more pesticides we further unbalance the ecology of our farm fields, and this increasing imbalance serves to support ever-increasing populations of pests.

The reason the pests increase is that pesticides disproportionately destroy predators in an environment. In any given area there are far more plant eaters and prey than animal-eating predators. When an area is sprayed there are always some survivors, but because the remainder are much smaller in number the predators of those insects are disproportionately set back, creating a burst of new plant-eating pests with few or no natural systems to keep them in check. That is, pesticides can actually cause outbreaks of pests. Only by restoring balance and biodiversity in the fields and gardens where we grow our food will we see a real reduction in food lost to such pests.

It's important to note that less than 0.1 percent of these pesticides actually reach the pests they're intended to kill.[199] That is, we're really just dosing our environment with the stuff in hopes that it will make slight improvements in crop yields. How slight you ask? Lappé and other suggest that, "for corn and wheat, together accounting for 30 percent of all pesticides used on US cropland, researchers estimate that crop losses from pesticides would increase only 1 or 2 percent if no pesticides at all were employed."[200] That is, we're enduring this poisoning for very, very slight gains.

It might further disturb readers to understand that vanity drives much of this exercise. Again Francis Moore Lappé et al.:

> Much of the problem with the use of pesticides is cultural: the cosmetic standards set by consumer preferences in industrial countries (especially in the United States) have driven producers all over the world into a never-ending search for the glossiest apple and most unblemished pear. In the United States it is estimated that from 60 to 80 percent of the pesticides applied to oranges and 40–60 percent of that applied to tomatoes is used only to improve appearance, with no improvement whatsoever to nutritional content.[201]

Why then, you might ask, have we allowed such a destructive process to enter into the way we grow food? We have again believed linear promises of technology that tell us we can completely manage complex biological systems. We have listened to the tales of the linear so carefully that many of us assume that pesticides have some benefit. And, of course, pesticides are enormously profitable.

In an especially insidious example of manipulation by the multinational agricultural corporations, new crops have been bred that are resistant to herbicides. This means that entire fields can be sprayed with herbicidal chemicals once under cultivation, destroying any other traces of plant life save the single species meant for cultivation. Though this might seem like an advantage for the farmer trying to increase the yields of his crop, the long-term effects are increasing dependency by farmers on these corporations as the ecological damage to his fields necessitates ever more such chemicals and their resistant seeds. And in the long term, it is impossible, in years when crops are destroyed, for farmers to harvest anything else from a field so managed. Unlike the Danish farmers who at least had brome seed to put in their bellies, in monocrops, the results are all or nothing.

Evidence suggests that resistant strains of super weeds are evolving that resist even this "take no prisoner" type of herbicidal approach to weed prevention. Thus chemical no-till agriculture is doomed to failure. Attempting to work against nature requires enormous quantities of energy, and generally only postpones the day on which we'll have to deal with the consequences. And again, our linear use of technologies has caused consequences that are intolerable: cancers, autism, reproductive disorders and other diseases are a logical consequence of our battles against nature.

It's worth pointing out that the benefits of a healthy diet are also compromised by these practices. The average US citizen has traces of 13 pesticides or the associated breakdown products in their bodies, with the highest levels in children. As Dale Allen Pfeiffer points out, "Many of these pesticides are present in amounts well in excess of established safety levels."[202] Which is to say that while the short-term outcome of increased yields might seem desirable, one of the long-term consequences is health complications for people participating in this agricultural experiment. The worst victims of our pesticide use are babies, whose tiny bodies can tolerate far less of these than the average human. Sandra Steingraber, in *Having Faith,* observes that nursing infants are at the very top of the food — and thus pesticide — chain. What is sprayed on plants makes its way into animals and fish we eat, and then into adult bodies, whereupon it passes into breast milk and damages our children in ways we do not fully understand.[203]

Tinkering with genetically modified organisms (GMOs) is another example of the technological manipulation of nature we undertake in an attempt to dominate. But such actions aren't without consequences. The wind and water don't accept direction on which way to flow, and already we've seen the seeds of genetically modified plants spread out from the fields where they were planted to areas in which they are unwanted.[204] It is our opinion that no scientist can say, definitively, what the long-term effects will be on the genetic makeup of the plants that humans have grown for food.

Some more sinister genetic manipulation has led to the creation of terminator seeds, or genetic manipulation that renders a plant sterile after just one generation. As noted, this prevents farmers from engaging in the millennia-old tradition of saving seeds and slowly breeding plants for characteristics beneficial to certain situations and localities. Were this mutation to spread into other plants not originally intended to become sterile after one year's time, the result could be catastrophic. It also leaves only those companies capable of producing such seeds with the power to hand out what each farmer needs at the beginning of each season of planting, the seed of the next harvest. We simply cannot permit large corporations to control something so basic as our right to food. Such a concentration of power is by its application anti-democratic.

The potential dangers of GMOs are best illustrated by the history of Elaine Ingham, who until recently was a professor of forest science at Oregon State University and is the founder of the Soil Food Web. Ingham writes about a narrowly averted disaster that might have starved everyone on the planet.

Ingham worked testing genetically modified organisms, exploring whether they had any implications were they to make it into uncontrolled use in the world. One of the organisms she tested was based on an incredibly common soil bacteria, *Klebsiella*. The bacteria had been modified to produce alcohol in its root systems, with the hope that this would be a new source of biofuels. Ingham did laboratory tests to see what would happen if this bacteria were to spread into fields. This is what she found:

> About a week later, we walked into the laboratory, opened up the incubator, and said, "Oops, what did we do wrong?" Many of the plants were dead and were turning into slime on the surface of the soil. In all the units with just water in the system, the plants were doing okay. In those that had been inoculated with the parent *Klebsiella planticola*, the plants were even bigger, because increased nutrient cycling in the root system makes more nitrogen available, causing the plants to grow bigger. Clearly the parent organism was a benefit to the plant. But where the engineered bacterium was growing, all the plants were dead. Later we tried this experiment using several different kinds of soils, but *the result in every case was dead plants.*
>
> Take that information and extrapolate it to the real world. Given that the parent organism lives in the root systems of all plants, what's the logical outcome of releasing this organism into the natural environment? Very possibly, we would have no terrestrial plants left. Some plants, such as riparian and wetland plants, have mechanisms for dealing with alcohol production in their root systems. But the logical extrapolation of that experiment is that we would lose terrestrial plants.[205]

The biotechnology industry has resisted any attempts to regulate it or to impose testing — and yet the stakes are as high as can be imagined. The loss of terrestrial plants would have killed most of humanity — and it came quite close to happening. GMOs have also failed to deliver on basic promises. The UNESCO report cited above recently confirmed that in fact most GMOs offer lower, rather than higher yields.

We should not believe the industrial agricultural corporations when they tell us they are smarter than nature and create only solutions, never problems, with their processes of biological consolidation. It is becoming more and more evident that in fact much of what they gained was not so much wisdom but access to nonrenewable resources — that is, it is not knowledge, but energy that made their processes most possible.

Today, despite all the energy we have injected to the system, despite everything the industrial model has cost us, more than 850,000 people worldwide do not have access to enough nutritious food.[206] According to the World Food Programme, 24,000 people die daily because of starvation and starvation-related illnesses. Even in the United States more than twelve percent of our population is food insecure.[207] So it is that industrial agriculture has not succeeded in its attempt to feed the masses.

> Millions go hungry around the world — nearly one fifth of humanity. At the same time, immense surpluses resulting from hypertechnologisation are being held or destroyed in other parts of the world. Yet the UN's Food and Agriculture Organisation is not embarrassed to call for more technology (genetic engineering), and further moves to an open world market, as the way to combat hunger in the Third World. The reality, on the contrary, is that hunger is a result of technologisation. The US grain surpluses used for so-called famine relief have destroyed the indigenous millet market for African peasants (Imfeld 1975, NACLA 1976). The boring of deep wells in the Sahel in order to raise the productivity and therefore the profitabiality of cattlebreeding has dangerously lowered the water table and compounded the desertification effects of overpasturing (J. O. Muller 1988; Comite d' Information Sahel 1975). The FAO's much-heralded Green Revolution, with its technologically generated maximum yields, has led India, Thailand, Mexico, and elsewhere to the concentration of land among those with the most capital, and to a veritable army of landless peasants (Shiva 1989; Pare 1979). If FAO president Diouff now admits that world hunger is a matter of unjust distribution trather than production

shortfalls, and therefore a social rather that a technolgoical problem he is still only speaking half the truth. It would appear that
techonologically and socially just distribution could be promoted
in parallel and independently of each other. But in reality, technology is anything but socially "innocent."[208]

That is to say, industrial agriculture and growth economics wasn't feeding the world *before* we started experiencing the problems of peak oil and
climate change. Those making money off of industrial agriculture will tell
you we need both more and technically better industrial agriculture to
solve these problems or we'll face starvation, never realizing that these solutions are already failing us. What makes such people think these two linear ways of producing food will somehow magically do so in the future in
these face of these looming problems?

It is suggested that a deviation from industrial agriculture will lead to
a decrease in yields and thus the fulfillment of a Malthusian prediction of
the world's inability to feed itself. This is, of course, another false dichotomy and one we will explore further in the next chapter — the notion that
we will prevail through technological advancement and strict adherence to
growth markets or perish from famine. But this false choice is perhaps the
most important of such choices we must reject as the future unfolds. And
we can do so with the knowledge and even the proof that an alternative exists. George Monbiot describes it in this way:

> We have, in other words, been deceived. Traditional farming has
> been stamped out all over the world not because it is less produc-
> tive than monoculture, but because it is, in some respects, more
> productive. Organic cultivation has been characterised as an en-
> emy of progress for the simple reason that it cannot be monopo-
> lised: it can be adopted by any farmer anywhere, without the help
> of multinational companies. Though it is more productive to grow
> several species or several varieties of crops in one field, the biotech
> companies must reduce diversity in order to make money, leaving
> farmers with no choice but to purchase their most profitable seeds.
> This is why they have spent the last 10 years buying up seed breed-
> ing institutes and lobbying governments to do what ours has done:
> banning the sale of any seed which has not been officially — and
> expensively — registered and approved.[209]

All this requires an unrelenting propaganda war against the tried and tested techniques of traditional farming, as the big companies and their scientists dismiss them as unproductive, unsophisticated and unsafe. The truth, so effectively suppressed that it is now almost impossible to believe, is that organic farming is the key to feeding the world." [210]

Get Small and Go Home

The best place to seek God is in a garden. You can dig for him there.
— GEORGE BERNARD SHAW —

We now recognize that there are other, more useful, choices on the spectrum between "the current agricultural model" and "cannibalism." The time has come to move toward an alternative agriculture, simply made up of many more small gardens and farms. Instead of one approach applied to every model, this would entail using appropriately scaled technologies and tools on many different types of land with variety of people growing and husbanding a much wider variety of food. Now, as the resources that support industrial agriculture make that way of growing food less likely in the future, small-scale agriculture can begin to take root again.

A more productive model of farming per unit of land will prove necessary in the future. Peter Rosset, in his report, "Benefits of Small Farm Agriculture In the Context of Global Trade Negotiations," estimates that a four-acre farm is 200 times more productive than four acres of a 1,000-acre farm. That is, growing food with more people on lots of much smaller plots of land is much more productive, and that is welcome news as we're entering into an era when we're going to need more food.

Rosset observes also that small farming operations are "multi-functional" — more productive, more efficient, and contribute more to economic development than large farms. [211]

By focusing on polyculture instead of monoculture, small farms foster biodiversity and promote a healthy ecology. This helps not only to stabilize the resources loss and degradation described earlier in this book but also to increase food yields. As natural balances are allowed back into play, small-scale food production is able to reduce waste by taking advantage of the absence of extremes. A small number of harmful insects might cause some damage, but a roughly equal number of beneficial insects will likely keep the situation within tolerable bounds. The large numbers of harmful

insects associated with acres and acres of a single crop will never material-
ize and therefore never experience such dramatic loss.

Diversity of ownership too is fostered by more small farms. This kind
of system creates choice instead of limiting selection as each small producer develops different skills and experience and produces more and new
varieties of food. Such a system promotes food security because it doesn't
focus the dietary needs of people on a small, centralized group of growers
but rather on a large network of decentralized small-scale growers. If a single farm, or even several farms in such a decentralized system, fail in a given
year, such a network has the ability to respond with flexibility in a way that
the current monolithic organization of industrial agriculture does not.

Smaller farms also mean a more intimate relationship with the land. No
one can properly understand and adequately care for thousands of acres of
land and the soil, water resources and other ecological resources present
on such a large tract. To care for and coax food from a much smaller parcel of land means gaining an understanding of one's ecosystem. Knowing
that you and future generations depend on this place means protecting and
defending one's land base from degradation and working to build biodiversity and the resources that might make the such a small farm even more
productive. Farming at such a scale becomes more than just using the right
chemicals at the right combinations. It means striving for a knowledge and
an understanding of how best to steward the land. The result is more sustainable land management than is possible by industrial agriculture — an
agriculture that contains its own incentives to reduce soil and water damage and create productive, sustainable systems.

Rosset suggests,

> Decentralized land ownership produces more equitable economic
> opportunity for people in rural areas, as well as greater social capi-
> tal. This can provide a greater sense of personal responsibility and
> feeling of control over one's life, characteristics that are not as read-
> ily available to factory line workers. Land owners who rely on lo-
> cal businesses and services for their needs are more likely to have
> a stake in the well-being of the community and the well-being of
> its citizens. In turn, local land owners are more likely to be held ac-
> countable for any negative actions that harm the community.[212]

Such thinking is sorely needed in the US at the beginning of the 21st
century.

We need more people with a greater connection to food and the process of producing it. We need older people with this wisdom to share it with new young gardeners and farmers-to-be and the next generation of children who could grow up with an understanding of how to farm and a connection to their land base that is invaluable. With a little faith and a bit of fear, we're hoping through this book to point the way toward an alternative that is flexible, malleable and adaptable so that we can move away from the current broken model of feeding ourselves and take up the enormous challenge of addressing worldwide hunger.

Another result of such a shift will be a much better diet. That is, this isn't all about saving ourselves from starvation or even saving ourselves from the clutches of evil industrial agriculture but about eating food that is healthier, more diverse in abundance and just flat out tastes better. The current model focuses on poor quality food of dubious nutritional value, eaten in ways that destroy communities rather than create them. Acres of cheap corn and soy turn into the prepackaged microwavable dinners that provide families all over the US with an excuse to forgo the home-cooked family meal for the convenient concoction that is a TV dinner. The result of this is the loss of that iconic American time around the dinner table.

Food has historically been a socially organizing activity with family and friends sharing food preparation and meal time. Prepackaged meals don't so much disassociate us from the art of cooking as package the art of food production and cheapen it, transforming acts of love into acts of factory production.

How We Eat Now

The most remarkable thing about my mother
is that for 30 years she served
the family nothing but leftovers.
The original meal has never been found.
— CALVIN TRILLIN —

If you were born after the 1940s, you were probably raised, to one degree or another, to believe that domestic work, including food production, is monotonous, brain numbing, unskilled, and pointless. At the same time that we look enviously at the image of Norman Rockwell's family lovingly sitting down to the turkey we also feel that the regular production of that meal is impossible for us and that it is work that is not merely time consuming but valueless. In many families, home food production is something to fight about, a tedious conflict at the heart of your family life where you and your spouse debate yet again who will microwave the macaroni and cheese and clean up afterward.

Even if we don't believe this, we often know that our jobs/busy schedules means that we can't help picking up fast food or pizza or eating out three nights a week. We have to have money to buy food, and that means we have to go to work all day and commute a long distance, and we are simply too tired to do anything else. And of course, this is true — but it is also true that most of us think more quickly of making more money than we do of needing less, of being able to buy more and better food than of growing it ourselves or cooking more basic foods from scratch, and thus reclaiming a bit of our time. Is that unrealistic? Probably for some people. For others, it isn't.

The wealthiest 20 percent of Americans eat out for more than 60 percent of their meals. The poorest 20 percent eat out for the exact same percentage of their meals.[213] The difference exists on only three levels: 1. how likely the restaurant is to be a fast food chain and how nutritious the meal is; 2. how many unused cookbooks are on the shelves of the kitchen they do not enter; and 3. how likely they are to say they "love" to cook, without ever actually doing it. (In the US, people who say they "hate" to cook actually eat in slightly more often than people who "love" it.)

One out of every three Americans eat in a fast food restaurant on any given day, and we spend 110 billion dollars on fast food each year.[214] More than half of all Americans eat six or more meals per week at a fast food restaurant. So it is impossible to talk about our food choices without talking about the fact that most of our meals aren't eaten at home at all. The first step to a better system must be to go home to our families and share food with them there.

Of meals eaten at home, 65 percent involve the use of pre-processed or "prepared" ingredients, and 75 percent involve a microwave. Seventy percent of Americans have no idea how to make stuffing not from a mix; 41 percent cannot make mashed potatoes from actual potatoes, rather than a box; and 90 percent buy boneless chicken breasts because they can't figure out to debone them.[215]

A vast majority of American meals involved at least two of the following six ingredients — white bread, chicken breasts, ground beef, potatoes (more than 75 percent of which come in the form of either boxed potatoes, chips or frozen fries/tater tots), milk, ketchup.

We suspect a lot of people reading this feel rather superior at the moment. "*I* bake my own bread," we say. "I don't eat out that often. I never, ever go to McDonalds (just Taco Bell, and that only once in a while, right before a meeting, you know.)"

But the truth is that most of us are implicated in this problem in complex ways and unsure of how to get out of the energy-consumptive, destructive way we eat and cook. We want to cook, but we are ambivalent about it and overwhelmed by the idea. As Jean Zimmerman argues, we want to be the sort of people who cook everything from scratch, but can't get there in our harried lives, and we resent the idea we should to do all this drudgery. But, of course, the idea that it is drudgery is something we've been sold.

> Between the 1920s and today, Americans bought the argument that we no longer have time to cook — and, even if we did have time, it was drudgery we'd rather avoid in preference of leisure activities. We use this phrase all the time: kitchen drudgery. What we don't realize is that it's a message promulgated by marketers for the processed food companies, beginning way back, almost a hundred years ago.... The American Can Company boasted that in the years 1951–1952, the use of frozen orange juice had saved American housewives 14,000 years of "drudgery." An inadvertent collaboration developed between the giant food companies and women eager to get out from under the feminine mystique.[216]

Zimmerman calls the collaboration inadvertent, but in her book *Depletion and Abundance: Life on the New Home Front*, Sharon argues that there was nothing inadvertent about it — that the version of feminism that succeeded was a corporate feminism that served the growth economy better than it served women in many cases. In fact, Americans did not get more leisure by going to work and outsourcing cooking; they got less. The drudgery they were freed of, which had been done to serve the families they loved, was replaced by drudgery in the workplace in the service of large corporations. This is not to say that the burden of this rests on women — men could have taken up this work as women went out into the public economy. The problem is that we were sold a bill of goods. We were told that domestic labor was unskilled, tedious and pointless. But was it?

Imagine yourselves required to do the simple job of making your own food for a month. Piece of cake — but wouldn't you be better off at your law firm or fixing cars and doing work that is "valuable?" But think about it for a moment.

You have to produce three meals a day, plus beverages and snacks entirely from whole foods in your storage, garden or barn, or easily obtained from local producers within 25 miles of your home. You must do so using sustainable methods, with no electric oven or microwave. You cannot go to the store more than once every few weeks; you must use what you have, and ensure that it will last. Or you can go to market every day, but buy only what your small daily wages can afford and what you can physically carry in your arms or on your back. You have no refrigeration, so each meal must be precisely the right size to ensure no waste. You need to pay special attention to the dietary needs and palates of the sick, elderly, children, pregnant and nursing mothers. You need to be sure that everyone gets enough to fuel increased physical labor (i.e., walking places instead of driving, growing food in a garden) and a balanced and varied enough diet to make sure they remain healthy. It also must be palatable enough to ensure adequate consumption and lack of waste. Meanwhile, you have to stretch limited food supplies and preserve supplies of fats, sugars, eggs, dairy and meats to ensure you will not go hungry later, if food supplies tighten.

Does this sound untenable, a ridiculous challenge? And yet, it is precisely how food is made in a vast majority of homes around the world today. And it was exactly how meals were produced throughout the entire world through all of human history up until the past 100 years. Nearly every person did a variation on this work. Mull that over for a moment.

Of course, part of the job was logistics and planning — did you start the sprouts on Friday, so that they would be ready for today's salad? Is the next batch of yogurt ready as the first one runs out? How early did you need to get up to get the bread baked before lunch? Did you plant a next crop of lettuce? How long can you keep those eggs warm? Did you grind enough flour for the pancakes, or do you have to go back and do it again? Are you sure that you've left enough baking soda for birthday cakes?

Meanwhile, besides the ordinary work of food production, you have to inventory, maintain, track, manage, preserve, protect and prevent rot on the food you have in storage and coming in. That means that besides three meals a day, you need to keep track of how much sugar is left, make applesauce when the last apples start to soften, dry or can those strawberries that come flooding in when the season starts, walk the six miles to the food market that is likely to have live chickens this week, forage for wild greens, kill the chicken, make six gallons of sauerkraut, figure out a way to make up for the absence of vanilla, white flour and eggs in your child's birthday cake, plan for extra guests and hospitality, as well as festival meals and special occasions.

Unskilled labor indeed. Try it for a month. Seriously, it will not only give you new appreciation for the value, intellectual pleasures and creativity of domestic labor and for the power of women (who do the majority of this work), but it will also point up the fact that only part of the project is knowing good recipes for whole wheat. The rest is figuring out how to make good, interesting, balanced, varied food out of what you have three times a day, 365 days a year, with your own hands, sustainable methods and local resources.

We are not suggesting that you must immediately move toward the way billions of poor people cook and eat now or that you give up all your appliances. But we do want all of us to recall that food looms larger in most lives than it does in our own and that that is normal and desirable, that most of the world's poor people work long hours and also feed themselves daily meals made as described above. It is, of course, challenging in the present economy to find time and energy to put food in its proper place at the center of our world, but it is both normal to do so, and probably necessary. Challenging does not mean "impossible." The good news is that that work is no less stimulating, engaging or meaningful than our present jobs — often more so. There's every chance that we will be better off with food in a different role in our lives.

Nor is it necessarily self-evident that we will suffer economically from doing so. Many estimates of the value of second incomes have found that when costs are sorted out, the second wage earner in the family brings in very little net income. If it were possible to make money growing food, or to need less by cooking from scratch and growing groceries, many, many households, heavily burdened by expensive commutes and the rising cost of trips to the store might find they came off better with only one person working. This will not apply to all families, to the poorest on the margins, to those most deeply in debt or those who depend on a second income for benefits. But it will apply to many households, and it might apply to even more if extended families were to combine housing and resources.

As much as we are tied to the growth economy, our beliefs about cooking and eating are just as tied to wrongheaded linear systems as our agriculture. As Michael Pollan and Marion Nestle have shown in their critiques of
"nutritionism," we have reduced foods to their component parts without
fully understanding that foods are not parts — that is, that garlic is more
than the sum of the few chemical components that we understand.

In the 1950s, science fiction stories routinely imagined that we would
be able to reduce food to nutrients and put it in pill form, meeting all needs
without the bothersome bits of actually needing food. But in fact, our attempts to turn food into components have been miserable failures — the
most startling one has been the turn to infant formulas, which kill 4,000
infants annually.[217] Not only is our attempt to mimic the nutrients in human breastmilk a failure, but there is growing scientific evidence that auto-
immune diseases may be promoted by formula feeding, and that hundreds
of common diseases and conditions are tied to lack of breastmilk. And yet
there remains a widespread perception among adults that formula is equivalent, that it "has all the nutrients" of breastmilk. But that only reveals what
we do not know and perhaps can never discover — the way that the whole
is greater than the sum of its parts.

If science over decades has failed to synthesize a single food, breastmilk,
or to create an adequate replacement, why is it that we imagine that our nutritional knowledge is in any sense sufficient to create processed, fortified
substances that substitute for food. In an essay entitled "Unhappy Meals,"
Michael Pollan detailed the ways in which nutritionism has directed us to
eat less healthily and moved us toward processed foods, more obesity and
more "lifestyle diseases" — the term used to describe the health problems
caused by the Western processed diet:

> The Year of Eating Oat Bran — also known as 1988 — served as a
> kind of coming-out party for the food scientists, who succeeded in
> getting the material into nearly every processed food sold in Amer-
> ica. Oat bran's moment on the dietary stage didn't last long, but the
> pattern had been established, and every few years since then a new
> oat bran has taken its turn under the marketing lights. (Here comes
> omega-3!)
>
>   By comparison, the typical real food has more trouble compet-
> ing under the rules of nutritionism, if only because something like
> a banana or an avocado can't easily change its nutritional stripes
> (though rest assured the genetic engineers are hard at work on the

problem). So far, at least, you can't put oat bran in a banana. So depending on the reigning nutritional orthodoxy, the avocado might be either a high-fat food to be avoided (Old Think) or a food high in monounsaturated fat to be embraced (New Think). The fate of each whole food rises and falls with every change in the nutritional weather, while the processed foods are simply reformulated. That's why when the Atkins mania hit the food industry, bread and pasta were given a quick redesign (dialing back the carbs; boosting the protein), while the poor unreconstructed potatoes and carrots were left out in the cold.

Of course it's also a lot easier to slap a health claim on a box of sugary cereal than on a potato or carrot, with the perverse result that the most healthful foods in the supermarket sit there quietly in the produce section, silent as *stroke victims*, while a few aisles over, the Cocoa Puffs and Lucky Charms are screaming about their newfound whole-grain goodness.[218]

Pollan's simple solution? Don't eat anything your grandmother wouldn't have eaten. That is, eat food, not things that claim to have magical health properties. Eat a varied diet, based mostly on plants in their whole form. And believe it or not, that's pretty much all we have to know about food.

But, of course, that's easy to say and harder to do, particularly in a world where we are constantly bombarded with advertisements, with "new" foods, and with cultural pressures to eat in particular ways. Eating cyclically, with the seasons, with what is fresh and available naturally in our area, cooking from scratch from whole foods, eating meat as a condiment, rather than the center of the plate — these things are simple in many ways, but it is hard to overcome the enormous pull of the linear upon us.

An Interview with Albert Bates: Spring 2008

Albert Bates is an early member of one of the US's oldest modern intentional communities, called The Farm, in Tennessee.

ANOF: Your most recent book, *The Post-Petroleum Survival Guide and Cookbook: Recipes for Changing Times*, talks about preparing for a transition to a new way of being, a new way of living. Could you talk in broad

terms about what that transition itself might look like? I think some people have the expectation that we're going to flip a switch and things are going to be post-carbon.

ALBERT: Yeah, it's not actually going to go that easily. I think that's kind of
wishful thinking, and I think the key theme that I'm harping on these days
when I go out and talk or lecture or give permaculture courses or speak to
groups of students is that what we need more of is resilience. That's essentially the quality of defense, in depth, that allows a community to provide
for most of its essential needs — food, energy, water, raw materials — from
multiple sources, most of them local. So that in the event of large-scale system failures, collapse is averted because there's smaller-scale, local community resilience that has the wherewithal to fend for itself.

Getting to that — that idea of resilience — actually means traveling
back on a development path that we had previously gone the opposite direction on. In a sense it's kind of a reversal, but at the same time, it's something that we are familiar with, that we know how to do, because we've
been there before. We actually have a lot of things that we've developed in
the last century of high-tech, fossil-fueled, civilized progress, and we can
apply many of those same kinds of things to this new paradigm of living locally and having multiple resilient systems.

To give you an example, the bicycle. The bicycle has advanced hugely
in the last 20 years and even more in the last 50 years. If you look at that
kind of progress and you say, okay, apply that now to getting to the post office to pick up the mail or the postman delivering the mail or the cop on
the beat instead of going around in a cruiser being on a bicycle. That kind
of thing is actually more doable now than it would have been back when
everyone had a single gear clunker that weighed a quarter of their own
body weight. At the same time, I don't want to completely throw out those
heavy-duty steel frame models. Arguably they won the Vietnamese their
independence. They were the workhorses that carried artillery shells up the
mountains to *Dien Bien Phu* and ran supplies down the Ho Chi Minh trail
through all the B-52 craters.

ANOF: Could you talk about cooking as an important building block of
the community? I'm thinking here of the technologies and the skills that
it takes, but also the sharing and the communal aspect of eating and cooking together.

ALBERT: If you look back in American history, you can see that there's been a lot of communal experiments over the years, a lot of weird strange cults and stuff that came over from various different countries and settled in North America, and a lot of those didn't survive. Most of them didn't survive, and several of them had fairly serious death tolls the first few years.

[At The Farm] we survived; we made it. And part of the reason we made it was we were able to feed everybody from soybeans. Soy was our miracle plant. It was the wonder bean of China, and for 2,000 years people in Asia had been developing a marvelous cuisine. The Indonesians had developed *tempeh;* the Javanese had developed *ontjom;* the Malaysians *yuba,* the Japanese *natto* and *sufu;* and the Chinese had *tofu,* soy milk, and yogurt and things like that. We just kept pushing that envelope and taking that into the hippy realms of California cuisine — soy burgers and soy burritos and soy cheesecake and soysage and soy pizzas and soy coffee and things like that. We were the Alice Waters and Wolfgang Puck of soy. And because soybeans in those days cost about three dollars a bushel, which is 60 pounds (today it's probably up to about seven dollars a bushel) what that means is that you can feed one person their protein needs for a year on three to seven dollars if you can make it tasty enough to repeat almost daily.

ANOF: But [in the stories we've heard about life on The Farm] it sounds like the eating was really an important part socially, a cohesion, a wonderful thing to look forward to.

ALBERT: There's actually been a study done by a guy at the University of British Columbia. A professor there did this lovely study where he looked at what is it that communities that have lasted the longest — intentional communities that lasted the longest — what are the factors that they have in common? And one of those that he signaled as being pretty important, that you can pretty much rank the longevity of any community based on, is common shared meals. The more often people come together, the better their odds. So if they come together daily, three times a day, their odds are excellent. If they come together a couple times a week, their odds are still good. If they come together once a month, they're still better than not coming together at all. There's a direct correlation there between people eating together and getting along in a community.

ANOF: And I certainly know sociologists who would say the same about individual families.

ALBERT: Probably so. You know, the other thing about it is that there is a joy in cooking. There's a joy in providing for others by the fruits of your labor. And you see that personal satisfaction of watching other people eat what you've just cooked and complimenting the chef and so on and so forth. All of that is a self-maintaining, self-gratifying kind of effort, but it's also very important from the standpoint of kids growing up in that and propagating that meme of the happy family out to larger and larger groups of extended family and community and so forth. We had lots of kids living in close confinement here. In the early days we didn't have much in the way of housing, so people were living thirty, forty people to a standard house — what you'd call a house in the US today. And so a lot of kids being raised there in those communal settings, going to meals three times a day with everybody else — all the other kids, all the other grownups — and seeing this kind of interaction over the food. It has an effect of making the community more stable from the kids up. As the kids grow into that, they grow up more stable in their social relationships.

ANOF: It's much maligned by a lot of modern Americans, the idea of growing their own food and cooking it, but there really is a joy that many people are missing out on.

ALBERT: That's right. You can go back — I don't know how old you are, but for me, I'm in my sixties now, and I go back to the early days of television. And I remember Mrs. Goldberg, you know, and the old 12-inch black-and-white TV and *The Honeymooners* and stuff like that? There were always people standing around the stove, right? There were always people who were making a pot of spaghetti sauce or something. That's what they did. You go to an Amish community and you see the same thing; you go to a Hutterite community and you see the same thing, which is that there are people who are the cooks. They're the ones who really take pleasure in making sure that everybody's well-fed all the time.

ANOF: Right. Well, and for the book, we're also going to talk specifically about Jeffersonian democracy because I feel like he had this idea of a nation of farmers, of a people who were marginally self-sufficient. They still interacted of course, and traded among themselves, but that certain level of self-sufficiency insulated them, gave them a certain amount of freedom because they weren't beholden to others for their basic needs.

ALBERT: That's right. Here's another piece of that, which is that one of the tensions that you always find in intentional communities, indeed anywhere that people are living together, is this continuum between privacy and public space, or personal space and public space. People want to be able to be left alone, but they also crave the company of people and the opportunity for conviviality. So you have to have a balance in your life, and you have to have a balance in your space, and you have to have the development of forms, patterns that allow for people to be in whatever place they want to be in that given moment and be able to move freely.

If you're successful in creating those kinds of forms where people have the option of being public or being private, where people have shared purse or common enterprise but they also have the ability to provide for their immediate needs or their families' immediate needs, then you get to a certain point where you can actually obtain enough happiness, enough contentment, that actually new creative energy comes forth that might be more synergistic, more multiplicative than what you had when everybody was just sort of contending for what they individually needed.

ANOF: It looks like we're going to have a shortage of arable land going forward, as our human population grows and as we salinate, and desertification and deforestation...

ALBERT: We've got a shortage now, and it appears that that shortage is growing. The thing about that is that there's this whole bugaboo about people saying that since the last ice age we've been depleting our soil and that we're in this irreversible decline now; we've past peak soil and we're now on this downslope, and so we're going to face this huge famine from that. My personal experience is, I know how to make soil. I teach people how to make soil. We've been making soil here at The Farm for years and years and years; we know how to make soil. It's not difficult to make soil, and I say the same thing for arable land. We can make arable land.

One of the things I do when I go out and talk is I go up there on the stage and I put up the projector and I have this short Shockwave Flash movie of Geoff Lawton making forest in the middle of the desert in Jordan. He is growing mushrooms in the soil and the mycelium is locking up the salt in the desert so that the soils have tilthe and come alive. And we can do that: we can take all of our deserts and turn them into farmland. Lately I have been researching the paleoclimatology of the Sahara and I am beginning to think it is even possible there. We can at least reverse the desertification trend in the Sahel, and it is possible we can reforest in Chad and elsewhere where there are aquifers.

ANOF: How about our suburbs?

ALBERT: Well, suburbs are poorly designed. Being an architect, you probably understand. They need some redesign — David Holmgren has some interesting ideas about that. You can take out every third house or every fourth house and begin to cluster up a bit and have connections between houses, and have land that has farming uses or other kinds of common activity. But the suburbs need redesign if for no other reason than they don't have essential infrastructure within walking distance. They need to have food production; they need to have water; but they need to have shops, schools, churches, theaters and clinics, a cemetery and things like that in every suburb.

Well, let me just close by saying something about the future for us. We may soon find that the model that we've created for a business here for the Ecovillage Training Center will not sustain past the period of no airplanes flying or people having the ability to travel long distances to come take a course here. And national currencies could become worthless also. So we're actually looking at a transition now, and some of our effort is directed toward the surrounding communities — going out to several counties around us and teaching these skills at the very simple level of where people are at in the surrounding areas rather than telling them that they have to learn permaculture or something. I have learned much from my friend, Rob Hopkins, and the Transition Towns movement, and I think that offers a strategy that is the next step after the experimental vessel of ecovillages. It is really a synthesis of ecovillage and relocalization, intentional community and sustainable development.

Then also, the example of The Farm has transitioned out of its early days of more self-reliance into much more bourgeois living in people's middle age or later years. And so we actually have to go back and say, "You know, we learned a whole lot back in those early days of the seventies; we sure could be doing a lot more of that now again." We're having to relearn or think about reclaiming some of that earlier skill set. So we're in a transition here. We're stable but not static. It's much tougher now, because our population has aged and our youth are still somewhat disinterested, but we're moving. We're in the process of changing ourselves. Events will force us to speed that up soon enough.

Best of all, we have tools we did not have in 1971. We have permaculture, biochar, E. M. (effective microorganisms), compost tea, biodynamic preps, aquatic garden systems, and activated water. We can terrace slopes with our bulldozers and road graders that can run on pond algae and used cooking oil. We have Japanese forest mushrooms, tempeh, and home-brewed beer.

I'm happy because the children have, to a larger extent than they may appreciate, already got it and they're turning around and heading in the right direction pretty quickly. My son, Will, is living in a passive solar house and farming; he's got several acres in CSA vegetable gardens now, and he's coming by all the time and asking for different bits of advice and tools and things. One of my next-door neighbor's kids, Biko, has spent several years living in ecovillages in South Africa and India and has returned with a whole new set of skills. That's the kind of thing that gives me real hope — that the next generation is hip, they're on board, they've got the vision, and they can see what's possible. And having done it all myself when I was young and full of crazy ideas, I don't worry that they can do it just as easily as I did. And everyone else can too.

—— RECIPES ——

Pawpaw Ginseng Wine   *by Albert Bates*

Equipment
- Large saucepan
- masher and mashing bowl
- cheesecloth
- secondary fermenters (could be stopped bottles or sterile canning jars)

Ingredients
- 2¼ pounds ripe pawpaws, very fresh, not green. The stem should wiggle easily. If they were picked green they can be refrigerated until ripe.
- 2 pounds granulated sugar or the equivalent in honey or stevia
- 1 small ginseng root, fresh or rehydrated
- 1½ tsp citric acid
- ½ tsp grape tannin
- 2 quarts good water
- 1 tsp pectic enzyme
- 1 tsp wine yeast

Directions
1. Bring water to a rolling boil while peeling and fine dicing the fruit. Fine grate the ginseng root. Wrap and bind fruit and ginseng into a cheesecloth and immerse in boiling water for 5 minutes.
2. Remove. Add sweetener to fruit. Mash and return to the boiling for 5 minutes.
3. Remove and cool to room temperature. Add remaining ingredients except yeast, and mash once more. Cover and store in cool place (not refrigerator) for 12 hours.

4. Add yeast. Watch for bubbles, monitor the smell (should be sweetly fermenting) and stir twice daily for a week. Press cheesecloth, reserving liquids and discarding pulp. Fill secondary fermenter, seal air-tight and rack in cool place (not refrigerator), top-up, for two months. Transfer to clean secondary and rerack for three months. Check wine for clarity. If it has not cleared, transfer to clean secondary and rerack three months or until clear. Best if consumed within two years.

Raw Zucchini Hummus   *by Bonnie Silvers*

This is a delicious way of using up extra zucchini in the summer!

Ingredients
- 4 zucchinis washed and peeled.
- 4 cloves of garlic
- juice from a lemon or two
- ¼ cup of tahini
- ¼ cup olive oil

Directions
1. Put all ingredients into a blender.
2. Blend until smooth, serve with warm, home-baked bread or sliced vegetables.

Authentic Alaska Root Stew   *by Shelley Finkler, a Chugak, Alaska, mother of five*

Here in Alaska if you don't like root vegetables a lot you really can't eat local. We don't have the ability to grow many things, but potatoes, carrots, turnips and so on thrive! We also have a lot of wild meats to choose from, including seafood. This recipe is extremely adaptable to what you've got on hand, and hearty and warming in the cold.

Ingredients
- 4 potatoes
- 2 onions
- 3 stalks celery
- parsley
- 2 tsp salt
- 4 carrots
- 2 turnips or rutabagas
- 2 quarts water
- 2 tbsp butter
- 1 tsp pepper
- whatever game meat you have nearby (grouse, moose, etc.) cooked and chopped

Directions
1. Saute onion in butter until translucent. Add salt, pepper, and sliced vegetables. Saute briefly and add 2 quarts water. Simmer vegetables until soft. Add cooked chopped meats, parsley or whatever herbs you have available. Cook until water is reduced by one-third.
2. If you have a lot of available meat, you can make a rich bone broth or stock of it and use that instead of water.

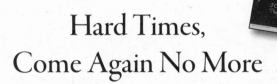

CHAPTER 5

Hard Times,
Come Again No More

Feeding the World

Let us pause in life's pleasures and count its many tears
While we all sup sorrow with the poor.
There's a song that will linger forever in our ears;
Oh, hard times come again no more.

— STEPHEN FOSTER —

SHARON: It is early spring here in rural, upstate New York, and signs of the change in season are still faint and small. But of course, in a cold place like this, these very small things — the spring peepers, the crocuses, the red winged blackbirds, the wood trillium — are huge, and each sign dwarfs the gray remnants of winter. When I look at a crocus or hear the sounds of the birds, the entire background seems greener, more awake, more alive, ripe with potential. The world is waking up.

There are other kinds of waking up going on as well. As I work on this book, reports are coming in as fast as I can read them from the front lines of a worldwide food crisis. The World Bank reports that 37 nations face major unrest because of rising food prices. Energy analyst Stuart Staniford recently posted an analysis at the energy website The Oil Drum suggesting that growth in biofuels could result in the starvation of up to 3 billion people in the near term. The World Food Program is unable to meet demand from the millions of new urban hungry, and more Americans are receiving food stamps than ever before.

I try to imagine what this looks like through the eyes of someone reading this book — does it seem too far away to recognize?

Are you part of the face of the new food crisis, going hungry now and again at the end of the month like so many formerly middle-class denizens of the Global North? Or are you merely among those who complain about high grocery price — and pay them? Most of us can only imagine what it means to be a Haitian woman, first cutting back on the too-occasional meat and vegetables, then serving only rice, and that once a day, and finally offering your children cookies made of mud and shortening to quiet their hunger enough that they can sleep.

Or we can only imagine it now. The hardest part of writing is to make real the truth — the truth that the line between you or I and that Haitian woman is nowhere near as thick as we have come to believe it is. Our food, so abundant, depends on a host of delicate links — energy, climate, even money — and the links are falling apart. We are further from the edge than that woman in Haiti, our children protected by a set of safety nets. But the nets are being removed one by one, or falling apart from neglect, and there is the very real possibility that one day we will walk over the precipice only to find that all the nets are gone and there is no food for us.

Even I find it hard to believe sometimes. My toddler, Asher, is small, sweet, sticky and round, as toddlers should be. He comes to me wearing his wizard's hat, holding up a wooden stick and announces he's ready to go outside and find "worms and tigers" in the garden. The idea that his world could be rocked by hunger, as the world of other toddlers who never got to be round or sticky already is, is both terrifying and alien. It would be easier for most of us who have never had to imagine such a thing to close our eyes, to imagine we are invulnerable, to write a check to some hunger relief agency and to believe that that is all that will ever be asked of us. Unfortunately, that is not enough.

Spring is here, and soon I will be planting peas and spinach. I will take my children into the garden with me, and we will press the seeds into place and watch and nurture them. We will see in those seeds hope of delicious food, of new life, pleasure, time together. They will not see those seeds as a hedge against a hunger they have never known, and it is not the job of parents to burden small children with these things. But I will see in them hope for the future — the hope that I share with that Haitian woman — that there will be enough for my children. And if I grow my own, I can take the money I would have spent on food and give it away; I can give some of what I grow to my local food pantry. And if enough of us do this, perhaps all parents, rich and poor, will know the satisfaction of having had what mothers and fathers need most — hope for their children. We will nurture our seeds, and in turn, they will nurture and comfort us.

Can We Feed the World?

It ain't what you don't know
that gets you into trouble.
It's what you know for sure that just ain't so.
— MARK TWAIN —

This is by far the hardest chapter in this book for us to write. Not only are we attempting to deal with a complex mix of factors, but to do so honestly this chapter requires that most of us confront our underlying assumptions about a host of subjects. As Mark Twain observes, we have our deepest difficulties when we are forced to alter or discard ideas we've come to believe are true but that may not be. This chapter will require most readers to confront new versions of what they "know for sure," just as writing it has done for us.

In addition, we must distinguish very carefully here between what is possible and what is likely. That is, the issue of whether a new agrarianism can feed the world must be addressed on three fronts. The first is by answering whether it is pragmatically possible, with minimal use of fossil inputs, to produce enough food to feed a world population projected to grow and stabilize at around 9 to 10 billion. This is the easiest of the questions to answer, as you will see, and ultimately, our answer is a qualified yes.

If we answer yes to that, the second question is whether we can continue to do so over hundreds and thousands of years — that is, whether doing so is sustainable. We take as a given that if this is not so, we must postulate some way of coming to a sustainable solution, with a transitional period leading in that direction. But postulation is not the same as accomplishment. A full-scale analysis of how this might happen on a world scale is outside the scope of this book. We believe it is within the realm of the possible, but outside the likely, that this could be managed. We will discuss later in the book some thoughts about how so great a transition might be approached, but these are necessarily limited suggestions.

Finally, there is the question of whether it is possible to imagine creating systems to enable us to distribute food fairly. Both of us harbor some real doubts about the likelihood that we will change our practices sufficiently to ensure that everyone has access to food. But despite those doubts, we believe passionately that we must try to do so, that we must find ways to change both the way we grow and eat food, and also, how we distribute it.

Let us also be very clear about what it is we are attempting to claim here. We are not attempting the perfection of human nature in any sense — that is, we are not fundamentally interested in idealistic solutions but in ones that are achievable. We do not claim that any solution we propose will eliminate problems of access, make all poverty disappear or make the world a nobler place. What we do claim is that we can feed the planet as well or better without fossil fuels, and in relocalized, sustainable agriculture.

It is easy to "know" that a world in which a human right to food is enforced is "unrealistic" or "naïve." It is easy to know that there are simply too many people and that the powers that be are too entrenched to turn around. And it may, unfortunately, turn out to be true that we fail to create a society that would permit these things. But we would fail either because we did not try or because we did not try hard enough, not because it was never possible. Beginning from the assumption that greater equity is impossible naturalizes disaster — it says that the reason people starve is because we can't do anything about it, and it makes it easy for us to wash our hands of the whole project of justice. This is wrong. What we can accomplish in terms of equity is debatable, and accomplishing it will be challenging. That does not free us from the moral obligation to attempt the project.

It is simply true that there have been times and societies that were better at equitable distribution than we are at present. It is true that people have at times been willing to do with less so that they could share with others. It is also true that human rights, once established, can be fulfilled. And there is no question that a universal right to food is an acknowledged and extant principle worldwide. As George Kent, University of Hawaii professor and author of *Freedom from Want: The Human Right to Adequate Food,* argues, having acknowledged such a right places an obligation upon all of us.

The human right to adequate food and all other human rights imply strong obligations on the part of national governments to their own people. However, if the obligations were limited to those of one's own national government, the idea of global human rights would be little more than a cruel joke. Human rights do not end at national borders, and neither do the corresponding obligations. Thus, the second major message here is that all of us have obligations in some measure to ensure the realization of all human rights for people. A child may have the misfortune of being born into a poor country, but that child is not born in a poor world. The world as a whole has the capacity to sharply reduce global hunger and malnutrition. It is obligated to do that.[219]

Where are these mystical, strange societies that have shown such concern for others that they were willing to allocate resources based on something other than personal greed? We imagine they must be faraway indigenous populations or the residents of lost Atlantis. In fact, however, there is a credible example in our own recent past — the response of Americans after World War II. Among the populations willing to endure hardship to increase the equity of people far from them were your own grandparents and great-grandparents.

As Amy Bentley documents in *Eating for Victory: Food Rationing and the Politics of Domesticity*, there was a time, about 60 years ago, when Americans were prepared to endure food rationing and hardship in order to keep other people alive. Here we are not talking about World War II, but shortly after it, during the last time in our history that so great a percentage of the world faced death from famine.

At the end of World War II, in 1945, the US was thriving, but up to one-quarter of the rest of the world's population was facing hunger. Whole economies had been destroyed by the war, and a subsequent drought dramatically reduced crop yields. In 1945, food production world wide was 12 percent below pre-war levels, and the 1946 harvest was similarly affected.

Europe's harvest levels were 25 percent below normal. Mexico was in the grip of massive inflation, with tortilla prices out of reach of many; more than half of all Mexicans were spending 90 percent of their income on food. In Korea, the whole year's food donation supply was consumed by June. Rations in Japan were at 520 calories per person, per day — well below starvation level. Worldwide, 500 million people faced death by starvation. Only a few nations, most notably the US, were in any position at all to export grains for relief.

Meanwhile, the US was newly released from wartime rationing, and food consumption rose to 3,300 calories per day on average. People celebrated unlimited meats, sugars and fats that they'd been denied during the war. And Americans were preoccupied with the return of family and the re-creation of American society. In the winter of 1946, Harry Truman gave a radio address on the world situation, asking Americans to help conserve food in order to earmark 16 percent of the total US harvest for food relief. His policies included the prohibition of wheat use in alcohol production and strict limitations on feeding grains to livestock. He also asked Americans to voluntarily restrict their food consumption in order to free up more food to be sent for relief.

What is remarkable is that when Americans turned their attention to the subject, they showed willingness to endure even stronger restrictions than the voluntary ones that Truman and his aid czar, Herbert Hoover, proposed. Seventy percent of Americans indicated their willingness to endure shortages of meat, butter, sugar, gas and other goods to give food to the hungry in Europe.

Herbert Hoover gave the following speech, after traveling to famine-struck regions:

> I have seen with my own eyes the grimmest spectre of famine in all the history of the world. Of the Four Horsemen of the Apocalypse, the one named War has gone, at least for a while. But Famine, Pestilence and Death are still charging over the earth.... Hunger hangs over the homes of 800 million people — over one-third of the people on the earth.[220]

Americans were further moved by this — and by the recognition that much of the world viewed them as gluttonous and selfish. Critics who claimed that the US could meet its commitments to provide food aid only with rationing demanded its reinstitution. Americans wanted to see rationing instituted to ensure fairness, as they reduced their consumption.

In 1944, in the heart of World War II, 85 percent of all Americans believed that rationing should be retained after the war to prevent hunger and shortages. In March, 1946, 59 percent of the American public was willing to reinstitute full-scale rationing to be able to relieve hunger in other nations. Think how radical that is. After Truman's eloquent radio address about the world's suffering, the numbers rose to 70 percent.

Perhaps the most astounding statistic was that almost one-third of the American public acknowledged a willingness to reinstitute rationing *to save the starving Japanese* — that is, despite national fury at the most demonized enemy we may ever have had, those who bombed Pearl Harbor, fully one-third of the American population was willing to give up food to save the lives of their enemies.

Women's consumer groups spoke out in favor of national rationing. The Office of Price Administration (OPA) consumer advisor committee, made up of many well known and powerful women castigated Truman for not reinstating rationing, saying,

> The first step is immediately to withdraw large quantities of these foods from the domestic market for shipment abroad.... Simultaneously measures must be taken to so allocate the domestic supply so that all the people will be able to get their share at home.... Voluntary rationing is patently inadequate...[221]

This suggests that it is possible to imagine a society in which people are, in fact, willing to make sacrifices for greater food equity, particularly when they come to understand the relationship between hunger and the violence in can engender.

Did We Ever Care About Feeding the World?

It is well that thou givest bread to the hungry,
better were it that none hungered and that thou haddest none to give.
— St. Augustine —

We began with the question, "Can we feed the world?" but what needs to be said first off is that the question itself is fundamentally misleading in a number of ways.

First of all, "feeding the world" is a moving target. Are we talking about feeding the current population of 6.6 billion? Or the projected 2050 population of 9.1 billion? Are we talking about 9 billion mostly vegetarians, or 9 billion people who try to eat like most Americans, including heavy consumption of meat and processed foods? What about the cars? Are we imagining that we must also feed more than a billion cars that consume grain and legumes in the form of ethanol and biodiesel?

What level of equity are we imagining? Will we continue the progression of inequity on which we've embarked, with wealth concentrated in the hands of smaller and smaller numbers of rich people? Are we going to ration food by price, as we do it now? Under the current system, if you have money, you eat, if not, you don't. Or might we work under some other system, one that recognizes the established universal right to adequate nutrition?

Moreover, we believe it is fundamentally and utterly in error to believe that the current industrial system has ever had the goal of "feeding the world." That is, much of the rhetoric of the Green Revolution was merely rhetoric. As George Kent has documented in his book *The Political Economy of Hunger*, while grain yields rose, most of the benefits of Green Revolution yields went into the mouths of rich world denizens, in the form of meat and cheap processed foods.

Setting up a scenario in which we compare the ability of industrial agriculture to "feed the world" against the ability of small-scale, food-sovereign, localized agricultures begins from the premise that agribusiness has the noble goal of feeding most of the world. But this is manifestly untrue.

Helena Norberg-Hodge makes this argument about the idea that we need to think of this in terms of "feeding the world":

> The myth is that [The Green Revolution] is necessary to provide cheap food for this very large global population. In actual fact, if you look at what goes behind it, you will see that large chemical and pharmaceutical corporations got involved — particularly in a major way after the Second World War — in food production, turning the same chemicals that we use for bombs, to the land. And that the system did become dominated by the need for profits for corporations, not the need to feed the global population. And that, whether you go back to the earlier days of the Green Revolution and look at how many farmers were destroyed because Green Revolution technologies demanded ever more expensive inputs: large scale technology, lots of petroleum, lots of toxic chemicals, chemical fertilizers, pesticides, antibiotics, hormones.
>
> All of this destroyed the farmer's ability to produce, generation after generation, without spending any money, without being beholden to either banks or large corporations. The net result was whole parts of the world suffering from famines. Sometimes a generation earlier, sometimes many generations earlier, those same parts of the world had been flourishing agricultural areas as well as with a lot of wilderness. And of course, the population at that time in many places was lower, but the main reason for the change was not some kind of sudden explosion in the population. The main

reason was the concentration of food production in the hands of for-profit corporations.[222]

In commercial industrial agriculture there is an enormous amount of rhetoric about "feeding the world." But this conceals the fact that industrial food companies have been more than willing to sacrifice the lives of the hungry in the name of enormous profits — and to increase the thing most responsible for famines: economic inequity. For example, the agricultural speculation divisions of large companies in 2008 made billions in profit — mostly by driving up food prices and putting millions in danger of starvation. Any of these companies could easily have met the World Food Program's call for 700 million dollars in hunger relief to keep the world's poorest from starving. None did. Instead, they continued raising prices through speculation and sought further agricultural subsidies by enforcing commodity food programs — that is, they asked to be paid again.

Yes, we must feed our people. But feeding the world is as much about equity and economic justice as it is about absolute food supplies. The 2007 rice harvest was a record, and the 2008 projected to be larger still. And yet despite this plenty, 175 million new poor found themselves unable to afford a simple bowl of rice by autumn 2008. This has nothing to do with our practical abilities to feed the world, and everything to do with issues of distribution and justice. And equitable distribution and justice cannot be achieved when multinationals seek to profit on hunger — that alone should be sufficient justification for deindustrializing agriculture — because it willfully, consciously causes hunger.

The Limits of the Green Revolution

The seed is starting to take shape as the site and symbol
of freedom in the age of manipulation and monopoly of life.
The seed is not big and powerful, but can become alive
as a sign of resistance and creativity in the smallest
of huts or gardens and the poorest of families.
In smallness lies power.
— Vandana Shiva —

Although there have long been critiques of the Green Revolution, many people assume that without the work of scientists who brought us new

hybrids and who convinced much of the world to convert to chemical fertilizers and pesticides, we could not feed the world. Suspicious. It is certainly true that grain yields rose dramatically during the Green Revolution,
but despite the tendency to imagine that "grain" is equivalent to "all food,"
it isn't certain how much, if at all, food supplies truly increased.

The first part of the story, many of us already know. Many of us know
that the introduction of massive quantities of fertilizer, the replacement of
traditional staple crops with hybrids, and the other changes of the Green
Revolution meant total grain yield increase of 250 percent over 35 years,
with an increase in fossil energy inputs of 50 percent over traditional agriculture. It would seem that that rate of return was quite gratifying — put
in some energy and get 2.5 times the total food. That was, however, a short-
term success, one that couldn't be sustained. The quantity of fossil fuel
inputs required to maintain these increased yields and keep up with population growth has grown steadily, and as Dale Allen Pfeiffer observes in
Eating Fossil Fuels, "Yet, due to soil degradation, the increased demands of
pest management, and increasing energy costs for irrigation…, modern agriculture must continue increasing its energy expenditures simply to maintain current crop yields. The Green Revolution is becoming bankrupt."[223]

For those who don't think much about agriculture, the last bit of information should disturb you. The world's population is set to grow for
some time, and we are only just holding steady (actually, there's been a bit
of a decline lately) in the amount of food we're able to grow in relationship to energy inputs and population. This matters. Right now we still produce more than we need, but the population is growing steadily, and the
climate is changing steadily, and the day is not so far away when our total
food yields may not feed the world. And if oil and natural gas peak soon, as
seems not unlikely, one might assume that yields will decline still further.
That's a scary prospect.

But that's not quite the end of the story. Because the Green Revolution actually cost us something too — and not just the costs we've already
discussed in fertility, soil erosion, aquifer depletion, etc. A whole realm of
food that we once used to grow and eat was lost to us.

Though the Green Revolution increased grain yields, it also cut back
on other food sources. For example, the pesticides required for the cultivation of the miracle rices produced in the 1960s killed fish and frogs that
provided much of the protein in the diets of rice-eating people, resulting
in, as Margaret Visser points out in *Much Depends on Dinner,* "the sadly

ironic result that 'more rice' could mean 'worse nutrition.'" The same can
be said of the loss of vegetables often grown in and at the edges of rice pad-
dies. The famous "golden rice" that was supposed to alleviate blindness due
to vitamin A deficiency, a common problem among poor people who have
little but rice to eat, ignored the fact that one of the reasons for the decline
in vitamin A consumption was that nutritious vegetables and weeds traditionally grown or harvested with rice were no longer available or were contaminated by pesticides and nitrogen fertilizer runoff.

The same is true of food grown in the US, in our very own breadbasket.
As our corn and wheat and soybeans were produced by larger and larger
farms, with more and more industrial equipment, we began to stop producing other, smaller crops that were less amenable to industrialization but
that made up a significant portion of people's diets.

For example, virtually every farm family in the US had a garden in the
first half of the 20th century, and most of those gardens produced most
or all of the family's vegetables. In a time when one-third to one-fifth of
the US population lived on farms, that was an enormous quantity of produce. The significance of gardens is easy to underestimate, but it would be
an error to do so. During World War II, 40 percent of the nation's produce
was grown in home gardens. The figures were higher in Britain during the
same period. Much of home-grown produce was lost to industrial agriculture, either directly, in the transformation of family farms from polycultures to monocrop farms, or indirectly, through agricultural subsidies that
made purchased food often nearly as cheap as growing your own, and even
through social policies that encouraged suburbs to become places of lawns,
not vegetable gardens. What was the point of growing food when buying
it cost so little? And how were we to grow food when our time was now
needed for more "valuable" work. We went from producing 44 percent of
our produce to less than 2 percent in home gardens over four decades.

When evaluating the importance of our gardens, it would be a mistake
to see produce as watery vegetables like lettuce, and thus believe that few of
our calories came from our gardens — among the vegetables lost were also
calorie-dense crops such as potatoes and sweet potatoes, which can substitute for grains in the diet. As writer and community organizer Pat Murphy
observes, over the years many of the most nutritious vegetables have effectively fallen off the government agricultural statistics, in part because of
changes in our eating habits but also because so many of these were originally grown primarily not in thousand-acre fields but in backyards and

truck gardens.[224] So collards and kale, once a staple in the South, and their nutritional value were lost in the industrialization of agriculture.[225]

Going back to what the Green Revolution, and its ugly step-child globalization, did to the American farm family, the exhortation by US Secretary of Agriculture Ezra Taft Benson to "get big or get out" and the systematic farm policies that favored large commodity growers and regional specialization cut back enormously on the quantity of food we produced. Small farmers in the 1940s might have raised corn or wheat as their central crop, but they also grew gardens, had an orchard, raised some pigs for sale and milked a cow. The loss of all that food value, spread over millions of farm families, was a significant one.

A farmer might have tapped his sugar maple trees and sold the syrup and would probably have sold some eggs. He might also have sold a pig to a neighbor or had a calf butchered and shared the meat. The industrial commodity farmer rarely does these things, and in many cases, the areas allotted them — the woodlot, the barn, the chicken coop — have been removed to allow unhindered access to more acres. In a bad crop year, a farmer might have planted a late crop of sunflowers for oil seed, lettuce or some other vegetable, which is also not calculated into our total consumption. In many cases a family member might also operate a small truck garden and sell produce locally — even children did this routinely.

All these are foods that were removed from the food stream, and this systematic deprivation over millions of households represents an enormous loss of total calories and, most importantly, nutrition.

The economic pressure of farms to specialize also took its toll. Joan Dye Gussow documents that before World War II, the state of Montana was self-sufficient for 70 percent of its food, including fruit.[226] Montana is one of the harshest climates in the US and has very little water, comparatively speaking, and yet this degree of sufficiency was possible in part because the economic pressure of big business had not yet persuaded small farmers that they couldn't grow fruit effectively in Montana but should leave it to Washington and Florida. None of us know how much food was lost this way, but it is almost certainly an enormous quantity. And this systematic removal in the name of efficiency and specialization happened all over the world to one degree or another.

All this is particularly important because of the distinction between yield and output. Peter Rosset has documented that industrial agriculture is, in fact, more efficient in terms of yield of a single, monocrop. That is, when five acres of soybeans and five thousand acres of soybeans are compared, you usually get more soybeans per acre by growing 5000 acres. But when you compare output — that is the total amount of food — and fiber you can get from a piece of land using small-scale polyculture, the five-acre farm comes out not just ahead but vastly ahead. That is, although a small-scale farm produces less of any single crop destined for the processed food system, it produces more calories, vitamins and minerals ready for cooking in our kitchens. It isn't just that five acres are more productive in terms of total output, they are often 2–200 times more productive.[227] Rosset's figures are not in dispute, as Rosset points out here:

> Surveying the data, we indeed find that small farms almost always produce far more agricultural output per unit area than larger farms. This is now widely recognised by agricultural economists across the political spectrum, as the "inverse relationship between farm size and output". Even leading development economists at the World Bank have come around to this view, to the point that they now accept that redistribution of land to small farmers would lead to greater overall productivity.[228]

This difference in total output rises further when you talk about garden models. A half-acre garden is often tens or hundreds of times more productive than the same acreage in industrial agriculture. A small farm is generally more productive per acre than a large one. And when fossil fuels are, by necessity or choice, removed from the picture, the distinctions become even more dramatic. The displacement of home and farm gardens by industrial agriculture represents a dramatic loss in important food crops. On a given acre of land, the Green Revolution might have increased rice or wheat yields by several times (although organic agricultural techniques have since caught up), but because the garden, henhouse and berry bushes that could have been on that acre would have been many times *more productive in total* than what was granted to us by fertilizers and hybridization, what we are experiencing is a net total loss, not a gain in many cases.

Grain crops are important, but so is the enormous diversity of food in our diets (or that should be in our diets). And many of the vegetable crops that have been lost were significant sources of food, oil or flavoring (now displaced by corn syrup and soybean oil) in the not-so-distant past. We cannot correctly assess the global food supply by focusing only on grains or by failing to recognize how much of the calories produced in grain were

once produced, often more nutritiously, by vegetable and fruit crops. As
Hope Shand notes,

> There is no doubt about the global economic importance of these
> major crops (rice, maize, wheat and soybean) but the tendency to
> focus on a small number of species masks the importance of plant
> species diversity to the world food supply. A very different picture
> would emerge if we were to look into women's cooking pots and if
> we could survey local markets and give attention to household use
> of non-domesticated species. [229]

In the US, during most of the past 50 years, we have had enormous
grain surpluses, mostly of corn, and as Michael Pollan documents in *The
Omnivore's Dilemma*, industrial food production has been challenged to
keep finding new ways to use up our spare corn. Processed foods are all
sweetened with our extra corn, made of processed corn or made of meat
from corn fed to livestock. And we have seen a rise in obesity, type 2 diabe-
tes and heart disease — all associated with high-meat, low-vegetable, processed-food diets. We kept raising our yields, at the cost of our outputs, and
our diets came to reflect that — we ate fewer kinds of vegetables and fruits,
and fewer of them. To a large degree, what happened was that we gave up
foods that we did need to be healthy and have good, varied, tasty diets,
and replaced them with a couple of grain crops that we did not particularly
need more of, and we harmed ourselves in the process.

Not only have most of the benefits of the Green Revolution accrued
not to the poor but to the already rich, but most of the plans for future
yield increases involve trying to increase food production in places where
there is already plenty of food — the US corn crop, for example, doesn't
need to be increased if our primary goal is feeding people. But even if
GMO seeds or new fertilizers could raise yields, the odds are excellent
that already-strapped poor farmers could never afford them. Our focus
on high-technology agriculture creates greater inequity by concentrating
food yields in places that currently have enough and to spare, if only we
would allocate it wisely.

This also ignores laws of diminishing returns — the truth is that pushing up yields in areas where they are already quite high is challenging. Increasing them enough to compensate for continually stripping the soil and
contaminating the water is nearly impossible. However, increasing yields
in poorer countries by increasing the level of organic matter in the soil,

introducing new techniques and teaching integrated pest management systems has potentially enormous returns. Historically though, economists have disdained enriching poor farmers by helping them to farm better. Techno fixes are far shinier and more exciting, though ultimately less effective.

It is impossible to discover precisely how much food was lost to us worldwide during the Green Revolution and the subsequent shift to industrial agriculture. But there is no question that it was enough food to feed millions, maybe even billions of people. We must, in our analysis of what the Green Revolution cost us, recognize that we lost an uncertain but enormous quantity of future food, mortgaging the future to overfeed the present.

Stealing from the Future

Whenever people say "we mustn't be sentimental,"
you can take it they are about to do something cruel.
And if they add, "we must be realistic,"
they mean they are going to make money out of it."
— BRIGID BROPHY —

The price of industrial agriculture is uncalculated quantities of food that future generations will not have to eat. How is this so? Well, for example, though cities grew up in good spots for trade, they also by necessity grew in areas surrounded by fertile, productive agricultural land that could support large populations. The displacement of large populations of agrarian people into cities has meant that all over the world, more and more land is transformed into city and suburb, paved over and no longer producing.

As the ability of soils to hold water decreases because of erosion and climate change, arable land becomes desert. As soils are depleted of nutrients and the price of natural-gas-based nitrogen fertilizers rises, untold people will find the cost of growing their own food in their depleted environment prohibitive. We are seeing this already.

As artificial fertilizers produce nitrous oxide and feedlot meat production warms the planet with methane, millions risk losing the sources of water that allow them to grow food. As we deplete aquifers by growing inappropriate crops in regions that cannot sustain them over the long term, we risk future hunger.

That said, however, we should not underestimate the resilience and power of local, indigenous, sustainable agriculture. For example, in *Bringing the Food Economy Home* Helena Norberg-Hodge, Todd Merrifield and Steven Gorelick cite several World Bank and FAO papers that indicate that as recently as the mid-1990s, *2 billion* people — 35 percent of the world's population — were being fed by traditional agriculture with minimal or no fossil fuel inputs.[230]

Often these farmers do so on marginal land, because the best agricultural land in the Global South has been turned to non-food or luxury food items. Shrimp farms displace rice farms in coastal India; coffee displaces small polyculture farms or food providing forests in Latin America and Africa; flowers displace food in much of Latin America and Asia; cotton to feed our endless appetite for cheap clothing displaces food in many nations. It will be a non-trivial problem to return this land to sustainable food production, but it is possible. These statistics, along with the others here should at least raise some significant questions in those who believe we know what the earth's proper carrying capacity is. That does not make the issue of population irrelevant, but it does mean we may have time and choices that we did not know we had. And if 2 billion people can feed themselves on the poorest available land organically and with minimal inputs, how many could do it if sustainable agriculture received the same supports commercial agriculture now does?

Vandana Shiva describes (and we will quote this at some length, because it is very important) what the Green Revolution has done in the third world, but it is important to remember that the loss of calories that occurred there also happened to us. For us, the cost came in the form of our loss of nutrition. That is, though we had more calories than we needed, we replaced nutritious foods with non-nutritious ones, to our detriment. For the poor of the world, it came as a significant loss of food value, as well as nutrition.

> Industrial agriculture has not produced more food. It has destroyed diverse sources of food, and it has stolen food from other species to bring larger quantities of specific commodities to the market, using huge quantities of fossil fuels and water and toxic chemicals in the process.
>
> It is often said that the so-called miracle varieties of the Green Revolution in modern industrial agriculture prevented famine

because they had higher yields. However, these higher yields disappear in the context of total yields of crops on farms.

Green Revolution varieties produced more grain by diverting production away from straw. This "partitioning" was achieved through dwarfing the plants, which also enabled them to withstand high doses of chemical fertilizer. However, less straw means less fodder for cattle and less organic matter for the soil to feed the millions of soil organisms that make and rejuvenate soil.

The higher yields of wheat or maize were thus achieved by stealing food from farm animals and soil organisms. Since cattle and earthworms are our partners in food production, stealing food from them makes it impossible to maintain food production over time, and means that the partial yield increases were not sustainable. The increase of yields in wheat and maize under industrial agriculture were also achieved at the cost of yields of other foods a small farm provides. Beans, legumes, fruits and vegetables all disappeared both from farms and from the calculus of yields. More grain from two or three commodities arrived on national and international markets, but less food was eaten by farm families in the Third World.

The gain in "yields" of industrially produced crops is thus based on a theft of food from other species and the rural poor in the Third World. That is why, as more grain is produced and traded globally, more people go hungry in the Third World. Global Markets record more commodities for trading because food has been stolen from nature and the poor.[231]

This may be the most important point we can make — drawing down future food and starving our children and grandchildren should not be an option in an agricultural system. High yields for us now and hunger for them later is not a viable choice in a growing world — period.

There is, in truth, no way to be certain what we gained and what we lost in the Green Revolution. What is virtually certain is that its gains were overstated and that allocation of resources, whether from future generations or from poor to rich, were inequitable. When someone makes the statement that grain yields rose by so much, that looks impressive. But the practical realities of that are very different. We have to ask whether those yield increases actually made it from fields to the mouths of the hungry and whether it was possible to duplicate them through any other method.

Organic Agriculture Can Feed the World Better

It's really very simple, Governor. When people are hungry they die.
So spare me your politics and tell me what you need
and how you're going to get it to these people.

— BOB GELDOF —

To discover whether we can feed the world, first we need to ask whether increased yields have actually meant more available food and nutrition. In fact, this question has been answered — even the World Bank admitted in 1986 that more food does not mean less hunger. Access to food is the primary issue — if it were not, the US would have no hungry people instead of 35 million food-insecure people. Food access is the most important issue in feeding the world, as economist Amartya Sen, among other people, has discussed at length. In Donald Freebairn's analysis of more than 300 research reports on Green Revolution results, he found that 80 percent of them showed that inequity increased with the adoption of Green Revolution techniques.[232]

If the Green Revolution had responded to real material shortages of food worldwide, the environmental costs might be worth it. But it did not. As Freebairn documents, the food supply was sufficient to feed the world's population in 1950, just as it is now. Claims that Norman Borlaug and the Green Revolution saved "a billion lives" are almost certainly wildly overstated — there was sufficient food to go around before the Green Revolution, had equitable distribution been in place, just as there is now. In fact some analysts have suggested, whether rightly or wrongly, that population growth itself is a product of that growth. (That last is a subject we'll return to shortly.)

And, as we've noted, industrial agriculture actually undermines our ability to continue to feed the world, by contaminating soil, increasing global warming, depleting water stocks and promoting erosion.

Dissecting figures about hunger in *World Hunger: 12 Myths*, Lappé, Collins, et al. note that though figures at first seem to suggest that the Green Revolution made real gains in hunger reduction because total food available between 1970 and 1990 rose by 11 percent and the estimated number of hungry people fell from 942 million to 786 million, this is not really true.

In South America, while food supplies rose almost 8 percent, the number of hungry people also went up, by 19 percent.... In South Asia there was 9 percent more food per person by 1990, but there were also 9 percent more hungry people. The remarkable difference in China, where the number of hungry dropped from 406 million to 189 million almost begs the question: which has been more effective at reducing hunger, the Green Revolution or the Chinese Revolution? [233]

Removing China from the equation, the number of hungry people in the developing world rose from 536 to 597 million. This suggests that first of all, though absolute food availability is relevant, it is not as relevant as distribution and economic justice. And because China was a comparatively late adopter of Green Revolution seeds and techniques, it also suggests that the Green Revolution itself may be less important than improved agricultural techniques that apply just as much to organic agriculture as to chemical agriculture.

It is a commonplace to assume that organic agriculture yields less than conventional agriculture and that we would have to endure enormous losses in yield were we to give up chemical inputs. The yield increases of the Green Revolution are commonly articulated in isolation, without discussion of comparisons with organic yields. To determine how important the Green Revolution was, then, we need to go through the outputs of the Green Revolution and ask whether increased agricultural yields depend upon Green Revolution techniques. If, for example, agricultural yields depended on mechanization, we would expect mechanized agriculture to consistently outyield hand labor. If they depend upon chemical inputs, we would expect organic agriculture to be heavily outyielded by conventional industrial agriculture. And if they depend on plant breeding, we would expect older varieties to be outyielded by newer ones.

Are these things true? Well, not in absolute terms. That is, small farms, which generally speaking use much less mechanization, fewer inputs and are more likely to use older plant varieties and save seed than large ones, actually are more productive per acre in total output than large farms. At the extreme ends of this, we can see this disparity in Ecology Action's biointensive gardening methods, which offer yields per acre much, much higher than industrial agriculture can achieve — without fossil fuel inputs, using open-pollinated seeds.

But on a larger scale this is true as well. In *Deep Economy* Bill McKibben argues that the 2002 Agricultural Census confirms this greater productivity of small farms using more hand labor — small farms produce more food per acre by every measure, whether calories, tons or dollars.[234] What mechanization does do is reduce the amount of human labor required. However, in a world with 6.6 billion humans and growing, human labor is a widely available resource.

It is also true that organic agriculture as a whole can consistently match yields with conventional agriculture, suggesting that we do not depend on artificial fertilizers or pesticides. In a 2007 paper, "Organic Agriculture and the Global Food Supply," the authors demonstrated that organic methods would offer a substantial net increase in yields in the Global South, while continuing comparable yields in the Global North. In a world-wide organic-only policy, "farms could produce between 2,641 and 4,381 calories per person per day compared to the current world equivalent of 2,786 calories per person per day."

In other studies, agronomist Jules Pretty studied 200 sustainable agricultural projects in 52 countries and observed that, per hectare, sustainable practices led to a 93 percent average increase in food production. Grain yields, as discussed in his volume *Agri-Culture*, had an average yield increase of 73 percent over studies including 4.5 million farmers.[235]

The Rodale Institute has been running test plots of conventionally farmed corn and soybean rotations (the practice of most Midwestern farms) against organically grown plots, where soil is maintained wholly by cover crops, and another where a fodder crop is grown and fed to cows whose manures are returned to the soil. The difference in total yields between the three plots is less than 1 percent. And during drought years, the organic plots dramatically outyielded conventional ones because of higher organic matter in the soil. The cover-crop-fed plots produced twice as many soybeans as the conventionally farmed ones.[236] As we go into increasingly difficult times, one of the great strengths of organic agriculture is its resilience in the face of less-than-optimal conditions; when fertilizer prices spike, in drought or flooding years, organics can continue to produce successfully. In times of stress, organic agriculture tends to outyield conventional — and what is coming is many more stressful years.[237]

Even the much-touted problem of lowered yields as fields stripped by conventional agriculture are converted to organic methods can be overcome, as a German study found. Making the first crop a nitrogen-fixing legume can prevent an initial drop in yield.[238]

Moreover, most of those assuming that industrial agriculture must "feed the world" are assuming that a few grain-exporting nations — the

US, Canada, Brazil — must feed the poor world. But yields could be doubled in poor nations. Not with commercial fertilizers, already out of the reach of many poor farmers, but by using organic cover crops, composting and new techniques that could have dramatic results in enabling poorer nations to feed themselves and in creating an agriculture of richer soil, higher in humus, that can withstand difficult weather. For example, in Benin in the 1990s, the government experimented with subsidizing seed for cover cropping and found that eroding soils could be repaired with a comparatively small investment in velvet beans, which also reduced weeding. Maize production tripled, without the importation of expensive commercial fertilizers.[239]

So although, seen in isolation, the Green Revolution did increase yield of grain, organic and sustainable agriculture have kept pace and in some cases exceeded the results of Green Revolution techniques. We need not depend on chemical agriculture, mechanization or any other fossil (or eventually renewable) fueled technology to feed ourselves.

How Many Can We Feed...And For How Long?

MALTHUSIAN, adj. Pertaining to Malthus and his doctrines.
Malthus believed in artificially limiting population,
but found that it could not be done by talking.
— AMBROSE BIERCE —

At present the world produces enough calories to feed everyone on earth about double the amount of food they actually need.[240] This is an easy thing not to understand, particularly as hunger spreads and the food crisis accelerates. It looks as though we are coming up against real limits to the food supply, what we will call "absolute scarcity." This is different than the kind of scarcity some Americans have recently experienced at Costco — that's a supply chain failure, where there isn't enough of the particular brand of rice that a company has contracted to buy to go around. But there is plenty of rice in the world. The problem is that millions of people can't afford to buy any of it.

As of this writing, the planet has about 6.6 billion people on it, and because we produce about twice as many calories as they need, this means that in a world where food was perfectly distributed, relying on techniques that simply matched and maintained presents yields, we could feed about twice as many people as we have now. Since perfectly equitable distribution cannot ever happen, however, we need a cushion — that is, we need to make sure that there's enough food for everyone in the world, plus extra to compensate. How much extra is a question of what lifestyle people live — 10 billion vegetarians, who ate mostly whole foods, farmed sustainably, didn't use biofuels and had a high degree of equity could live quite well (for a while — more on this later) at the present rate of food production. Three billion heavy meat eaters who drove cars using biofuels would probably rapidly overwhelm resources, leading to an environmental crisis even more acute than the one we currently face.

To look at this another way, let's imagine that right now we have perfectly equitable distribution — that everyone gets a "share" of resources equivalent to living on $2 a day (approximately the world average). If everyone used resources in the same way, to get the impact that we have now, we'd have effectively 52 billion people in the world, the vast majority of whom were located in North America, Western Europe and Australia. Discussions of population tend logically to trend toward discussions of poor world nations, where people have more children, but the greatest impact comes from smaller numbers of people consuming more. On the other hand, the larger the numbers, the lower each person's individual share is.

But it is important to note that 5 percent of the world's population produces almost 25 percent of the world's carbon — that is, as environmental writer Kyle Schuant points out, even if everyone in the world except for the denizens of the US and Australia were to disappear, we would still cross the climate change tipping points if we did not change our rate of consumption dramatically.[241]

The problem, of course, is that most of us in the rich world don't want to live on $2 a day. We think about how that would work in our society (in the US, the equivalent is $7 per day, and it is actually disturbingly common), and we recognize there's no way it could — at least not while we have to have cars and private health insurance and a host of other things. So even if we believe in equitable distribution in principle, it is hard to find a way to get there. And that leads us back to the question of population — after all, we think, if there weren't so many people, there'd be more resources to go around.

Now that $2 a day figure is a bit misleading — it can cover a surprising range of life situations, from the hellacious to the pretty comfortable. That is, $2 a day sucks pretty badly if you live in an urban slum, and have to spend 90 percent of that on food and rent. On the other hand, if you live on a small farm and grow almost all the food you eat, produce the heating and cooking fuel you need and need just a little money, you might not have such a tough time. For example, the average savings rate for poor Chinese farmers is a full 20 percent of their income — they are able to put aside a reserve, in large part because they don't need their money for the most basic things.

So maybe there's a glimmer of hope in here — because a lot of us could get a lot closer to equity if we could meet more of our needs at home. But that still doesn't get us all the way to equity, and most of us are a long way away from having an inherited small farm, passed down from family to family, and a property tax assessor who accepts eggs and zucchini.

If perfect equity isn't going to happen anytime soon, why bring it up? Because there are a host of fairly simple ways we could make the food go further. The first would be to minimize biofuel production, unless we develop a method that doesn't compete with people food. Cars simply shouldn't get a share of the world's food — when cars compete with people, the cars win, because most people who own cars can out purchase those who don't. So biofuels as we do them now can't exist on any scale.

The next culprit (bigger than biofuels, but more ethically defensible than feeding cars) is meat, egg and dairy production. We are not suggesting that everyone become a vegetarian, merely that we in the US could easily cut our consumption of animal products by half, and reduce the feeding of grain to cows and other animals that not only don't need it but don't thrive on large quantities of grain.

Is that so hard to imagine? That's still more meat than our grandparents ate. And we'd still have as much fuel as our grandparents had for a good while. If we were to do this, along with raising outputs by capturing animal manures and human urine, intensive small-scale agriculture and a host of other strategies, there's a good chance we could feed 9 billion people without any more poverty and starvation than we have now, maybe less — probably.

Why probably? Well, the big caveat here is climate change. As we showed in Chapter 1, the vast majority of the implications of climate change for agriculture are bad. Though there will be some areas that benefit (growing tomatoes in Siberia, for instance, will become easier), those benefits will probably be overwhelmed by losses. If we stabilize the climate (one of the reasons small-scale agriculture is preferable — because it does

double duty in both reducing emissions and storing carbon), we can probably feed 9 billion people — for a bit.

The next biggest challenge is the ability of wealthy people (which includes most of us reading this, even if we don't feel wealthy) to recognize
that a real drop in some measures of standard of living is to their benefit,
and this is a very hard thing indeed. For example, if we allow the rainforest
to be destroyed in order to make more farmland, we will pay a heavy price
as climate change decimates future generations. The loss of biodiversity is
already harming us economically. All of this is another important reason to
say the land we most need to use is the land on our house lots and public
parks and all the places that are already disturbed heavily by man.

And there are other caveats. Feeding the world depends on the availability of oil to transport food from areas that will have surpluses to the
areas that don't. We can do a great deal to make many areas more food secure than they are, but some regions will always rely on imports. It would
be easy to say that there is no point to food sovereignty then, but this is
false — the more a region can feed itself, the smaller the surpluses needed,
the smaller the quantities of energy needed to transport it and the more
likely it is that food will move to where it needs to be eaten.

An equitable future also depends on the ability of people in areas that
have surpluses to contain their appetites for meat and fuel and to recognize
that the world is not served by the upheaval created by billions of starving
people. It depends on a set of economic assumptions completely different
from the ones currently in place.

As mentioned above, fairly inexpensive organic inputs and training
techniques could dramatically raise yields in many poor nations. This is
perhaps the best hope of sustainable agriculture — that it could result in
equal yields all around the world, yields not dependent on the rising market prices of fertilizers. Thus, instead of poorer nations in the Global South
depending on large grain producers to offer them increasingly unafford-
able grains, nations could feed themselves and their regions.

As we said early on, the distinction that applies here is between what is
technically possible and what is likely. We both reluctantly conclude that it
is unlikely, unless we are truly able to alter our present path quite quickly,
that we will avoid more famine. But we want to emphasize that if we fail
to do so, this will be a decision made by the world, largely by the world's
wealthiest and most powerful citizens — the starvation of millions or billions will not be an accidental tragedy but a conscious choice.

We would also point out that even if we are unable to perfectly avoid the death of many hungry people, it makes an enormous difference whether millions or billions starve. That is, the perfect cannot be the enemy of the good here.

Reallocating food would make it possible for the world's population to reach 9 billion (about the midpoint of UN projections) by the middle of the century, with no more hunger than there was in 2006 — that is millions of people would die of hunger every, day, but this would be ordinarily horrible rather than extraordinary.

But let's go from there. Yes, it is possible to match and exceed existing agricultural output — and without failing forms of industrial agriculture. Yes, it is possible to produce enough food to feed 9 billion people, if the richest ones were willing to give up some of their privileges both because it is right and to reduce inevitable conflicts.

But once we'd done so — could we keep on feeding 9 billion people forever? Almost certainly not. Even if all of us were willing to reduce our standard of living dramatically, the wealthy among us are unlikely to be content to live like Keralans or other poor-world denizens. And as long as the wealthy are unwilling to do this, then others will try to become like the wealthy. And though it is possible to feed 9 billion people without more destruction of rainforest, it is not possible to begin the process of repairing land and restoring our losses with 9 billion people. We're going to be struggling just to keep up, and undoubtedly, while sustainable agriculture can do much to mitigate climate change and peak oil, we're also going to lose a great deal of biodiversity. We will deplete our fossil water supplies from underground aquifers in this scenario, even if we use them more wisely.

We have chosen, with some ambivalence, for the purposes of this book, to say that protecting human lives is more important than losing wildlife of all sorts. Although we've chosen here to say that preserving human lives outranks preserving biodiversity, to the extent that we can have both, we've chosen both. That is, we've chosen to use the most productive, most sustainable, most climate mitigating, least fossil-intensive way of feeding 9 billion people, but we recognize that in doing so we're going to do harm.

We have debated with ourselves the ethics of this, but have come to the conclusion that it is necessary. First, we both broadly derive from ethical traditions that prioritize human lives. We're both aware of the ambiguities of saying that humans outrank gorillas and polar bears and other creatures whose whole populations may become extinct, but for better and for worse, we prioritize the minimization of human suffering — whether we should be able to or not, we can't live with ourselves if we allow human beings to starve, though horribly and perhaps shamefully enough, we can live with ourselves if the sockeye salmon becomes extinct. It would be more pleasant and easy to cloak our decision in nobler language, but this is the ugly truth. We hope that there's another choice, which we will discuss in a moment, but if the choice is between children and salmon, children win.

We also make this choice for pragmatic reasons — because starving people often lay waste to landscapes even more than ordinary people, eating grass, stripping bark from trees, killing any animal they can to feed their families. Hunger also leads to resource wars and violence — and the potential ecological destruction of nations battling over water and the remaining food is far vaster than the ecological destruction of feeding everyone. For example, scientists recently suggested that even a small-scale exchange of nuclear weapons between India and Pakistan would be enough to plunge the world into a nuclear winter.

The other pragmatic reasoning is that a die-off, the starvation of billions, wouldn't fix the problem. That is, it would certainly leave more food for everyone else in the very short term, but as long as the world had a burgeoning group of people who wanted to live like middle and upper class Americans, we would still end up struggling with the food issues for a long, long time.

As we've seen, the majority of the carbon emissions per person come from the Global North, where people are richer. The majority of hungry people come from the Global South, where people are poorer. But those in the Global South don't use very much of the fossil fuels or make very many emissions. So even if we imagine the world's population dropping by half in famine (horrifying image though that is) it doesn't fix the problem. It doesn't create enough world resources to manage the problem of rich people's ever-growing appetite for fossil fuels. And it doesn't do enough to mitigate climate change — we would still get to the disaster point, and fairly quickly. And as that happened, yields of food would fall — that is, we'd eventually be struggling just as hard to feed 3 billion in this scenario as we will be to feed 9 billion. No matter how the scenario goes, we have to find a way to increase equity *and* deal with the population issue.

If we can't accept world-wide famine, and we can't feed 9 billion people forever, without harming the oceans and running out of water, what options do we have? The only possible choice is a managed population decline.

The best hope we can see is to try and stabilize population by using the best techniques available to us. What are these? They involve more education and power for women all over the world, access to basic medical care so that children survive infancy and women who want contraception can get it, and basic food security. And if you translate that, it comes down, generally speaking, to greater equity. That is, the things we need to do in order to stabilize the population problem are also the things we need to do for reasons of justice and for ecological stability.

Reproducing Security

It is known that there are an infinite number of worlds,
simply because there is an infinite amount of space for them to be in.
However, not every one of them is inhabited. Any finite number
divided by infinity is as near nothing as makes no odds, so the average
population of all the planets in the Universe can be said to be zero.
From this it follows that the population of the whole Universe is also zero,
and that any people you may meet from time to time
are merely products of a deranged imagination.
— Douglas Adams —

Over the past few decades, reproductive rates have halved worldwide. It is almost impossible to overstate how important this fact is — and, except in China, it has overwhelmingly been achieved by women choosing to have fewer children. One ecologist called it "women's gift to the planet." In many versions of UN population projections, world population begins to fall rapidly after its peak at 8.5 to 9.5 billion people, reaching as low as 5 billion by the end of the century.

Reproductive rates fall fastest in societies where women have access to basic security. For example, the state of Kerala, with its high well-being, medical care and food security has a dramatically lower TFR (total fertility rate) than the rest of India. But in most of the rest of India, literacy rates are lower, women are less politically engaged; and, as Vandana Shiva points out, without social-security-like programs and with high infant and child mortality, a woman has to have five children to ensure that she will have a living adult child to support her in her old age.[242]

In many very poor countries, children begin to produce more than they consume by the time they are six, and are producing as much as an adult by the time they are 12. That is, for very poor people, children are the one hope of economic stability. If we can give people greater security and stability, more hope that the children they do have will grow up, evidence suggests they will choose to have fewer children.

Birth control has a role here too, but not in isolation from these larger issues of food and other forms of security. Taken in isolation, Western medical care and birth control engender resentment and take power away from women — that is, they work in exactly the wrong direction. Consider this example from Bangladesh, where sterilization is often offered as a bribe to women, whether they want it or not, taking away control of their bodies, and stripping them of power in the interest of outsiders' goals.

> The trend towards enforcing final solutions is aimed particularly at women. This is borne out by the fact that, in Bangladesh, food-aid earmarked for distribution among the most distressed women is used to blackmail them into accepting sterilization in exchange for a few kilograms of wheat. Thus, the Vulnerable Group Feeding Programme (VGF) has been used to force the poorest women to be sterilized.... Old women, women already sterilized and widows are not entitled to food relief.[243]

Birth control has value, but only if it is offered to women in combination with the power to make good choices. If birth control strips women of political power, then the larger social goal of creating a society where women voluntarily constrain childbirth is impossible.

Jim Merkel, author of *Radical Simplicity,* has calculated that if everyone on earth had one child, we could reduce the population to 1 billion by the end of this century.[244] Even if we were to have two children and encourage somewhat delayed childbearing (the later you begin having children, the fewer generations in a period, and the smaller the total impact of your children), we could get the planet down to about 3 billion people, voluntarily, without famine or war. Three billion people willing to live a lower-energy life, without the expansionist economy, is probably within the range of the planet's carrying capacity, and a two-child self-limit would further reduce the world's population over time.

Many nations in the Global North are already at or about 2.0 TFR, and others are well below. For them, the challenge is going to be reducing consumption — as long as the average American uses 30 times the resources of the average Kenyan, Kenyan reproductive practices simply don't have the same impact that the consumption patterns in the rich world do. Most Kenyans have four children, and their four children together use the same amount of resources as about one-eighth of one American kid. As long as that's true, it is much more important that people in the rich world voluntarily constrain their consumption, and, if they can't get their usage down to a fair share, that they also constrain reproduction.

There are bound to be people reading this discussion who know that Sharon has four biological children and who are concerned about the hypocrisy of calling for voluntary reproductive restraint. She discussed this issue at length in her book *Depletion and Abundance,* and we will not rehash it here. We will simply observe that for Sharon, whose children preceded her understanding of population as an issue and whose biology exceeded the expected limits of quite a few forms of simultaneous birth control, this issue allows her to illustrate the power of reduced consumption. Her family lives on between 10 and 15 percent of the average American's energy use, meaning that her four children combined currently consume about half as much as one ordinary American child. This does not eliminate their impact, nor does it suggest that everyone on the planet can do as she does — but it does suggest that for those who, like Sharon, came late to an understanding of population issues or those whose religious convictions don't permit them to use contraception, there is at least some substantial power to mitigate one's impact.

The good thing is that it isn't necessary to create a perfect world or to bring about lots of fossil-fuel usage or high-energy economic development. The world had schools for thousands of years before fossil fuels. Women's access to political power does not require lots of fossil energies. Access to birth control and to basic medical care, including sufficient food, hygiene and oral rehydration syrups that prevent death in early childhood are really quite inexpensive to provide. But to imagine that a society reducing its energy use would provide these things to billions of people, we must imagine a world in which there is greater equity. Again, we come back to this large question of equity.

And this question of equity is, in the end, the thing that will determine what kind of future we have. If the rich world can give up its privileges; if we can eat a diet based mostly on plants with some grass-fed animal products; if most of us can give up our cars and stay closer to home, carpool, walk and bike; if most of us can grow gardens; if we are prepared to have less money but perhaps more time, more freedom, more democracy, stronger families, better food — if we are prepared to make those choices, there's a way forward.

How Does "Relocalization" Work on a World Scale?

Charity begins at home,
and justice begins next door.
— CHARLES DICKENS —

Most of us raised in a biblical religion have some vague memory of the story of Joseph and his brothers, if only from the Donny Osmond musical. Genesis 39–47 will refresh your memory if you are interested in the details. In the story, Joseph, who was sold into Egypt becomes the powerful advisor of Pharaoh, who is having bad dreams. In one dream, Pharaoh dreams of seven fat cows devoured by seven starving cows. In the second, seven ripe, healthy sheaves of wheat are devoured by seven shriveled, dry ones. Joseph correctly predicts what this means:

> Immediately ahead are seven years of great abundance in all the land of Egypt. After them will come seven years of famine and all the abundance in the land of Egypt will be forgotten. As the land is ravaged by famine, no trace of the abundance will be left in the land.... And let Pharaoh take steps to appoint overseers over the land, and organize by taking a fifth part of the land's produce in the seven years of plenty. Let all the food of those good years that are coming be gathered and let the grain be collected under Pharaoh's authority as food to be stored in cities. Let that food be a reserve for the land for the seven years of famine which will come upon the land of Egypt, so that the land may not perish in the famine.[245]

Joseph's understanding and forethought enable Egyptians, and ultimately his own family, to survive the famine, in which "...there was no bread in all the world."

One of the fascinating things about the way that this story is told is the linguistic linking of land and people here — that is, we are told that we should store food so that "the land may not perish." Of course, this means the people of the land, but it also is a reminder that famine is enormously destructive to the land itself — in the face of famine, land that should not be cultivated is brought into cultivation (we are seeing this already in the US as Crop Protection Land is brought into production and elsewhere as the world's poor are pressed onto increasingly marginal land), and desperately hungry people will eat whatever they can, including protected animals and plants. Famine isn't just destructive to the hungry, but to the earth they devastate in the quest for food. In a real sense, the preservation of the people can be the preservation of the land itself.

It is also a reminder that the current food crisis derives, in part, from the fact nations all over the world have reduced their stockpiles and ceased to regard good harvests as a means of creating long-term security for their populations. Instead, we've wasted grain surpluses on livestock, biofuels and market dumping. Somehow, we forgot about the danger of famine.

Whatever anyone can say about pharaohs, the one in the story seems to have a laudable sense of obligation to his own populace — one that wildly exceeds that of the leaders of many present-day nations, who have allowed stockpiles to collapse in times of comparative prosperity. Right now world grain reserves are well below what is considered to be a "safe" level to keep populations fed in a time of shortage — and this can be seen by the concern that nations are showing about expanding and safeguarding what reserves they do have in the present crisis. For example, Thailand recently announced it will not consider selling grain from its stockpiles, and the Philippines negotiated a deal with the US and Vietnam to buy a large reserve. Meanwhile, some softening in the rice crisis finally came when Japan, forced by the rules of globalized trade to buy imported rice it neither wanted nor needed to feed its populace, opened up its enormous surplus of imported rice to help feed the world's poor.

We raise the issue of the importance of building food reserves because there's a growing backlash, mostly by free-trade absolutists, who are blaming world hunger on the attempts of individuals and nations to feed themselves and become food secure. One example is a recent *Washington Post* article, which looks like a strong propaganda component, warning people about the danger of stockpiling grain.

> Cambodian Finance Minister Keat Chhon last week called for people to be calm. He urged them "not to stock up on foods, which could make the situation even harder."
>
> Some experts say that building reserves to protect against future shortages only makes the problem worse.

"Of course, if every country, or individual consumer, acts the same way, the hoarding causes a panic and extreme shortage in markets, leading to rapidly rising prices," said Peter Timmer, a visiting professor at Stanford University's program on food security and the environment.

For example, he said, "the newly elected populist government in Thailand did not want consumer prices for rice to go up, so they started talking about export restrictions from Thailand, the world's largest rice exporter.... So last Friday, rice prices in Thailand jumped $75 per metric ton. This is the stuff of panics. [246]

Now, there is some truth here — if billions of people attempt to build up a food reserve in a time of short supplies, they will make the situation worse, driving up prices and increasing shortages. It is also true, however, that the root cause of these shortages is not people trying to buy now so that they can be sure that they will have rice to eat if the price continues to jump. Instead, as we've seen, meat consumption, biofuels and economic speculation have driven food prices far more than hungry people attempting to get ahead of rapidly rising food prices.

Now, the difference between hoarding and stockpiling is this — once you are already in a crisis *and* there is a meaningful and rational system for ensuring people have access to food, building up stores can disrupt the existing system. This is hoarding, and it is wrong. That is, if there's just enough rice to go around, *and it is going around in a fairly just way*, those who are wealthy enough to build up private stocks can disrupt the system, but shouldn't. That, however is not the case now. First of all, there's more than enough food to go around, and second of all, justice has not been the major concern — that is, there has been no concerted world attempt to get poor hungry people their food.

We have no existing system to enforce even the most basic idea — that human food, grown by humans for humans, should go to human beings first. The reality is that rich people effectively consume grain three times. They eat some grain. Then they eat meat fed on enough grain to feed an ordinary person many times over for the same meal. Then they feed grain or grain-fed meat to their cars, their pets, the birds and occasionally burn some grain and legumes in their stoves.

Which is why people are vulnerable to charges of hoarding. Most hoarding (there are always exceptions) represents an attempt at securing food by already hungry or worried people in a world that rations food by price. If the price of rice or wheat or cooking oil is going up, anyone with common sense recognizes that if they can buy extra now, they can save more later. But because we ration by price and believe that the ability to pay is what gives one the right to food, we have no way of distinguishing between, say, the right of cars to eat and the right of people to eat, or the right of rich people to eat a pound of steak, created with 8 lbs. of grain and the right of poor people to eat a pound of that grain. What we need is a system of rights that recognizes that food is for people first. It seems so simple and obvious. For example, US biofuels usage could have fed 250 million additional people last year, had we simply believed that people not starving is more important that our ability to drive.

Building up supplies to be consumed in times of comparative prosperity and surplus is not hoarding — it is simply a wise idea, and has been since Pharaoh and Joseph were doing it. Keeping a solid reserve of food means that you are not as vulnerable to disruptions and crises. But national stockpiles have been falling steadily for the past decade, with world reserves currently at their lowest since records have been kept. Just as we're not saving money any more, we are not reserving our staple foods for hard times.

Not only is building supplies in times of comparative prosperity morally okay, it is not, ethically speaking, hoarding if there is no system of equitable distribution. That is, hoarding is the retention of food supplies that disrupts an already fair system. Hoarding is not an accurate way to describe the attempt of desperately poor and hungry people to make sure that they are a little less desperately poor and hungry next week; nor is stockpiling an unreasonable response to a crisis in which there is no just system of making sure that the hungry are fed. In that case, when governments and larger institutions are not ensuring fair distribution, it is more than reasonable for people to try and make sure they and theirs are fed. Can this cause problems? Absolutely. Is this root cause of present problems, and should those who inadvertently exacerbate problems with deeper root causes be held up as responsible? Hell, no.

The extended discussion of individual hoarding, which takes up nearly half the *Washington Post* article, implies that political unrest is primarily caused by governments acknowledging there is a problem and attempting to avoid starvation in their countries, and by people who want to eat trying to continue doing so. We do not believe that Americans who preserve and store food should be made to feel guilty about it, as the above article and dozens like it imply. Storing food for periods of poor harvest is a human norm. It always has been, and food sovereignty implies that we will prepare for lean times. Eaters should always have first rights to food. Moreover, those of us who are concerned about the failure of our nations or regions to stockpile food during our fat years have a reason and a responsibility to take on that role for ourselves.

The thing is, organizing and keeping grain reserves is one of those "comparatively good uses for government" things — at every level from the national to the local. Thus, moves by nations to stabilize or increase their reserves — though a day late or a dollar short — are not the root problem. Yes, they are driving short-term price rises. But they are also responding to the real danger that people will starve to death. Market analysts who talk about the problem of people holding back food and creating subsidies are ignoring the fact that nations are responding because a substantial portion of their populace is in danger of death from hunger and hunger-related disease.

But implicit in this assumption is the belief that it would be better to let some people starve than to start the cycle of driving up prices or having governments stabilize them. This is a form of free market orthodoxy that doesn't tolerate any dissent. Are people dropping dead of starvation? Well, the solution is to let the market handle it, which, of course, it will — in due course. Pay no attention to the corpses on the side of the road. This is, of course, nonsense.

The answer is a much greater degree of food sovereignty, not less. That is, the answer to world hunger is both to prioritize food for human beings and to encourage localities to be able to meet as many of their needs as possible. This gives everyone a hedge against famine and disasters — if crops fail in one place, surpluses can move from another. And food sovereignty, the idea that the people who have the right to the production of a piece of land are the people who tend and nurture it and participate in that community, is a means of getting at a greater degree of equity, ultimately the only hope we have for avoiding disaster in the coming decades.

There is a story in the Mishnah (a rabbinical text that explores biblical stories) that says that after Joseph and his brothers were reunited, Jacob and his sons made their way to Egypt where there was food. On the way to Egypt, one day, Jacob awakens and tells his sons to get up and plant cedars in the desert. They ask him why? Jacob answers that someday they will come out of Egypt again at the end of some terrible times, and when they do, their descendents will need those cedars. "So rise up now and plant seeds. For you are planting on this day the seeds of your own deliverance."

In telling the truth of our present circumstances, we have encountered many painful truths — perhaps as painful to you as they are to us. But we also recognize that the seeds of our deliverance are in our hands — and they are the seeds of a new Nation of Farmers.

An Interview with Helena Norberg-Hodge: Spring 2008

Reading Helena Norberg-Hodge and her thoughtful critique of industrial agriculture in *Bring the Food Economy Home* will make you yearn for another way of eating. Hearing her speak will further inspire you to take up the cause yourself. We were delighted to get to spend a few hours talking with her in preparation for writing this book.

ANOF: You're formal training is as a linguist. Could you tell me why you chose that path? How has it shaped your work?
HELENA: The interest in linguistics was really not an interest in linguistics, it was an interest in different languages and different cultures. My awareness of the primary importance of food and farming arose out of an interest in different cultures and from questioning the so-called Americanization of other cultures. In 1975, when I arrived in Ladakh, I did come equipped with quite an unusually broad cultural experience, but it was there that I became fully aware of the role of farming and the ways that the modern economy systematically removes people from the land and cuts off their ecological literacy.

In Ladakh I had this unusual experience of seeing a very ancient culture whose primary economic activity had been getting food from the environment, and I saw this very ancient culture suddenly dramatically changed.

ANOF: Could you tell me a bit more about your experience in Ladakh?
HELENA: I saw this very dramatic and very unusual situation of a culture that had not been affected by colonialism nor by modern development. As late as 1975 it had been sealed off for political reasons. Traders went through, but the area remained essentially an area where people were providing for their own needs as a priority and trading where it made sense

on their terms and according to their needs. We sort of know this and we are aware that colonialism and slavery had a very profound effect on people, but I think we forget that colonialism is the background to this modern economy and economic growth. There is a tendency both within the West as well as outside to think of our wealth as being a function of our very clever education system, science and modern technology, but that is leaving out a very big part of the story — that it could never have happened without this essentially robbery of other people's resources and their labor.

To find a place that, unlike most of Africa, India or South America, has not been affected by that process [of colonialism] was very unusual. And then I saw in a very graphic way that the global economy would bring in subsidized food and almost overnight destroy the market for local producers in favor of this artificially constructed market basically favoring monopolies. In just a decade that created not only massive ecological problems but also unemployment and local conflict between groups that have lived peacefully side by side for at least 500 years. That was a very dramatic lesson that showed me that what we do economically to agriculture is absolutely fundamental either to our well-being or to our destruction.

ANOF: I think understanding the economic connections you mentioned is important in considering a different form of agriculture here in the US or anywhere for that matter. Growth capitalism can completely change subsistence culture.

HELENA: Yes. I would also add to that, though. I think it's very important that we realize that communism or capitalism or even socialism are all large-scale, centralized systems, and therefore I prefer not to talk about the problem as being capitalism. The reason why I don't is that it in many minds conjures up the notion that socialism or communism are better — and I personally believe that the intentions behind communism and socialism are broader and in a certain way more noble. But I don't think it's just that the centralized power they entail, in both socialism and communism, was the problem socially, but I also see them as fundamentally anti-ecological, because they were top-down, centralized systems that also then foisted monoculture in terms of agricultural production. But when we talk about agricultural production, we're basically talking about all the activities from which we derive our basic needs: forestry, for building, fiber, building materials.

ANOF: So this not a question of favoring a particular economic system but that the tendency of top-down centralized economic systems to be ecologically destructive?

HELENA: Yes. My point of view is different from many people in the Anglo world — I see a tendency even among many deeper thinkers to still partly not to want to let go of the industrial experiment, and to see Scandinavia and socialism as the ideal. It is very rare to have a global perspective from grassroots experience, and it's very sad that that's the case, that the grass roots that are very close to the realities on the ground, whether it is the soil or the cultural and community experience, tend not to be born of people who have global experience.

ANOF: Could you talk about fact that in the Global North we are more wealthy in terms of material wealth and yet many studies show we are in fact less happy?

HELENA: I am working on a film now which I am calling *The Economics of Happiness*. I think we have increasing poverty in the most industrialized, urbanized parts of the world, and as part and parcel of that we have less time to enjoy our friends and families. In every culture, in studies that I am familiar with from around the world, people describe well-being and happiness as depending on good social relationships, family and friends. They are now starved and mutilated into far too rapid, far too stressed and therefore also much less positive experiences. Then you add to that the poverty in terms of our relationship to nature, to the natural world; as we are isolated in big cities, it is not just that we don't see the beauty of the sky and the trees, but we also have so much less contact with other beings, with animals.

There is so much evidence that people want more time and more contact with other people and positive relationships with family as well as with animals and nature; so you can see a tendency, where people do have a lot of money, to spend time in nature, whether it is sailing or riding horses or buying huge areas of wild land, there is a tendency for the wealthier classes, throughout the industrialized world, to demonstrate with their feet, with their money, that this is something desirable. And yet their rhetoric and the dogma is that this is all romantic nonsense. Another indicator is to look at what do people do when they have a holiday? Where is the general tendency to go on your holiday? It is to more natural places. So yes, I think we're very deprived and increasingly poor.

Then you add to that that in addition to that very fundamental spiritual, psychological poverty, even in terms of the food we eat, the clothes we wear, the houses we live in, the types of furniture, pottery, whatever, around us, the mass-produced stuff that comes out of this consumer culture is not as satisfying as the more adapted and crafted materials and the folks who are also robbed of space, in terms of our living space, as we are herded into bigger and bigger cities and suburbs; and then we are also surrounded by materials that are very dead.

ANOF: How do your concerns about issues of energy and the environment intersect with your concerns about food and farming?

HELENA: For about 30 years I have been coming to the West every year, mainly giving lectures with the message that we really need to look at what's happening to farming. I would talk about farmers as a threatened species and say we need to have a T-shirt that says not just "Save the panda" but "Save the farmer." In the 1980s and 1990s there was a big shift towards a commercializing, corporate world view, but in the last at least six or seven years there is a clear trend towards more interest in food and farming, which is very heartening. Just recently now there is a UNESCO World Bank report where something like 200 scientists have essentially concluded that we need to go back to more adapted, localized systems, using indigenous seed varieties and so on if we want to feed the world.

But I worry about this blind leadership which now you can see in virtually every country — governments are having to recognize at least global warming as a major problem, but they are still locked into an economic trajectory that promotes more globalized trade. They are completely schizophrenic and just turning a blind eye to the fact that more global trade is the antithesis of what we need. And, as you can see, many of their solutions focus on nuclear power, biofuels and genetic engineering, in the name of, "We have to adapt to global warming." I see a worldview born of almost total ecological illiteracy and wedded to a notion of growth that also comes out of the artificially low price for oil, so my concern right now is for the small players. The small players, whether the individual home owners or the small, local businesses, will be bearing the brunt of higher prices of oil and other regulatory changes.

ANOF: What do you think about the public discussion that's emerging concerning global warming?

HELENA: From Al Gore to virtually every major voice, the solutions for dealing with global warming are ridiculous, like the light bulbs. Those light bulbs [account for] something like 2% of the electrical use; in addition they're highly toxic, and not only toxic in terms of the mercury, but they are, as we have known for a long time, fluorescent lights are linked to epilepsy and other neurological problems. I'm very worried about the way that the analysis of the cause of global warming is steering away from the fundamental problems with the global food system and other really significant factors.

The food system should be the primary thing we should be looking at when we talk about global warming, including shipping other products back and forth that could be manufactured locally, regionally or nationally.

ANOF: There's a growing understanding that growing food organically isn't good enough in terms of having a more healthy agricultural system, in every sense of the phrase. The system monocropping is at the heart of the problem.

HELENA: There is a very clear link between the long distances that food travels and the structural need for monoculture at the production end. In a huge supermarket chain in New York or London, the longer the distance, the more difficult for them to deal with diversity on the farm, so we end up talking about container ships. We're [already also] talking about the huge harvesting technologies and ways of transporting and storing the food, and so the pressure on the production end is towards monoculture in these systems and, as a consequence, we are losing, every day, agricultural biodiversity. We don't even know how much we're losing, but it's very, very frightening.

Every day we are losing species, never to be recovered again; and yet on the shelf it looks like this fantastic range. Then there's also, at the processing end, the range of, for instance, different cheeses or different wines that were produced in regions, whether in France or Italy; we're more familiar with that. Those too are becoming more and more standardized and... the relationship between the human care and intelligence and the speed at which things are produced is under commercial pressure to scale up and to simplify; so, whether it's how long the wine stays in the barrel or what you do to balsamic vinegar or how you make a Camembert cheese, all of these things are under pressure of standardization, homogenization; so we are very rapidly losing that richness.

ANOF: Could all the bad news about how unhealthy our food system has become cause us to make positive changes?

HELENA: I feel that the bad news that I've witnessed around the world is also a tremendous source of hope. The local food system in this area is nothing like as rich as it could be, so in the area where I am now in Australia, in a climate where you can grow food the year round, you could grow an amazing range of things. The possibilities are very rich. Even in less warm climates, we can all grow far more than we can even dream. Every area has been encouraged to specialize, going back hundreds of years, so there is just tremendous potential for regions around the world to suddenly shift their economic focus towards diversifying and enriching their own economies.

ANOF: How about all the bad news related to energy issues, especially the pending global oil production peak. Could that actually help to create change — push us to grow food differently and change the way we cook and what we eat?

HELENA: Here I differ from a lot of peak oil people. There's a tendency to think that oil allowed us to feed more people. That, I would argue, is absolutely not true. Thank goodness there is an emerging grassroots movement of people who are contesting this. There is actually now quite a body of literature that shows that when you diversify production on the land almost anywhere you will be able to increase yields while reducing the ecological footprint and ecological damage.

As I was saying, you could actually increase the ecological wealth beyond what is needed for human use. So if you take that into reverse, what oil did was never to increase productivity in terms of the land use, the use of nature, it was to increase productivity *vis-à-vis* the use of human labor, so what happened was that we were able to replace human care and intelligence and hands-on nurturing of plants and animals with blind, stupid machines, that at the same time as they took over from the human care and labor, they also created a lot of pollution and a lot of damage and actually decreased the productivity from a given unit of land or water.

I see a potential for decentralization, for people in the South or less industrialized parts of the world to be allowed to stay in villages and smaller towns and remain more connected to the land. Also, we can start a process of re-ruralization or decentralization in the North, which is not going to happen overnight, but it could happen probably roughly at the rate of suburbanization and urbanization that's going on now. So instead of continuing to break down smaller towns in the North, there would be the infrastructure, and subsidies and taxes would be shifted to support a ruralization, localization or decentralization. Does that make sense?

ANOF: Would you mind sharing a recipe for our book? Perhaps a meal you might have in Ladakh?

HELENA: A meal that I might have in Ladakh? Well, you know, it's interesting. Here, again, is where I was talking about this potential for enriching ourselves and can I also just add that I came to realize that no traditional, indigenous group ever strove to increase its abundance as a major goal.

My sense is that most indigenous cultures did really quite well on what was there, and there were places like Ladakh where they had settled agriculture and they had a range of products and so on, but they didn't set out to think, "How can we really optimize this situation, really get the most out of this ecosystem without destroying it?" That is now our modern task. We're rather spoiled, but there is a way now of looking at the situation, of a lot of people on a crowded planet, how can we optimize this situation? The traditional cultures didn't do this, and we've never done this. In the modern era, the entire model has been, "rape nature to amass wealth for a few."

I would say from my point of view and from the point of view of most Ladakhis, the typical diet has been improved by the introduction of greenhouses, which means that what was a four-month growing season now means that there can be fresh green leaves surviving in very simple greenhouses 10 or 11 months of the year. When I sit down to a meal in Ladakh, I eat the best and most delicious vegetables I ever tasted anywhere in the world, mainly wild vegetables, of a range that I don't know how to translate into English — nettles was one of them — and then grain, a lot of grain, especially barley and meat and dairy products. But the food was wonderful.

—— *RECIPES* ——

Warm Potato, Egg and Tomato Salad   *by Helena Norberg-Hodge*

This first appeared in the book *Gaia's Kitchen: Vegetarian Recipes for Family and Community* by Julia Ponsonby, published by Green Books.

Also known as the Henhouse Hotch-potch, this salad is a very quick and delicious way of creating a meal. Using cubes of boiled new potatoes as your base, add whatever other delights your garden and hen house offer you — and which appeal to you. The delight of using warm potatoes is that they will suck in the salad dressing, marinating themselves in a delectable brew of fresh flavors. So, even if you prefer to serve the salad cold, dress it while the potatoes are still hot. The typically Scandinavian inclusion of protein-rich eggs not only tastes good but makes the meal nutritionally balanced. Serve with a fresh green salad.

Ingredients

	For 5–7 servings	For 35–40 servings
• potatoes	1 lb (450 g)	8 lb (3.6 k)
• firm red medium-sized tomatoes	4	4½ lb (2 kg)
• medium eggs	5–7	35–40
• spring onions	6	4 bunches
• freshly chopped parsley	3–4 tbsp approx.	2 oz (55g / ¾ cup) approx.

Dressing:

	For 5–7 servings	For 35–40 servings
• lemon juice	3 tbsp	6 fl oz (150 ml / ¾ cup)
• organic lemon zest	½ tsp	2–3 tsp
• olive oil	5 tbsp	10 fl oz (300 ml / 1¼ cups)
• pommery or grainy mustard	1 tsp	2 tbsp
• garlic cloves, crushed (to taste)	1–2	8–15
• sea salt (to taste)	2–3 pinches	3–4 tsp
• freshly ground black pepper (to taste)	1–2 tsp	

Directions

1. Place the whole eggs carefully in cold water and bring to the boil. Boil for six minutes, then remove from heat and plunge eggs into cold water until cool. This is supposed to stop a green ring forming around the yolk.
2. Scrub the potatoes. Use organic potatoes and leave on the skins. Cut the potatoes into ¾" (2 cm) cubes. Place these in boiling water and cook quickly for a five to ten minutes, until tender. Don't wait until the skins start flaking off. If fresh mint is available, plunge a generous bunch into the cooking water when potatoes are half way through cooking, for extra flavor.
3. Prepare the dressing, using a hand whisk or blender to combine all ingredients, and hopefully obtain a light emulsion.
4. Drain the potatoes and let them drip in the colander for a few minutes. Then put them into a mixing bowl and pour the dressing over them. Gently stir with a wooden spoon until all the potatoes are coated.
5. Cut the tomatoes into generous pieces, compatible in size with your potatoes (or use cherry tomatoes whole or halved).
6. Peel the eggs. Cracking and peeling them under cold water can make things easier. Halve about a quarter of the eggs lengthwise and reserve them on a plate for decorating the salad later on. Roughly chop the rest, making four to six pieces from each egg.

7. Chop the spring onions into approximately ¼" (½ cm) rings. Put a few aside for garnishing.
8. Chop the parsley fairly finely. Reserve a little for garnishing.
9. Add the tomatoes, roughly chopped eggs, spring onions and parsley to the potatoes. Stir very gently (so that the egg does not become completely mashed in). Everything can be added to the potatoes when still warm — or even quite hot! Taste and add extra salt and pepper if needed.
10. Tip the salad into your serving bowl. Decorate with chopped parsley, spring onions, and a ring of egg halves around the edge. Avoid pressing the salad down — let it sit chunkily, even mountainously, with all its garnishes sprouting like wild plants on its surface. Finish off with a sprinkling of paprika if you like.

Greens with Sweet Soy and Mushroom Sauce   *by Sharon*

Ingredients
- greens — your choice
- Kecap Manis, or sweet soy sauce
- mushroom "oyster" sauce

Directions
1. Steam or sauté as much of your favorite greens as you can cram in a pan for as long as necessary to get it to the just tender stage. For tender greens like spinach, mustards or kailaan it will take just seconds; for something like Brussels sprouts, chopped cabbage or kale stems this might take a bit longer. Consider using greens that we usually discard — broccoli stems, the stems of chard, the wrapper leaves of cabbage. Add a tablespoon or two each of mushroom "oyster" sauce (or the real stuff) and Kecap Manis, or sweet soy sauce. Serve over rice, barley or quinoa.

Urban Chicken with Roasted Vegetables
and Tossed Salad   *by Wendy McCrady, who blogs as "Chile" at*
chilechews.blogspot.com

All ingredients are locally available from her desert Southwest gardens. Wendy is actually a vegan, but a practical one. If times get tough, all of us may have to get a lot less picky about what we eat.
Prep time: 2 weeks

Ingredients
- pigeons — 2 per person
- ¼ cup minced cilantro
- 2 apples, diced
- zest and juice from 3 limes
- 1 quart crumbs from whole wheat bread
- 1½ tsp salt
- 1 jalapeno pepper, minced
- 3 tbsp toasted chopped pecans

- 2 dried red chili peppers, powdered
- red potatoes – 2 small ones per person
- onions – ¼ medium one per person
- 1 quart fresh greens (arugula, mizuna, etc.), washed and roughly torn
- oil pressed from 1 cup dried sunflower seeds (reserve 2 tbsp oil)

Directions

1. For one week, toss bread crumbs in a small area of your yard to attract pigeons.
2. After a week, set up a box trap in the feeding area and continue to toss bread crumbs. Do not trip the trap.
3. Once the pigeons are habituated to the feed and the trap, you should be able to easily catch a few for dinner over the course of a morning.
4. Clean and dress pigeons. Cut into parts (breasts, legs, back, etc.)
5. Mix lime, chili powder, salt, cilantro, oil, and jalapeno. Marinate the pigeon in half the marinade, reserving remaining mixture for salad.
6. Preheat solar oven for 1 hour.
7. Clean potatoes and onions. Quarter. Toss with reserved oil and sprinkle with a little salt.
8. Place pigeon and vegetables in large roasting pot, cover tightly, and place in solar oven. Cook until meat is no longer pink and vegetables are tender, 1–2 hours.
9. Toss together greens and apples. Drizzle with remaining dressing and top with pecans.
10. Serve with roasted pigeon and vegetables.

CHAPTER 6

The Landslide
Brings It Down

Feeding Ourselves

Well, I've been afraid of changin'
Cause I've built my life around you.
But time makes you bolder
Children get older
And I'm getting older too

— STEVIE NICKS —

AARON: I'm ashamed to say that when my family moved into our home, more than three years passed before I met the woman who lives across the street from me. As soon as we arrived, I began to talk regularly with the folks next door, but it was quite a while before I met Jean, the flat black asphalt of the road between us somehow proving a more formidable fence than the one that separated me from my next-door neighbors.

And I should go ahead and admit that when, one Sunday afternoon, I did decided to break the ice, I was driven not purely by altruistic intentions. I was curious to meet my neighbor and I did fully intend to offer her any assistance a younger neighbor might be able to provide. She's an elderly lady whose health keeps her from going out much. I was embarrassed not to have been over to meet her sooner, and I wanted to make that right. But when I headed over to her house, I was also in search of something. I was looking to borrow some sun.

Jean is a kind, bright-eyed woman who is not afraid of silence. She's easy to talk to and has plenty worth hearing to say back. When I visit, my older daughter, Keaton, often goes with me, curiously

259

picking up knickknacks and joining in the conversation as two-year-olds do. My neighbor never seems to mind the intrusion or the busy hands of a toddler. And whenever I visit Jean, I leave thinking I should do it more often. We're a neighborhood that respects privacy — but maybe a little too much sometimes. It is fair to say I was hoping some sun might improve that.

On my first trip to meet my neighbor we didn't talk about peak oil or the tragic loss of topsoil in our country. We talked about neighborly things, dancing around the question of what our relationship might be. Jean's backyard was wide open. From the sidewalk I could see the sunshine that fell on it, and I wanted to know if she had ever gardened there or if she ever would again. I wanted to see what my neighbor thought, just in general, about growing our own food.

It turned out that my neighbor had seen my chickens on occasion when they ventured into my front yard. She told me about how living in our small, southern town used to include keeping backyard poultry and sometimes even larger livestock. She lamented that folks no longer garden; that people aren't as neighborly and don't get together to share as often. She was not admonishing me for not visiting sooner; she just couldn't help talking about state of things. I apologized for not having visited before, and I brought up the idea of my gardening in her backyard. She liked it.

Jean is no longer able to do the physical work of growing food and was happy to hear the idea of my using her former garden to do so. It turns out her late husband used to garden in the very spot I had in mind. It's a small fenced-in backyard with an awful lot of sun, especially compared to my own yard. She has a detached building just right for potting and storing tools, the roof of which now collects water we use for irrigation. I say we because several other neighbors now grow food there. Ed, Kelley and Kylie were already starting a garden when I inquired. They helped plant and water and mulch and harvest during those first few years. We have added rain barrels and raised some beds. Jean's fence now has a gate that leads to Eric's yard, who gardens on his property and on hers, combining his efforts with those of others to grow food in a few places throughout our neighborhood. We share a tiller, several compost piles and the best fertilizer our neighborhood chickens have to offer. Add in Jodi, Martha and her husband, Richard, my new neighbor Eric and his wife Amanda, and the beginnings of a crew have taken shape. And there are others, who just haven't quite made up their minds yet.

If all this sounds like a well-oiled, community gardening effort, then I've sinned again. I have painted too pretty a picture about what changing a modern American neighborhood looks like. Sometimes it gets messy, and almost never does it look like the picture on a postcard.

The job of growing food has become the job of organizing schedules, deciding who will serve as home to the piles of fallen leaves we collect to use as mulch, and making up our minds about what to grow where, with whom and how. There are now a string of backyards — some sharing soil, others labor, one simply allowing passage for our wheel barrows, but that's okay too. Much of it is in the initial stages, with beds being built and systems being established — in short people learning as we go.

It is accurate to say that we are growing our shared garden every bit as much as we are growing our own food. I went across the street to meet my neighbor and to see if she would let me grow food in her backyard. From there on I began to discover — or maybe rediscover — where I live, who shares my neighborhood with me and what we might do about meeting more of our own needs. I'm glad I did.

Bull's-eye Eating

The best time is always right now;
the best place is always right here.
— GREG HICKMAN —

The Oxford Word of the Year for 2007 was *locavore*. The term was coined by a group of "concerned culinary adventurers" in San Francisco who, in 2005, started eating locally and advocating that others do the same, recognizing that, "the choices we make about what foods we choose to eat are important politically, environmentally, economically, and healthfully." Like a growing number of Americans, they elected to live on the "100 Mile Diet," eating only local food from their bioregion.

The 100 Mile Diet (or variations of 200 miles or 250 miles) is becoming more and more popular as more people consider the high costs of industrial agriculture. In contrast to the 100 Mile Diet, there's the ubiquitous 1500-Mile Caesar salad — ingredients flown from all over at enormous energy costs. As the true cost of our food becomes evident, we need to find a new model and a way of sorting a system of ethical eating in a world of great complexity.

The volatility of the times in which we live shape our response as well. As people learn about peak oil, climate change and food insecurity, many of us have decided to grow more of our own food. The Dervaes family of California, for example, produces thousands of pounds of food a year on a city lot. They call it the "100-foot diet." As food prices rise, more small farmers will pop up. There is a growing movement of eaters and growers trying to create local eating systems. How do we pull these threads together?

It is unlikely that most of us living on small to mid-sized lots will be able to grow all of our own food, and even more unlikely that many of us will want to. Even the most dedicated subsistence grower enjoys the occasional treat from far away. Many of us are capable of growing much more of our own food, but the idea is not that every household in the US could become food self-sufficient. Instead, we need to focus on quality, local economies, local systems and food security. Even people committed to more home production are going to have culinary needs and wants better served by others, and recognizing this can help to foster cooperation and local markets for small-scale food producers — we need systems that can help us figure out how to eat well in a low-energy world.

Recognizing this need for interdependence can help bring about all sorts of new and potentially enriching food production arrangements. The local, regional, national and even international trade in food is probably not going to disappear entirely, even in a world more tightly constrained by resource depletion and climate change. Regional differences will most likely be magnified in our diets in the coming decades, but some trade will persist as it always has.

This trade can be an awfully rewarding experience. The problem we have been articulating is not trade itself, but dependence. We have lost the balance of self-sufficiency and interdependence that creates healthy market relationships. Those relationships themselves can prove very rewarding for many reasons, as Maria Mies describes,

Subsistence trading in Juchitan, is itself a craft that requires partic-ipants to learn how to handle the social relationships network of exchange. It is a fine art that also creates obligations, so it cannot be replaced by wage labour. The logic of subsistence trading is pre-cisely not one of profit maximisation without regard to long-term relationships among producers, traders and customers. Subsistence relations are just as important as the supplies themselves — and in any case, more important than money — for the survival of the par-ticipants.[247]

The economics of local eating require a combination of security, plea-sure and positive market relationships — something lost under the current globalized system. It begins in relationships, in communities, where we are. It is about tying together all the threads of the system — in this case, gar-deners, farmers, cooks, eaters.

So, moving forward, we will need Victory Gardens and local farms, ur-ban food security and markets for rural farmers. Most of all we need re-lationships between growers and eaters. The question is how to build networks that serve all the involved parties. Finding a balance between the 100 Mile Diet and the 100-foot diet requires a really new way to think about how we eat, how we shop, how we grow and consume. What should we grow ourselves? What should we buy locally? What is okay to import from far away?

We need a means to think about the relationship between local and distant foods, a strategy for eating in the long term, even in places that will never be perfectly food self-sufficient. We'd like to suggest one — the Bull's-eye Diet. Think of your diet as a dartboard and your choices as aim-ing to get as close to the center as possible.

The center ring is the bull's-eye — our own *Home Production Ring*. For people with land and ability to grow gardens, that could include a surpris-ing amount of intensively grown food. A quarter-acre suburban lot, care-fully managed, might produce most of a family's diet. For others, especially those with restricted access to land, the center ring may be a smaller part of our diets, but the principle is to eat as locally as possible when making de-cisions about where our food comes from. It is worth remembering how powerful container gardening can be for those with minimal land access — planting rooftops, balconies, stoops, and sprouts in the windowsills — can provide a surprisingly large amount of food.

The next ring from the center represents food from very close by. We'll call it the *Neighborhood Ring*. It includes shared food from neighbors' yards and gardens, community gardens, city farmers, food grown at our schools, parks and on the lawns outside businesses and halls of worship. Wild foods gathered from parks and from other sources such as fruiting street trees can be part of the picture. "Guerilla gardening," a new movement that calls on people to plant untended areas and produce food on land they don't own, can expand this even further. In urban areas around the world, guerilla gardeners plant food-producing plants in traffic circles, in vacant lots and other unused spaces — claiming their right to beautify and bring food security to a region. The idea is to gather as much food as possible from as close to home as you can. Within walking distance is a good way to think about the geographic boundaries of this ring.

Next out from the center would be the *District Ring* of our dietary dartboard — the food grown by gardeners and farmers throughout your bioregion. This would probably include all producers in your town or city, and areas of rural land immediately surrounding them. Many of the small farmers that might make up your District Ring will probably participate in farmers' markets, run CSAs that deliver to your region, and sell to local restaurants. It might be helpful to consider the geographic boundary of this eating region as the distance of a reasonable bike ride on a Saturday afternoon, perhaps a ten-mile round trip. Here we're still talking about people with whom you might have a regular relationship, if not a daily one. This is a place for want-to-be farmers to consider starting their farms — and if you can't afford land near a city, consider renting unused lots. It isn't necessary that your farm be made up of large, contiguous spaces.

Further from home, but still within a practical distance of travel is the next ring of the bull's-eye, your *Region Ring*. This area is defined as places from which your food might come in large shipments, infrequently but consistently. People within a few hundred miles of the coast would include the seafood likely to be shipped to where they live. Another example might be the apples of the Southeast, grown primarily in the Appalachian Mountains where it is cooler but which are within a hundred miles or so of many of the more densely populated cities of the Southeast. This isn't a region you might visit weekly or even monthly, but one from which you might buy apples annually to store and eat, use in sauces, ciders, pies, and the like all winter long. This might also include grains imported from the nearest grain-growing regions. One option for larger farmers who want to tie their food to a particular region would be to contract to neighborhood co-ops, or even neighborhoods, for bulk grains or other agricultural products.

Specialty foods from even further away might compose part, if only a small measure, of our diets. We might call this the *Fair Trade Ring*. For example, high-value goods that are transported dry, such as spices, coffee, tea and chocolate would be part of this ring. These are good ways for people in the Global South to make a supplemental income from those who dream of such products in the North. In fact, it is possible to imagine tropical CSAs, where communities support a particular coffee farmer in Kenya or Java, skipping the middleman and creating a mutually beneficial partnership, one in which it would be feasible to have a true omnivore's Thanksgiving and give a name to the person who grew your breakfast drink or the cinnamon for your pie.

Another part of this ring might be occasional treats, such as pineapples, bananas and citrus. We tend to take them for granted now, but once upon a time they were rare and treasured delights, the proverbial orange in the Christmas stocking. In the future, however, such fruits of far away places will probably be much less available. The difficulty is that moving fruit long distances often involves air shipping, which is incredibly fuel expensive and energy intensive. It also creates tremendous amounts of carbon and amounts to shipping water, often from dry places to wet ones. So we are likely to eat such treats less often and enjoy them more.

What might eating this way look like? Well, on the morning we're writing this, we decided to look at our menus and see where things are coming from.

On a warm, sunny morning in late May, Sharon had oatmeal for breakfast; the rolled oats were grown in Quebec, about 300 miles from Sharon's home. She also drank bulk, fair-traded, organic green tea, and had home-canned peaches, grown in the Hudson Valley, about 30 miles south. Sharon has two peach trees in her yard, but they are not yet bearing. The oatmeal was flavored with fair-traded cinnamon from Madagascar and sweetened with honey from the bees of a neighbor down the road. With it went an apple that was picked a mile from Sharon and has been stored since autumn.

For lunch for Sharon there's a sandwich made of local cheese from an Amish dairy 30 miles to the west. She buys it at a farm stand down in the valley below her house. The sandwich will be garnished with home-made hot-pepper pickles from her garden, fresh sorrel and lettuce from the kitchen garden, and mustard originating in some grocery store (remember, neither of us are perfect!), and served on bread made by her husband from wheat grown in Pennsylvania. With it is a bowl of rhubarb compote from fresh rhubarb picked from her garden and a glass of lemon-balm/lemon-verbena iced tea.

Later, her boys will make a bowl of purple (!) popcorn, grown on farms in the valley six miles from her. They will butter it with homemade butter, made from cream milked in a local dairy. Sharon actually grows popcorn, but sometimes choices are made by other than purely bull's-eye standards — the boys wanted to try the purple kind.

Dinner will be baked potatoes covered with steamed fresh mixed greens — all homegrown (chard, kale, spinach and dandelion) — coated with a chipotle (from the organic co-op) cheese sauce, made with milk from the local dairy and cider vinegar from the apples that went wrinkly this spring. For dessert they will eat the first strawberries of the season, with reverence.

Soon the garden will be booming and there will tomatoes and peppers, zucchini and more, but now things go slowly. Even for Sharon on the farm, there are foods that come from far away. But as the season rises, the bull's-eye will get closer and closer to the center.

Aaron's breakfast was collard greens from his CSA, delivered from 15 miles away, and mixed with lambs quarters weeded out of his garden. Eggs came from the chickens Aaron keeps (somewhat illicitly) in his backyard, and bread from a local bakery (although when he's not finishing books, Aaron bakes his own from flour grown in the Midwest or makes cornbread from corn grown and milled in South Carolina). When he takes the dog for a walk later, Aaron will pick figs from a neighbor's fig tree (with permission) and enjoy them. So far Aaron's coffee comes from far away, but he has an indoor coffee tree, and his region includes tea camellias, so both could be grown near him.

His family will eat sweet potatoes, which grow as a cover crop to shade out weeds in their yard, and which proliferate wildly. His infant daughter, Salem, will get them steamed and mashed as one of her first solid foods, and the rest of them will enjoy them baked. Strawberries grow in the yard, and the peach trees are loaded with fruit. The pears and apples are losing to the squirrels, but Aaron still expects to get a crop. Salem will also nurse — and that too is local food.

Aaron is a vegetarian, but his wife and daughter eat some meat, raised locally; so everyone will have stir-fry for dinner, Jennifer and Keaton with local beef, Aaron with vegetables from their CSA basket and with chives, chard and new potatoes from their yard. Aaron's blackberries are ripening, but aren't quite ready yet. But the ones over the fence are, and Aaron has permission to harvest as he likes.

One of the things that you'll notice from the above is that our food choices aren't just shaped by our personal tastes, but by where we live — by the soils and climates that we live in.

As it becomes less feasible to ship food from all over the world to our doorsteps, we can expect a wider diversity of crops to be grown closer to home. Creative gardeners always push limits, and they will have more incentive to do so. Simultaneously we can also imagine that our diets will become more specific to our region. Those in the South will likely not have to survive on corn, collards and sweet potatoes alone; those in the Northeast won't have to make do with cabbage, potatoes and parsnips. Farmers and gardeners are notorious for experimenting and pushing the limits of what they can grow. It is reasonable to expect that even as we become reacquainted with the wonderful varieties of the foods that grow best locally in the seasons of our area, we will still occasionally enjoy special foods from farther away or specialties grown locally in unique conditions.

The bull's-eye diet can help us make decisions about where our food should come from. The closer the better — shooting for as close to the bull's-eye as possible means we'll be striving to eat as locally as we can, while recognizing that no man, no region, no neighborhood, no city is an island.

What about the 'Burbs?

We look at the present through a rear-view mirror.
We march backwards into the future.
Suburbia lives imaginatively
in Bonanza-land.
— MARSHALL McLUHAN —

But where will we grow all this food? In his book, *The Long Emergency*, social critic James Kunstler argues that we will ultimately be hobbled, and perhaps destroyed, by what he calls "the psychology of previous investment." That is, Kunstler argues that we tend to believe in the inherent value of things we've poured resources into already, and we are thus reluctant to abandon them even when abandonment is the right course. In a more recent essay, Kunstler has argued that this psychological force is nearly impossible to resist,

> The psychology of previous investment is, for us, a force too great to overcome. We will sell the birthrights of the next three generations in order to avoid changing our behavior. We will blame other people who behave differently for the consequences of our own behavior. We will not understand the messages that reality is sending us, and we will drive ourselves crazy in the attempt to avoid hearing it.[248]

We think Kunstler is absolutely right about the sheer power of attachment that our prior works will have for us. In fact, we are seeing signs of this already, as discussions of global warming and energy depletion have focused on how to keep the cars on the road and the rest of the infrastructure of rich world society going. Since it is virtually impossible to do so, much more urgent goals of cutting carbon and addressing peak energy have been essentially abandoned. That is, because we do not seriously consider solutions to global warming and peak oil that involve a smaller economy, a vastly lower-energy society and fair share solutions, we work ourselves into a situation where we are back to linear choices — technofix or doom.

Our whole investment in an auto-based society is so great that we are blind the fact that we cannot simultaneously address global warming and energy depletion and keep the cars on the road and our society structured as it is. We are increasingly suffering from this, bound by the psychology of our previous investments.

Kunstler is describing a real psychological phenomenon — we are like gamblers who begin losing money and play more and more, hoping to repair their losses. We bet on the car, on the housing bubble, on high technological solutions and free markets, and now that we've begun to lose, and lose big, it is hard for us to recognize the deep unlikelihood of our ever hitting the lottery and replacing what we've lost. There comes a point at which the best action anyone can take is to cut his losses, get up from the table and cease to gamble — to put the money he has left into a safer cause.

Is it all hopeless, then? That is, now that we've gambled away a good part of our own inheritance and our children's, are we doomed to sit around playing and losing until the game becomes Russian roulette, and the gun is pointed at our temples? Or is it possible that the psychology of previous investment isn't so much a gun as a double-edged sword and might be put to good use? Is it possible to find a new game, one that doesn't involve abandoning what we've invested in but using it differently?

There is little doubt that during that past 60 years we here in the US have transformed our self-made landscape in disturbing ways. Consider the suburbs, on which Kunstler lavishes much of his venom — and for good reason. Kunstler calls them "the greatest misallocation of resources in the history of the world" — and that is almost certainly true.

We spent more than 60 years building an energy-intensive, fossil-fuel-dependent, carbon-spewing landscape that doesn't work very well without those fossil fuels. The ability of most citizens to cheaply own and operate an automobile means we've had access to a level of mobility never before experienced. The outgrowth of that access has been a sprawling pattern of living that changed the rules about how and where we live, work, and play and how we get there and back. We are now more spread out than ever before, mostly getting back and forth from one place to another by driving alone in our cars. All signs say this could turn out very badly — that it already has turned out badly. We have invested enormous resources in this system. Is it possible that some of this investment could be made to serve us?

It is absolutely the case that we ought to have designed better than we did, to have chosen more wisely. As the cost of fueling our automobiles increases, it's becoming obvious we've put too many of our eggs into one basket. And as the US wakes up to the realities of a changing climate, it's also painfully obvious that soloing around in a huge fleet of carbon emitters isn't the most thoughtful way to transport ourselves from one side of our towns and cities to the other. The question is, as the expansive nature of suburban life becomes too expensive, both economically and ecologically, what will we do with this great "misallocation" of resources?

Will we, as some suggest, simply abandon this experiment? The likelihood of moving everyone out of suburbia and into mixed-use, walkable communities is quite remote — to do so would involve spending more of our limited resources than we can likely afford on building new infrastructure. Likewise moving everyone from the suburbs into the countryside and onto farms is unlikely. To be sure many, many people will move. Becoming a farmer in a hungry world is likely to be a very wise choice. But many of us have other ties and other goals — our agriculture is only part of what we do to live.

Some people are already choosing to move to places where they can safely walk and bike to meet more of their daily needs. Others are choosing to reruralize. But completely depopulating the US suburbs is a project we have neither the fiscal resources nor the fossil fuel energy necessary to accomplish. It seems reasonable to assume that lots of people are going to continue to live in the suburban communities we've created all over this country during the past 60 years.

Will these places simply devolve into slums, with roving bands of thieves stripping building materials and other valuables from abandoned homes and formerly homeless drug addicts burning them down while trying to keep warm? There will probably be some of that, especially if the course of the housing crisis isn't arrested by some strategy that keeps people in homes. The following is from a recent article in *The Atlantic*:

> At Windy Ridge, a recently built starter-home development seven miles northwest of Charlotte, North Carolina, 81 of the community's 132 small, vinyl-sided houses were in foreclosure as of late last year. Vandals have kicked in doors and stripped the copper wire from vacant houses; drug users and homeless people have furtively moved in. In December, after a stray bullet blasted through her son's bedroom and into her own, Laurie Talbot, who'd moved to Windy Ridge from New York in 2005, told *The Charlotte Observer*, "I thought I'd bought a home in Pleasantville. I never imagined in my wildest dreams that stuff like this would happen."[249]

This question of what will happen to the suburbs is already on the table. And with more people defaulting on their mortgages and losing their jobs as the economy slumps, we're likely to see this scenario play out repeatedly. It is not, however, inevitable. Though banks may object, the truth is that no one, including the banking industry, benefits from seeing our existing investments destroyed, as properties go into foreclosure and are abandoned. The only sensible solution is to enable people to live in these properties — whether by helping the present owners stay or by making them accessible to low-income families who couldn't afford houses any other way.

It's important to take a moment and assess the possibilities presented by the problem. That is, if we're going to do anything other than watch while a large number of the communities in this country turn into the slums of the 21st century, we're going to have to comprehensively address the problem. That means starting with an assessment of not only the disadvantages of the suburban communities in the US but the advantages.

In 1994, David Pimentel of Cornell University and Mario Gampietro of the National Institute in Rome published a report entitled "Food, Land, Population and the US Economy." In it they observed that at present rates of population growth, by 2050 the US will have only 0.6 acres of available arable land per person to grow food, fiber and biofuels. Right now, the average American's diet requires 1.8 acres, three times as much land as will be available in the future. The minimum considered necessary for a lower-energy but roughly familiar diet is 1.2 acres. We will have only half that, because of a combination of land lost to highways and housing, population growth, and the destructive practices of industrial agriculture.

Indeed, the numbers may be more disturbing still — Pimentel and Gampietro's analysis preceeded much of what we now know about climate change. With the drought in the US Southwest predicted to last until the end of the century, and with climate change reducing both land availability and water available for irrigation, the forecast may indeed be even more dire. Abandoning the suburbs is incompatible with imagining a future without hunger.

The suburbs are full of problems that could turn into solutions, depending on our choices. Consider, perhaps the problem of water, becoming acute in many parts of the US. The suburbs have large quantities of impervious surfaces, or surfaces that shed water — driveways, rooftops, parking lots, strip malls, sidewalks, streets. This is a problem in many communities. If too many rooftops and roadways shed too much water during a rainstorm, the result is a high volume of water that has to be diverted out of these neighborhoods before rushing into our creeks, streams and rivers. This often leads to flooding and/or substantial amounts of soil runoff, the number one water pollution problem in many communities. It is ironic that many locations simultaneously struggle with water restrictions because of drought and capacity problems because of excessive storm runoff. But this is precisely the kind of problem that could be solved.

The rooftops and roadways of suburbia could be used to gather the water we need to grow food for ourselves. This could be especially important as global climate changes throw weather curveball after curveball at us. The solution is to design simple, elegant ways to collect this water for use during times between rain storms. Six hundred gallons of water can be collected from 1,000 square feet of rooftop in just a 1" rainstorm. Many McMansions are much larger and have the capacity to gather much more rain into cisterns. It's worth noting that 65 percent of the water we use in our homes each day goes to irrigation, toilet flushing and laundry. Rainwater could be used to do all three with simple filtration. Doing this could go a long way toward restoring the health of our waterways. And this is just one example of how the disadvantages of suburbia might be turned into advantages.

But that's not the end of the story. It seems increasingly obvious that we're going to have to grow food differently if we have any chance of adapting to a low-energy lifestyle with any semblance of grace. And it is also true that over the past decades we have often taken as many as a million acres a year and put them into suburban development. In many cases houses were built on some of the best farmland available, as small farmers were driven out of business. The land may have been sold to developers, but it remains the same land. Parts of it now have roads, driveways and McMansions on them, but the lawns are still capable of producing enormous amounts of food, fuel and even fiber.

Our own rough calculations suggest that there is just about as much land in suburban properties — parks, corporate greenspaces and similar locations — as there will be arable land per person by 2050; that is, we can essentially double our food base from the absolutely minimal to something well within norms by simply growing food in suburbia. We cannot afford to abandon suburbia, because we may starve without it. The next decades are going to require us to make use of all the food-producing land we have.

Without tractors or draft animals, most healthy, able-bodied people will be able to farm/garden no more than one or two acres intensively, working full time. Some people will want to farm this much, maybe on large suburban five-acre lots or by sharing, as Aaron and his neighbors do, several lots owned by those unable or uninterested in growing. We might use animal agriculture but on a smaller scale, raising rabbits or chickens in our suburban backyards. Instead of relying on feedlots, each household might produce its own eggs and a small portion of its meat.

Most suburban lots fall somewhere between one-quarter and one-half an acre, just about right for an older couple or a young family to produce a large portion of their own food and some for sale while still holding down other jobs. Permaculture techniques, which emphasize growing perennial food plants, can help reduce the workload, as can containers, raised beds, and a host of other techniques for accessibility and ease. It is easy to assume that the work will be too hard — but it doesn't have to be.

It almost certainly would have been better had we used wiser patterns of development, but having put enormous quantities of energy and resources into suburbia, subdividing highly productive land into parcels ranging from a few hundred feet to ten acres, we have done a large part of the labor of subdividing land into small-scale, human-sized plots to be farmed and gardened. These plots have houses on them — not the superinsulated, reasonably sized houses we might have built if we had been wiser, but large houses eminently suited to consolidating families into a single home, renting out space, turning rooms or garages into small businesses, and creating small-scale food producing and manufacturing infrastructure.

The suburbs were born out of an idea that each person could have his own cottage and his own garden of Eden, her own unmolested paradise outside of the nastiness of the industrializing cities, and still go to work in those cities each day. It never quite worked out that way, but the end result is that a lot of people live on small amounts of land in communities that aren't completely paved over with asphalt and concrete. Is it possible to imagine that we might change our dreams about what the suburbs are to something more in line with what they could potentially become?

One historic problem of agrarian societies has been the mistreatment of agricultural workers and the consolidation of land and its wealth into the hands of rich owners. The question of how we might avoid a new feudalism has engaged many thinkers — when we will have to grow food to avoid hunger, how do we create Thomas Jefferson's imagined nation of independent and empowered farmers rather than a class of new serfs, mistreated migrants or virtual slaves? One possibility is "distributism" — a form of capitalism in which capital (natural resources) is not controlled by governments or a few wealthy private individuals but is shared as widely as possible among the general population. Or as G. K. Chesterton put it, "Too much capitalism does not mean too many capitalists, but too few capitalists."[250]

The simple fact is that we have more suburban houses on large tracts of land than we will need. At the same time, the amount of space taken per person for housing has risen dramatically, from 293 square feet per person in 1950 to 893 square feet per person in 2000.[251] We have fewer people per house, yet they have more space. Thus the opportunity to consolidate housing resources while more widely distributing the task of growing food stands at hand.

Many of us in this country could have access to land — albeit in small parcels — and while the housing boom excluded millions of younger people, the bust opens up possibilities in that regard, depending on how we manage it. To do this, we would have to overcome the foreclosure crisis and avoid seeing millions of Americans displaced from their homes. At the same time, we will have to find a way to bring those who have been unable to enter the housing market into these now-abandoned houses. Correctly managed, our present circumstances might lead to a fairly nifty way of developing and maintaining a moderately democratic land ownership policy here in the US. More from Leinberger's article:

> Arthur C. Nelson, director of the Metropolitan Institute at Virginia Tech, has looked carefully at trends in American demographics, construction, house prices, and consumer preferences. In 2006, using recent consumer research, housing supply data, and population growth rates, he modeled future demand for various types of housing. The results were bracing: *Nelson forecasts a likely surplus of 22 million large-lot homes (houses built on a sixth of an acre or more) by 2025 — that's roughly 40 percent of the large-lot homes in existence today.* [emphasis added][252]

What do you do with a surplus of more than 22 million large-lot homes during a period of failing industrial agriculture and rising food costs? You establish new micro farms of course. Those people who do continue to live in the suburbs, either because they cannot move or they don't want to, could use this land to grow food for themselves and their neighbors. The food could be grown with minimal or no fossil-fuel inputs and would be produced very close to the people who will eventually eat it. This solves two of the really big problems associated with the industrial model of agriculture. It is conceivable that our previous investment might be made to serve our needs. That is, we might take what we have valued and turn it into something genuinely valuable.

What Can We Accomplish in the 'Burbs?

The most noteworthy thing about gardeners is that they are always optimistic, always enterprising, and never satisfied. They always look forward to doing something better than they have ever done before.
— VITA SACKVILLE-WEST —

Tell all of this to the average citizen unaware of the prospects of energy shortages and environmental disaster and you're likely to get a host of responses about how unlikely or unreasonable such a solution might be. It's likely we haven't reached the pain threshold necessary to get the real attention of many Americans, but one response certainly will be that we can't grow very much food by just tearing out our lawns. This, of course, isn't true at all.

In a previously mentioned study titled "Organic agriculture and the global food supply," University of Michigan professor Ivette Perfecto and Catherine Badgley, a research scientist with UM's Museum of Paleontology, set out to test the "objections to the proposition that organic agriculture can contribute significantly to the global food supply [because of] low yields and insufficient quantities of organically acceptable fertilizers." The results of their study found that instead,

> [M]odel estimates indicate that organic methods could produce enough food on a global per capita basis to sustain the current human population, and potentially an even larger population, without increasing the agricultural land base. These results indicate that organic agriculture has the potential to contribute quite substantially to the global food supply, while reducing the detrimental environmental impacts of conventional agriculture.[253]

It is important to recognize that 85 percent of all the world's farms are small farms, and the average farm size in all of Africa and Asia is only about four acres — that's the average, which obviously means that many are smaller. In the Soviet Union 95 percent of all farms are less than 2.5 acres.[254] The US still contains more than 66,000 farms smaller than five acres.

In many, many nations a substantial number of farms are pretty much the same size as a suburban lot. And it is worth noting that most terminology, including that of the UN and the World Bank, calls those people farmers. The average Bangladeshi farms half a hectare. (A hectare is about 2.5 acres.) In Barbados the average piece of land is 1.6 hectares, in China 0.67 hectares, in India 1.34, Lebanon 1.2, Japan, 1.2, Egypt 0.95. And of course, averages mean that many, many of these farms are quite a bit tinier. In India, small farms of less than two hectares don't just grow vegetables — they produce nearly half of all food grains. So we can see the enormous potential of small-scale, suburban agriculture.[255]

Even in the US the line between farmer and suburbanite is growing fainter. In her glorious book *The Earth Knows My Name: Food, Culture, and Sustainability in the Gardens of Ethnic America*, Patricia Klindienst notes that there is no clear boundary between those who call themselves "farmers" and those who call themselves "gardeners" — some of the gardens are bigger than the farms, in fact.[256] Even in the US, there are thousands of small farms, being worked by thousands of small farmers, and size doesn't seem to be the defining factor.

A system of small farms can go a long way toward feeding itself and producing surpluses. The Dervaes family, who created the website "Path to Freedom," provides an excellent example of what is possible in our front and backyards. This family lives on a suburban lot of about one-fifth of an acre in Pasadena, California. They cultivate about one-tenth of an acre, or about 4,400 square feet. That's an area roughly 67 feet square, and yet they consistently produce more than 6,000 pounds of vegetables annually. The four adults living there eat about 85 percent of their vegetarian diet from the yard during the summer months and are able to get more than half of what they eat out of their garden in the winter. They also sell some produce to nearby restaurants.[257]

It should be noted that the Dervaes family lives in southern California, where the weather is extremely generous to those who grow food (and have access to water). But Eliot Coleman and Barbara Damrosch point out in *Four-Seasons Harvest: Organic Vegetables from Your Home Garden All Year Long* that even people living in Maine are capable of growing food year round, using fairly simple season extension techniques.

In *Garden Agriculture: A Revolution in Efficient Water Use*, David Holmgren notes that "Australian suburbs are no more densely populated than the world's most densely populated agricultural regions."[258] American suburbs are similarly populated. This suggests to us that it is at least within the realm of possibility that the suburbs could be transformed in a way that helps us a) take advantage of new soil for growing food, b) foster self-sufficiency and democracy by freeing Americans from corporate control over their food, c) provide a reasonable amount of food self-sufficiency for families during the coming era of change and volatility and d) capture the rain water necessary to address the deepening water crisis. We may find that in a time in which we are unable to build out grand new responses to peak oil and climate change, agriculturally at least, we may not have to.

It's also likely that many Americans will face trouble finding work during an era of declining energy and resource availability. Politicians and a lot of well-meaning business-as-usual types will undoubtedly put together all sorts of plans to try to re-employ those people who lose their jobs in the post-carbon economy.

There is already a growing call for some sort of "green" Works Project Administration (WPA) like the WPA seen during the New Deal era. At one time the WPA, created as a way to build up American infrastructure while simultaneously providing desperately needed jobs to hungry people, was the largest employer in the country. Van Jones, activist and writer, has called for the creation of millions of new urban "green" jobs to benefit urban minorities. White-collar technical and financial sector urban jobs are also taking a huge hit. It is conceivable that the solution for both the newly unemployed rich and the urban working poor could be the creation of our new, low-energy infrastructure and agriculture. However, any response that doesn't include a large measure of self-sufficiency for the average American would be missing out on a great opportunity to give back power to ordinary people. It is painfully obvious that we are at our greatest disadvantage when we are in debt to others for the basics we need to survive.

And the green jobs solution is also a way to re-energize local economies in the wake of the failure of the big-box model of warehouse-on-wheels commerce. As it becomes less profitable to make stuff cheaply in China and then ship it half way around the world, we're going to have begin rebuilding our capacity to provide for ourselves, starting with our dinners.

Not only can the suburbs potentially provide that necessary measure of self-sufficiency but they also can sell surpluses to the cities around them. The places we most need people to grow food are the places where people live right now. On May 22, 2007, for the first time in history, more people were estimated to live in cities than in rural areas. In the year 2000 there were 388 cities whose population exceeded 1 million residents. By 2015 that number is expected to increase to 554, with three-quarters of them in developing countries.[259] Today, 72 million Americans live in the country's 200 largest cities.[260] Getting food from the countryside to the cities will be one of the major challenges of a newer, lower-energy society. The first step will be making the suburbs bloom and turning our previous investment into something we can continue to value.

Urban Food Production: A Case Study

The sun was enough to maintain life on earth for millions of years.
Only when we [humans] arrived and changed the way we use energy
was the sun not enough. So the problem is with our society,
not with the world of energy.
— Bruno Henriquez —

Havana, the capital of Cuba, is home to more than 2 million residents and is the largest city in the Caribbean. With the collapse of the Soviet Union in 1989, the Cuban national food distribution system experienced substantial shortages of fuel oil for agriculture. These food shortages were further aggravated by the Toricelli Bill, passed by the US Congress in 1992, effectively banning trade between foreign subsidiaries of US companies and Cuba by disallowing ships that visited Cuba to visit the US for six months. As a result, hunger became systemic in Havana and throughout Cuba. Raquel Pinderhughes, Catherine Murphy and Mario Gonzalez describe the response in "Urban Agriculture in Havana, Cuba."

> Havana had no food production sector or infrastructure, almost no land dedicated to the production of food. Worsening food shortages motivated Havaneros to spontaneously begin to plant food crops in the yards, patios, balconies, rooftops and vacant land sites near their homes. In some cases, neighbors got together to plants crops — beans, tomatoes, bananas, lettuce, okra, eggplant and taro. If they had the space, many began to raise small animals — chickens, rabbits, even pigs. Within two years there were gardens and farms in almost every Havana neighborhood. By 1994 hundreds of Havana residents were involved in food production. The majority of these urban growers had little or no access to much need [sic] agricultural inputs — seeds, tools, pest controls, soil amendments. Nor did they have knowledge about the small-scale, agro-ecological techniques that urban gardening requires.[261]

This grassroots response was the beginning of an agricultural revolution in Cuba. In addition to the food imports Cuba enjoyed before the Soviet collapse, cheap oil imports had allowed Cuba to industrialize its agriculture even more than the US has today. Thus the lack of energy for agricultural equipment after the collapse compounded the food shortages. There are multiple accounts. IEA data suggests that oil imports dropped in the 1990s by only 20 percent.[262] Others who were on site, suggested that imports may have fallen by as much as 50 percent.[263] Imports of fertilizers and pesticides dropped by roughly 80 percent.[264] The Cuban people had to remake their system of agriculture to thrive without the oil and other hydrocarbon inputs previously enjoyed.

The Cuban Ministry of Agriculture responded to people's need for information and agricultural inputs by creating an Urban Agriculture Department in Havana. The Department's goal was to put all of the city's open land into cultivation and provide a wide range of extension services and resources such as agricultural specialists, short courses, seed banks, biological controls, compost, and tools.[265]

It's interesting to note that the approach even within the city was very local. For example, in their new system, "[t]he majority of extension workers are women who live in the neighborhoods in which they work; they know the residents in the neighborhoods they work in, keep track of ongoing needs and concerns, and continually encourage people to consider using available land for food production."[266]

It's also interesting to note that the scale and variety of the farms and gardens varied according to need.

> There are small backyard and individual plot gardens cultivated privately by urban residents (huertos populares). There are larger gardens based in raised container beds by individuals and state institutions (organoponicos). There are work place gardens that supply the cafeterias of their own workplace or institution (autoconsumos). There small family-run farms (campesinos) and there are farms owned and operated by the State with varying degrees of profit sharing with workers (empresas estatales).[267]

As other urban areas around the world begin to grapple with intertwined increases of food and fuel costs, cities are likely to need flexibility and adaptability. In all likelihood some combination of the tools used by Cuba to address their famine will be needed in most of the world's cities.

Most cities in the Global South, including comparatively wealthy ones like Hong Kong and Singapore, already produce large quantities of their food within city limits. Eighteen major cities in China produce at least 80 percent of their vegetables within city limits. Sixty-five percent of the population of Moscow have gardens. Hong Kong and Singapore produce nearly 40 percent of their poultry within city limits.[268] Urban farming is a norm — there are 200 million urban farmers world-wide, and they produce food and income for 700 million people.[269]

Even in the most densely populated urban areas in the US there are small private areas that could be adapted for food production. The row houses of the Manayunk neighborhood just outside of city center Philadelphia is an example of a very densely populated community where many residents still have small backyards that could support some home food production. Of course, the climate of Philadelphia is a bit different than that of Cuba. But the larger principles are applicable.

Or consider the state of New Jersey, mostly made up of small cities and large towns, with a comparatively small amount of agricultural land. How might the Cuba model work there?

In *For Hunger Proof Cities*, Michael W. Hamm and Monique Baron ask whether New Jersey could become food secure. Their answer is that it would require the existing agricultural land of New Jersey along with either 115,000 additional acres of agricultural land or 6.8 million gardens of 100 square feet or 3.4 million gardens of 200 square feet, or a balance among those configurations. One hundred or 200 square feet is a very small garden. In addition, were existing farms to be used more efficiently, using intensive organic agriculture, even more people could be fed. That is, there is excellent reason to believe that New Jersey could produce enough produce to feed itself and a not-insignificant percentage of neighboring New York City — mostly by gardening.[270]

Differences in local climatic and sociopolitical atmosphere will mean tailoring local solutions to local conditions. It will require the participation of local residents to make decisions about how best to use green space. But this process holds within it the potential to connect communities during a period of change and uncertainty. It is, after all, through food that cultures have grown and developed throughout our history. Other problems associated with peak oil and climate change can begin to be addressed through the organizational strategies put together to address access to local food.

A combination of private and public options for urban food production were used in Cuba. For urban dwellers without yards, rooftop gardens are an option and can help reduce the heat-island effect. Porches, patios and balconies are all excellent candidates for container gardens, and well-managed containers can provide an enormous amount of food.

The Power of Self-Help — Cities, Suburbs, Countryside

City areas with flourishing diversity
sprout strange and unpredictable uses and peculiar scenes.
But this is not a drawback of diversity.
This is the point...of it.
— JANE JACOBS —

One of the most powerful tools for urban food self-sufficiency and for urban democracy is the community garden. The American Community

Garden Association doesn't mention peak oil or climate change, but it does offer a list of other benefits to the community gardening approach including the following:
1. improves the quality of life for people in the garden
2. provides a catalyst for neighborhood and community development
3. stimulates social interaction
4. encourages self-reliance
5. beautifies neighborhoods
6. produces nutritious food
7. reduces family food budgets
8. conserves resources
9. creates opportunity for recreation, exercise, therapy, and education
10. reduces crime
11. preserves green space
12. creates income opportunities and economic development
13. reduces city heat from streets and parking lots
14. provides opportunities for intergenerational and cross-cultural connections [271]

Despite the existence of more than 10,000 community gardens already in American cities, many city residents find themselves on the waiting list to participate. Rising housing prices have created strong incentives for cities to develop vacant lots rather than use them for food production. But the collapse of the housing bubble is likely to change that.

Community gardens (which are not just a phenomenon of highly urbanized regions but exist in many cities and towns) aren't just a way of getting land to the comparatively landless — they are means of self-organization, a way that communities can organize themselves to meet needs that the state has not. At their root, they articulate the claim that public land is for public interests and that the right to eat is real. They also can help people lost in the system, overwhelmed by the complexity of large systems find a simple, accessible way of getting food.

The right to eat, and the power of food access is also being taught in schools, as public education is being turned toward the needs of a growingly food insecure and agriculturally disconnected population. The idea that children will need to understand where their food comes from and how to feed themselves is becoming increasingly prevalent in schools struggling to deal with the health consequences of industrial food systems and with growing hunger in poor families.

For more than a decade the Edible Schoolyard program at Martin Luther King Jr. Middle School in Berkley, California, has been developing a closer relationship between students and agriculture. Fostered by chef Alice Waters, the program is an excellent example of how spaces such as schoolyards can serve not only to produce food for school kitchens but also help to connect children with their food.

> Student participation in all aspects of the Seed to Table experience occurs as they prepare beds, plant seeds and seedlings, tend crops, and harvest produce. Through these engaging activities, students begin to understand the cycle of food production. Vegetables, grains, and fruits, grown in soil rich with the compost of last year's harvest, are elements of seasonal recipes prepared by students in the kitchen. Students and teachers sit together to eat at tables set with flowers from the garden, adults facilitate conversation, and cleanup is a collective responsibility. They complete the Seed to Table cycle by taking vegetable scraps back to the garden at the end of each kitchen class. The Seed to Table experience exposes children to food production, ecology, and nutrition, and fosters an appreciation of meaningful work, and of fresh and natural food.[272]

This program shows the potential of using extant local systems to foster food production. Besides making use of underutilized public space, the edible schoolyard program helps create desperately needed new farmers.

Perhaps even more importantly, this program and thousands like it show that a democratic right to food can be integrated into our history and our political narratives of self. For example, the growing guerilla gardening movement asserts that the community can reclaim under- or mis-used public space, which cannot afford to be sacrificed by those who do not use resources wisely.

Much of the work of feeding those who already experience hunger in this country falls on the shoulders of religious communities. Often working in coordination with local businesses and government programs, these groups help to gather and distribute food from donations and waste. Some faith-based relief organizations are already working with hunters and farmers to use food surpluses to feed the hungry. These programs could be expanded and new ones started in coordination with the growing local food movement. On property they own, churches, synagogues and mosques could set aside land for cultivation, either for use by members or for donation, and could organize their membership to create linked gardens within communities to create local food security and perhaps prevent, rather than ameliorate, hunger. Such gardens are also potentially profitable and offer the possibility of raising people out of poverty.

But the outreach effort must also focus on education, not just of children but of whole communities — teaching people how to gain access to land and how to farm efficiently and sustainably, and also helping people see the connections between personal empowerment and democracy. During the Cuban food crisis, the Australian organization Permaculture International worked with the Cuban Council of Churches to teach citizens how to more effectively grow food through systems like permaculture (more on this shortly).

Self-help and community education programs have a long history of successfully empowering towns and cities. For example, during the Great Depression, almost 300,000 people participated in self-help groups all over the country. As Howard Zinn writes,

> In Seattle, the fishermen's union caught fish and exchanged them with people who picked fruit and vegetables, and those who cut wood exchanged that. There were twenty-two locals, each with a commissary where food and firewood were exchanged for other good and services: barbers, seamstresses and doctors gave of their skills in return for other things.[273]

Zinn suggests that the New Deal may actually have arisen in part from a growing awareness by politicians that if they did not help the people, the people would help themselves — and perhaps decide they did not need the politicians.[274] Meanwhile, during the same period, Detroit city workers who had not been laid off donated a portion of their salaries to help unemployed urban dwellers begin "relief gardens" to feed themselves.[275]

The power of self-help and urban agriculture to work on reducing hunger is as much about learning, again, to see what we have that we are wasting as it is about gardening.

> The growth of urban agriculture is largely due to the Cuban government's commitment to making use of unused urban and peri-urban land and resources available to Cubans interested in farming. The issuing of land grants of vacant space in the city resulted in the conversion of hundreds of vacant lots into food producing plots. Although there is now intense competition for land uses in Havana,

new planning laws place the highest land use priority on food production.[276]

From cities to the suburbs, much of the land we leave unused could go
for food production. Each year municipalities plant millions of trees and
shrubs as part of public beautification projects. Many thousands of pounds
of nuts and fruit could be harvested in cities were there a concerted effort
to plant edibles and make use of the output. Plants that once served primarily aesthetic purposes could be pressed into the service of food production, as olive trees on the campus of the University of California at Davis
have been.

> For years, oily fruit dropping from the university's 1,500 olive trees
> created hazardous conditions on bicycle paths. Weary of the haz-
> ards and the high costs of tree maintenance, the university decided
> in 2005 to take a more sustainable approach and began harvesting
> the olives to produce olive oil.[277]

Urban and peri-urban agriculture often involves the use of land and
food that is generally wasted. Weeds can be harvested from the margins
of roads to feed chickens and rabbits; crops can be grown on vacant lots
and in reclaimed spaces. Because sustainable agriculture requires few inputs, many of which are otherwise wasted (manures that provide fertility,
discarded containers that can hold food producing plants, small animals
that consume roadside weeds), urban gardening not only increases local
food security, but reduces waste build up, improves aesthetics and builds
community structures.

Cuba is hardly the only example of urban communities being saved by
urban agriculture. For example, in the 1990s, the city of Kampala, Uganda
was essentially blockaded, and urban agriculture largely fed the city, preventing mass starvation.[278] Since 1985, hundreds of desperately poor
women in danger of starvation in Bogota, Columbia have formed a cooperative, producing food on urban rooftops that they have claimed as a public resource.

In all of these cases, self-organized self-help programs kept hungry people fed when state-led solutions failed. As we have seen, our state solutions
are already failing in the US — the number of hungry is steadily increasing.
We need new grassroots self-help solutions that will enable people to eat
in the coming hard times. Ultimately, we are perhaps most handicapped

by the perception that we are powerless — and yet there is ample evidence that we are not. Resistance is not only not futile, it is inevitable. As H. Patricia Hynes writes,

> If anything, the community gardens…are not a way out, for most who live there can't leave, and some don't want to, but a bridge back to a neighborhood they had nearly lost, back to hope, community, friendship and pride…"place attachment" — glue that binds people to place [and] is characterized by drawing neighbors together as a community, lessening stress, crime, vandalism and flight and stimulating public involvement, self-governance, and altruistic behavior.[279]

The simple truth is that we will never get through the coming decades without fostering precisely these virtues, without self-help, without meeting basic needs through self-sustaining communities.

Expanding the CSA Model

When Hitler's armies overrode Europe,
even while the armies trod down the grass,
there were forces beyond those powers of destruction.
There were the same forces that still went out
and made the trees bud and the leaves come out.
— CLARE LEIGHTON —

Even using our whole tool chest, most individual urban and suburban citizens won't be producing all their own food. How, then, do we ensure that cities are fed and that farmers are paid fairly? How do we avoid what occurred during the Great Depression, when the link between producer and consumer was horribly, disastrously broken? It is a link that is important to both parties — the exploitation of farmers who are underpaid and disregarded is possible only when you don't know any farmers, when you don't care what they have to do to make your dinner. And urbanites who have lost touch with natural rhythms need to get in touch with them, to have a relationship not only to their food but to land itself.

The US has an unusual gap between city and country. In many places in Africa, Asia and Europe, even urban people have a "country place." This does not imply a recreational second home, as it does here, but a simple shack or other shelter designed to allow you to gather or grow food during the correct season. In much of southern Africa, middle-class urban dwellers keep cattle and go out the land to tend them on weekends. In Russia, summerhouses allow people to collect mushrooms and wild plants.

In the US, there are still vestiges of this culture. Hunting and fishing camps are now recreational to a large degree, but there are still millions of Americans who rely on deer and fish as sources of food. The community garden in the undeveloped areas of urban centers is a metaphor for this — the going out to "the land" where you are. But the overwhelming assumption is that the first step to agriculture is ownership of rural land. That's wrong. It is wrong because many of the people who most need to grow food cannot afford to own land, and because many of those who most need to grow food have been consciously displaced. For example, the world's women produce 50 percent of the world's total food, but women hold legal title to only 1 percent of all the world's agricultural lands.[280]

And it is wrong, we think, because our response cannot be about any one piece of land. It is about all the land. Our society can survive the coming crises only if we make the nation — and the world — bloom, if we use land productively, wisely and carefully. But it is also wrong because understanding what is going on depends on having a populace that is connected to its own agriculture. We cannot afford to leave millions of city and suburb dwellers out of the project of creating a sustainable agriculture. And as few people can afford to live in expensive cities and also own large quantities of rural land, we need to think of more creative ways than traditional ownership to draw those connections.

Both to save money and build relationships with farmers near cities, many people have already turned to direct relationships with farmers through CSAs. The Community Supported Agriculture (CSA) model is one of the most successful local food initiatives. It was founded in Japan, where its name means "Food with a Face." Participants sign up to receive a weekly allotment of in-season food. Many CSA programs focus largely on vegetables, but others offer fruits, nuts, eggs, and even meat. Farmer's benefit because participants pay in advance, ensuring them a stable income and enough money to buy needed seeds and inputs. CSA subscribers benefit with higher-quality food and a connection to land — a connection we desperately need to foster.

Many CSAs encourage visits to the farm, and there is often a weekly dialogue about what is included and how to cook it. Some CSA shares include seedlings, to encourage home growing. Shareholders often find themselves eating new vegetables and expanding their diet. It is a way that people who are fond of food and looking to go local can jump-start their participation.

The model has extended to include some staples as well. Community Supported Grain (CSG) programs are beginning to spring up, allowing grain farmers to get higher prices by direct selling their grains. This is a model that could be vastly expanded, allowing families, communities, bakeries and restaurants to ensure a reliable supply of grains.

The community support model also works well on the other side of the culinary coin. Many states have laws that make it very expensive for individual cooks to prepare small batches of homemade treats for sale locally. One response has been the CSK or Community Supported Kitchen. These might be created in churches or community centers or make use of existing public kitchens when they are not being used. For example, most public schools have kitchens that are unused during summers and weekends. Once certified, use of the kitchen is offered to the community for large-scale home canning or those who want to create value-added goodies to sell to other people.

How else might we expand the CSA model? Community Supported Fiber programs (CSFs) might make it possible for people to support local textile initiatives and financially support those talented souls who raise sheep, rabbits or alpaca, or grow cotton and flax for use in spinning. Imagine if you could pay such people to provide the raw material for someone who might make your next winter scarf, favorite pair socks or even the embroidered dress your young daughter might wear for the next holiday festivities.

The model has even been applied to other human needs, most notably the creation of the Community Supported Electricity program (CSE). The Farm in Tennessee created the first CSE in 2006, installing solar panels on outbuilding roofs and channeling electricity back to the local grid. Participants get more of their electricity provided by decentralized sources and a rebate from the provider to reduce their electricity bills. As many farms have outbuildings or good wind sites, the possibility of creating "Bob's Sunshine Hut" electrical generation on your local farm is a real one.

This model of exchange seems strange to us only because of our experience over the past few decades. Once it was more common than not to deal directly (or at least more directly) with the person who was providing us with a product or a service. In rural areas with low population densities people have traditionally needed to know how to do a more varied assortment of tasks. If you or one of the few neighbors near by didn't know how to build something, it might mean that product coming from far away — often too expensive or time consuming to be feasible. Relying on neighbors, then, was a necessity.

Farmers' markets, community currencies, locally owned business alliances, barter arrangements — it is impossible to detail all the possible mechanisms of creating sustainable relationships between producers and consumers, or better yet, between whole societies of producer/consumers. These relationships represent the beginnings of new economies as well — or perhaps it is the other way around — the new economy is the beginning of a host of new relationships. As Bill McKibben writes,

> It's extremely hard to imagine a world substantially different from the one we know. But our current economies are changing the physical world in horrifying ways. It's our greatest challenge — the only real question of our time — to see whether we can transform those economies enough to prevent some damage and to help us cope with what we can't prevent. To see if we can manage to mobilize the wealth of our communities to make the transition tolerable, even sweet, instead of tragic.[281]

It is that sweetness that we begin to get at as we tie together eaters (all of us) and producers (most of us) in bonds that build something new.

The Forest for the Trees

Why are there trees I never walk under
but large and melodious thoughts descend upon me?
— Walt Whitman —

The ties between city and country aren't just born in market relationships and community gardens. In the Northeast, where Sharon lives, urban, suburban and rural regions are tied together by the great Northeastern forest, one of the most remarkable expanses of trees in the world.

Why is it so remarkable? Because in 1850, when we stood on the cusp of our transition from a mostly agrarian to mostly urban society, it was almost wholly deforested. Tree cover has increased from 35 percent of Vermont in 1850 to almost 90 percent in 1995.[282] That growth in forest occurred despite vast population increases and for a host of complicated, sometimes troubling, reasons.

In part it was because we stopped farming in the Northeast and moved agriculture to the Midwest, leaving large chunks of the Northeast bare of trees. In part it was because we found other fuels to burn — coal, oil and natural gas, which, of course, created environmental consequences that may, in the long term, be worse than the prior deforestation.

But that doesn't change the fact that those who grow up in the Northeast now see flocks of wild turkeys regularly, that the beavers are back, that coyotes den in Central Park in New York and in the mid-1990s, while Sharon was living in Boston, a moose wandered across the subway lines, having followed the forest corridor down from Maine or New Hampshire.

The trees are part of one vast forest, the largest in the US. They are also part of a million different individual towns, neighborhoods, roadsides, backyards and communities — they encompass the outskirts of Manhattan and the winding rural dirt roads where Sharon lives, the leafy suburbs of Boston and the great pine forests of Maine. They are mostly contiguous with one another, and that contiguity makes them a whole, tended and permitted by individuals and collectives who often do not realize that they are engaged in a vast project of reforestation.

One of the questions raised by our present situation is this — is there hope that we can optimize our use of resources, that we can transform our landscapes in ways that prevent us from having to decide between feeding ourselves and creating a barren landscape in which the forests have been burned for fuel and the wildlife eaten or chased away? Is it possible to have both things?

We think it is, but it will require that we manage our environment in productive and positive ways. Up until now, we have, to a large degree, seen the management of our environment as a choice between stripping and ignoring — that is, either we chop down all the old growth forests for paper mills or we preserve them in perpetuity as wild spaces. That leaves us with a constantly diminishing quantity of "useful" land, as things are stripped of their resources and there is constant pressure to move into new areas.

But what if we were to truly manage our resources in a sustainable way? What if a forest — and the links between chunks of forest that are suburban street trees and forested personal land — were used carefully and mindfully? For example, non-extractive use of forested land on a property can provide fallen and coppiced wood for heating (coppicing involves cutting branches from a living tree that will regrow), mushrooms, fruit, nuts and acorns, woodland plants, medicinal plants, and other materials. Pigs and other animals can forage within them for food.

Moreover, treed land can be managed for crops — chestnuts, for example, have nutritional values similar to many grains, and can produce large yields when intensively managed on land, while also maintaining forest cover, providing wildlife habitat and sequestering carbon. Orcharding is a form of tree cropping, but monocropped orchards historically have been magnets for insects and diseases, so polyculture is as essential in tree farming as it is in any other form of agriculture.

As tree farmer "Greenpa" writes on his blog,

> All of our plantings have species mingled, a couple rows of this, then 8 rows of that. We've specifically striven to include diversity in species and genetics and physical structure, just for the sake of the diversity. More diversity means more critters can live here. The more species living here, the more stable the entire system is. That's an ecological dogma. But humans have never acted like we believe it. It's true, and it works.[283]

That is, it is possible to imagine moving the forests to our farms and to conceive of farming our forests, while still allowing space for, indeed depending on, livestock. The same is true of systems of pasturage in which animals graze on land that is not suitable for cultivation. With the use of these animals a little more food can be produced — but human food isn't the all. Diverse pasturelands provide open spaces for nesting birds and often contain as many species as similar forests. As we've seen, they also sequester carbon in similar ways.

Is it possible to imagine an intertwined, contiguous network of gardens (which diversify our yards and open spaces, soften the impact of roofs and parking lots, and provide habitat for small species, and also produce food on land that was already in use, so that more doesn't have to be cleared), and forests and pastures as one whole, one net ecology in which more is put in than taken out?

We think it is, that, as Wendell Berry puts it,

> In the recovery of culture and nature is the knowledge of how to farm well, how to preserve, harvest and replenish the forests, how to make, build, and use, return and restore. In this double recovery, which is the recovery of our humanity, is the hope that the domestic and wild can exist together in lasting harmony.[284]

Permaculture, which places both ecology and care for human needs at its center, and which argues that it is possible to restore and repair and have sufficient surplus for equitable distribution, is a design strategy that has placed tree culture at the center of much of its analysis, in large part because tree-based agriculture represents long-term food security and long-term ecologies. The term *permaculture* is a contraction of "permanent agriculture" and "permanent culture," and is defined by author Toby Hemenway as, "a set of techniques and principles for designing sustainable human settlements."[285]

In Chapter 3, we wrote about vegeculture and the power of roots, but it is worth remembering that those small African gardens, ones that looked, to European eyes, as though there was nothing there, were simply part of a vast, farmed forested landscape. Research has begun to understand how much North American Native peoples also managed their landscapes. Indeed, it may not be possible to live sustainably simply practicing agriculture — that is, we can sustain ourselves only if we manage our landscape. This does not mean claiming our whole landscape and our right to strip it, but creating cyclical systems that enable us to optimize the use of resources for human creatures and wild ones, so that we actually do, for perhaps the first time in human history, feed the whole world.

An Interview with Faith Morgan: Spring 2008

Faith Morgan, along with her husband, Pat Murphy, is one of the driving forces behind the Community Activist group The Community Solution. They focus on finding ways to adapt to a lower-energy life and providing local solutions to energy descent. Faith directed the remarkable film *The Power of Community,* which explored how Cuba survived and thrived in the face of a sudden, radical drop in oil imports. Faith has consistently led the way in preparing for our future.

ANOF: Faith, you co-wrote, co-produced and directed *The Power of Community: The Cuban response to Peak Oil.* Could you describe the peak oil event that Cuba experienced and the reasons behind it?
FAITH: It happened very suddenly as the Soviet Union collapsed. Part of the agreement between the Soviet Union and the United States for aid was that the Soviet bloc would stop shipping any resources to Cuba. Cuba was

a large producer of sugar for the Soviet bloc. The exchange rate Cuba enjoyed was better than it would have gotten with the rest of the world for everything it was producing. And it was also getting oil at a subsidized rate. Cuba would get oil cheap from the Soviet Union and then it would sell it; so it was a way for the Soviet Union to give it money.

When that went away and they had to sell their sugar on the open market, that caused a financial collapse. Within six months, which is a very short period of time, the US tightened its embargo on Cuba. There'd been an embargo on Cuba since the revolution, but this new embargo said that any ship that docked in Cuba couldn't dock in the US for six months. The Cuban diet before peak oil was meat based and had lots of imported food, much of it canned, so it was difficult when Cubans were no longer able to import food from the Soviet bloc. There were ships on their way to Cuba and they stopped in Mexico and never came to Cuba. They had food and medicine and goods that were on their way there. That is when the food situation became really desperate.

ANOF: How did agriculture in Cuba and the Cuban diet change immediately after, and then later on as they were able to adjust to the life with fewer fossil fuels?
FAITH: Cuba was very industrialized in terms of how it treated its agricultural land. It used a lot of chemicals and a lot of fungicides, herbicides, pesticides and fertilizer — all from petrochemicals. And anybody who knows about agriculture knows that that destroys the natural productivity of the land.

Cuba serves as an example of what happens when you withdraw petrochemicals — initially the land doesn't produce anymore. And organic farmers in [the US], years ago, people who for whatever reason decided to go from conventional practices to organic farming, found the same thing. They had to intensively rebuild the soil for a minimum of three years before it would start growing food productively. So that's what happened in Cuba from 1990 to 1993. Their production, their whole economy, just dropped to the bottom and then it started to climb back up, and you can see in a production graph that they started to come back up. And then by the time we went to Cuba in 2003 some crops were producing better with organic methods than they had been under conventional. So it's what we will be facing in this country.

You asked about how Cuban food had changed, and I think one of the things that's worked very well for Cuba has been to have a combination of both state markets and private farmers' markets, and the reason for this is, if we have a financial collapse and there isn't food, food prices are going to skyrocket, and then the rich get to buy all the food and the poor get to…suffer; it's harder for them to get [the food]. There is a need in a time of hardship to have some sort of government monitoring to keep prices down, and one of the things [Cuba] did that served them through, (sometimes I've heard it written about very scathingly)…is actually saying, food is a basic right and everybody gets a minimum of rice and milk and beans and you know, whatever, and then they have to supplement that with what they purchase.

ANOF: In Cuba there was an instantaneous disruption of the fossil fuels on which their agriculture was dependent, but here in the United States it may be a slower process of declining availability. Was that ultimately an advantage for Cuba, that it happened so fast? And what should we hope for here in terms of how quickly change happens?

FAITH: I think that is an important point, that if it had been just up to the Cuban government, people probably would have starved. It would have been much worse. But people took action. And it wasn't people individually taking action but people collectively. There was always somebody in charge who was elected as part of their neighborhood group, and they would say, "We have some land over here, and who has time?" and they would go to Havana and get some seeds. There was one person who would make sure that they had what they needed, and they'd start gardening and they'd use every available land. Sometimes it would be a group of women saying, "If we clear that land can we use it to garden?" I met a group of women who had to clear really noxious weeds off a piece of the land, and it's a gorgeous urban farm now. If the government had said, "You need to garden" it wouldn't have been as effective as people saying, "We can grow food here." For the first time, Cuba started seeing a transformation happen. We don't have enough meat; we can grow vegetables. We didn't think we liked all these vegetables but now, some years later, all the people I spoke to said, "I wouldn't go back. This is so good. I love it."

One of the fascinating things is that there are farmers' markets all over Havana, but the growers also sell to their neighborhood. They will sell to their neighborhood cheaper than when they take it to a farmers' market. So right at the farm they have a little stall and their neighbors come in and buy stuff. It makes more sense because it's more effort to take it to a farmers' market. But it's real support of the neighborhood. And that's one of the reasons we call ourselves Community Solutions — because we want to encourage people to think neighborhood. How can I do this? I'm gardening two backyards and this year we're going to expand to a third backyard. There are elderly people who own land saying, "Would you garden my backyard too? We're not using it. Please, we want to be part of this."

ANOF: Do you think we'll see a return to community through the American experience of peak oil, given the differences between the Cuban sense of community and ours?

FAITH: Basically, I think, there is a difference. When the Great Depression happened and the people were closer to farms, people left cities and went back to the farms they had come from. There were a lot of roaming people. My mother remembers people stopping by, and they'd always come to the back door and her mother would give them a sandwich…. So we have a precedent for becoming more community, for supporting others when we're all down and out and things are rough. I think we're much farther from that. I mean this idea of "We don't need anybody else" will be a detriment for people who want to live that way or think that's the way they're going to live. I'm not so worried about it. When the Great Depression happened, in the town that I grew up in, Yellow Springs, Ohio, my sense is that the town didn't just suffer. It turned into "How do we work together?" Everybody worked together.

ANOF: When some people talk about these issues they say, "Well, when food increases in price — doubles or triples — that's when we'll see change. That's when we'll see the market respond."

FAITH: I think people who say that are fairly well off. They haven't really suffered. The price can go up and they can buy it. But what's happening is that as gas prices go up and people need to get to work, they're buying cheaper food for their families. Basically the poor are saying "Okay, I have to get to work," so they're buying cheaper food, less nutritious food because it's very cheap. So what we're having is an increase in malnutrition in the poor of our society. So the people who are wealthy who are saying something like that are really keeping the blinders on. They don't want to look at what's happening. *And it's not going to be talked about in our major media. They talk about the glass ceiling when women or people of color can't move*

up in business. Well, we also have a an opaque floor. We don't really look be-
low and see what's happening to the poor in society. And we don't probably
want to, especially those of us who are well off. I sometimes make the com-
ment that in societies historically which have survived for a long time, the
people — the politicians, the wealthy, the people of power — have suffered
the consequences of their actions just like everybody else. And when you
have a society where the people with money and power don't have to suffer
the consequences of their actions, the society ultimately collapses. I think
that's where we are in our society. And the people say, "Oh, the market —
it'll drive it." But the suffering of getting to the point where the market will
drive it leaves us very, very vulnerable. I think that's what we saw in New
Orleans. There wasn't really consideration. All the people of wealth and
power could get out of there. They didn't really have a plan for the poor.

ANOF: Do you keep chickens in your backyard?
FAITH: People think of them as farmyard animals, but fortunately our
town considers them pets, and so they're allowed. And I don't keep a
rooster because I don't want to disturb our neighbors at four in the morning. The first [thing] I did was talk to all my neighbors and said, "Is this
okay?" I wanted to be a good neighbor and make sure everyone was fine
with it. They were thrilled (except for when [the chickens] got out and
started scraping in my friend's flower garden). I was really glad when the
next door neighbors sold the house, moved out, and [the people who
moved in] put up a fence to keep their dogs in. I didn't have to worry about
my chickens running free. My chickens run out into the street and into the
college at the back and nobody seems to mind.

ANOF: What other local foods are you able to take advantage of?
FAITH: I raise so much food in the garden. A friend has a big garden out
in the countryside. We buy our staples — rice and beans and spelt. We buy
it in bulk and keep it. And I grind my own flour. And at this point I'm still
using a freezer. And I can all the tomatoes I use; and I can applesauce; and I
canned lots of sauerkraut this year for the first time — sauerkraut with lots
of different things in it, not just cabbage. I've learned it's a very versatile
thing. And then I freeze all sorts of things out of the garden — wild greens
and regular greens, green beans and broccoli, asparagus — and make stews
and I use them as the basis — that and the butternut squash — as the basis
for various kinds of soups and stews.

I grew up with gardening. My mother loved to garden, and when I was three she had polio and she couldn't any longer. She'd tell us what to do and we'd go out and dig the garden, plant everything and harvest it. It's been a part of my life forever. But I really want to since I have so much skill and experience gardening. I mean, I want to be an example that people can look at and say, "Oh, that was tasty. How did you do that?" or "I'd really like to start a garden. How do I do it?" So that it's just inspiring by doing. If people can, even if they're just doing it for flowers, if people can start making some part of their yard into a garden and start planting fruit trees or raspberry bushes instead of just herbaceous stuff just to look nice then they will have some of the variety when more difficult times come. They will have some variety; they will have soil that's prepared, that's healthy.

—— RECIPES ——

Wild Greens Frittata   *by Faith Morgan*

I love making this in the spring when lambs quarter and red root (wild amaranth) are rampantly growing. I also keep a few plants of each of these in the garden all summer and pick off the new tender buds until they finally go to seed in September. This way I have spinach-like greens all spring and summer. I also end up with enough to freeze and then I make this dish in the winter as well. I also use rainbow chard, broccoli, asparagus, or any cooked green stuff I might have leftover in the fridge. Cook the greens before starting the frittata and never worry about having too many, as you can always serve them for some other meal or freeze them for a winter meal.

I use a 15" non-stick (or well seasoned) frying pan and 5 eggs. If using a smaller frying pan, use fewer eggs.

Ingredients
- 5 eggs
- ½ tsp salt (to taste)
- pinch of thyme
- ½ cup of soy, rice or almond milk
- ground mixed peppers to taste
- 2 tablespoons of local goat feta cheese, crumbled
- 2 cups of cooked, chopped greens, approximately (I don't usually chop asparagus as it looks nice long)
- ½ to ¾ cup of hard goat cheese grated (Gouda or manchego are both good)

Directions
1. Beat eggs with a fork. Whisk milk and seasonings into the eggs.
2. Put just a little cold-pressed cooking oil in the frying pan, distributing it with your fingers or brush it over the bottom and up the sides a little. Turn on the heat. After a little water sizzles in the pan (I flick it with my fingers), pour in

the egg mixture. Make sure the heat is not too high. (It needs to be about the same as for cooking pancakes.)

3. Sprinkle the feta evenly in the egg.
4. Spread the chopped greens evenly over the feta and egg, making sure you can still see some of the egg. (Too many greens can overpower the other flavors.)
5. Pat the greens gently into the eggs and spread the grated cheese on top.
6. Cover and cook for two to three minutes. Basically you want most of the egg to be cooked before the next step.
7. Using a spatula, slice the frittata into six equal pieces. Lift an edge of the one piece to see how done it is. (I like it golden underneath.) Turn each piece, putting the cheese side down and the golden underside up.
8. Cook until it is done to your liking. (I like mine a little moist.)
9. I use this for a main dish with a garden salad.

Oatmeal in a Thermos   *by Jena Becker of Becker Farms, in Michigan*

What about cooking in a vacuum bottle, a.k.a. a Thermos? Here's a simple recipe.

Ingredients
- ¼ cup steel cut or rolled oats
- hot water to fill Thermos
- cinnamon (optional)
- 1 cup water
- dried apples (optional)

Directions
1. Put oats and 1 cup water in a saucepan. Bring to a boil. This could be done over a fire or other places rather then a traditional stove. In the meantime have your vacuum bottle sitting full of hot water. You may want to heat this water first and just leave about a cup in the pan and add the oats to that.
2. Once the oats come to a boil pour the hot water out of the bottle and replace it with the oat/water mixture. (You could use the warm water from the bottle to make something else. I have a special jug in the kitchen to discard water and I use it to water plants or fill the dog dish.)
3. Put the cap tightly on the bottle and lay it on its side. If you do this at night you'll have fresh oats in the morning, possibly still warm. I tried it this morning and had my oats for dinner. I added some of my dehydrated apple slices, all broken up, and a bit of cinnamon to the mix and when I ate it they were nice and soft and rehydrated

Here's why I like this:
- You only have to have a heat source for a few minutes instead of around 20 minutes like it would normally take.
- Almost everyone has a Thermos or could get one cheap enough. (You want a nice metal or glass-lined one though, no plastic.)
- It is flexible — you can do this with rice, beans, etc.

Thai Salad   *by Sharon*

We especially enjoy making this dish in the summer, when we are able to get most of the salad ingredients from our garden and the eggs from our own chickens.

Salad Ingredients
- whatever you like to put in a salad — lots of greens and whatever is in season
- 1 small bunch broccoli, lightly steamed
- ½ cup pineapple chunks, fresh or canned, or fresh fruit in season
- 4 eggs, hard boiled, peeled and quartered
- 1 pound fresh or fried tofu, sliced (you can replace this with more eggs, or the eggs with more tofu)

Dressing Ingredients
- 1 can coconut milk
- 1 tbsp rice vinegar
- ½ cup peanut butter
- 2 tbsp sugar
- 1 tbsp Thai or Vietnamese fish sauce (you can substitute soy sauce)
- 1 tsp Southeast Asian chili sauce, such as sambal oelek (or chopped hot peppers to taste)

Directions
1. Assemble the salad, including the standard salad items mixed with the broccoli, pineapple, eggs and tofu.
2. Heat the coconut milk in a small saucepan over low heat until warm. Add the peanut butter, fish (or soy) sauce, rice vinegar, sugar, and chili sauce.
3. Divide the salad into individual portions and serve with warm peanut dressing spooned over it. This dish goes nicely with brown rice or barley on the side.
4. Makes 4 salads.

CHAPTER 7

FOOD WILL WIN THE WAR
You came here seeking Freedom
You must now help to preserve it
WHEAT is needed for the allies
Waste nothing
UNITED STATES FOOD ADMINISTRATION

The Hands
that Built the Country
We're Always Trying To Keep Down

Extending the Table

*People are always talking about their comfort zones,
you ever heard that expression?
"This is outside of my comfort zone."
Grow your goddamn comfort zone then, okay?
Cause we are running out of time.
My suggestion is, grow the comfort zone.*

— VAN JONES —

AARON: Last Autumn was a busy time for my family. Besides the day job, family life, growing food, harvesting discarded bagged leaves in my neighborhood (that being one of my hobbies) and attending a conference on sustainable community design (which was inspiring), we had our house reinsulated. Or rather, it would probably be more accurate to say we had it insulated — as much of it had no insulation at all.

You might think it is strange that someone who is convinced we're embarking on a worldwide energy downturn would live in an under-insulated house for years. But like everyone else, our budget is far from unlimited. It has long been on the to-do list. The other reason is that we weren't sure we were staying here.

My wife and I had been planning to build our own home for several years. Since my first day of architectural studies, I've dreamed of building my own home. In recent years I've studied alternative construction methods and have fallen in love with straw bale building. I've read books, I've taken classes and even worked on a few such structures. We were investigating a land purchase and organizing a few folks to help with the permit process.

But last fall we realized the situation had changed — or maybe we had. The peak in global oil production appeared imminent, and the effects of climate change are more rapidly headed our way. I became convinced that with more than 90 million homes already in existence here in America, what is really needed is less building new and more making do. Several people have suggested that I could be more useful to my fellow citizens by offering an example of effective strategies for sheltering "in place," and last fall I started to believe them.

And there was still another reason we decided to stay put and reinsulate. My wife was expecting our second child and our other daughter was then almost two years old. Keaton can already pick up a hammer and swing it quite effectively but hasn't yet learned what to hit and when. My family building a new home during the coming year, what with a pregnant wife, then a brand new baby and helpful toddler might make for a great reality TV show, but I wasn't sure we'd find it funny.

I wasn't willing to give up forever the dream of building our own home. I think using straw for home construction makes sense for lots of reasons: easy to work with, sequesters carbon, insulates very well, burns more slowly than wood and is available almost everywhere. I think we need more people who are exploring sustainable building techniques. I'd like to be one of them, but for now it looks like we are staying put, and that means more closely examining our current conditions and making reasonable adjustments. Sounds prudent right? Well, it is, but here's the thing — prudent change isn't sexy. Building something new comes with all the possibilities of perfection or at least improvement over what you've had before. We were to create the home of our dreams and point the way toward a future of sustainable building techniques — and that, my friends, is sexy! But reinsulating an old house? Not quite as exciting

What it means is that I spent three days with a crew who shoved insulation made from recycled newspaper into the framing of our home. When they first arrived they hooked up a device to the front door and pressurized the whole house to get a sense of how airtight it was. The answer was not very. That part was fun to watch, but then came hours of hard work caulking and sealing and weather stripping. The real work took a long time and wasn't much fun.

Another contractor used an infrared camera to find out where the big heat leaks were located. This too was pretty neat. But then it was back to the grindstone. The flooring in the attic had to be removed, and then insulation was blown in. The crawlspace below the house had to be cleaned, plastic sheeting laid against the ground and insulation strapped to the underside of the floor joists. The best part, I say with my tongue firmly planted in my cheek, was when the crew drilled two-inch holes all along the exterior walls of our home every 20 inches or so. That is, they drilled holes through my wife's beautiful painting handiwork (more on this in a moment) before blowing insulation into each wall cavity.

It was necessary. It will make for a much more energy-efficient home. We are doing our part! And yet the work itself was mundane. And some of it was downright uncomfortable, just regular hard work. And the mess! Let's just say that my wife, Jennifer, was not happy. And the caulking of each tiny hole didn't make me happy either.

In contrast, my time at the sustainable community design conference was great. But all the talking and learning didn't actually produce anything tangible. Both experiences were useful. The knowledge I brought away with me from the conference will certainly come in handy, but the real change came by getting down and dirty in the attic and the basement.

Hopefully much of what we're talking about in this book is inspiring, and that's great. But it is also time to move on from talk to action. It's all fine and good to talk about peak oil and climate change, to track the progress of these issues and discuss the need for more gardens and farms. We need to spread these ideas around. But for most of us, responding to the converging calamities of the 21st century should be more work and less talk, even if the work isn't sexy. As Mother Theresa put it, "There should be less talk; a preaching point is not a meeting point. What do you do then? Take a broom and clean someone's house. That says enough."

Having said that, I did film the transformation of my home. It will be turned into a video and uploaded onto the Internet some time early next year. Hopefully it will help inspire other people to begin making similar hands-on changes. My family will continue to share our progress with other people. In fact, I think we have an obligation to do so. But as much as possible I think we need to get to work — not online but in our homes and in our communities. It isn't always sexy, but it matters.

Farmers and Their Gardens

My father was a farmer and my mother was a farmer,
my childhood was very good. I am very grateful for my childhood,
because it was full of gladness and good humanity.
— Roberto Benigni —

One of the major difficulties facing us is bringing a new agriculture to a host of populations that, for one reason or another, face bigger-than-average barriers to being integrated into a new agrarian society. The truth is that the food crisis knows no bounds — the need to produce some of our own applies to all populations in the US, except, perhaps Fortune 500 executives. And that applies disturbingly enough, even to professional farmers.

We recognize, as we write this book, that many farmers are going to be wondering who the heck we think we are. We've talked to a lot of them, and some aren't thrilled to see their job title taken by anyone with a backyard garden. And they've got a point. Little farmers like Sharon and big garden-farmers like Aaron are annoying, particularly when we tell the people who feed everyone what we think needs doing. Who the hell are we, and why are we talking? We don't blame them for their reactions. And yet, that doesn't change the fact that farmers in the US are in just as much danger as the rest of us, and in some ways, more. They've been squeezed so much that we're in danger of seeing farmers all over the country driven into even more disaster — and that's potentially deadly for all of us.

When the dryness, heat, and grasshoppers destroyed the crops, farmers were left with no money to buy groceries or make farm payments. Some people lost hope and moved away. Many young men took government jobs building roads and bridges.[286]

That is how the website of the Wessels Living History Farm describes the 1930s and the effects of that decade on the farming community of York County, Nebraska.

But then it adds, "Many farm families raised most of their own food — eggs and chickens, milk and beef from their own cows, and vegetables from their gardens." Note the distinction, even among those who raise food for a living, between the garden, where they grow food for their own consumption, and the farm, which provides an income with which to buy goods to fulfill their needs. That is, the crops failed, because they were produced on a scale that prevented close management — but the garden succeeded for many, even in the worst of times. How often do you hear stories about Depression life on farms that start by saying "We were poor, but we never went hungry." That is what the farmer's garden can do.

Over the past half century there has been a shift in the US in the way we think about the work that professional (as opposed to home) farmers do. This disconnect between what farmers grow for themselves and what they grow for sale seems best illustrated, and indeed underpinned, by the lopsided support for certain kinds of crops in the US commercial food industry. The habit of subsidizing agriculture is a product of the Depression. Agricultural subsidies began as a set of policies designed to boost crop prices and provide a safety net for farmers during rough times. It has come to overwhelmingly favor the large-scale production of just five crops: corn, wheat, soybeans, rice and cotton. Even excluding cotton, when you put these together, you don't so much have the makings of a wonderful meal as the feedstock for a processed-food industry and feedlot meat.

During the course of industrialization, the idea that farmers grew food to eat and a surplus to sell changed. Instead, farming became the growing of feedstock for the production of industrial food, which was then sold back to the farmer at much higher prices. Decades into this process, we think of a food market primarily as a place that sells frozen pizzas and soft drinks — final food products — rather than as a place to buy ingredients. The link between the farmer's table, the market and our tables has been to a large extent disrupted.

This shift away from growing foods to producing feedstock is a way of thinking that leads logically to the biofuels debacle (because if what we are growing is not food, it has no special status and can be burned even as people go hungry) and to hunger and to increased rural food insecurity.

This is not to say that all farmers must produce everything they need. Farmers are like everyone else, and their tastes have been shaped by global marketplaces. There are plenty of ordinary needs and wants that can't be produced on just any farm. Coffee and sugar are examples of foodstuffs that are better suited to production in warmer climates. There are substitutes for those who live further north — dandelion root, for example, as an alternative to coffee, and sugar beets or honey as sweeteners. Maple syrup has long been used in colder climates to add sweetness in the kitchen. But white cane sugar has its pleasures. And many coffee addicts will probably never prefer dandelion roots. Moreover, some farmers don't want to garden.

However, the decrease in farm self-sufficiency now goes beyond the long-standing practice of purchasing specialties, and it isn't motivated by personal preferences. That is, farmers once sold a wide variety of food products, but in their struggle to survive an extraordinarily hostile economy, market forces have driven them to single crops, increasing their economic vulnerability to price drops, input rises and crop losses. And as the market narrowed through industrialization, so too did the farmer's garden shrink.

We know of lots of farmers who still grow some vegetables in their gardens, but without a market for the extras from those gardens, that task becomes subservient to the constant, exhausting project of raising some large-scale cash crop to pay the bills, including the grocery bills — which, incidentally, are on the rise.

Though everyone is now paying more for food, it's important to point out that farmers aren't necessarily making more money. The main reason, as we've discussed, is an increase in the cost of all the inputs industrial farmers have come to depend on. In a linear system like industrial agriculture, those rising input costs mean rising output costs as well. Conventional farming might become even more of a seasonal gamble with pricey pesticides and fertilizers — not to mention higher fuel costs — serving as the ever more expensive "ante up" in the bet on a big harvest. Per acre input costs have doubled in the past few years. Farmers are also stuck with higher interest rates on the loans they must take out each year for those inputs along with higher insurance premium on crop insurance as more and more extreme weather events occur.

All of which means that though more money is coming in as a result of a good harvest, more money is necessary to stay in the game. Or as Owosso farmer George Zmitko put it, "You handle more money. You don't get to keep much more, but you handle more money."[287] Farmers are, of course, acutely aware of their tremendous vulnerability; most do not believe that the current high prices are stable, and they fear the day that markets pull the rug out from under them, leaving them with enormous input bills and not enough revenue to pay the loans. It is this system that has been driving farmers out of business, and their children off the land, for decades, and we cannot afford to lose any more farmers.

Besides their ordinary hardships, farmers find themselves in the same boat as the rest of us, caught up in the rising cost of fossil fuels and food. The extent to which professional farmers are now working away from the farm to make money is a complicated issue to sort out, but evidence seems to suggest that farmers are increasingly dependant for more of their daily needs on money coming in from outside the farm. We shouldn't be surprised at the expanding divide between the farm and the farmer's garden. Increasingly, there's the farm and the job that enables farmers to keep farming — that is, the outside subsidy that keep the agricultural way of life going.

> Off-farm income received by farm operators and their spouses has risen steadily over recent decades as job opportunities have grown and mechanization and other technological innovations have lessened on-farm labor needs. Off-farm income as a share of total U.S. farm household income rose from about 50 percent in 1960 to more than 80 percent over the past 10 years. On average, a farm household received about $81,500 in 2004, netting only $14,200 from farming activities. Earned off-farm income averaged $48,800 and unearned income was about $18,500 (Social Security, interest, etc.). Fifty-two percent of farm operators worked off-farm in 2004, up from 44 percent in 1979. Over the same period, the share of spouses working off-farm grew from 28 to 45 percent.[288]

The farmer's wife is now working full time to provide the family with health insurance, and the farmer is driving a truck on the side. And this is very important because the fact that farmers are increasingly leaving their fields to earn income to provide for their families has a direct impact on how they farm.

> A recent ERS study finds that the adoption of time-saving technologies, such as herbicide-tolerant (HT) soybeans, is associated with higher off-farm incomes. On the other hand, the adoption of time-intensive technologies such as precision farming is more

closely associated with lower off-farm incomes. These findings confirm a trade-off between the time spent on farm and off-farm activities, which, in turn, translates into a trade-off between expanding farm operations and increasing off-farm income-generating activities.[289]

The rise of "convenience agriculture" can be blamed in part on this divide between growing food and growing industrial food feedstock.

When asked what motivated their adoption of GE crop varieties, farmers often respond that these varieties are simply easier to use. Cultivation of these crop varieties is characterized by simplicity and flexibility. A great advantage of adoption is that it saves time... and takes no extra thought. It is convenient.[290]

But as we've suggested, the price of this time saving is millions of former farming families displaced, less care of the land and farmers themselves being reliant on the same shaky food chains as non-farm families. Increasingly, industrial farming fails to provide enough income even for those who did get big, and more farmers are unable or unwilling to play this high-stakes game commodity farming.

Thus, increased food costs hurt farmers as much as the rest of us. "Junk Food Nation," a Newsweek article near the end of 2007, described the problem of unhealthy rural eating habits but failed to grasp the underlying cause.

This is the real world of eating and nutrition in the rural United States. Forget plucking an apple from a tree, or an egg from under a chicken. "The stereotype is everyone in rural America lives on a farm, which is far from the truth," says Jim Weill, president of the nonprofit Food Research and Action Center (FRAC). New research from the University of South Carolina's Arnold School of Public Health shows just how unhealthy the country life can be. The study, which examined food-shopping options in Orangeburg County (1,106 square miles; population 91,500), found a dearth of supermarkets and grocery stores.

In an ideal world, says Weill, more people would take advantage of nutrition and financial education programs, like those offered by the USDA, that teach consumers how to make a food budget and use recipes. The 2007 Farm Bill would increase food stamp access and benefits and allocate an additional $2.75 billion over 10 years to buy fruits and vegetables for the USDA's nutrition assistance programs.[291]

Actually, in an ideal world we would work toward a food system that rewarded farmers and gardeners alike for producing a variety of tasty, healthy foods that they and we could eat. All over the world, farmers who buy food and sell their products at commodity prices have the worst of both worlds — and experience severe nutritional deficits because of it. In the poor world, they are hungry; in the rich world, they are merely eating empty calories. But we are still stuck on the idea that the answer is more grocery stores and more anti-poverty programs, rather than helping rural people make use of the enormous resources embodied in the land they live on.

There is nothing wrong with offering help to people who need it — we have a moral obligation to do so. But help should involve more than creating dependencies on food stamps while subsidizing the industrial food system that undermines our health and our food security. Real help would involve teaching people how to grow more of their own food and cook with whole ingredients. It would also include a farm bill that actually supports small-scale, sustainable agriculture. Many rural towns suffer because there is no work for the children when they grow up; they have to leave. It would be so simple to turn the billions of dollars we spend annually ensuring that small farmers can't make a living to ensuring that they can. Treating the problem of unhealthy eating in rural America by building more grocery stores that sell processed foods and handing out more food stamps is like putting a Band-Aid on a gaping chest wound.

We need an approach that values growing and selling local food as a real and lasting way to address the hunger of those who grow and eat food and those who traditionally have been only eaters. Because, as we are seeing, those two groups are much more alike than they are different.

Farm operators are likely to be as appreciative of convenience as is the busy, multi-tasking member of the average U.S. household. In fact, farm households are increasingly similar to nonfarm households in terms of working spouses, diversity of income sources, and dependence on the general economy.[292]

This is at once a bad and a good similitude. It means that farming families are increasingly dependent on the industrialized, globalized, corporate world of need-meeting. That is, the typical American household gets almost everything it needs from corporations at high cost both economically and environmentally. The typical household is dependent on supply chains that are deeply vulnerable to disruption. But it also means that farm and nonfarm household are increasingly bound together by common ground, more alike than not. As Gene Logsdon suggested in a recent interview,

> The biggest problem, in my opinion, is that our society, our culture, does not understand that food is everyone's business. We have decided, as a society, to let a few people worry about our food while the rest of us worry about money, and so food production has more or less become the domain of a few very large international corporations. The only cure for it is what is now happening. Food prices and food shortages and fuel shortages will force people to take back their lives.[293]

Thus, if farmers are struggling to buy food for their own tables, rising food prices will bring back farm gardens and cause even farmers who haven't had time and energy to work on these issues to become active in bringing about change in the way we think about, grow and eat food in this country. Nonfarm and farm families are increasingly united by decreased food security

Bringing Urban and Rural Poor Together

The world is so empty if one
thinks only of mountains, rivers and cities;
but to know someone here and there who thinks
and feels with us, and though distant, is close to us in spirit —
this makes the earth for us an inhabited garden.
— GOETHE —

Many rural families, farming and non-farming, are increasingly at risk of hunger — as are the rest of us. The first and most serious victims are those who are already poor all over the world. And herein is, perhaps, the beginning of an alliance between those in rural areas who are struggling to keep enough nutritious food on the table and those in the cities experiencing the same problem. That is, the rural poor and the urban poor share the same burdens — a growing hunger that cannot be met by industrial food.

The connection between the two is longstanding. The industrialization of agriculture decreased the number of people working the fields, and most of them went to cities — usually to low-wage jobs because the complex skills that make them able to make good use of land are of little value in urban areas. Many of the urban poor are immigrants, often from rural areas around the globe, or African-Americans whose access to land was always troubled and constrained and who moved to cities during the brief burst of wartime equality, which promised economic opportunity not always delivered.

How might we tie the rural and urban poor together in economic alliance to meet the needs of both groups? How can we bring together the access to land that the rural poor have with the markets that the urban poor provide? The aggregate value of low-income households' economic activity is quite large. As Michael Shulman observes, the desperately poor Anacostia neighborhood of Washington DC has a combined household income of 370 million dollars a year. That's a lot of buying power.[294]

What if rural poor people with access to land (and we believe that access to land may be the defining political issue of the coming decades) use a variety of tools to move toward being more food self-sufficient while simultaneously raising their incomes by selling surplus food directly to nearby urban populations? What if this relationship meant that the urban poor could not be outbid for a secure food supply and thus were insulated from rapid price rises? It would be possible also to reduce the enormous health costs of poverty, in part caused by bad food.

One of the ways we might do this is through new, "green-collar" jobs. As Van Jones writes, such jobs benefit both urban and rural poor, and ensure stable, middle class incomes. Small-scale farming has been largely impoverishing in the US, but if it were possible to change practices and diets and market relationships enough to cut middlemen, both urban and rural poor would benefit enormously.

Thus far green-collar jobs have focused on renewable energies and infrastructure adaptations, and these are essential projects too — it is not our intention to suggest otherwise. But agriculture is the ultimate green-collar job, and we need to both find ways for the urban poor to make money growing food where it is needed most — in population centers — and also to reduce poverty all the way around. We need work that brings people out of poverty, even as forces try to drive us back into it.

As Jones puts it:

Green-Collar Jobs Rebuild a Strong Middle Class
Green-collar jobs are good jobs. Like blue-collar jobs, green-collar jobs pay family wages and provide opportunities for advancement along a career track of increasing skills and wages. A job that does something for the planet, and little to nothing for the people or the economy, is not a green-collar job. The green economy cannot be built with solar sweat shops and Walmart wind farms.

Green-Collar Jobs Provide Pathways Out of Poverty
Most green-collar jobs are middle-skill jobs requiring more education than high school, but less than a four-year degree — and are well within reach for lower-skilled and low-income workers as long as they have access to effective training programs and appropriate supports. We must ensure that all green-collar jobs strategies provide opportunities for low-income people to take the first step on a pathway from poverty to economic self-sufficiency....

A Green-Collar Job Strengthens Urban and Rural Communities
Urban and rural America have both been negatively impacted over the past decades by a failure to invest in their growth — green-collar jobs provide an opportunity to reclaim these areas for the benefit of local residents. From new transit spending and energy audits in inner cities to windmills and biomass in our nation's heartland, green jobs mean a reinvestment in the communities hardest hit in recent decades.[295]

The simple truth is that it isn't clear how many renewable jobs there will be if the economy fails, or what scale of energy build out we'll be able to manage. But it is clear that we desperately need more skilled, talented, smart people to grow food. And the first major shift is finding ways to pay them well enough to make sure that farming gets you out of poverty, as it once did.

In our vision, cities and rural areas combine to address poverty and hunger while the suburbs (more poor people now live in the suburbs than in cities) serve as a middle ground, sometimes net provider, sometimes net consumer of food, depending on available resources.

Currently for every dollar spent on food, only $0.20 goes back to the farmer.[296] The rest goes to middlemen. From a 2008 article in *The Independent*,

> The World Bank says that 100 million more people are facing severe hunger. Yet some of the world's richest food companies are making record profits. Monsanto last month reported that its net income for the three months up to the end of February this year had more than doubled over the same period in 2007, from $543m (£275m) to $1.12bn. Its profits increased from $1.44bn to $2.22bn.
>
> Cargill's net earnings soared by 86 per cent from $553m to $1.030bn over the same three months. And Archer Daniels Midland, one of the world's largest agricultural processors of soy, corn and wheat, increased its net earnings by 42 per cent in the first three months of this year from $363m to $517m. The operating profit of its grains merchandising and handling operations jumped 16-fold from $21m to $341m.[297]

There is enough wealth here to provide economic security for millions of poor Americans — and millions or billions of poor small farmers worldwide. We simply have to reclaim it from corporate hands.

Poor urban dwellers might also prosper where farmland meets the city. Cities and towns dealing with sprawl often now hold parcels of land that cannot be developed. There is no reason why such community resources should serve only the tax rolls, why cattle cannot graze the local commons again, why farms rescued from the bulldozer should not be transformed into smaller truck farms or be farmed by tenants or be turned into community gardens. Reclaiming public land for the public good and for food security must be one of the main projects of extending the table.

To end the monopoly of industrialized food means that we need to fight for food everywhere in the following ways:

- Promote an increase in the basic food self-sufficiency of urban dwellers through the support of food-centered land-use policies and a multitude of agricultural resources in the form of experts, education, seed banks, organic pest controls, composting programs, tools and access to land.
- Strive for more complete food self-sufficiency among rural people with greater access to land by offering similar agricultural resources and by providing financial incentives that help would-be part-time farmers dedicate more time and energy to their land base

- Promote direct trade of food between those in rural areas with more access to land and those in urban areas with less such access. This would include:
  - supporting local and regional food transit networks
  - supporting local and regional food markets
  - providing financial incentives to growers who sell locally
  - supporting regional communication between farmers and eaters in the form of food stewardship councils, agricultural extension offices, websites, public service announcements, pie eating competitions, bikini contests, free beer at farmers' markets and more.
- Promote whole foods or home value-added food products that support nutritious eating and healthy living. This means addressing rules and regulations that unfairly support gigantic food companies at the expense of small local producers. These would include:
  - reasonable regulations regarding the processing and packaging of local meat
  - reasonable rules about home-cooked products and access to free or cheap certified commercial kitchens for producing such products
  - reduced fees regarding the certification of agricultural practices including the processing, packaging and the cooking of food
- Permanently eliminate food subsidies and other legislative barriers that unfairly support the overproduction of commodities crops, including corn, wheat and soybeans.
- Increase (if only temporarily) subsidies for fruit and vegetable production that can help to jump start a return to more sensible crop selection.

Paving the Road to Hell: Racism in the Food System

*Lukewarm acceptance is more bewildering
than outright rejection.*
— MARTIN LUTHER KING —

The overwhelming majority of people who are currently suffering disproportionately from the fallout of industrial agriculture and a consumer culture, both in this country and around the world, are not white. And the loudest voices in the food movement, including Sharon and Aaron, are white. The truth is that local community food systems are not going to grow where they are most needed without more non-white people in power.

Climate change and peak oil are operating to make non-white people poorer, more vulnerable, sicker and less safe. And the people who are preparing most and getting their communities organized are mostly white and comfortable. That disparity is bad for all of us for many reasons. The biggest one is that, for a long time, non-white communities have been in the situation where all of us are now headed — forced to use self-help because no one else will help them. We're going to need the help of those communities in learning to live in this new world.

We can't help but see that a book about food security written by and directed at middle-class white people who are currently food secure has its issues. We're sure as hell not going to claim we know what non-white communities need. Instead, we're going to speak about the way that our new farming communities and our collective new worldview has to change if we're to create really collective responses. And part of that is that we're going to have to learn to listen to other people better. As Van Jones writes,

> So we live together in these bubbles that touch, and we call that diversity, but we don't know each other. And when that bubble breaks for just a second and we're face to face with each other, it's very, very hard to hear that reality.
>
> But white supremacy, to use the provocative term, will reinterpret that experience for you; and make it not be about your inability to hear, but be about other people's inability to speak. This is one of the most remarkable things: if you can get this, all doors open. There is the assumption — this is deep, this is deep — there is the assumption that when there's a breakdown in communication between people of color and white people, that there is an deficiency but that the deficiency is not in white listening, that the deficiency is in black speech. "Why are they so angry?" People start critiquing, and then you find somebody who keeps themselves together just for a little bit and it's, "Oh that one's very eloquent, that one's very articulate." Right? Always the assumption is that the deficiency lies with the people of color. "Why don't they care about the environment? What wrong with them, don't they see the big picture? We've been talking at them about this for years? Don't they see that we have this big beautiful conference, this big

beautiful training? Why aren't they coming? What's wrong with them? We've been outreaching at them for years, I could show you the e-mails I've sent outreaching at them. I even make phone calls out reaching at them. What's wrong with them? Maybe they are just too poor or busy, because certainly there is nothing wrong with our speech!"[298]

We know that some readers will read this section of the book and feel that we are "merely" being politically correct. What we'd call it, perhaps, is two things. First, trying not to be jerks. We believe that always has value. But the other thing is this — the recognition that, to paraphrase Christ, "Whatever they do to the least of my brethren, people will feel quite free to do to you."

What do we mean by this? The privileged have had limited success on casting off privilege and connecting with non-white people out of noble motives. Now we *have* to get to know our non-white neighbors because we're about to be a lot less privileged, and if we allow the already poor and disadvantaged to get hurt, the next victims will be us. This is self interest, and perhaps less than noble, but it is nonetheless true. We have to get over our assumptions and our internalized bigotry and our jerk behavior because we're all about to get our asses kicked by rich people, and we need all the allies we can get.

One of the biggest reasons that peak oil and climate change have not engaged the poor is that in our focus on future scarcity, we have been leaving out people who are already experiencing scarcity. The only way to change that disparity is to engage African-American, Native American, Asian and Latino people in finding real, local, community solutions for themselves. Externally imposed solutions are likely to be both inappropriate and smack of condescension.

Many poor, non-white communities have been using less energy than we have all along. They've been making do and adapting to food availability challenges, budget cuts and loss of utilities and food security for a long, long time. Poor people of all races in the US and the rest of the world have created lifestyles that use less energy and fewer resources, and we are going to need to model our lives on theirs.

The single most important skill set of the future may be one honed in poor urban and rural communities around the nation, and still remembered and honored in the homes of millions of first- and second-generation immigrants — making things last, making the food go around, and practicing community self-help.

Race, class and immigration are high-tension issues in our society; and in the face of hard times we can expect those tensions to rise. We're going to need to watch our worst impulses. We wrote earlier about the dangers of linear thinking and the assumption that we're all doomed. Apocalyptic visions tend to naturalize and increase existing divisions along race, class, religious and social lines.

For example, if we're all doomed, if we're struggling to keep our very lives together, then there is certainly no reason to try and improve the lot of the already poor — it is hopeless, why bother? No reason to worry about the hungry — too late for that. Thus, all our obligations to one another are erased, and the rise of our worst selves is naturalized. This is a bad thing.

The "war of all against all," as writer Harvey Winston put it, ends with everyone dead in their bunkers. And the language of "them" ignores the fact that some of us *are* "them." That is, we cannot go along assuming that the only people we are talking to are all white middle-class people who can afford a solar system on their roof.

The extreme version of the "there's no hope" vision is the idea that "they" will be rioting in the cities and come out of "the cities" to steal your food and attack your family. The word "they" is rarely clarified, but we don't think there's very much doubt about who "they" are. Most apocalyptic visions see a *Mad Max* hell in the cities, where, not coincidentally, a lot of non-white people live. It envisions disaster as inevitable, irrevocable and irresolvable. Thus, there's no point in talking about things like reducing infant mortality, health insurance for the poor, better democracy, sustainable urban food systems — the end of the world is already inevitable, and because it is inevitable, we white folks can just sit around and lament, without actually feeling responsible for any of it.

Well, that's nonsense, and we all know it. Will the coming decades be difficult? No doubt. Is it hopeless? Absolutely not. If we use peak oil and climate change as an excuse for doing harm to others, or not mending that harm, we're being cowards or worse. In doing so, we are not bowing to inevitability — we are choosing to believe what we prefer to hear, that remedying our present ills is simply too difficult.

Cuba is living proof that it is possible for an energy-poor society to give priority to health-care and food security. Our society could choose those things as well. We could choose them right now and use our resources to create infrastructure that would diminish inequities today, make our energy descent much less painful for tens of millions of people and create food security.

We have not done so — mostly because we have a long tradition of choosing policies that can best be summed up as "less for the poor and more for the rich," supported by a lottery mentality that we are all just one play away from winning the big one. Even if we aren't rich today, we might be so any time now. Or so we believe. This polarized way of thinking is not inevitable. It is a choice, and every single participant in our democracy is morally responsible for it. We cannot vacate that responsibility by moaning that it is hopeless.

We have a lot of choices, and we need to call our choices by their correct names. If we pick high food prices instead of rationing, let's be explicit about what we've chosen — we've decided to ration by price and starve the poor again. If we end up not doing anything about food systems in urban centers because we're unwilling to demand that cities hold back development in favor of growing food or because we care more about parking than the fact that many kids don't get dinner, we need to admit that we chose not to feed poor hungry kids so that we'd have parking. Making all the bad stuff seem inevitable is lying, and it's weak.

When talking about inequity, there's a lot of dismissal of the possibility of change. It is easier to believe that we cannot make substantive change, because then we don't have to give anything up. Frankly, most of us are afraid of losing what we've got. There's a lot of instinctive fear of living like poor people. Some of that is justified. But how do you tell that to real poor people — "Yeah, we're just not prepared to redistribute the food and other goods. Sorry, too bad — we don't want to be like you."

We are still willing to justify what we do for personal reasons — "Well, I *have* to use more than my share because of: insert job reason/family reason/personal problem/medical problem." We need to be absolutely clear about how such rationalizations sound to people who are already experiencing real rationing of things like medical care, good food, safe housing, transportation — people who are already priced out of those things that we say we desperately need because of our personal reasons. It's not as though none of them have long trips to their jobs, or health problems, personal justifications or family issues. What they don't usually have is the luxury of using that justification.

There is no question that if rich people give up some privilege, they are going to be giving up some things they may not be happy about losing. The only possible argument here is that there's a greater good involved. It wasn't that long ago that such an argument was enough for a lot of us. We should make that argument more often, and we should not apologize for making it.

Realistically, if we're talking about something more than the survival of the richest, we're talking about equitable redistribution, and that means finding a way to each live on our own share — period. It doesn't mean saying "Oh, well, I'll just take a little more — the poor people won't mind." They mind — so don't cover it up with icing and call it cake. None of us is perfect, and in many ways it is as hard to get the comfortable down as it is get poor people raised up. But we need to shake off the lies we tell ourselves.

Again, it would be helpful if privileged and well-educated white people would turn to the poor Native American, Black, Asian and Latino people and ask, "How do you do it? Can you teach me?" instead of assuming that they won't mind if we just use a little more than our share, because after all, we're very busy and very important, and our reasons count more than theirs.

For example, Southern California has seen a substantial influx of Hispanics during the past few decades, with their percentage of the population rising from 27 percent in 1980 to 74 percent in 2000. This has also meant a change in the sights and sounds of South L.A.

> For many, the image of South Los Angeles is that of a paved, parched, densely packed urban grid. But increasingly, it is also a place where untold numbers of barnyard animals — chickens, roosters, goats, geese, ducks, pigs and even the odd pony — are being tended in tiny backyard spaces.... The cacophony of cock-a-doodle-doos south of the 10 Freeway is one of the louder manifestations of a demographic change that has transformed South Los Angeles.[299]

The culture of keeping animals as part of a garden even in dense urban areas has followed immigrants from Mexico and Central America. Here is set of skills — raising animals for meat, eggs, pest control and garden fertilizer — that we can learn from people who have a history and knowledge of caring for animals in an urban environment. This type of adaptation is a knowledge base we should make use of. Without some kind of recognition that we are being led by our own poor communities, our relationship with them will always be one of dismissal.

One of the things we believe most powerfully is that most of us, whether poor now or poor soon, are not going to be able to choose strategies that involve spending thousands of dollars. In this sense, gardens and small farms have a remarkable degree of equity — organic production can be done with a few tools and many waste materials. Gardens and farms can be — if we can ensure land access — the territory of millions of low-income people. Thus our society's emphasis needs to be on agriculture because of its enormous accessibility.

There are a lot of non-white people who need jobs, and many, many who have skill sets that would be extremely useful and valuable to us as we learn to grow food differently. But these people are not being welcomed or encouraged. How many of us are seeking to bring Latino farmers into our neighborhoods and preparedness communities or to provide jobs for refugee immigrants with agricultural skills? How many of us think of migrant laborers as skilled farmers who produce much of our food? How much of the discourse on immigration and poverty has recognized how very dependent we are on the skill sets of people we often disdain?

In Amherst, Massachusetts, Cambodian refugees "have translated a three-thousand-year-old farming tradition into the local idiom of a New England field,"[300] blessing the land each spring as their king would do at the start of each growing season in their homeland. Originally a garden to help feed the more than 150 Khmer people in the area, the garden now produces food for local Asian restaurants, grocery stores and the local farmers' market.

We could and should be welcoming whole communities of poor people who already know the things we need to know. There is a story of a group of recent Hmong immigrants who went to visit Plymouth Plantation, a historical re-enactment museum. When they saw the huts made of wood and thatch, the chickens and the gardens, the head of the group asked if, instead of being relocated to their apartments in Providence, they could simply live there. They noted that this was all they wanted — a simple place to live and land to farm.

Instead of placing agrarian immigrants in agrarian environments, we have overwhelmingly displaced poor, non-white people into cities. If we continue this, it will mean a repeat of our history in which agricultural migrants unsuccessfully compete for jobs with people who have urban skills. This is the root of dependency — the devaluation of desperately needed skills. We simply can't afford to have that happen again to this generation's immigrant farmers — we need them too badly.

Ruhan Kainth, an Indian immigrant who first arrived in America in the late 1970s, describes the creation of her Punjabi garden that blossoms with 50 or so varieties of edibles. She says, "For years, nothing would grow here, The soil was dead." Her neighbors' yards explain why, with their manicured, chemical-laden lawns. Ruhan describes a lesson learned in her native country, "Nothing goes to waste in those Indian villages." [301]

Most of us probably think of any revolution in agriculture in terms of our own heritage and our own experience of food and farming. But the history and future of our agriculture are more complex.

We need to make sure that when we're talking about broad, national solutions, we aren't just talking about the middle class, the healthy and the fortunate. We can't just talk tax cuts — poor people often don't benefit from them. We need to talk subsidies, redistribution, justice. We need to grasp right now that peak oil and climate change are justice issues — as much as civil rights were. In fact, they are civil rights. If we price people out basic human rights — such as access to food — and those people "just happen" not to be white, we're no better than those guys with the fire hoses shooting at African American kids during the civil rights movement. We're just better at hiding our responsibility.

The one bright spot in this future is that peak oil and climate change represent the greatest hope for reallocation of wealth and justice in the world, but we probably won't do it without someone to keep us honest. How about we do that for ourselves? This is going to take everyone.

Is this All a Commie Plot?

When I give food to the poor, they call me a saint.
When I ask why the poor have no food,
they call me a Communist.
— HELDER PESSOA CAMARA —

The peak oil movement has occasionally been called the "liberal left behind" movement — the apocalypse of the left. Of course, it is no such thing, and never has been. Former Bush energy czar Matthew Simmons is no leftist radical; Republican Congressman Roscoe Bartlett never dated Abbie Hoffman; and the US Army is not, as far as I know, handing out "Free Mumia" buttons with its rifles. And yet all are among the first to recognize the imminence of peak oil. And though climate change may once have been the province of the left, the truth is that everyone — even the Bush administration — has been forced to acknowledge the scientific truth of anthropogenic global warming.

Though it is true that the peak oil and climate change movements have their share of aging hippies and tree-huggers, we're also flush with survivalists, petroleum geologists, biologists, investment bankers and other bastions of the right and center. And this is all to the good — the end of cheap oil and the climate disaster is not a political fact; it is a simple, practical reality. The hard, scientific truths about sea level rise, aquifer depletion and drought really don't care whether you prefer Bill O'Reilly, Thom Hartmann or Stephen Colbert.

It is insufficient to say that these issues cross party lines, because what they actually do is destroy party and political lines and the divisions we've carefully worked out to decide who is "left" and who is "right." It is worth noting that these have always been artificial distinctions for most people. Both of us have been described as "leftists" in our time. And sometimes we take pride in that designation. We value the history of leftism, of justice movements, and believe profoundly that food security is a justice issue. But "left" has never been more than a shorthand for some positions on some issues — and had we drawn the circles in other ways, we might have spoken, at times, for other constituencies, even, perhaps, for some segments of the much dreaded "other side." All of which is simply proof, that, though it isn't true that we're all exactly the same under the skin, most of us are political hybrids, with opinions and beliefs that don't fit neatly into one category.

The past decade or so has blurred things further. Which party is the big government, tax-and-spend one? Which party is the party of genocide — the Democrats who killed half a million children in Iraq with the embargo or the Republicans who killed a million civilians in Iraq with the war? Now it is the left who is screaming in horror about the dangers of big government (and some of the right screaming along with them). Conventional political lines are shifting.

And at the same time that this shift is happening, those of us who foresee the coming crisis have to make major internal political shifts as well.

For example, in *The Upside of Down*, Thomas Homer-Dixon observes that to address the coming crises, we'd have enact,

> A global society that I've come to call "Holland times ten," with vastly more sophisticated, pervasive and expensive rules and regulatory institutions than anything the Dutch live with today. Do we really want such a future for ourselves and our children?[302]

Homer-Dixon, not exactly a man of the right, recognizes the simple reality that a vastly more repressive bureaucracy might actually be worse than collapse. He observes, following Joseph Tainter, the author of *The Collapse of Complex Societies*, that institutions created to deal with crisis invariably stay with us forever, leaving us laden with ever more oppressive, expensive and resource intensive layers of government. What is remarkable about Homer-Dixon's book is that it shakes off conventional left/right thinking and simply allows the data to lead him to a conclusion that is neither.

The same could be said of Rod Dreher's book, *Crunchy Cons*. Dreher too is motivated by the honest recognition that peak oil and the environmental crisis have simply changed things, shifting old political lines. He tries very hard to slip all the good stuff under the rubric of conservatism, arguing, for example, that traditional social welfare programs that support families are conservative. We're not convinced he succeeds, but he provides one of the most remarkable analyses I've imagined, and his work has real power among conservatives. Dreher is one of the first people to seriously reconsider, in a popular and accessible way, how to reconfigure politics to deal with the future. Even more importantly, Dreher ties religious ideas of stewardship to environmental responses to the future.

The reality is that for many people who work in these issues, left and right stop becoming fully explicatory categories. Richard Heinberg writes about the problem of addressing our crises in *Powerdown*, where he discusses his preference for minimal government while arguing simultaneously that no full-scale response to peak oil can proceed without a national government push like World War II. Moreover, Heinberg also acknowledges that we have to expand government only to make it smaller — that the large social structures necessary to make the transition must ultimately hand out power voluntarily to smaller, localized units of government. This represents a remarkably hybridized vision of power.

At the risk of alienating people on both the left and the right who read this book, and ending up with absolutely no readers at all, we're going to

argue that none of the problems we are facing can be fixed from the right
or the left, or even by discussion in those terms. As long as we are divided
by fairly superficial political divisions, we cannot successfully address our
present crisis. So, although we nominally have ties to the left, let us consider some ways in which we stand also with the "right," or rather, ways in
which most of us can and should stand together.

1. We believe passionately in the importance of personal responsibility
and of fair accounting for one's choices. By this we do not mean that one's
situation is wholly a product of one's personal choices, and thus tough pa-
tooties if you were born poor. We mean that all of us have allowed ourselves to become overly passive and dependent on powers that simply don't
have our interests at heart. And the solution to this is to stop depending on
them as much as possible. Each of us needs to take greater responsibility
for our present, societal circumstances than we do, and that includes what
we put on our tables.

What we eat, where we get it, who grew it and how — these are all important decision that are too important to be left up to government agen-
cies with a stamp. The importance of "organic" as a stamp of approval is, in
a certain way, a license not to have a personal relationship with your food,
not to know the farmer or how it was grown.

We often hear people lamenting the power of corporations — as though
that power does not derive from our dependency and willingness to give
them cash. Walmart and Monsanto aren't powerful because they are evil
corporations — they are powerful because they have great stinking wads
of money and those wads came from you and me. Stop buying from them.
It is true they receive corporate subsidies and have lobbying power — but
that too derives from the money we pay them

We also hear many voices calling out for public policy solutions, when
what they really mean is that they want the government to take care of
peak oil and climate change for them, without being personally inconve-
nienced. Again, this is a failure of personal responsibility, because if we tell
governments that what we want is solutions without personal sacrifice,
we will get only inadequate solutions, which will fail us and the next generation.

Full-scale, straight-out, honest accounting of responsibility is important. That means that people are responsible for what they do, and the most
responsible people are the most privileged people in the world — and that

means us. We must seek environmental solutions that use fair accounting, that don't try to find ways to explain how we deserve just a little more.

Those of us who are in a position to do more to facilitate change in the way we eat have more of a responsibility to do so. Those of us with wealth should be financially supporting the fledging farmers attempting to grow food differently. Those who teach must share the extent of the problem with their students and help shape attitudes of change. Any and all of us with influence over municipal policies that promote local food have an obligation to do all we can to see that support put in place. And all of us who are fortunate enough to be healthy should be out in the garden, getting to work and asking "How can I change things?"

2. We don't expect the government to save us in a crisis, and we believe that anyone with the ability to do so shouldn't either. We don't understand why it is that people in Florida don't have any bottled water or boards for their windows and are standing in line for it the day before the hurricane. For cripes sake, you live in Florida! The same is true with people who are unprepared for blackouts during winter blizzards in the Northeast or for earthquakes in California. It is true that one of the better uses for government is to get the helicopters up and make sure people don't die of typhus after the disaster, but we shouldn't be betting on it — we should be betting on ourselves and our communities.

We all watched the footage of Hurricane Katrina, and it confirmed what everyone on the right has been saying for generations — our present government isn't going to save our behinds in a crisis. Now, we should try and improve national emergency response, because there are always going to be people who can't protect themselves and situations we can't prepare for. But many of us can — and we need to store and preserve food and have resources and a backup plan for hard times.

Ultimately a certain degree of self-sufficiency is merely common sense. There are people who may not be able to afford extra food or blankets or a means to get out of a dying city; we need to help those people. But it would be really useful if those who aren't elderly or disabled or desperately poor would get their acts together and be prepared to meet their own damned needs for predictable situations, so that they won't clog the system.

This goes for garden and farm systems. The truth is that change is coming, and coming fast. We've spent a lot of time in this book explaining why we should want a smaller-scale agriculture — as energy prices rise and food

A NATION OF FARMERS

gets scarcer, we're going to need one. Once we understand what's going on, if we don't get to work, we'll pay the price and bear the responsibility for not responding.

3. We don't want to see power centralized any more than strictly necessary. Okay, let's be honest — this used to be the big old left–right debate — social welfare or not, big government or little government. It is no longer a right–left issue — no one has a monopoly here.

We need smaller solutions in larger numbers and to get as much power out to as many people as humanly possible. Let's be honest, whether you hate the Clintons or the Bushes (or both equally), every single one of us can see exactly why we want to decentralize power and exactly why we should be getting rid of political dynasties and the system that locates private armies, our food system and our own right to justice in the hands of any one person.

In fact, both peak oil and climate change require, absolutely mandate a reduction of scale of government — just as conservatives have been calling for. Yes, we also need to expand some central projects — but the general movement has to be toward local sovereignty and local power and resources being kept in the communities.

4. We're going to have to develop better family relationships and a strong focus on family units. We're not talking about getting into people's bedrooms here, but about getting into people's kitchens and dining rooms, and getting us to work and eat together. We are going to need to take care of our own aging parents and disabled family members, stop whining "What about *myyyyyy* needs?" and start thinking a bit more of other people. Those of us who have ordinarily screwed up families (as opposed to the ones that are so awful you can't do anything about it) are going to have to start getting along again and recognize that biological and chosen family are going to be much more important in our lives for a long, long time. And we're going to have to start to value and honor the work of caring for others; instead of acting like helping Grandma to the bathroom or breastfeeding your kid is a pain in the ass to be shoved off on other people, we have to start realizing that this *is* the point — the reason we're here. To be of use. To do good work. To care for others. To keep everyone fed.

Whether we live in nuclear families, extended ones or chosen families, we're going to have to concentrate on bringing families together with ties that go beyond our old disagreements. As Albert Bates notes, "Shared meals are a cornerstone of human culture. Sitting down to eat with people, people you love and people who drive you crazy, is one of the ways we organize ourselves."[303] When describing the founding of The Farm, Bates pointed out,

> If you look back in American history, you can see that there's been a lot of communal experiments over the years, a lot of weird strange cults and stuff that came over from various different countries and settled in North America, and a lot of those didn't survive. Most of them didn't survive, and several of them had fairly serious death tolls the first few years.

We survived, we made it. And part of the reason we made it was we were able to feed everybody.[304]

In a *Vanity Fair* article about The Farm, one of the stories told about Farm founder Stephen Gaskin is that he insisted that biological ties mattered, even in the face of a culture that sometimes wanted to overthrow them.

> The next day Gaskin called a meeting and issued a decree: "If you're sleeping together, you're engaged. If you're pregnant, you're married." Six or seven men who had joined the Caravan for the free love split.[305]

That recognition that older patterns of human organization still have value, and that children require parents to survive and thrive may also be why The Farm is still going. We anticipate that all sorts of new ties and arrangements will grow up in the coming years. Our survival will depend on how these serve as an enhancement to what we already have.

We're also going to have to parent better. We need to stop telling our kids how special and perfect and wonderful they are and tell them to move away from the TV and get to work helping grow food. Instead of telling Jimmy and Jenny that the best thing they can do is to get good SAT scores and go to Tae Kwon Do, tell them the truth — that you want them to grow up to be good and righteous people who care about others, are hard workers, honorable and generous. And that means participating in meeting basic family needs. The good thing is that children need meaning as much they need as food and shelter — they deserve to be proud of their work and their value to their family.

5. If you harbor any lingering prejudices about blue-collar work, doing it yourself or getting down and dirty, get over it now. It is not, in any sense of the word, more noble to be a tax lawyer than a plumber or farmer, and your expensive education doesn't mean you are smarter than people who grow your food. If you call the middle of the country "flyover states" cut it out now — you won't be flying much of anywhere anyway, and they grow your dinner.

The reality is that most comparatively well off, well educated people have been doing things that aren't very useful and are soon going to stop being done. Most of the people we have been told we are smarter than are actually doing good and useful work — feeding people, keeping houses running, building things, making things, growing food. It is likely that we have been so firmly told we are smarter simply because it was a good way to avoid pointing out that we are, as Sharon's husband likes to put it, "the surplus population."

6. Religion may not be something you approve of, and that's just fine. But agrarian religious culture is going to be powerful. If you think all religious people are the same, that religion is the cause of all problems and religious people are idiots, that's your privilege; but shut up about it. As we're less and less able to control our future, more and more people are going to be praying in their foxholes, maybe even you. Get over it, and stop feeling superior.

And if you reject religion and don't want to see it flourish but you aren't working to provide community support, food for the hungry, care for the sick and dying, festivals of celebration and release, and a way to think about why the world is so screwed up, then expect to spend a lot of time wondering why you aren't as successful as religious groups. Don't blame it on religion — blame it on the fact that you aren't very good at doing the things that religion does very well for many of us.

7. We need a new sense of personal freedom, one in which limits in the form of things like honor, self-discipline, modesty, courtesy, and public order are perceived not as acts of repression but as structure in which culture can bloom. The notion that there are things we ought not do is likely to be a painful one to those who spent their youth practicing iconoclasm. The notion that we should follow our bliss, support our own self-esteem and do what feels best to us has to be replaced with the notion that we should

regulate our desires, limit our choices and do what is best for the community and the planet.

Our culture has grown to reject hypocrisy as the ultimate sin. Hypocrisy in the popular (rather than the moral) sense, of course, is defined as doing things that you don't believe in, expressing feeling you don't have for the sake of the community. But, of course, communities run on just such self-restraint, and in tighter-knit, more strongly bound communities how you feel about things may not matter that much all the time. It may be that what you do, how you treat others and how you regulate your own feelings and intentions is more important to your own survival and success than following your bliss.

Capitalism has enthusiastically supported the notion that we should follow our hearts all the time — just as it has rejected modesty of ambition, of lifestyle, of desire. Because if we believe that our feelings are authentic, immutable and natural — that is, that we feel the way we do about things for some fundamental reason of self — then there is no reason to limit our desires. But if we come to see our desires as manufactured, a product of the industrial economy itself, the product of a massive devaluation of the collective over the personal, then we begin to shift our vision and to trust, instead of our manipulated instincts, the idea of a greater good.

Now that we've traumatized everyone on the left, eliminated all readership and caused our publishers to curse the day they signed our contract, we'll stop for the moment. But we hope that the readers who were cursing us as commie pinko hippie tree huggers now, at least, feel that we've adequately insulted everyone else. Just doing our job.

An Interview with Gene Logsdon: Spring 2008

Along with Wendell Berry, Gene Logsdon has been a central leader of the American agrarian movement for decades. He is the author of many books, both practical and philosophical, and it is impossible to read any of his writing without being overcome with the desire to grow food.

ANOF: Given the rising cost of fossil fuels because of their declining availability, the climate change associated with using those fossil fuels, the problems of soil erosion and water degradation and all the other problems with the way we grow food and eat it at this point in history, what do you think is the biggest challenge facing the American agriculture? And how can we address it?

GENE: The biggest problem in my opinion is that our society, our culture, does not understand that food is everyone's business. We have decided, as a society, to let a few people worry about our food while the rest of us worry about money. And so food production has more or less become the domain of a few very large international corporations. The only cure for it is what is now happening. Food prices and food shortages and fuel shortages will force people to take back their lives. There's an old saying that goes "People won't do the right thing until they have no other choice." I'm afraid that is true for the majority.

ANOF: Do you think it makes sense to grow food in the suburbs — in former farmland turned neighborhood? And do you have any suggestions for people interested in this sort of suburban homesteading?

GENE: Yes, this kind of "homesteading" is possible and admirable, and if you watch what is happening as food prices climb, it is taking place more and more. You will run into the same problem, however, suggested by the preceding question. Most of the people who live in these enclaves of urbanism out in the countryside, wasting good land in the process, do not have a vocation to farming and gardening and will therefore not do it or fail at it. I was talking to one such person just yesterday. She was full of enthusiasm for putting out a big garden because of rising food prices. But she had not turned a spadeful of dirt yet when the real food producer with a vocation to the work has his or her early garden already planted and growing. People who don't really like gardening and farming do not understand the first principle of successful food production. You do not do it at your convenience. You do it when nature dictates. The secret of success is timeliness, and nature drives the clock.

ANOF: Could you describe the interplay between plants and animals — wild and domestic — on a small farm?

GENE: I think, contrary to what vegans say, that a really natural and economical garden or farm must have both animals and plants on it. If you don't have domestic animals, you will have plenty of wild ones. In fact you will have plenty of wild ones anyway, and the biggest threat to home food production right now is wild animals. They are overpopulating without enough natural predation. Humans should be hunting and eating them, or replacing their niche in the natural order with domestic animals. Unfortunately our over-civilized society thinks I am a barbarian for saying that. People can't be convinced that all life belongs to the food chain and that the food chain is a giant dining table around which all things sit, eating and being eaten. I guess our society is going to have to learn that the hard way.

ANOF: Books on food production are often either too local in scope, and therefore useful only to people living in a certain area, or too broad, and therefore not detailed enough to be helpful. What's the best way to establish information-sharing systems to encourage more small-scale, backyard food production? And how can we best share information in the age of the Internet?

GENE: I probably shouldn't say this but libraries and the Internet are choking full of information necessary to raise backyard food. That is not the problem. The problem is that the literate world thinks success in food raising (or anything else) can be attained by reading information. Information does not make one successful in farming and gardening. *Experience* does. We have been led to believe that a college degree brings success; not having a degree brings failure. That is so stupid. If everyone had a college degree, then you would see real fast that the degree does not bring success. Love and bullheadedness bring success, especially in food production. There are a zillion books out there for information sharing. You don't need to establish anything more.

ANOF: What are some of your personal garden favorites? Would you share a recipe using some of them?

GENE: I really don't have personal garden favorites. If it's fresh, I like it. The best part of it all is that you can eat these things without any recipe — just raw or heated up. I mean, what kind of recipe would enhance a strawberry or an ear of sweet corn?

—— *RECIPES* ——

Stuffed Eggplant   *by Gene Logsdon*

If you are a meat lover, as we are, this is a good meat substitute if you want to eat less meat and not feel hungry for meat.

Ingredients

- 1 large eggplant
- 2 tbsp grated onion
- ½ cup half and half (about)
- ⅛ tsp pepper
- 1 egg, well beaten

- 4 tbsp butter
- 1 tsp chopped parsley
- ¼ tsp salt
- ¾ cup of ground pecans
- ½ cup of Ritz cracker crumbs

Directions

1. Wash eggplant. Cut off one-third, lengthwise. Remove pulp, leaving ½-inch wall around. Dice the pulp. Rub inside of shell with lemon juice.
2. Melt butter, add parsley, onion and cubed eggplant. Cook, covered, over low heat, stirring often, until tender.
3. Add remaining ingredients with enough half and half to moisten well. Pour into shell. Bake for 45 minutes at 350° or until crusty on top.

Honey Mead or Metheglin   *by Colleen Collins of North Carolina*

This summer I have been playing with making metheglins and melomels, which are the oldest form of liquor known — and delicious. Metheglin is honey mead made with herbs and/or spices; melomel is honey mead made with fruit.

I have made a number of variations: lemon thyme metheglin, blackberry melomel, blueberry melomel, blueberry melomel with lemon verbena, strawberry melomel with lemon verbena, plum melomel, pawpaw melomel, peach melomel with cinnamon, slippery elm and maca.

These were all "wild ferments" started with the yeast on the fruits and in the air. I adapted Sandor Katz's recipe from *The Revolution Will Not Be Microwaved*. After I got my first good ferment going, I used a few teaspoons to innoculate the next batch. And so on.

Here is my basic recipe.

Equipment

- a glass or ceramic mixing bowl
- cheesecloth or towels

Ingredients

- 1 tbsp or so of fresh herbs
- 1 cup fruit (whole, chopped or sliced)
- 1 cup local honey (sourwood is my preference for its light flavor, but I've also tried wildflower)
- 4–7 cups of purified water (4 for a mead I intend to drink "young" — within a few weeks or months after fermenting starts — 7 for a mead I intend to bottle and age)

Directions

1. Mix ingredients in bowl. Cover with towel or layers of cheesecloth.
2. Put it in a warm but easy to reach place.

3. Stir every day to incorporate yeast from the air.
4. When bubbly, start tasting.
5. When you like the taste, strain, bottle and refrigerate. Or strain, rack (siphon off liquid leaving sediment behind), bottle and age. If aging, use an airlock to allow CO_2 to escape, or put a balloon on top of bottle and release when full of CO_2. Or put a screw cap on the bottle and remember to release the CO_2 manually — often in warm weather, less often in cool weather.

Challah   *by Sharon*

On Fridays we make two loaves of this traditional Jewish festival bread, a staple on the Sabbath table. When we were delivering weekly baskets of fresh home-grown produce and eggs to our CSA customers, we would include a loaf or two of home-baked challah. There are many variants, but this is the recipe we perfected for our customers, and we figured it was good enough for us too. Challah is a festival food — not just plain bread, but rich and sweet with honey and eggs. The idea was that the rest of the time you were eating plainer, heavier breads, and that once a week, everyone got a simple but delicious festival food.

Ingredients
- 1 cup warm water
- 2 pkg active dry yeast
- ⅓ cup local honey
- ½ tbsp salt
- pinch of sugar
- ¼ cup oil, melted butter or other fat
- 2 eggs, beaten
- 4 cups fresh ground wheat flour (if you aren't grinding your own, you might want a little white flour to lighten purchased wheat flour)

Directions
1. Dissolve a pinch of sugar in the water, and add the yeast. Allow the yeast to start eating the sugar. After five minutes or so the mixture should start to froth on the surface.
2. Add the canola oil, sugar, eggs, salt and bread flour and mix well with a spoon. Add the wheat flour and mix until well blended. Knead for a few minutes or until dough is stretchy.
3. Divide the dough into six portions. Roll each section back and forth between your palms and stretch until it forms a thick rope. Transfer three dough ropes to a lightly floured surface and braid them. Repeat with the remaining three ropes.
4. Transfer the two braided loaves to a greased baking sheet and bake in a 350° oven for 45 minutes or until golden brown on the outside and hollow-sounding inside when tapped.

CHAPTER 8

Keep Your Hand
on the Plow

Transformations

Took Paul and Silas, put 'em in the jail,
Had no one to go their bail.
Keep your hands on that plow, hold on.
Paul and Silas, they begin to shout,
Jail doors opened and they walked out.
Keep your hands on the plow, hold on.

— UNKNOWN —

SHARON: I was recently told that some people read me because I'm a "sweet-natured mother who cares about the earth and her children" and that I "appeal to people's better nature." So if that's the case, and that's why you are reading this book, I want to suggest that you take a break and go read something else. In fact, I beg of you, avert your eyes! Because by the time you finish this, you will think I'm one Machiavellian bitch, someone who could probably have dated Karl Rove. And you probably will want to go read someone nicer and fuzzier. I have no wish to disillusion you.

The truth is that I am a mother who cares about the earth and her children (too many of my friends and family will read this for me to even try to get away with "sweet natured"), and I do truly and sincerely believe that we can change the world and that we should. I also am extremely practical, which is a term I prefer over the laden word, "Machiavellian." But it means much the same. As my sister once said to me, "Sharon, you are surprisingly good with a carrot, and not too bad with a stick." As for Karl Rove — we're too far apart in age, I fear, but if we were closer.... I will note that I did date a whole lot of debate geeks over the years, many of them as unattractive as Karl Rove, so it isn't out of the question. I will simply note that I have little doubt that if I had, Karl would be a leftist serving the Gore presidency. Practical is powerful.

Because I am not a nice girl, or maybe not merely a nice girl, I feel that I should point out that the peak oil movement and the climate change movement are losing the race to plan the future. To a large degree it is because we are refusing to be practical, or perhaps Machiavellian. We tend to think that practical tactics are immoral tactics. And, like all high-minded people, we're getting our asses kicked by the low-minded ones.

Since I am not all that nice, I have no trouble with practical techniques of moving public opinion in the ways I think are wise, provided I am telling the truth. The good thing is that I don't have to lie; the other side of these issues has to lie, but I don't — I have the truth on my side, along with a firm taste for low culture and low tactics, within certain parameters. Personally, I think we should all get much more practical, very quickly.

Most of the strategies that have been proposed for dealing with peak oil and climate change involve lots of new, expensive technologies. Unfortunately, these probably won't work. Politically, what we need most is to admit that the basic unit of currency for dealing with our ecological crisis is not burning fossil fuels — that is, turning things off and getting rid of them. The basic project of dealing with peak oil and climate change is adapting our infrastructure to dealing with life turned off and gotten rid of. Many people fear this outcome so deeply that they are willing to destroy billions of lives to avoid it.

Thus, our task is to reassure people while telling the hard truths. We need to offer a vision and alternative to the choice between hell and hell, and point out that the life without stuff is not a bad one. We need to tell that story. If we don't get this message out, we will lose in the most literal sense — we will die. Our kids will die. Our grandkids will die. This is losing. And I personally don't much give a damn if I use low tactics (within reason) to keep that outcome from happening. I'm willing to go to hell for using propaganda — better than going from not using it and letting the world burn.

That's because the opposition is on message and way, way ahead. "Trust us," say BP, Shell and Exxon. "We have your interests at heart." "Trust us," say the idiots who pervert science and lie like rugs in the Bush administration. "Climate change can't hurt us. Don't look at the NASA scientists, read this nice novel." And always the message is "We just need good new technologies."

Well, guess what — technology doesn't work like that. You don't put in a coin and get out a prize.

Now, it is true that we have done this twice — we made it to the moon, and we built nuclear bombs. But the nuclear bombs took something we don't like to admit we once had — a centrally planned, tightly managed economy. Yup, the US was once as centrally planned as the Soviet Union — we had rationing; farmers were told what to plant and when to plant it; clothing manufacturers were told what kinds of clothing they could offer; people were told what they could waste and penalized for not abiding by it. We had black markets and price stabilization, and manufacturing was told what to make and where to bring it and at what price they could sell it. Niels Bohr said that the only way we could make the bomb was to turn the entire country into a factory — and we did. The whole nation worked together on one goal and used all its resources towards that goal — as opposed to the way we operate now. We may yet do this again — but for that to turn into anything but a hellacious dictatorship, we would need both a better government and an intellectual and propaganda foundation.

We may need a WWII-style economy to powerdown. But we can't let the current holders of power and thieves of democracy decide who gets screwed; we need to take control of the discourse, of the why and how, not just at the high level but at the low level, at the practical, guy-on-the-street level, so that when the time comes, most folks on the street are on our side. Because all the protocols on the planet won't help if ordinary folk don't buy it.

Now that we know that peak oil is now or about 10 minutes from now and that climate change is a disaster that is happening today, we need a massive change in policy — that is, we need millions of people in the US to come to a rapid consensus about what constitutes the American way of life and how we should change it to be compatible with our survival. We have no choice, because we have no time. But while Exxon and Shell are getting out their message — "We're working on new technologies, don't worry about the rising temps and the rolling blackouts" — we're not getting a unified message.

Ultimately, we are plagued by the basic fact that even many of the people offering alternatives don't believe that large-scale change is possible. But, of course it is. You only have to look at human history to see that we've tried just about every form of change that there could be — we've held all property in common (no, I'm not talking about communists, but early Christians); we've had unfettered markets and fettered ones; we've believed kings were divine and then overthrown the kings and instituted democracy; and then we've lied our way out of democracy. We've believed homosexuality was an abomination, and we've let gay people get married (nope, not talking about Oklahoma and Massachusetts, but the medieval Catholic Church vs. the early Catholic church, which had lovely rites for gay couples to marry with).

We've changed everything we think and how we live so many times that I can't count them all — we've had a billion revolutions, and we can have another. Yes, it would be radical, radical change. So what? So was the American revolution, the anti-colonialist movement, the worldwide women's movement. All of those things took unthinkable things and made them real.

And what makes the unthinkable politically normal? Whether you live in a true democracy or, as we do, in one with a thin candy coating of democracy over a dark chocolate totalitarian filling, ultimately, the people have the power to determine what is politically possible. When they care about something or decline to care, when they respond one way or another, they make political possibilities.

And how do people come to decide what political options they consider to be on the table? Hmmm…well, through the shaping of public opinion, once called agitprop or propaganda, like the posters you see at the beginning of each chapter. Most people see the world in fairly superficial terms, except for the things of great interest to them. You and I are no different. Most people don't do deep research — they want to know what everyone else knows. And if the answer is "Nothing" or "Exxon will fix it," that's what they will believe.

On the other hand, most people could be persuaded to care about food. It matters to them. We would have to persuade most people that growing food, getting food from new sources, and cooking and eating differently is necessary and that they should want to, for reasons that might vary from better food or less war to a more relaxed pace of life or patriotism or better sex. Without a single lie or misrepresentation, I could compellingly argue that all of the above are logical results of cutting our consumption, changing our economy and changing what the American way of life is.

Practical public relations, then, is the next big project for all of us. Thus far, people who have spoken have, for the most part, been scientists — very good, very smart, very wise scientists, but often a little boring. We cannot afford to be boring with the truth. The lies that are being told are not boring — they are very carefully crafted. Time to compete. Better yet, time to win.

Ultimately, everything is told in the form of stories. And good stories usually trump bad stories. The stories of fun writers trump the stories of not-so-fun writers. This is why James Kunstler writes for *Rolling Stone* and Matthew Simmons doesn't, even though both are very smart. The future that we face, and what we could accomplish, makes a superb story — all the elements of edge-of-your seat fiction, survival against all odds, courage, self-sacrifice, nobility, honor, strength, love, heroism. We need to tell it that well, well enough that the stories that corporations and governments sell seem flat and dull by comparison. We can do this.

Transitional Moments

It wasn't raining when Noah built the ark.
— HOWARD RUFF —

Are any of these strategies going to be enough to bring about change? Maybe not today. It is common to respond to plans for radical change by stating that it is impossible to get this or that change enacted. This, of course, is manifestly wrong. We have only to look at historical events to see that it is perfectly possible, for both good and ill, to radically change circumstances in a host of ways that looked completely impossible not very long before.

The question is, how does that happen? And is it possible to imagine that we could, in fact, change things and, for example, bring about a relocalized economy or 100 million farmers and 200 million new home cooks? Is all of this even feasible? More importantly, could it possibly happen before it has to? That is, we all know that we'd be a lot more secure if the transition to a sustainable agriculture happened a little before we were all out of food. Is that within the realm of possibility? We think so, but it requires a change in our perspective.

Now, generally speaking, radical change is enacted in one of two ways. The first is by revolution of one sort or another — a violent (not always warlike, but always violent) and deeply disruptive overthrow of what has gone before. In a very short time, the casting off of what has always seemed inviolable — slavery, colonialism, the divine right of kings — transforms the landscape.

The problem with revolutions is that the costs are extremely high. Even a non-violent revolution means that large chunks of the existing population in power are simply cast out and often come back to haunt you (Cuba's wealthy landowners, for example). Revolutions are vastly destructive, and anyone who simply isn't ready either adapts or is overrun.

The other option is culture change — the gradual transition of a society from old values to new ones. It starts as a small movement, growing gradually, until ideas permeate the culture. Most of those who resist are given the chance to acclimate, and they eventually come to accept, if not like, the dominant culture view. Eventually, cultural norms make it impossible even for those who espoused previous views to acknowledge them or to express them. Think, for example, of the American Civil Rights movement. Racism was once a cultural norm in the US, but now if you ask around, only about four people will admit to ever having expressed racist views.

The difficulty with this method is that it is far too slow for our present purposes — the major advances of the Civil Rights movement, for example, came over a period of 20 years. We simply don't have 20 years of marching and gradually changing cultural norms.

Now, it is necessarily the case that every movement contains elements of both of these — that is, the Civil Rights movement did include revolutionaries, and revolutions often begin with demonstrations. It is impossible to describe historical courses in the space we have here — but for the purposes of our discussion, we believe our generalities fit.

Are those our only choices — taking up arms or marching and singing? Both might work or they might not. We may well be able to transition our culture — given enough time or enough will and anger — to a society that can adapt to the new environmental norms. But we do not have multiple decades to make such a transition. James Hansen, for example, notes that most of our environmental changes will have to come rapidly over the next decade. And because almost all our changes take some major lead time, that means the period we have in which to change attitudes is very short.

As for revolution, it is simply too destructive, even were it not a bad idea for a host of other reasons. The human costs of radical, sudden transformation are resistance — lots of it. And lots of resistance means either the failure of overall goals or repressive responses that destroy what is created from the inside out.

So are there any other choices between the complete rupture of prior experience and the gradual transition to a new way of thinking? We think there is another option, but it depends upon being prepared to take hold of a moment and claim it as your own.

The third choice is something we're calling "threshold moments" — those points at which history intervenes and something that was unimaginable the day before becomes entirely possible. At those moments, it is possible to make a larger step forward than could previously have been imagined — people are poised for radical change and then it happens.

Such moments occur in two ways. The first is when events demand a particular change — such as in Cuba when the cutoff of oil supplies demanded a rapid-fire deindustrialization of agriculture and the transition to a new economy. In that case, cause and effect were direct. That is, the systemic response to food shortages was the institutionalization of a new food system. The bombing of Pearl Harbor also had a direct outcome; it led to a military response and US participation in World War II.

But there is another kind of threshold moment, one in which we perceive we are at a transitional moment and in which it is possible to imagine a number of possible responses, where what matters is that the populace is poised for response. Multiple, flexible, scaleable, successful responses are possible. Here is the moment at which it is possible to advance a new agenda — and possible to override other public agendas by laying claim to that moment and advancing one's agenda as a logical response.

The obvious example is 9/11. If you are not American, I think it is hard to understand how desperately Americans were casting around after 9/11 for some way to make their own response match up to the radical change in their world that they experienced. And there is nothing logically contiguous with the event about, say, invading Iraq or going shopping. That is, what was most notable about 9/11 was that people were willing to make massive changes, but were never asked. Unfortunately, no one made a strong, unified attempt to wrest the narrative of 9/11 away from the government. Individuals resisted the story we were being told, but theirs was not a fully formed attempt, say, to recast our response to 9/11 in terms of oil and energy and to use it as a major call for real and lasting change. Some attempts were made, but there weren't enough people working together.

Such threshold moments come around fairly often in history, and are likely to come more often as we enter what have been called "interesting times." In the past decade, we've had both a large-scale threshold moment, 9/11, and a smaller one in which some significant cultural changes might have been enacted, Hurricane Katrina.

Does that sound strange and unlikely? We think it is true that had Americans been told after 9/11, "We want you to go out and grow a victory garden and cut back on energy usage" the response would have been tremendous — it would absolutely have been possible to harness the anger and pain and frustration of those moments.

Even after Katrina, it would have been possible for a concerted narrative that ran the pictures from the superdome over and over again, saying "And if you want this never to happen again, you must..." Katrina would not have been nearly as effective as 9/11, but a great deal of change could have been made with it, regardless. And making use of the momentum of such events could have enabled us to be that much further along in the adaptation process before a moment comes at which a particular response is truly necessary.

Naomi Klein notes that this is precisely the claim of Milton Friedman's "Shock Doctrine," which says that at a moment of crisis you can sweep away the old and transform things utterly.[306] Up until now, such a system has been mostly used for ill, for market reforms that are utterly destructive to our public life. That is, while we have consistently underfunded our public school system here in the US for decades, Congress had no trouble coming up with *trillions* of dollars in bailouts to help bankers during the stock market failure in the fall of 2008. We know such events will be used and that those who make the most money by keeping us consumers will try their best to use them for selfish and greedy ends. It only makes sense for us to beat them to the punch and use them for good.

Moreover, as Klein points out, the *Shock Doctrine*'s essential message, overthrowing the past, is destructive to the ordinary people who are victims of a crisis. That is, those who live through such threshold moments in history and are directly affected by them want to cling to what they have of the past, to restore what they have lost. The *Shock Doctrine* model destroys, rather than reclaims the past.[307]

Here sustainability advocates have an enormous advantage in being able to claim the narrative from those who want to overthrow the past. Because ultimately our propositions are always tied to the past, to previous successful responses to hard times and disaster. We are tying our propositions to what people dreamed of in suburbia, the small slice of personal Eden that never was, and saying you *can* have that thing you once sought, as part of the promise of restoration. Those who claim that we are merely advocating a return to the past are missing the point — it is never possible to go back, but it is feasible to anchor the future in the past, to offer a narrative in which we do not have to give up what we value but can retain it and take it with us into a new and radically different world. *Sankofa* is an African word that means to go back and retrieve wisdom and use it to move forward. In it lies the key to our future.

To do this, we will have to prepare and watch for the next such threshold moment. The peak oil and climate change movements were simply not organized enough at 9/11, and we mishandled Hurricane Katrina. There were plenty of individual attempts to tie it into climate change, but there was no unified attempt to create a single narrative account of Katrina.

If we are to imagine sustainable, relocalized agriculture changing the world, if it is possible (and we do not say that it is, merely that we cannot fail to try), we must be absolutely prepared for the next threshold moment and to explain how it is about oil (and it will be, we won't have to lie), about the climate, and how it demands a particular response, not blowing up another country far away, but a change in us and our society.

We have no idea when that moment will come, and neither does anyone else. It could happen tonight and have us wake up in a changed world. Or it could leave us hanging for years, and the next such threshold we cross could be the transition into a real disaster, one in which our options are limited and we are struggling to feed ourselves. But regardless, because it is always possible to screw things up worse than necessary, sustainability advocates of every kind must be prepared to take one story and echo it back across media and blogs, to tell it and tell it and tell it, and teach others to demand a hopeful response, one that does not leave people behind.

It is worth remembering that none of this change works in a linear way. The process involves going along making small changes, and adding a few new recruits and tiny incremental alterations for a good long time. At first it seems like you aren't making any progress at all — that the change is so vast that the little moves can't get you there. But you must always keep in mind that you are doing the advance work for something that is likely to make great change, not slowly over time, but in a moment, and there's no telling when that moment might arrive. That is, we're doing what we can now, so that when the right time comes, we can do vastly more.

University of Michigan Professor Thomas Princen describes the way these kinds of advance plans help shift whole societies. He writes,

> I discovered in my earlier research on international conflict reso-
> lution that however intractable an intersocietal conflict might
> be, there are always people working on the solution. Pick the dir-
> est time in the Middle East conflict, for example, and you can find
> someone hidden away in a basement drawing up maps for the wa-
> ter and sewer lines, the lines that will connect the two societies and
> that must be built *when peace is reached*, as inconceivable as that is
> at the time. Someone else is sketching the constitution for the new
> country, the one that is also inconceivable at the time. And some-
> one else is outlining the terms of trade for the as yet unproduced
> goods that will traverse the two societies' border. We do not hear
> about these people because it is the nature of their work, includ-
> ing the dangers of their activities, that make it so. Surrounded by
> intense conflict, hatred and violence, these people appear the fool,
> idealists who do not know or cannot accept the reality of their so-
> cieties' situation. If they really knew that situation, others would
> say, they would be "realists"; they would concentrate their efforts
> on hard bargaining, economic incentives and military force. But,
> in practice, when a threshold is passed, when leaders shake hands
> or a jailed dissident is freed or families from two sides join together,
> everyone casts about for new ways to organize.
>
>   My prognosis, foolish and idealistic as it might seem to some, is
> that that threshold, that day of biophysical reckoning is near. And
> with it, serious questions about humans' patterns of material provi-
> sioning, their production, their consumption, their work and their
> play. Then, the premises of modern industrial societies — capital-
> ist, socialist, communist — will crumble.... Some will gravitate to
> the extremes — religious fundamentalism, survivalist homestead-
> ing, totalitarian government. Many, though, will seek paths that are

familiar, if not prevalent. Notions of moderation and prudence and stewardship will stand up, as if they were just waiting to be noticed, waiting for their time, even though, in many realms they were always there.[308]

Paul Hawken has called the sustainability movement the largest movement on the planet, and that may well be true. There are tens of millions of people drawing maps and growing gardens, and more every day.

So while we wait, we grow our Victory Gardens and build our movement and educate our neighbors and plan and wait. It won't be too long in coming. And then it will be time — time to pass the word and make our move, to try to take control of the story and say "This is what is needed as a response, to make us better." And everything we do in the meantime, every experiment we undertake, every working model we create, every program we start, every change we make in our homes and neighborhoods, gets us that much more ready to seize the day.

We've seen the movement to small-scale food production critiqued as essentially favoring those who were already blessed with natural resources, with gardens, and abandoning those who have the least. The accusation they make is that we are saying, "I've got mine, screw the rest of you." Or that we are abandoning politics to luxuriate in our gardens.

It is possible that this may be a fair critique of a few strains of the movement. But what we've seen is the contrary — thousands of people out there are reaching out to protect their own but also to extend their preserve to include some small piece of the world that belongs to them because they have claimed its preservation as their own work. They don't always own it. They don't always get to claim the rewards of tending a piece of land or a person. But they extend their wings above it no less. That is, I think most of us, once we begin to move past our immediate panic response to the changes in front of us, realize that we serve ourselves by serving others, that our communities matter as much as our homes and families, that there is no future in which we merely feed ourselves.

There is a degree to which creating a Nation of Farmers as a response to potential collapse focuses on personal responses. But instead of imagining the majority of this work as a kind of clutch-fisted self-preservation at the cost of the society, we see it far more often as a host of birds taking flight, men and women stretching their wings, reaching as far as they can to cover, with their preparations, as large an area of "my own" as they can.

When eagles do this, riding the rising warm air, it's called kettling. Some-times their wings can overstretch only their own territory and a small bit beyond. Others find ways to make faraway people and places part of "their own." But the net effect of enough outstretched wings is a vast, sheltered place, our own kettling effort, growing larger by the day. And in the shelter of those wings, hopes are nurtured, futures born, and the possibility of sur-viving, thriving, retaining and growing begins.

Quick, Change.

It doesn't work to leap a twenty-foot chasm in two ten-foot jumps.
— AMERICAN PROVERB —

In recent years the primary response to the US's rapidly rising rate of heart disease has been to perform bypass surgeries and angioplasties. Though these traumatic surgeries temporarily relieve the immediate problem, a clogged artery in the heart, they fail to address the cause of the disease, and many of these arterial clogs return within a months or years. The medi-cal profession has long known what we really need — a radical change in the way we live. We need a new lifestyle that doesn't lead to increased in-cidence of heart disease. However, most medical attention has focused on repair surgeries because of the apparent overwhelming odds against chang-ing human behavior. After all, research suggests that only 1 person in 10 will make a lasting behavioral change even when faced with the prospect of death as an incentive.[309] Even when such an obvious threshold moment arrives, many people choose not to change. Why is that? We think that it's not that such change is undesirable or even unachievable but rather that we have been trying to motivate change with failed methods.

In 1993 Dr. Dean Ornish, professor of medicine at the University of California at San Francisco and founder of the Preventative Medicine Re-search Institute, conducted an unconventional medical trial. Dr. Ornish set out to study the need for an unorthodox approach to helping patients make significant lifestyle changes. It seems that when doctors try to appeal to a patient who has a life-threatening illnesses with a straightforward, fact-based plea for change, they often fail. That is, even when people know they must change or face grave consequences, they often don't because of the way the change is framed. In his article "Change or Die" Alan Deutschman describes it this way. In the past,

[D]octors have been trying to motivate patients mainly with the fear of death....and that simply wasn't working. For a few weeks after a heart attack, patients were scared enough to do whatever their doctors said. But death was just too frightening to think about, so their denial would return, and they'd go back to their olds ways.[310]

This isn't hard to understand. The fear of death is strong enough to motivate short-term change but too scary to tap into on a daily basis. Making all our daily decisions based on avoiding death is just too heavy to handle over the long run. In Ornish's trial however, the emphasis was placed not on avoiding death, but on the rewards that would come from making change. It also focused not on slow, incremental, "baby steps" change but on radical change that took place quickly. This turned out to be hugely important because Dr. Ornish was able to deliver on the promises of pleasure in short order. In his words,

People who make moderate changes to their diets get the worst of both worlds: They feel deprived and hungry because they aren't eating everything they want, but they aren't making big enough changes to quickly see an improvement in how they feel, or in measurements such as weight, blood pressure, and cholesterol.[311]

The same is true of other lifestyle changes. Moderate changes involve the uncomfortable nature of doing things differently *and* not realizing pleasurable results quickly. However, the people involved in Dr. Ornish's study undertook rapid changes in their life that translated into a more pleasurable way of living very quickly. As incidence of chests pains decreased and as mobility increased, patients felt better and proved, as Dr. Ornish suggests, that "joy is a more powerful motivator that fear." With such rapid and tangible results, the changes in behavior lasted longer because those participating could feel a difference in quality of life and didn't want to go back to their old habits of living.

When people who have had so much chest pain that they can't work, or make love, or even walk across the street without intense suffering find that they are able to do all of those things without pain in only a few weeks, then they often say, "These are choices worth making."[312]

Although research suggests only 1 in 10 patients stick with changes for one year when doctors said "change or die," the results of Dr. Ornish's trial showed that 77 percent of his patients were sticking with their life-style changes after three years, even though the changes were more time consuming and required more effort. In addition to meeting with groups of other patients, they also received care from "dieticians, psychologists, nurses, and yoga and meditation instructors," not exactly a list of the specialists often thought responsible for successful treatment of patients with heart disease.[313]

This illustrates how drastic lifestyle changes have a greater chance of being adopted permanently when support systems are available. Though fear failed to bring about lasting change, pleasure coupled with social support networks to facilitate that change succeeded in motivating people to drastically reorient their lives and make real changes last.

This is important because any threshold moment we experience in the future is likely to be at least a little scary. Certainly 9/11 was terrifying. Katrina, even for those of us not left behind in New Orleans, was frightening because it forced us to imagine a major US city destroyed and abandoned and that the same could happen to us. If we're going to take advantage of future threshold moments though, we're not going to be able to make lasting change just by tapping into the fear such events cause in all of us. We're going to have to be ready with a story about all the pleasures of doing things differently.

We are suggesting that it's time to change the way we eat in this country and that US citizens should adopt a greater role in the ways we feed ourselves. This isn't a book simply saying that we must make these changes or we'll starve. Certainly the case has been made that these changes are of the life-and-death variety, but if you're at all buying into the idea that we have to eat differently and planning to help us create a Nation of Farmers, then we're all going to have to get beyond the gloom of describing what will happen if we don't change and get on with the work of showing how great this change will be.

Notice we don't suggest *telling* people how great the change will be but suggest *showing* them. Sure, we need more people talking about these ideas, but we specifically mention *showing* people because we think it will take that action to create real and lasting change. We're trying to create a world where growing more of our own food locally and cooking it ourselves is not an outlandish idea, and the facts themselves won't be enough.

Change will come in large part when we begin to reframe our thinking in radical ways and reinforce this change with pleasure — that is, by making ourselves happier by actually doing things differently.

Dr. Ornish's study is relevant because although we may be afraid of what will happen if we do not change, the driving force of change must be the pleasure we will gain from such a change — the message that change will create a better nation and will make us happier. If that's the case, even very radical change, as we are suggesting, is possible.

Googling Luffa

Learning is what most adults will do for a living in the 21st century.
— S. J. Perelman —

Even as we write this book hoping to spur a change in the way this nation thinks about how we eat, we understand it's unlikely that any grand new agricultural structure will emerge. That is, the likelihood of such a change happening in a coordinated, top-down manner is near zero — and how boring would that be anyway. From an historical standpoint, the Victory Garden movement itself might resemble such a coordinated response, what with all the posters and propaganda coming from our centralized government at the time. The truth is that the US government initially resisted the Victory Garden movement, which originally sprang from the personal needs of average Americans and spread virally. In fact the USDA didn't want to put the precious agricultural resources of seeds and fertilizer into the hands of ordinary citizens with little experience in growing food. Only after the movement proved itself successful and Eleanor Roosevelt planted her now most famous of Victory Gardens on the lawn of the White House did the government jump on the bandwagon. This is important beyond pointing out that governments are often slow to react to crises. This example suggests that when change comes, there often isn't any single person or group in charge. It is much more likely that people everywhere will adopt new ideas about how to feed themselves and their communities and that these changes will happen in varied ways and will be communicated through a horizontal network of information sharing. Or, as David Holmgren described it in an interview,

> One of the things I think a lot of the urban planners miss is that
> they assume that any future framework will be driven by public

policy and forward planning and design, whereas I think given the speed with which we are approaching this energy descent world and the paucity of any serious consideration planning or even awareness of it, we have to take as part of the equation that the adoptive strategies to it will not happen by some big sensible long range planning approach but will happen just organically, incrementally by people just doing things in response to immediate conditions.[314]

Does this mean then that there is no reason to fret, that the best strategy is to just wait and see how all of this shakes out? Of course not. In fact the opposite is true. We will need a system of coordination and cooperation for sharing resources and information, and we should get to work on it now. It will likely prove necessary that to quickly spread information about growing local, sustainable food in the wake of any threshold moment of the future we will need a flexible network for sharing inspirational examples of successful local-food initiatives already in place and the information needed to replicate such examples. We'll need a great way to get new farmers and gardeners started and successful as quickly as possible.

There is a wealth of information already available about how to garden and farm. As more people tap into this information and begin eating differently even more examples of creative adaptation will be created. As Clay Shirky puts it, "The way you explore complex ecosystems is you just try lots and lots and lots of things…" And as all of us explore growing and eating food differently, we're bound to experience a wide range of outcomes. It's important for everyone who succeeded to share those successes but also, "…you hope that everybody who fails fails informatively so that you can at least find a skull on a pikestaff near where you're going."[315] Sharing examples of what citizens can achieve is important to help establish a trend that transforms the way we consider what is normal in terms of how we eat. We're hoping for a responsive, systematic, cooperative network for sharing the changes of becoming a Nation of Farmers.

So what would such a network look like? In September of 2006 Aaron published a blog post about sponges, specifically *Luffa aegyptiaca*, the tropical vine species grown for its gourd-like fruits whose innards can be dried and used as a sponge. The story was roughly 15 sentences in length, included three pictures and took ten minutes to write.[316] It received tens of thousands of Internet hits over the next few days, more than 100,000 during the first week alone and still shows up as one of the most prominent search results for the term "Luffa" on Google. A large number of those who commented on the post and sent e-mails said that they had no idea that luffa (or "loofah") sponges were, in fact, made from the fruit of a plant. Most thought luffas came from the sea. Not so, and in fact it is possible in much of the US to grow your own luffa in your yard. As readers realized they too could grow their next shower sponge, you could almost feel the excitement over the Internet.

It wasn't that we were experiencing a national a shortage of shower sponges. It wasn't that the facts surrounding luffa sponges and their cultivation were carefully guarded secrets. Nor that the article itself was superbly written. It was an easy-to-read description of how anyone could grow her own sponge. Sure you can buy one for less the price of two cups of coffee, but that's not the point. The point was that the article, which years later still gets consistent traffic and generates regular comments and e-mails, is an example of well-shared, do-it-yourself information that sparked the curiosity of people from all over the world.

The process didn't involve paying for a class at the local community college or attending a weekend permaculture workshop, although both of those are worthwhile endeavors. Gaining enough information to begin growing luffa sponges required just turning on a computer and reading for about 60 seconds. A quick trip to an online seed store and the postal service could soon deliver the seeds of one's next shower sponge.

All it would take is for one person in your neighborhood to read this luffa article and successfully grow just one vine to maturity. Luffa vines often yield 20 or more fruits and each fruit yields hundreds of seeds. The result would be enough luffa seeds to outfit everyone in that neighborhood with seeds for the following year's sponge needs. Such is the bounty of the natural world. Recapturing local sponge self-sufficiency is only a few growing seasons away and it starts with sharing information in the form of an example.

The Internet does a superb job of this but it isn't the only way to share such information. In World War II, long before the advent of computers, the US government struggled to help people adapt to new rationing strategies. This wasn't merely altruistic. The success of the system depended on people's ability to participate — if people found rationing overly onerous, they would seek out black markets. The solution was neighbor-to-neighbor training, block captains and ties into existing social networks of women's groups and labor unions.

It's important to point out that the wonderful world of computers could be made instantly useless by a widespread electrical blackout, a virtual virus or large solar flares that could destroy large quantities of virtual knowledge in an instant. We rely on a technology that is at utterly dependant on cheap electricity transported over long distances, includes fragile, hard-to-build components and is subject to malicious attacks or government restrictions. How precarious this system seems when its weaknesses are examined, and therefore how shaky our situation appears concerning all the knowledge we have tied up on our computers. What would you lose if it all suddenly went away?

But as the example of the luffa shows, any idea adopted over the Internet or put into action through the efforts of other social networking systems can turn into an idea adopted and spread among neighbors. The Internet won't completely replace the kinds of conversations that take place while leaning on a fence post, nor will it replace buying or borrowing a good book, which is not subject to the concerns above. It is likely though that through books and conversations and classes and sharing over the Internet, this revolution in agriculture will get started by people everywhere doing and sharing what they're doing; what works and what needs work — as we get underway.

We want to emphasize that though it starts with sharing information about how to grow food, store it, share it and cook it, the best possible action for bringing about food security is to get at it. Grow food, work with your local farmers to create new systems, work for food security and economic justice. There are plenty of things we cannot know by studying and that will require the power of experience. And sharing these experiences can become the basis for the change in others. It's a pattern whereby individuals learn new information and put it to good use while gaining experience. By sharing their newfound experience they can help others gain the knowledge necessary to become more successful more quickly.

Recently a Massachusetts bakery decided to try to include their customers in the process of making bread by helping them to grow wheat. Writer Steve Balogh described how the bakery "started to distribute wheat berries (seeds) to customers so they could plant 100 sq. ft. plots of wheat in their yards. They plan a hand-scythed harvest in the summer.... [I]t will be interesting to see how productive the 10 × 10 plots of "front yard" wheat are."[317]

The bakery is enabling its customers to make a shift from being simply consumers to being producers as well, making their economic relationship run both ways by both buying bread and selling flour. How successful will such efforts be? That's a great question, but the exciting part is the width and breadth of the experimentation that's going on. The customers will gain experience concerning the growing and harvesting of wheat. The town will be able to gauge the amount of wheat it might be possible to produce in the front and back yards of average homes. No doubt problems like how to process the wheat will pop up and need to be solved. All of this is the process of taking information and turning it into experience, and this particular example shows just how creative we can get in making these changes.

When describing the program, the owner of this Massachusetts bakery said, "We have to be an agricultural state, because we eat." The owner understands the relationship between growing and eating and he's helping his community to envision a more local food economy. Coverage of this experiment on the Internet — news stories, audio interviews and blog posts about it — represents the transmission of experience to potentially millions of people, and the result could be a better understanding of how a local community might meet its needs for flour in the future. It might prove a phenomenal success, total failure or something in between, but regardless, it helps as an example of change and a reminder that if we're going to be successful at changing the way we eat in this country we must simultaneously make changes and share our changes with others. It well demonstrates the makings of an interwoven web of participation in a new type of agriculture as experience grows out of information and as those experiences are shared with others.

Practical Suggestions for Getting 100 Million New Farmers

It is not necessary to change. Survival is not mandatory.
— W. EDWARDS DEMING —

So we've convinced you. We must, we should and we will recreate agriculture in the US, and you're ready to help; you're ready to take your place as one of the 100 million new farmers needed in this country, or you live elsewhere and want to participate too. This obviously means you've got to get outside and get started in the garden. But as we've mentioned above, it's important not only that we get out in the garden but that we share this change at every step along the way so that we can band together and make these changes stick. We're going to need some help.

For just a moment, before you run out the door hoe in hand, let's talk about how much more fun and exciting this will be if we can convince other people to join us. Of course we suggest that when you finish this book a few pages from now that you give it to a friend. However, there are other ways we think will be helpful in getting this movement off to a rolling start. Here are ten ways to share the Agrarian Revolution.

We need video — lots of it. There is no question that that's how most of the world is accustomed to seeing things. We need to persuade people that what we are offering is better, prettier, nicer, cleaner, healthier, happier, more loving. We need video. I don't mean YouTube video of people sitting in darkened rooms talking about peak oil and climate change, but agitprop video — inspiring music, beautiful images of what can be. People immediately think that giving up their comforts means living in a degraded, filthy hell. We've got to show them that isn't true, and let them envision this as a better life.

We need funny videos — anyone who saw the Massachusetts Gubernatorial "Head Up Their Asses" campaign ad in 2006 knows that there is a lot of opportunity for good, smart, funny video out there.

And there's a lot of material out there for beautiful videos. One of the things we are selling is a better life. We need to show pictures, still and moving, of people living better, being healthier, being happier. Sell it like a patent medicine, with testimony and pictures of what can be. If we don't give people a "Morning in America" image of their own, of little Johnny walking down the street to pick up his eggs and fruit at his neighbor's garden and skipping home, people will be vulnerable to whatever stupid lies they are told that give them that dream. Let's beat them to it.

We need to make fun of the stupid people and bad ideas. When Exxon puts out an ad saying that they are our clean-air experts, deface it! Make fun of it. When government says that ethanol will save us, we need to remix the lie and add nasty commentary. Every time they lie, we show them and we call them liars to their faces. Throw homemade pies at them. Paint horns on them. Draw cartoons. We need a whole group of people devoted to mocking the lies being told to us — not just a rational debunking, or blog sarcasm, but dead blunt, dry, funny mocking of the liars.

We need famous people. People trust familiar faces. Get 'em moving. If Willie Nelson or Ed Begley, Jr. or Florence Henderson cares about climate change, get them into some ads, dammit. Noble and brilliant as they are, Sir David King and Peter Rosset aren't going to get the masses going in the same way. If we can't get famous people, get impersonators — they have to be cheaper. Make it funny — say "We believe the US government has Elvis in a Cuban Gulag. Here is an Elvis impersonator to tell you just how to grow peas."

Or get people who just look reassuring. We've seen enough aging hippies at the conferences to know there must be one out there who could grow a mustache and look like Wilford Brimley, and there have to be 50 who look like Willie or John Mellencamp or someone. If you make music, write a song — not a bleak song of grief but one about how great it is to grow your garden and hang your laundry on the clothesline. The rest of us will save up cash to hire the Dixie Chicks, but make your music video and put it out there. And dammit, grow those mustaches. David Crosby's is good.

We need to get better about using the Net to create buzz. We need more gardens on Myspace and Facebook. We need to make it clear that all the cool kids care about food. Peer pressure is good (this time). And remember the stupid, stupid, *Snakes on a Plane* movie? Without the Internet it would have been merely a contribution to a movie studio's annual tax writeoff. Come up with a slogan. Do something funny. We can't afford to be boring.

In 2006, at the conference we wrote about in Chapter 1, Sharon suggested that the famous men of peak oil should all pose naked for a calendar "The Men of Peak Oil." She was joking of course, but now she's threatening. If you people out there who read this book don't get to work and come up with something funnier and smarter (how hard could that be?) she's going to hunt down every famous peak oil and climate change researcher on the earth and make them pose naked. So if you wish to avert the tragedy of seeing these pasty men, for the love of George Washington Carver, do something funny to get people growing, make it public, and send it round the Internet.

We need good fiction. One of the ways that people envision the future is through books. We've got some sci fi out there, and there are a few good pieces on the Net, but we need our own Michael Crichton. We've got Barbara Kingsolver and Jim Kunstler already, but let's get some more! Write your damned novels, people. Tell people what the future will look like, but most of all, what it *could* look like. No one will start dreaming to get to *Mad Max* — they want *Little House on the Prairie*. And we should give it to them — what was Laura Ingalls Wilder but a reminder that life was not hell without all the stuff we have?

We need to sell it to children and to adults who read children's books. This can't just be about high culture. And we need genre fiction — romance, Christian, children's books. Again, all of this is how you tell the story folks. Yes, we need the apocalyptic fiction, to tell us what will happen if we don't, but more than that, we need an alternative to the end of the world.

We need to start using all the good iconography we already have on our side. Speaking of *Little House on the Prairie* — that's ours. Someone dust off Melissa Gilbert and get her a dress! So is Norman Rockwell and the World War II Victory Garden material. Ben Franklin and Thomas Jefferson are ours if we want them — we are recreating the Nation of Farmers that the founding fathers dreamed of. We get to use them whenever we want.

We have the best music! Benny Goodman, Tom Waits, the Dixie Chicks, Willie Nelson, Bob Dylan, Bruce Springsteen, the Working Man's Blues!

We have our agrarian past, cute lambs, sexy dairy maids, half naked farmers stripped to the (sexy) waist, we have agricultural festivals and down-home music, we have the country, and nostalgia, delicious home-grown food, Mom, apple pie, happy kids running in fields, cute baby ducks — we have all the good images. They have smokestacks and George Bush's face and trucks — but we've got the real cowboys. If we can't beat them with what we've got, we're not trying. But we have to take the iconography and make it ours.

We need sex. Sex sells. Use it. Okay, no one wants to see naked engineers, we all know that, but there are a lot of hot farmers and gardeners out there in the movement. Most of what we are asking people to do is get sensuous — that is, get down in the warm soil, eat ripe fresh vegetables, spend more time in nature and less time at the mall. In the sensual delights we are offering there is no reason, while we show the young woman cheerfully hanging her laundry while the song "Suds in the Bucket" plays in the background, that them who want to shouldn't be looking at her behind.

In order not to seem like sexist pigs, we note that we're all for seeing lots of tight male behinds hanging laundry and picking tomatoes as well.

And not just sex — drugs and rock 'n roll are good too! The energy party may be giving out, but people parties run on laughter, dance, music and beer. No wonder we aren't filling the stands — more beer, more dancing, more laughter, more music, more waggling of behinds! There's a lot of bending in a garden — take advantage.

We need to invite more people into the club. People who feel alienated from the peak oil movement listen to us because we're not 55-year-old engineers. Now let us be fair — most of those 55-year-old scientists know more about climate change, peak energy and agronomy than either of us ever will, but there's something about talking to your approximate peers, or at least your sex.

We need a lot more people writing and talking and singing and making noise who don't look like your average petroleum geologist or climate scientist. We need more non-white people and young people; we need Christians to talk to religious Christians and moms to talk to moms and people taking and sharing across national borders. And we need to put a lot more of those people's *faces* out there as the image of the New Home Front — we need people to realize that farms can happen anywhere, and the best ones happen where you are, in your neighborhood.

Older white scientists can do it too, even if we've got your demographic covered — we're only making fun because we know you'll forgive us! We need to talk in ways that other people can hear us; we need to go out looking for new, interesting voices. And then shove them up on the stage.

We need to get out the coleslaw! Throw a really good party — not just the music and dancing kind but a backyard barbecue with lots of local beer to get things flowing. We need this to come to our neighborhoods — we need to get the idea that these are immediate, imminent and serious issues that we can fix by working together. The first step to working together is to get past the barriers that keep us apart, get our neighbors into our lives and us into theirs. The first step is to sit down and eat together — as often as we can manage.

So invite the weird neighbors over for a beer. Maybe you hate each other's politics and your kids don't get along. That's okay — you don't have to love each other to work together. The guy up the road who mows his lawn in a Speedo and does karaoke to Ted Nugent songs at one in the morning may not be the person I dreamed of forming my perfect community with, but who cares? He needs to eat too. He has a sunny front yard! And he cares about the future too and has kids he loves. Find that common ground — the rising food prices or the health issues in the neighborhood. It doesn't matter where you live — some of your neighbors are always going to be assholes. But they are your assholes now, and you need each other.

We need to connect the dots. Peak oil and climate change are justice movements. If you want to get regular folk out into the street, angry and outraged, we need to connect the dots between the energy we burn and the people it hurts. We need to point to the hungry people and the displaced people and make it clear that justice for those people is what matters here. Every successful people's movement has, at its root, been about justice. We need to show people how peak oil and climate change hurt them — and just *who* is doing the hurting. We need to point fingers at the folks who have blown this off and show everyday people who will suffer and who profits. We need to make this very clear — *this is about who eats, who drinks, who lives and who dies.*

We will never get people to the streets and to congress based on a movement that is about oil — we will only ever get them there if we draw the connection between *justice* and these issues. And we don't have to tell a single lie for that. We need to take our lessons from the food crisis and the civil rights movement. We need to teach the people who are most vulnerable — the poor, women, the elderly and non-white people — just how vulnerable they are about to be and make them angry enough to take to the streets demanding justice. We need to connect the dots — over and over and over as clearly as possible — that peak oil and climate change mean poverty and suffering, hunger and diminished opportunity. And we need to do that fast. Enough with depletion rates. Yes, they matter; yes, they are important. But what people need to know is this — this is a human rights exercise. Our right to live, our right to a bright future and our right to feed our children are not negotiable.

If any of this seems revelatory to you, if it has never before occurred to you that poor black women in Kenya or New Orleans are like you and are the face of your future and your potential allies, it is time to wake up! If you've never thought of peasant farmers and people who are shot for trying to unionize in Ecuador as your brethren, people whose rights and needs should be a part of your focus, it is time to wake up. If you don't see the problem of immigration and the loss of manufacturing jobs for poor white people in the south as linked to each other and to you, wake up. If you don't recognize that justice for everyone means justice for you, it is time to *wake up!*

There are a lot more regular people than there are rich folks, politicians and corporate powers. So of course they want us to be balkanized, divided, debating. They want feminists to see poor southern white men as their enemy, instead of allies and victims of corporate greed. They want peak oil tarred as something only for "liberals," and climate change advocates to be "hippie environmentalists." They want churches to fight over whether or not to deal with climate change and Jews and Muslims to wonder if they have any common ground at all. Guess what — we do! And it is the simplest common ground in history. We want to live, to go on, to prosper, to have enough, to live in a just society, to have peace, and hope for the future. That depends on unity. Getting over our differences and finding common ground will be hard work. The only reason to do it is because it is so necessary.

Those in power are terrified of ordinary people and their anger, their fear and their passion for justice. Of course they want as many ordinary people as possible fighting over things like gay marriage and Don Imus. Of course they don't care if poor people die or go hungry — hungry people are too weak to fight, and dead people can't call out for justice. This is about rallying around food. That we can all work together and eat the fruits of our labor should be our rallying call.

Sooner or later we're all going to wake up and notice, because the future will be slapping us in the face. We vote sooner. We vote now. We vote today. We vote we scare the hell out of them, and save the world.

Paul and Silas Bound in Jail

*Two people can keep each other
sane, can give support, conviction,
love, massage, hope, sex.
Three people are a delegation,
a committee, a wedge. With four
you can play bridge and start
an organization. With six you can rent a whole house,*

eat pie for dinner with no
seconds, and hold a fund raising party.
A dozen make a demonstration. A hundred fill a hall.
A thousand have solidarity and your own newsletter;
ten thousand, power and your own paper;
a hundred thousand, your own media;
ten million, your own country.

It goes on one at a time,
it starts when you care
to act, it starts when you do
it again after they said no,
it starts when you say We
and know who you mean, and each
day you mean one more.
— Marge Piercy —

All of the chapter titles in this book come from songs we like, songs that have something to do with the way we're thinking. But the last chapter's title was chosen because "Keep your hand on the Plow" was the original title of the African-American spiritual that became "Eyes on the Prize." We thought it was worth remembering that one of the most iconic songs of the Civil Rights movement began, in fact, with agricultural metaphors. That is, justice was conceived not just as keeping watch on what we're seeking but on the physical labor of growing food. Because, of course, "who eats" is a question of justice and freedom.

From the question of whether we can feed ourselves, we're back again to what kind of world we're trying to feed — back to the old question of abolition and freedom. We're back to justice. Or maybe we never left. Because as we've been saying from the beginning, it isn't about how much food there is, it is about how we allocate it. And ultimately the question of allocation comes down to the simplest issues — what do we want in the future? Do we have the strength to make it happen?

We don't know the answer — and we won't deny that the future is a troubling place. We don't know if we can avoid hunger in the future, if our children will have any future at all — and that is frightening. We're driven by the hungry people in the world, but we don't even know, some days, if we are the ones to help them. And I suspect that's true of you as well.

A lot of us are in the same boat — we spent our lives preparing for a different world and life than the one we're faced with. And now we know this stuff about peak oil and climate change and the world, and we have to do something. But how can we? How can *we* do something when we're not trained or prepared or ready? When we're not activists or leaders by nature? When we have fears and doubts and weaknesses?

There's so very much work that needs to be done that it can get overwhelming. How do we narrow things down? None of us can do it all, so how do we know what to do, when to step up? How do we put ourselves forward into places we aren't fully prepared to go, into roles we aren't wholly ready for?

Writer Annie Lamott has said, "one of the immutable laws of being human is that the people who show up are the right people." Could this possibly be true? That is, could it be true that we somehow, trusting our intuitions and our guts, know what our proper work is, know better how to fix things than great minds or markets? None of us can do everything we need to in the world. Trying to do so will drive us mad. But all of us can find a piece of the project, a limited part of what desperately needs to be done, can trust the part of us that says "this is my proper work in the world" and pick that up and go on with it.

We don't know what your work is — but maybe there's more. Maybe your job is to start a small, local seed company that will serve your area, or to help families in need in your spare time. Maybe your work is to spread the word about climate change to your friends and family, or to write position papers for a senator. Maybe your work is a very small piece of everything — to tend this patch of ground, to care for these particular people who need you. Maybe your work is much larger — to transmit this idea or make that policy change. Maybe your work will change over time — maybe right now you are head down in a medical crisis or new fatherhood or school, and your work is to get yourself to a place where you can take on a little more later — and then you'll find what else there is. Or maybe you are moving from one kind of work to another to match your interests or your needs. Some of us will have a single immutable project, others a host of them, or a shifting pattern of pies we put our fingers in.

But, I would argue, all of us are the right people for some work. All of us have the obligation to show up, to the extent of our abilities, to stretch ourselves a little, to take on a piece of this, and maybe just a little more than we can possibly achieve. We often struggle with the questions of whether we know enough, are smart enough, are wise enough to do this work.

So, except that most of us need to reconnect with food, we can't tell you what you particularly should take on. We can only tell you this: the work is out there, and it is as much as all of us can do. And the right people are the ones, illuminated by consent, who take on a project and a vision of the future, claim it as their own and go forward, in all their limitations.

If you feel inadequate to the job, welcome to the club! If you feel you don't know enough, have enough strength or courage or skill, we're glad to meet you — we're in the same boat. If you think that this is a job for someone with authority, we're going to tell you our secret. The week before Sharon was a farmer, she was a grad student with a seed and some dirt she had no idea what to do with. The day before Aaron was an environmental writer he was a father trying to figure out how to keep the people he loved secure.

The transition from inadequacy to authority is only this — one more day of trying, one more experiment, one person who knows even less than you do, the willingness to try, at least, to help them, and the illumination of consent.

Are there enough of us? No, probably not yet, and the growth is slow. But if you are going to take this book, put your hand on the plow and grow something, then today we're one person richer.

How many gardeners are there in your community? Are there 100 in your city if you include everyone who plants some flowers or plays in the dirt? I know, most of them don't grow vegetables, and it can feel isolated. But everyone who plants something has at least touched the dirt, and there's a bond and a hope. What if you could get 20 people in your small town, 100 in your city? Fifty is enough to start a committee, to approach the town council, and maybe even to win new zoning laws about front yard gardens. One hundred is more people than started the American Revolution. What could you do with a hundred people?

Could this book reach 500 people who never grew food before? We think that Sharon and Aaron together have probably started that many gardens already. Could we get another 500 going, and bring together 1,000 new farmers, all across the country? There were fewer than 1,000 people who began the great Salt March across India that helped bring about freedom from colonialism. And what if those 1,000 new farmers each gave seeds and help to a few of their neighbors?

Five thousand people all over the US who grow their own food and buy sustainably would be a constituency, a PAC, a political power, a voice of quiet joy and anger. Five thousand people alone could save 25,000 barrels of oil from being burned, could grow 20,000 pounds of food annually in their gardens. Less than 5,000 people changed the 2000 US elections. Five thousand people can turn their cities into gardens

When 10,000 voices speak, you cannot help but hear. When 10,000 people stand up and say "We did it and you can too!" those who would rather not hear us have to pay attention. Ten thousand people have changed the course of history hundreds of times. Ten thousand people can make our biggest cities bloom, and the dollars of 10,000 people out of the hands of agribusiness would cause some bankruptcies.

Fifty thousand can change the government. One hundred thousand can change the world. One person can change the world if it is the right one — just not all alone. We don't know how many people it will take before our kids and your kids and everyone's kids get to live in a world with enough water and reasonable justice — but getting to that number starts with one and only goes up until we reach it.

The truth is that the civil rights movement seemed impossible — until it wasn't anymore. Overthrowing the colonial British in India seemed impossible — until it wasn't anymore. Defeating fascism seemed impossible — until it wasn't anymore. Making the US a country seemed impossible — until it wasn't anymore.

We don't know if we'll succeed. But the only way we will is the same way it happened every other time — long nights of talk and long days of hard work, struggle and strife, believing and falling momentarily into hopelessness, picking each other up and coming back to hope, and small numbers of people trying, and trying, and seeming to fail, and then succeeding. The only hope is to keep our eyes on the prize and our hands on the plow, and start the changes now.

An Interview with Bill McKibben: Spring 2008

What can we say about Bill McKibben? Since he wrote *The End of Nature* he has been a world leader in addressing ecological loss and climate change. His latest book, *Deep Economy*, explores the economic implications of a sustainable life. Like almost all ecological writers, we can't possibly express our debt to his work, and we feel enormously lucky that he took the time to talk to us.

ANOF: You spent an entire winter eating locally in your Vermont valley. Can you describe what you found most rewarding about this exercise in limiting your diet geographically? What would you describe as the most surprising part of that experiment? Most frustrating?

BILL: Most frustrating: no oats. (I finally cheated and found a small grower just across the border in Quebec. Apparently almost all oats now come from a mill somewhere in Saskatchewan.) Most rewarding: the large number of farmers that I met over the course of the winter and the deepening sense of the economic and social geography of my community. Most surprising: What a good spur it is to one's cooking to have a limited list of ingredients. It's like writing sonnets instead of free verse.

ANOF: So it changed the way you cook. What was that change like?

BILL: Much more creative. I was kicked out of my usual roster of fifteen or twenty dishes. I got to think more about how tastes go together and how the envelope might be pushed. And I learned everything that was possible to do with maple syrup.

ANOF: Lots of people are talking about models that describe geographic boundaries of eating. The 100 Mile Diet is one such model. How might we reshape this model to focus more directly on food production closer to home?

BILL: I just think eat from your neighborhood, the people who you can count on and who might count on you.

ANOF: It seems that there are two related problems simultaneously facing people who eat: the fossil fuel energy used to grow food is becoming less available and therefore more economically expensive, and using fossil fuel energy to grow food is, in part, causing our global climate to change and is therefore ecologically expensive. Is food the intersection of these issues? And could it be a catalyst for larger social change?

BILL: You got it on all counts. Food is the place where the limits on this planet are finally starting to pinch, and how we respond will determine how the century goes — either creatively or defensively.

ANOF: Where can we look for tangible examples to foster optimism?

BILL: Check out the farmers' market in Madison, Wisconsin, or the Intervale in Burlington; check out Kerala in India. There are a growing list of exceptions to the industrial rule.

—— RECIPES ——

Syrup Snow   *by Bill McKibben*

Directions
1. Tap a maple tree overnight.
2. Boil the sap for a number of hours.
3. Sprinkle the result on fresh snow.
4. Enjoy.

Mama Ruth's Chicken   *by Ruth Harwell & Margaret Irvin*

Ingredients
- 2 tbsp butter
- 1 cup milk
- 2 tbsp chopped mushrooms
- 4 tbsp flour
- 8 oz sour cream
- 1 tbsp grated onion
- One half chicken cooked, deboned and cut into pieces
- salt and pepper

Topping
- 1 sleeve Ritz Crackers (or bread crumbs)
- ½ cup butter
- 2 tbsp poppy seeds

Directions
1. Make a white sauce using the milk, flour and butter. Add the chicken, mushrooms, grated onion and sour cream. Salt and pepper to taste. For those who like stronger flavoring add 1 tsp of Worcestershire sauce or hot sauce.
2. Place in 2-quart casserole dish.
3. Mix the bread crumbs, butter, poppy seeds and drizzle over the dish.
4. Bake at 350 degrees for 30 minutes or until bubbly.

Wild Fennel and Dandelion "Risotto"   *by Dani Sevilla*

This can be cooked in an oven of any type (including solar) or over a flame. I live alongside a creek where a good old forage gives me all the vegetables for this meal. All I need is a bit of fat and some form of grain. Not only is it tasty but the golden flowers make it beautiful as well — food for the body and the soul.

Ingredients
- 3 cups sliced wild fennel bulb (cultivated would do just fine too)
- 2 tbsp fat (oil, butter, whatever fat you have is fine)
- 1½ cups grain, soaked overnight (this works with quinoa, pearl barley or rice; pearl barley is my favorite)
- 1 cup dandelion flowers (gather leaves as well for a side salad)
- 3 cups water

Directions
1. Place fennel in pan or baking dish and scatter fat over the top. Slowly cook until starting to brown. Add the grain and half the water and cook gently, stirring occasionally if cooking over a flame. Test after about 30 minutes, add more water as required. When grain is cooked, remove from heat and stir in dandelion flowers. Serve.
2. Dandelion greens can be served on the side as a salad, stir fried or cooked with a little bit of pork.

Recipe Index

A List of Useful Resources

Peak Oil and Climate Change

Darley, Julian. *High Noon for Natural Gas: The New Energy Crisis.* Chelsea Green, 2004.

Heinberg, Richard. *The Party's Over: Oil, War and the Fate of Industrial Societies.* New Society, 2003.

Heinberg, Richard. *Peak Everything: Waking Up to the Century of Declines.* New Society Publishers, 2007.

Kolbert, Elizabeth. *Field Notes from a Catastrophe: Man, Nature and Climate Change.* Bloomsbury, 2006.

Kunstler, James Howard. *The Long Emergency: Surviving the Converging Catastrophes of the Twenty-First Century.* Atlantic Monthly Press, 2005.

Monbiot, George. *Heat: How To Stop the Planet from Burning.* Allen Lane, 2007.

Romm, Joseph. *Hell and High Water and What We Should Do*, William Morrow, 2007.

Our Food System

Lappé, Francis Moore, Joseph Collins, Peter Rosset and Luis Esparza. *World Hunger: Twelve Myths.* Grove Press, 1998.

Menzel, Peter, and Faith D'Aluisio. *Hungry Planet: What the World Eats.* Material World Books and Ten Speed Press, 2006.

Patel, Raj. *Stuffed and Starved*, Melville House Books, 2007.

Pfeiffer, Dale Allen. *Eating Fossil Fuels.* New Society Publishers, 2006.

Pollan, Michael. *The Omnivore's Dilemma: A Natural History of Four Meals.* Penguin Press, 2006.

Salatin, Joel. *Everything I Want to Do Is Illegal: War Stories from the Local Food Front.* Polyface Inc., 2007.

Salatin, Joel. *You Can Farm: The Entrepreneur's Guide to Start and Succeed in a Farming Enterprise.* Polyface Inc., 1998.

Shiva, Vandana. *Soil not Oil.* Southend Press, 2008.

Shiva, Vandana. *Stolen Harvest: The Hijacking of the Global Food Supply.* South End Press, 2000.

Local Food Systems

Flores, H. C. *Food Not Lawns: How to Turn Your Yard Into a Garden and Your Neighborhood into a Community.* Chelsea Green, 2006.

Gussow, Joan Dye. *This Organic Life: Confessions of a Suburban Homesteader.* Chelsea Green Publishing Company, 2001

Kingsolver, Barbara. *Animal, Vegetable, Miracle: A Year of Food Life.* Harper Collins, 2007.

Klindienst, Patricia. *The Earth Knows My Name: Food, Culture, and Sustainability in the Gardens of Ethnic Americans.* Beacon Press, 2006

Nabhan, Gary. *Coming Home to Eat.* WW Norton, 2002.

Norberg-Hodge, Helena. *Bringing the Food Economy Home.* Zed Books, 2002.

Smith, Alisa, and J. B. MacKinnon. *Plenty: One Man, One Woman and a Raucous Year of Eating Locally*. Harmony Books, 2007.

Gardening and Small-Scale Farming
Ashworth, Suzanne. *Seed to Seed*. Seed Saver's Exchange, 1991.
Bartholomew, Mel. *Square Foot Gardening*. Rodale Press, 1981.
Coleman, Eliot. *The Four Season Harvest: Organic Vegetables From Your Home Garden All Year Long*. Chelsea Green, 1999.
Deppe, Carol. *Breed Your Own Vegetable Varieties: The Gardener's and Farmer's Guide to Plant Breeding and Seed Saving*. Chelsea Green Publishing, 2000.
Duhon, David. *One Circle: How to Grow a Complete Diet in Less than 1000 Square Feet*. Ecology Action Publications, 1985.
Hartung, Tammi. *Growing 101 Herbs that Heal*. Storey Books. 2000.
Jeavons, John. *How to Grow More Vegetables: And Fruits, Nuts, Berries, Grains, and Other Crops Than You Ever Thought Possible on Less Land Than You Can Imagine*. Ten Speed Press, 2002.
Lanza, Patricia. *Lasagna Gardening: A New Layering System for Bountiful Gardens: No Digging, No Tilling, No Weeding, No Kidding!* Rodale Books, 1998.
Logsdon, Gene. *Organic Orcharding: A Grove of Trees to Live in*. Rodale Press, 1981.
Logsdon, Gene. *Small-Scale Grain Raising*. Rodale Press, 1977.
Lovejoy, Sharon. *Roots, Shoots, Buckets and Boots*. Workman Publishing, 1999.
McClure, Susan. *Rodale's Successful Organic Gardening: Fruits and Berries*. Rodale Press, 1996.
McGee, Rose Marie Nichols, and Maggie Stuckey. *The Bountiful Container*. Workman Publishing, 2002.
Reich, Lee. *Weedless Gardening*. Workman Publishing, 2001.
Smith, Edward C. *Incredible Vegetables from Self-Watering Containers*. Storey Publishing, 2006.
Solomon, Steve. *Gardening When it Counts: Growing Food in Hard Times*. New Society Publishers, 2006.

Permaculture, Design, Landscaping
Creasy, Rosalind. *The Complete Book of Edible Landscaping*. Sierra Club Books, 1982.
Fukuoka, Mansanobu. *The One-Straw Revolution*. Rodale Press, 1978.
Hemenway, Toby. *Gaia's Garden*. Chelsea Green, 2000.
Holmgren, David. *Permaculture: Principles and Pathways Beyond Sustainability*. Holmgren Design Services, 2002.
Mollison, Bill. *The Permaculture Design Manual*. Tagari Publications, 1988.
Stamets, Paul. *Mycellium Running*, Ten Speed Press, 2005.
Toensmeier, Eric. *Perennial Vegetables*. Chelsea Green, 2007.

Water and Outputs/Inputs
Campbell, Stu. *Home Water Supply: How to Find, Filter, Store and Conserve It*. Storey Books, 1993.
Jenkins, J. C. *The Humanure Handbook: A Guide to Composting Human Manure*. Jenkins Publishing, 1994.

Lechner, Norbert. *Heating, Cooling, & Lighting: Design Methods for Architects.* John Miley & Sons, 1991.

Olkowski, Helga, Bill Olkowski, Tom Javits and the Farallones Institute Staff. *The Integral Urban House: Self-Reliant Living in the City.* Sierra Club Books, 1979.

Steinfeld, Carol. *Liquid Gold: The Lore and Logic of Using Urine to Grow Plants.* Eco-Waters, 2004.

Vittori, Gail, and Wendy Price. *Texas Guide to Rainwater Harvesting,* Texas Water Development Board in Cooperation with the Center for Maximum Potential Building Systems, 1997.

Gathering

Brill, Steve with Evelyn Dean. *Identifying and Harvesting Edible and Medicinal Plants in Wild (and Not So Wild) Places.* HarperCollins Publishers, 1994.

Gibbons, Euell. *Stalking the Wild Asparagus.* Alan C. Hood & Company, 1962.

Medsger, Oliver Perry. *Edible Wild Plants.* Collier Books, 1972.

Starting Seeds

Bubel, Nancy. *The New Seed-Starters Handbook.* Rodale Press, 1988.

Young, James A., and Cheryl G. Young. *Collecting, Processing and Germinating Seeds of Wildland Plants.* Timber Press, 1986.

Cookbooks

Dragonwagon, Crescent. *The Soup and Bread Cookbook.* Viking/Allen Lane, 1989.

Lewis, Edna. *The Taste of Country Cooking.* Knopf, 1976.

Longacre, Doris Janzen. *More With Less Cookbook.* Herald Press, 2000.

Robertson, Laurel. *The Laurel's Kitchen Bread Book.* Random House, 1984.

Wolfert, Paula. *Mediterranean Grains and Greens.* William Morrow Cookbooks, 1998.

Yin Fei Lo, Eileen. *From the Earth: Chinese Vegetarian Cooking.* MacMillan, 1995.

The Low Energy Life

Bates, Albert. *The Post-Petroleum Survival Guide and Cookbook: Recipes for Changing Times.* New Society Publishers, 2006.

Emery, Carla. *The Encyclopedia of Country Living: An Old Fashioned Recipe Book.* Sasquatch Books, 2003.

Hopkins, Rob. *The Transition Handbook: From Oil Dependency to Local Resilience.* Green Books, 2008.

Langer, Richard W. *Grow It.* Saturday Review Press, 1972.

Logsdon, Gene. *The Contrary Farmer.* Chelsea Green, 1999.

Warde, Jon, Ed. The *Backyard Builder: Over 150 Projects for Your Garden, Home and Yard.* Random House, 1994.

Robinson, Ed and Carolyn. *The "Have-More" Plan.* Storey Books, 1983.

Websites

A Nation of Farmers: anationoffarmers.com

   The website dedicated to this book and its call for 100 million new farmers and 200 million new cooks!

Better Times: bettertimesinfo.org
    An Almanac of Useful Information
Black Farmers and Agriculturalists Association: bfaa-us.org/
    Among other things powerful advocates for farm subsidy justice.
Community Solutions: communitysolution.org/
    An organization "focused on the values and virtues of small community living."
Cooperative State Research, Education and Extension Service: csrees.usda.gov/Extension/
    Dedicated to helping people connect with their local cooperative extension office.
Energy Bulletin: energybulletin.net
    The clearinghouse for information related to energy.
Global Public Media: globalpublicmedia.com/
    Public Service Broadcasting for a Post Carbon World
Hen and Harvest: henandharvest.com/
    Dedicated to supporting sustainable agriculture.
immag: immag.org/
    Refugee and immigrant agricultural support program.
National Sustainable Agricultural Information Service: attra.org
    The name tells the story- tons of great information.
Path to Freedom: pathtofreedom.com
    One family's amazing journey in an effort to become more self sufficient.
Rodale Institute: rodaleinstitute.org/
    A leader in the arena of sustainable agriculture since the 1940s.
The Riot for Austerity: riot4austerity.org
    Official website of a movement to reduce personal emissions by 90%, founded by Sharon and Miranda Edel.
Seed Savers Exchange: seedsavers.org/
    The major seed saving organization in the US.
The Farm: thefarm.org/
    One of the oldest intentional communities in the US.
The Oil Drum: theoildrum.com/
    A great ongoing, online conversation about energy issues.
Transition Culture: transitionculture.org
    A website dedicated to support of the Transition Movement.
The Women's Agricultural Network: uvm.edu/~wagn/
    A national organization working to increase the number of women in agriculture in the US.

Endnotes

Introduction

1. George Monbiot. *Heat: How To Stop the Planet from Burning.* Allen Lane, 2007, p. xii.

Chapter 1: A Fast Train

2. chron.com/CDA/archives/archive.mpl?id=2008_4558882 (accessed July 28, 2008).
3. economist.com/world/international/displaystory.cfm?story_id=11049284 (accessed July 28, 2008).
4. globalresearch.ca/index.php?context=va&aid=8877 (accessed July 28, 2008).
5. sharonastyk.com/2008/01/30/haitians-eat-dirt-cars-eat-corn/ (accessed July 28, 2008).
6. "Mexico's Poor Get Food Cash Boost," news.bbc.co.uk/2/hi/business/7421237.stm (accessed July 28, 2008).
7. globalresearch.ca/index.php?context=va&aid=8846 (accessed July 28, 2008).
8. economist.com/world/international/displaystory.cfm?story_id=11049284 (accessed July 28, 2008).
9. iht.com/articles/2008/05/04/business/adb.php (accessed July 28, 2008).
10. philly.com/inquirer/home_top_left_story/18479604.html (accessed July 28, 2008).
11. boston.com/news/globe/editorial_opinion/oped/articles/2007/10/21/the_heat_or_eat_dilemma/ (accessed July 28, 2008).
12. Evelyn Nieves, "Food Banks Face High Costs But Feeding More People," Associated Press, May 26, 2008. ap.google.com/article/ALeqM5hput8Lt-BOaDqn_jKVLlQRIR2lMswD90TIJLGo.
13. business.theage.com.au/japans-hunger-becomes-a-dire-warning-for-other-nations/20080420-27ey.html?page=1 (accessed July 28, 2008).
14. UK.reuters.com/article/lifestyleMolk/idUKTRE5135E320090204?pagenumber=34virtualBrandChannel=0
15. sharonastyk.com/2008/03/19/wheat-rationing-seed-shortages/ (accessed July 28, 2008).
16. afp.google.com/article/ALeqM5iW8zWM5yz55uuitWsc8DsUFZnbmw (accessed July 28, 2008).
17. adn.com/news/alaska/story/394730.html (accessed July 28, 2008).
18. Heather Scoffield, "High Oil Prices Will Hurt Trade, Report Says," *Globe and Mail Update*, May 27, 2008. theglobeandmail.com/servlet/story/RTGAM.20080527.woileconomy0527/BNStory/energy/home.
19. bloomberg.com/apps/news?pid=20601087&sid=aox4ZwDlWkvQ&refer=home (accessed Nov. 12, 2008).
20. chicagotribune.com/news/nationworld/chi-sun-inflation-may04,0,2037787.story (accessed July 28, 2008).
21. energybulletin.net/39100.html (accessed July 28, 2008).

22. news.bbc.co.uk/2/hi/asia-pacific/7239279.stm (accessed July 28, 2008).

23. timesonline.co.uk/tol/news/world/asia/article3863240.ece (accessed July 28, 2008).

24. timesofindia.indiatimes.com/India/Govt_Uranium_shortage_has_hit_N-power _plants/articleshow/3008504.cms (accessed July 28, 2008).

25. theoildrum.com/node/4092 (accessed Nov. 12, 2008).

26. ft.com/cms/s/e5e78778-a53f-11dd-b4f5-000077b07658,Authorised=false.html?_i _location=http%3A%2F%2Fwww.ft.com%2Fcms%2Fs%2F0%2Fe5e78778-a53f-11 dd-b4f5-000077b07658.html%3Fnclick_check%3D1&_i_referer=http%3A%2F% 2Fwww.energybulletin.net%2Fnode%2F47041&nclick_check=1 (accessed Nov. 12, 2008).

27. globalpublicmedia.com/saying_goodbye_to_air_travel (accessed August 13, 2008).

28. energybulletin.net/44253.html (accessed August 13, 2008).

29. Jim Drinkard, AP, "Research Budgets Cut Amid Food Crisis, Wheat Worry," May 27, 2008, ap.google.com/article/ALeqM5j3lWoI5WHE4waYWHLzquDlmo2H4 QD90U4MAG1.

30. earth-policy.org/Books/Seg/PB2cho3_ss2.htm (accessed August 13, 2008).

31. financialpost.com/story.html?id=428615 (accessed May 29, 2008).

32. theglobeandmail.com/servlet/story/RTGAM.20080423.WBwreguly2008042308 5316/WBStory/Wbwreguly (accessed August 13, 2008).

33. nytimes.com/2008/04/30/business/worldbusiness/30fertilizer.html?_r=3&oref=s login&oref=slogin&oref=slogin (accessed August 13, 2008).

34. independent.co.uk/environment/green-living/multinationals-make-billions-in-profit-out-of-growing-global-food-crisis-820855.html (accessed August 13, 2008).

35. Kenneth Deffeyes, "Join Us as We Watch the Crisis Unfolding" May 27, 2008, princeton.edu/hubbert/current-events.html.

36. livingonearth.org/shows/segments.htm?programID=08-P13-00004&segment ID=3 (accessed August 13, 2008).

37. Michael Antonucci, "Blood for Oil: The Quest for Fuel in World War II," *Command*, January–February 1993, p. 167.

38. James Howard Kunstler, *The Long Emergency: Surviving the Converging Catastrophes of the Twenty-first Century*, Atlantic Monthly Press, 2005.

39. peakoil.net/Oil_tsunami.html (accessed August 13, 2008).

40. eia.doe.gov/pub/oil_gas/petroleum/analysis_publications/oil_market_basics/ demand_text.htm (accessed August 13, 2008).

41. aga.org/Legislative/legislative+advocacy/issues/energy/Questions+and+Answers +About+Natural+Gas+and+National+Energy+Policy.htm (accessed August 13, 2008).

42. reuters.com/article/Utilities/idUSN2163310420050621 (accessed Nov. 13, 2008).

43. Matthew R. Simmons, *The Story of Natural Gas: Supply, Demand and a Brick Wall*, Enskilda Securities Institutional Investor Meeting, 2004.

44. Julian Darley, *High Noon for Natural Gas: The New Energy Crisis*, Chelsea Green, 2004, p. 183.

45. Pat Murphy, *Plan C: Community Survival Strategies for Peak Oil and Climate Change*, New Society, 2008, p. 8.

46. Darley, personal communication, September 25, 2006.

47. Executive Summary from Peaking of World Oil Production: Impacts, Mitigation & Risk Management, Dr. Robert Hirsch, February 2005.

48. Richard Heinberg, *MuseLetter*, May 24, 2006.

49. Eileen T. Westervelt and Donald F. Fournier, *Energy Trends and Implications for U.S. Army Installations,* ERDC/CERL TN-05-1, September 2005.

50. foodmuseum.com/nmffUSAFarmHeritage.html (accessed August 13, 2008).

51. United States Department of Agriculture (USDA), *Economic Research Service Report*, "Estimating The Net Energy Balance Of Corn Ethanol: An Update," number 814, 2002.

52. Murphy, p. 66.

53. Murphy, p. 84.

54. Murphy, p. 85.

55. Alvin M. Weinberg, "Science and Trans-Science" *Science,* July 1972, p.211.

56. Mark Diesendorf, "Can Nuclear Energy Reduce CO_2 Emissions?" sustainability centre.com.au/CT_nukes_CO2.pdf (accessed Nov. 12, 2008).

57. Personal correspondence with electrical engineer at the McGuire Nuclear Power Plant.

58. Rob Hopkins, *The Transition Handbook: From Oil Dependency to Local Resilience.* Green Books, 2008, p. 69

59. Richard G. Lugar and R. James Woolsey, "The New Petroleum," Council on Foreign Relations, Jan/Feb 1999, foreignaffairs.org/19990101faessay954/richard-g-lugar-r-james-woolsey/the-new-petroleum.html.

60. Geoffrey Lean, "Global Warming is Three Times Faster than Worst Predictions," *Independent,* June 6, 2007, p. 42.

61. news.bbc.co.uk/2/hi/science/nature/7139797.stm (accessed Nov. 12, 2008).

62. spiegel.de/international/world/0,1518,547976,00.html (accessed August 13, 2008).

63. uk.reuters.com/article/environmentNews/idUKTRE49T0AD20081030 (accessed Nov. 12, 2008).

64. guardian.co.uk/environment/2008/apr/07/climatechange.carbonemissions. (accessed Nov. 12, 2008).

65. cosmosmagazine.com/node/927 (accessed August 13, 2008).

66. Elizabeth Kolbert, *Field Notes from a Catastrophe,* Bloomsbury, 2006, p. 109–110.

67. Shaobing Peng et al, "Rice Yields Decline With Higher Night Temperature from Global Warming" Proceedings of the National Academy of Sciences, 2004, pp. 9971–5.

68. Monbiot, p. 7.

69. C. Ford Runge, Benjamin Senauer, Philip G. Pardey and Mark W. Rosegrant, *Ending Hunger in Our Lifetime: Food Security and Globalization,* Johns Hopkins University Press, 2003.

70. Runge, Senauer, et al., p. 60.

71. energybulletin.net/node/47048 (accessed Nov. 12, 2008).

72. "Global Warming: Methane," *U.S. Environmental Protection Agency,* 8 Mar. 2006.

73. kearney.ucdavis.edu/OLD%20MISSION/UC%20ANR-Growers%20can%20profit%20from%20parking%20carbon%20on%20farm.pdf (accessed August 13, 2008).

74. David Holmgren, *Permaculture: Principles and Pathways Beyond Sustainability*, Holmgren Design Services, 2002, p. 35.

75. rightpundits.com/?p=2748 (accessed Feb. 10, 2009).

76. Frances Moore Lappé et al., *World Hunger: Twelve Myths,* Grove Press, 1998, p. 9.

77. Amartya Sen, *Poverty and Famines: An Essay on Entitlement and Deprivation*, Oxford, 1982, p. 32.

78. Runge, Senauer et al., p. 171.

79. Vandana Shiva, *Biopiracy, the Plunder of Nature and Knowledge*, South End Press, 1997, pp. 115–116.

80. Monbiot, p. 22.

81. Sharon Astyk, *Depletion and Abundance*, New Society, 2008, p. 46.

82. Jeremy Seabrook, *The No Nonsense Guide to World Poverty*, Verso, 2004, p. 20.

83. Ibid, p. 24.

84. Murphy, p. 4.

85. Murphy, p. 23.

86. theautomaticearth.blogspot.com/2009/02/february-8-2009-let-us-pray-that-it
.html (accessed Feb. 10, 2009)

87. washingtonpost.com/wp-dyn/content/article/2008/04/25/AR2008042503096_2
.html?sid=ST2008042602333 (accessed August 14, 2008).

88. Peter Rosset, *Food is Different: Why We Must Get the WTO Out of Agriculture*, Zed Books, 2006, p. 5.

89. Lappé et al., p. 20.

90. sharonastyk.com/2008/04/28/peak-farmers-a-guest-post-by-elaine-solowey/ (accessed August 14, 2008).

91. Joan Dye Gussow, *This Organic Life*, Chelsea Green Publishing, 2004, pp. 170–171.

92. Yegor Gaidar, trans. Antonina W. Bouis, *Collapse of an Empire: Lessons for Modern Russia*, Brookings Institute Press, 2007, pp. 43–49.

93. Dmitry Orlov, "Keeping Fed" ClubOrlov, cluborlov.blogspot.com/2008/04/keep
ing-fed.html (accessed Nov. 12, 2008).

94. Ibid.

95. Dmitry Lyskov, trans. Dmitry Sudakov, "Famine Killed Seven Million People USA," *Pravda*, May 19, 2008, english.pravda.ru/world/americas/105255-0/.

96. *Historical Statistics of the United States: Colonial Times to 1957,* Statistical Abstract Supplements, US Bureau of the Census, 1961, pp. 22–23.

97. David A. Shannon, *The Great Depression,* Prentice-Hall, 1960, p. 36.

98. Ibid, p. 47.

99. Bernie Sternsher and Judy Sealander, *Women of Valor: The Struggle Against the Great Depression as Told in Their Own Life Stories,* Ivan R. Dee, 1990, p. 35.

100. Ibid, pp. 27–28.

101. ft.com/cms/s/0/cb8a989a-1d2a-11dd-82ae-000077b07658.html (accessed August 14, 2008).

102. ft.com/cms/s/f02c1e94-e4d6-11dc-a495-0000779fd2ac,Authorised=false.html?_i
_location=http%3A%2F%2Fwww.ft.com%2Fcms%2Fs%2F0%2Ff02c1e94-e4d6-11
dc-a495-0000779fd2ac.html&_i_referer=http%3A%2F%2Fsharonastyk.com%2F
2008%2F03%2F03%2Fthe-holy-crap-files%2F (accessed August 14, 2008).

103. dieoff.org/page55.htm (accessed August 14, 2008).

104. canada.com/vancouvercourier/news/story.html?id=efa784df-6ccd-4000-a0f4-204f698c22b4 (accessed August 14, 2008).

105. Jeffrey Brown, personal communication, June 18, 2008.

Chapter 2: Hands on the Wheel

106. Michael Pollan, *The Omnivore's Dilemma: A Natural History of Four Meals*, Penguin Press, 2006, pp. 409–410.

107. sidewalksprouts.wordpress.com/history/vg/ (accessed August 19, 2008).

108. Joseph Romm, *Hell and High Water and What We Should Do*, William Morrow, 2007, p. 235.

109. Lester Brown, *Plan B 2.0: Rescuing a Planet Under Stress and a Civilization in Trouble,* W. W. Norton, 2003, p. 263.

110. fao.org/docrep/X0051T/X0051t02.htm (accessed August 19, 2008).

111. Howard Zinn, *The People's History of the United States*, Harper Collins, 2003, p. 10.

112. Robert Shetterly, *Americans Who Tell the Truth*, Penguin, 2005, p. 4.

113. Pollan, p. 135.

114. Dale Pfeiffer, *Eating Fossil Fuels*, New Society, 2005, p. 9.

115. mindfully.org/Farm/Small-Farm-Benefits-Rosset.htm (accessed August 19, 2008).

116. i-sis.org.uk/RiceWars.php (accessed August 19, 2008).

117. fao.org/docrep/X0051T/X0051t02.htm (accessed August 19, 2008).

118. Gary Becker, "Addendum on Rising Food Prices," The Becker-Posner Blog, becker-posner-blog.com/archives/2008/04/post_7.html (accessed August 19, 2008).

119. Bill McKibben, *Deep Economy,* Times Books, 2007, pp. 35–36.

120. Richard Louv, *Last Child in the Woods*, Algonquin Books, 2005, p. 101.

121. Maria Mies and Veronika Bennholdt-Thomsen, *The Subsistence Perspective*, Zed Books, 2000, p. 116.

122. Hopkins, p. 69.

123. Ibid, p. 65.

124. Gary M. Walton and James Shepherd, *The Economic Rise of Early America,* Cambridge University Press, 1979, pp. 132–134.

125. Jonathan Bloom, "Labor Down, Waste Up," wastedfood.com/2008/05/13/labor-down-waste-up/ (accessed August 19, 2008).

126. Douglass Adair, *The Intellectual Origins of Jeffersonian Democracy,* Yale University Press, 1943, p. 7.

127. Roger Kennedy, *Mr. Jefferson's Lost Cause* , Oxford University Press, 2003, pp. 123–29.

128. Thomas Hartmann, *What Would Jefferson Do: A Return to Democracy,* Three Rivers Press, 2004, p. 86.

129. Susan Llewellyn Leach , "Slavery is Not Dead, Just Less Recognizable," *Christian Science Monitor,* csmonitor.com/2004/0901/p16s01-wogi.html (accessed Sept. 12, 2008).

130. "Child Protection from Violence and Exploitation" UNICEF, unicef.org/protection/index_childlabour.html (accessed Sept. 12, 2008).

131. "Fact Sheets on Gender Issues: Prostitution and Trafficking" UNIFEM, unifem-eseasia.org/resources/factsheets/Gendis2.htm (accessed Sept. 12, 2008).

132. Naomi Klein, *No Logo,* Picador, 2002, p. 36.

133. Ibid, p. 67.

134. Mark O'Brien, "Labour," in ed. Emma Birchim and John Charlton, *Anti-Capitalism: A Guide to the Movement,* Bookmark Publications, 2001, pp. 71–72.

135. Kenneth Stampp, *Peculiar Institution: Slavery in the Ante-Bellum South,* Vintage, 1989, pp. 89–90.

136. David Brion Davis, *Inhuman Bondage: The Rise and Fall of Slavery in the New World,* Oxford University Press, 2006, p. 182.

137. Mohandas Gandhi, "Hind Swaraj, Or The Indian Home-Rule (1909)," mkgandhi -sarvodaya.org/hindswaraj.htm (accessed Sept. 14, 2008).

138. Gandhi, 1958–1984, Vol. 85, p. 33.

139. Laura Schenone, *A Thousand Years Over a Hot Stove: A History of American Women Told Though Food, Recipes and Remembrances,* W. W. Norton, 2004, p. 344.

140. Rosen, Ruth "The Care Crisis: How Women are Bearing the Burden of A National Emergency" *The Nation* Vol. 284, No. 10, pp. 31–35.

141. Jean Zimmerman, *Made from Scratch,* Free Press, 2003, p. 153.

142. Ibid., p. 167.

143. Stan Cox, "Turning Your Lawn into a Victory Garden Won't Save You — Fighting the Corporations Will," alternet.org/story/86943/turning_your_lawn_into_a_ victory_garden_won%27t_save_you_--_fighting_the_corporations_will/ (accessed November 15, 2008).

Chapter 3: Ring the Bell

144. Chapter 3, alternet.org/story/56303/ (accessed Sept. 9, 2008).

145. Michael Pollan, *The Omnivore's Dilemma: A Natural History of Four Meals,* Penguin, 2006, pp. 17–18.

146. Michael Babaro and Eric Dash, "Recession Diet Just One Way to Tighten Belt," *New York Times,* April 27, 2008, nytimes.com/2008/04/27/business/27spend. html?_r=2&pagewanted=1&th&emc=th&oref=slogin.

147. Margaret Visser, *Much Depends on Dinner,* Grove Press, 1999, p. 175.

148. Pollan, p. 18.

149. Oksana Nagayets, "Small Farms: Current Status and Key Trends," ifpri.org/events/ seminars/2005/smallfarms/sfproc/Appendix_InformationBrief.pdf (accessed Sept. 9, 2008).

150. Gene Logsdon, *Small-Scale Grain Raising,* Rodale Press, 1977, p. 19.

151. Richard Westmacott, *African American Gardens and Yards in the Rural South,* University of Tennessee Press, 1992, pp. 10–11.

152. D. B. Grigg, *Agricultural Systems of the World,* Routledge, 1995, p. 37.

153. Lydia Pulsipher, "They Have Saturdays and Sundays to Feed Themselves: Slave Gardens in the Caribbean," *Expedition,* 2 No 2, 1990.

154. Pat Murphy, *Plan C: Community Survival Strategies for Peak Oil and Climate Change,* New Society, 2008, p. 187.

155. Peter Menzel and Faith D'Aluisio, *Hungry Planet: What the World Eats,* Ten Speed Press, 2005.

156. Marion Nestle, *What To Eat,* North Point Press, 2006, p. 28.

157. Joetta Handrich Schlabach, *Extending the Table: A World Community Cookbook,* Herald Press, 1991, p. 73.

158. geosci.uchicago.edu/~gidon/papers/nutri/nutriEI.pdf (accessed Nov. 25, 2008).

159. news.cornell.edu/stories/Oct07/diets.ag.footprint.sl.html (accessed Sept. 10, 2008).

Chapter 4: God's Away on Business

160. Maria Mies and Veronika Bennholdt-Thomsen, *The Subsistence Perspective: Beyond the Globalized Economy,* Zed Books, 1999, p. 25.

161. Thomas Friedman, *The Lexus and the Olive Tree,* Anchor, 2000, p. 39.

162. Joseph A. Tainter, *New Studies in Archaeology: The Collapse of Complex Societies,* Cambridge University Press, 1990, pp. 292–93.

163. Jared Diamond, *Collapse: How Societies Choose to Fail or Succeed,* Viking 2005, pp. 504–505.

164. Pfeiffer, p. 13.

165. Lappé et al., p. 45.

166. *Pimental Journal of the Environment, Development and Sustainability,* Vol. 8, 2006.

167. Pfeiffer, p. 12.

168. M. E. Ensminger, *Animal Science,* Prentice Hall, 1990, p .21 .

169. R. Lal, "Soil Erosion Impact on Agronomic Productivity and Environment Quality," *Critical Reviews in Plant Sciences,* 17, 1998, pp. 319–464.

170. Pfeiffer, p. 16.

171. Pimental and Giampietro, *Food, Land Population and the U.S. Economy,* dieoff. org/page40.htm (accessed Nov. 25, 2008).

172. David Pimental. et al., "Will Limits of the Earth's Resources Control Human Numbers?," *Environment Development and Sustainability,* Issue 1 1999, p. 4.

173. Letter to all State Governors on a Uniform Soil Conservation Law, February 26, 1937.

174. newfarm.org/columns/research_paul/2007/0107 /notill.shtml (accessed Aug. 25, 2008).

175. permaculturetokyo.blogspot.com/2007/02/healthy-life-from-healthy-soil.html (accessed Aug. 25, 2008).

176. Michael Tenneson, "Black Gold of the Amazon," *Discover,* April 2007, discover magazine.com/2007/apr/black-gold-of-the-amazon (accessed Nov. 25, 3008).

177. Peter Bane, "Storing Carbon in Soil: The possibilities of a New American Agriculture," *Permaculture Activist,* Autumn, 2007.

178. ICL Performance Products presentation, Concord, N. C., 1.10.08.

179. topix.com/world/canada/2008/04/potash-stocks-nourished-by-230-increase-400 -tonne-price-hike-but-canadians-where-profits-go (accessed Nov. 25, 2008).

180. energybulletin.net/node/33164 (accessed Nov. 25, 2008).

181. Personal communication with Ron Danise, a certified arborist who has worked in the field of arboriculture since 1964, during which time he has researched and developed organic soil amendments that develop living soil systems.

182. sahra.arizona.edu/programs/water_cons/home/bathroom_toilet.htm (accessed August 25, 2008).

183. epa.gov/newsroom/greenscene/transcripts/2008-01-28-greenscene.htm (accessed August 25, 2008).

184. waterencyclopedia.com/Re-St/Rivers-Major-World.html (accessed August 25, 2008).

185. news.bbc.co.uk/1/hi/world/676064.stm (accessed August 25, 2008).

186. Pfeiffer, p. 15.

187. Sandra L. Postel, "Water for Agriculture: Facing the Limits," *Worldwatch Paper 93*, Worldwatch Institute, 1989.

188. southernstudies.org/facingsouth/labels/nuclear%20power.asp (accessed August 25, 2008).

189. ncdc.noaa.gov/oa/climate/research/2007/sep/us-drought.html (accessed August 25, 2008).

190. edf.org/page.cfm?tagID=68 (accessed August 25, 2008).

191. Pfeiffer, p. 17.

192. Robin Wheeler, *Food Security for the Faint of Heart*, New Society 2008, p. 95.

193. Martin Jones, *Feast: Why Humans Share Food*, Oxford University Press, 2007, p. 162.

194. Schenone, pp. 8–9.

195. Jones, p. 241.

196. Pfeiffer, p. 22.

197. Ibid., p. 23.

198. David Pimentel and Hugh Lehman, eds., *The Pesticide Question: Environment, Economics, and Ethics*, Springer, 1993, p. 26.

199. David Pimentel and L. Levitan, "Pesticides: Amounts Applied and Amounts Reaching Pests," *Bioscience* 36, No. 2, February 1986, p. 90.

200. Lappé at al., p. 53.

201. Ibid.

202. Pfeiffer, p. 23.

203. Sandra Steingraber, *Having Faith: An Ecologist's Journey to Motherhood*, Perseus, 2001, p. 251.

204. counterpunch.org/montague01072006.html (accessed August 25, 2008).

205. Elaine Ingham, "Unnatural Selection: The Bacterium that (Almost) Ate the World," kjpermaculture.blogspot.com/2008/01/bacterium-that-almost-ate-world.html (accessed Nov. 25, 2008).

206. huffingtonpost.com/frances-moore-lappe-and-anna-lappe/the-right-to-food-means-f_b_68564.html (accessed August 25, 2008).

207. Mark Nord and Margaret Andrews, "Reducing Food Insecurity in the United States: Assessing Progress Toward a National Objective," *Food Assistance and Nutrition Research Report*, Number 26, 2 May, 2002.

208. Mies and Bennholdt-Thomsen, p. 82.

209. George Monbiot, *The Guardian*, August 24, 2000, monbiot.com/archives/2000/08/24/organic-farming-will-feed-the-world/.

210. Ibid.

211. Peter M. Rosset, "The Multiple Functions and Benefits of Small Farm Agriculture In the Context of Global Trade Negotiations," econpapers.repec.org/article/paldevelp/v_3A43_3Ay_3A2000_3Ai_3A2_3Ap_3A77-82.htm (accessed Nov. 24, 2008).

212. Ibid.
213. faqs.org/nutrition/Diab-Em/Dietary-Trends-International.html (accessed Nov. 25, 2008).
214. Eric Schlosser, *Fast Food Nation: The Dark Side of the All American Meal,* Houghton Mifflin, 2002, p.3.
215. Jean Zimmerman, *Made from Scratch: Reclaiming the Pleasures of the American Hearth,* Free Press, 2003. p. 156–158.
216. Ibid, p. 174.
217. Sandra Steingraber, *Having Faith: An Ecologist's Journey to Motherhood*, Perseus Publishing, 2001, p. 274.
218. nytimes.com/2007/01/28/magazine/28nutritionism.t.html?_r=1&ref=magazine &pagewanted=all&oref=slogin (accessed August 25, 2008).

Chapter 5: Hard Times Come Again No More

219. George Kent, *Freedom from Want: The Human Right to Adequate Food.* Georgetown University Press, 2005, p. 4.
220. Address by Hubert Hoover under the auspices of the Famine Emergency Committee, Sherman Hotel, Chicago, May 17, 1946.
221. Amy Bentley, *Eating for Victory: Food Rationing and the Politics of Domesticity,* University of Illinois Press, 1988, p. 151.
222. globalpublicmedia.com/transcripts/232 (accessed August 28, 2008).
223. Pfeiffer, p. 9.
224. Murphy, p. 260.
225. Murphy, p. 184.
226. Gussow, p. 82.
227. Rosset, mindfully.org/Farm/Small-Farm-Benefits-Rosset.htm (accessed Nov. 26, 2008).
228. Ibid.
229. Hope Shand, "Human Nature: Agricultural Biodiversity and Farm-Based Food Security," RAFI, 1997, p. 3.
230. Helena Norberg-Hodge, Steven Gorelick and Todd Merrifield, *Bringing the Food Economy Home*, Kumarian Press, 2002, p. 4.
231. Vandana Shiva, *Stolen Harvest: The Hijacking of the Global Food Supply*, South End Press, 2000, pp. 12–13.
232. Donald Freebairn, "Did the Green Revolution Concentrate Incomes? A Quantitative Study of Research Reports," *World Development*, 23, No. 2, 1995.
233. Lappé, et al., p. 61.
234. McKibben, p. 67.
235. Jules Pretty, *Agri-Culture: Reconnecting People, Land, and Nature,* Earthscan Publications, 2002, pp. 59–66.
236. Donella Meadows, "Our Food, Our Future," *Organic Gardening*, Vol. 47 No. 5, September/October, 2000, p. 54.
237. Ibid., p. 55.
238. Ibid., p. 56.
239. Ibid., p. 54.
240. fao.org/docrep/010/ah876e/ah876e01.htm. (accessed August 29, 2008).

241. greenwithagun.blogspot.com/2007/12/its-not-how-big-it-is-its-what-you-do.htm (accessed August 29, 2008).

242. Maria Mies and Vandana Shiva, *Ecofeminism*, Zed Books, 1993, p. 286.

243. Ibid., p. 191.

244. Jim Merkel, *Radical Simplicity: Small Footprints on a Finite Earth,* New Society, 2003, p. 183.

245. Genesis 41:29–30.

246. Ariana Eunjung Cha, "Rising Grain Prices Panic Developing World" *Washington Post*, April 4, 2008, washingtonpost.com/wp-dyn/content/article/2008/04/03/AR2008040304054.html.

Chapter 6: The Landslide Brings it Down

247. Mies and Bennholdt-Thomsen, p. 115.

248. jameshowardkunstler.typepad.com/clusterfuck_nation/2007/09/crunch-time.html (accessed Sept. 10, 2008).

249. Christopher B. Leinberger, "The Next Slum?" *Atlantic Monthly,* March 2008.

250. G. K. Chesterton, *The Uses of Diversity*, Kessinger Publishing (May 30, 2005), Dodd, Mead and Company, 1921.

251. Pat Murphy, *Plan C: Community Survival Strategies for Peak Oil and Climate Change*, New Society, 2008, p. 146.

252. Christopher B. Leinberger, "The Next Slum?" *Atlantic Monthly,* March 2008.

253. *Renewable Agriculture and Food Systems*, 22:86–108 Cambridge University Press, 2007.

254. ifpri.org/events/seminars/2005/smallfarms/sfproc/Appendix_InformationBrief.pdf (accessed Sept. 10, 2008).

255. Ibid.

256. Patricia Klindeist, *The Earth Knows My Name: Food, Culture, and Sustainability in the Gardens of Ethnic America,* Beacon Press, 2008, p. 8.

257. pathtofreedom.com/urbanhomestead/ataglance.shtml (accessed Sept. 10, 2008).

258. David Holmgren, "Garden Agriculture: A revolution in efficient water use," *Water,* Volume 32 No 8, December, 2005.

259. *Meeting the Urban Challenge, Population Reports,* Volume XXX, Number 4, Fall 2002, Series M, Number 16, Special Topics.

260. citymayors.com (accessed Sept. 10, 2008).

261. "Urban Agriculture in Havana, Cuba," Urban Studies Program at San Francisco State University, August 2000.

262. tonto.eia.doe.gov/country/country_energy_data.cfm?fips=CU (accessed Sept. 10, 2008).

263. Peter Rosset and Medea Benjamin, "Two Steps Back, One Step Forward: Cuba's National Policy for Alternative Agriculture," *Gatekeeper Series* No. 46, International Institute for Environment and Development, 1994.

264. Peter Rosset with Shea Cunningham, "The Greening of Cuba," *Earth Island Journal*, Winter 94, Vol. 10 Issue 1, p. 23.

265. Scott G. Chaplowe, "Havana's Popular Gardens: Sustainable Urban Agriculture," *WSAA Newsletter*, A Publication of the World Sustainable Agriculture Association, Fall 1996, Vol. 5, No. 22.

266. "Urban Agriculture in Havana, Cuba," Urban Studies Program at San Francisco State University, August, 2000.

267. Ibid.

268. R. Marsh, "Building on Traditional Gardening To Improve Household Food Security," UNFAO, fao.org/docrep/X0051T/X0051t02.htm (accessed Sept. 10, 2008).

269. H. Patricia Hynes, *A Patch of Eden: America's Inner City Gardeners*, Chelsea Green, 1996, p. 156.

270. Michael W. Hamm and Monique Baron, *For Hunger Proof Cities*, International Development Research Centre, 1999, p. 56.

271. communitygarden.org/learn/ (accessed Sept. 10, 2008).

272. edibleschoolyard.org/about.html (accessed Sept. 10, 2008).

273. Howard Zinn, *The Twentieth Century*, Harper Perennial, 2003, p. 121.

274. Ibid., p. 122.

275. Leslie Heimer, "Depression Relief Gardens 1929–1939," sidewalksprouts.wordpress .com/history/relief-garden/ (accessed Sept. 10, 2008).

276. "Urban Agriculture in Havana, Cuba," Urban Studies Program at San Francisco State University, August, 2000.

277. oliveoil.ucdavis.edu/ (accessed Sept. 10, 2008).

278. R. Marsh, "Building on Traditional Gardening To Improve Household Food Security," UNFAO, fao.org/docrep/X0051T/X0051t02.htm (accessed Sept. 10, 2008).

279. H. Patricia Hynes, *A Patch of Eden: America's Inner City Gardeners*, Chelsea Green, 1996, p. 114.

280. Ibid., p. 155.

281. Bill McKibben, *Deep Economy: The Wealth of Communities and the Durable Future*, Henry Holt, 2007, p. 232.

282. Bill McKibben, *Hope, Human and Wild*, Milkweed Editions, 1995, p. 14.

283. "The Water is Back" Little Blog in the Big Woods, May 5, 2008, littlebloginthebig woods.blogspot.com/2008/05/water-is-back.html.

284. Wendell Berry, "Preserving Wildness," *Home Economics: Fourteen Essays,* Harper Collins, 1987, p. 142.

285. Toby Hemenway, *Gaia's Garden*, Chelsea Green Publishing Company, 2000, p. 4.

Chapter 7: The Hands that Built the Country...

286. livinghistoryfarm.org/farminginthe30s/life_01.html (accessed Sept. 11, 2008).

287. mlive.com/news/index.ssf/2008/05/farmers_say_they_arent_reaping.html (accessed Sept. 11, 2008).

288. Jorge Fernandez-Cornejo, "Farmers Balance Off-Farm Work and Technology Adoption," Amber Waves, Volume 5, Issue 1, February, 2007, ers.usda.gov/Amber-Waves/February07/Features/FarmersBalance.htm.

289. Ibid.

290. Katherine R. Smith, "Does Off-Farm Work Hinder 'Smart' Farming?" Economic Research Service/USDA Agricultural Outlook, September, 2002.

291. newsweek.com/id/76929 (accessed Sept. 11, 2008).

292. Katherine R. Smith, "Does Off-Farm Work Hinder 'Smart' Farming?" Economic Research Service/USDA Agricultural Outlook, September, 2002.

293. Interview, May 2008.

294. Michael Shulman, *Going Local: Self-Reliant Communities in a Global Age,* Routledge, 2000, p. 106.

295. Van Jones, "Memo to Candidates: Green Collar Jobs Mean Standing Up for People and the Planet," *Gristmill,* January 25, 2008, gristmill.grist.org/story/2008/1/24/145628/140.

296. *Buy Local Food and Farm Toolkit, A Guide for Community Organizers,* Oxfam America, p. 3 oxfamamerica.org/resources/files/Food_and_Farm_Toolkit.pdf (accessed Nov. 28, 2008).

297. independent.co.uk/environment/green-living/multinationals-make-billions-in-profit-out-of-growing-global-food-crisis-820855.html (accessed Sept. 11, 2008).

298. hopedance.org/cms/index.php?option=com_content&task=view&id=337&Itemid=98 (accessed Dec. 5, 2008).

299. articles.latimes.com/2008/may/25/local/me-rooster25 (accessed Nov. 1, 2008).

300. Patricia Klindienst, *The Earth Knows My Name,* Beacon Press, 2006, p. 104.

301. Ibid., p. 171.

302. Thomas Homer-Dixon, *The Upside of Down,* Island Press, 2006, p. 17.

303. Interview, April 2008.

304. Ibid.

305. Jim Windolf, "Sex, Drugs, and Soybeans…and Click Here for the Rock and Roll," *Vanity Fair,* April 5, 2007, vanityfair.com/politics/features/2007/05/thefarm200705?currentPage=1.

Chapter 8: Keep Your Hand on the Plow

306. Naomi Klein, *The Shock Doctrine: The Rise of Disaster Capitalism,* Henry Holt, 2007, p. 8.

307. Ibid.

308. Thomas Princen, *The Logic of Sufficiency,* MIT Press, 2005, p. 360.

309. fastcompany.com/magazine/94/open_change-or-die.html (accessed Sept. 14, 2008).

310. fastcompany.com/magazine/94/open_change-or-die.html?page=0%2C1 (accessed Sept. 14, 2008).

311. fastcompany.com/magazine/94/open_change-or-die.html?page=0%2C3 (accessed Sept. 14, 2008).

312. Ibid.

313. fastcompany.com/magazine/94/open_change-or-die.html?page=0%2C4 (accessed Sept. 14, 2008).

314. Interview April, 2004, by Adam Fenderson.

315. shirky.com/herecomeseverybody/2008/04/looking-for-the-mouse.html (accessed Sept. 14, 2008).

316. groovygreen.com/groove/?p=689 (accessed Sept. 14, 2008).

317. groovygreen.com/groove/?p=3018 (accessed Nov. 28, 2008).

Index

About the Authors

SHARON ASTYK is a writer, teacher, blogger and small farmer. A former academic, her unfinished doctoral dissertation focused on the ecological and demographic catastrophes explored in Early Modern Literature. Abandoning Shakespeare to work on the ecological and demographic catastrophes of the 21st century, she began by running a small CSA and right now seems to write books, including *Depletion & Abundance: Life on the New Home Front* (New Society Publishers 2008). In her copious spare time, she raises vegetables, fruit, livestock, children and havoc with her husband in rural upstate New York.

AARON NEWTON is a land planner and a participating farmer at the Elma C. Lomax Farm Incubator in Concord, North Carolina. He directs the Greater Goods Garden Co., a non-profit garden installation organization helping to feed the hungry. He helps operate a CSA serving forty families locally. Aaron is the co-founder of *Groovy Green* and *Hen and Harvest*, two online journals discussing issues related to food, energy and the environment. He rides a bike and helps his wife raise their two daughters.

If you have enjoyed *A Nation of Farmers*, you might also enjoy other

BOOKS TO BUILD A NEW SOCIETY

Our books provide positive solutions for people who want to
make a difference. We specialize in:

Sustainable Living ◆ Ecological Design and Planning
Natural Building & Appropriate Technology ◆ New Forestry
Environment and Justice ◆ Conscientious Commerce
Progressive Leadership ◆ Resistance and Community ◆ Nonviolence
Educational and Parenting Resources

New Society Publishers
ENVIRONMENTAL BENEFITS STATEMENT

New Society Publishers has chosen to produce this book on recycled paper made
with 100% post consumer waste, processed chlorine free, and old growth free.
For every 5,000 books printed, New Society saves the following resources:[1]

39	Trees
3,575	Pounds of Solid Waste
3,933	Gallons of Water
5,130	Kilowatt Hours of Electricity
6,498	Pounds of Greenhouse Gases
28	Pounds of HAPs, VOCs, and AOX Combined
10	Cubic Yards of Landfill Space

[1]Environmental benefits are calculated based on research done by the Environmental Defense
Fund and other members of the Paper Task Force who study the environmental impacts of the
paper industry.

For a full list of NSP's titles, please call 1-800-567-6772 or check out our web site at:

www.newsociety.com

NEW SOCIETY PUBLISHERS